DanaTerr

D0904843

EMDR

AND THE RELATIONAL IMPERATIVE

EMDR

AND THE RELATIONAL IMPERATIVE

The Therapeutic Relationship
in EMDR Treatment

Mark Dworkin

Foreword by Francine Shapiro

 Routledge
Taylor & Francis Group
New York   London

Published in 2005 by
Routledge
Taylor & Francis Group
270 Madison Avenue
New York, NY 10016

Published in Great Britain by
Routledge
Taylor & Francis Group
2 Park Square
Milton Park, Abingdon
Oxon OX14 4RN

© 2005 by Taylor & Francis Group, LLC
Routledge is an imprint of Taylor & Francis Group

Printed in the United States of America on acid-free paper
10 9 8 7 6 5 4 3 2 1

International Standard Book Number-10: 0-415-95028-7 (Hardcover)
International Standard Book Number-13: 978-0-415-95028-2 (Hardcover)
Library of Congress Card Number 2005004356

No part of this book may be reprinted, reproduced, transmitted, or utilized in any form by any electronic, mechanical, or other means, now known or hereafter invented, including photocopying, microfilming, and recording, or in any information storage or retrieval system, without written permission from the publishers.

Trademark Notice: Product or corporate names may be trademarks or registered trademarks, and are used only for identification and explanation without intent to infringe.

Library of Congress Cataloging-in-Publication Data

Dworkin, Mark, 1950-
    EMDR and the relational imperative : the therapeutic relationship in EMDR treatment / Mark Dworkin.
        p. cm.
    Includes bibliographical references and index.
    ISBN 0-415-95028-7 (hardbound)
    1. Eye movement desensitization and reprocessing. 2. Psychotherapist and patient. 3. Psychic trauma--Treatment. 4. Post-traumatic stress disorder--Treatment. I. Title.

RC489.E98D94 2005
616.85'210651--dc22   2005004356

Taylor & Francis Group
is the Academic Division of T&F Informa plc.

Visit the Taylor & Francis Web site at
http://www.taylorandfrancis.com

and the Routledge Web site at
http://www.routledge-ny.com

To the loving memory of my mother Annette Dworkin for teaching me the values of caring for my fellow humans;

and

To the loving memory of my father Harry Dworkin for teaching me to live as a man in this world.

The carpenter has a hammer, the surgeon has a scalpel, the clinician has the self. The clinician's professional experience, theoretical knowledge, clinical skills, and personal history will shape the therapeutic self, and, in turn, affect the process of therapy.

—Hayes and Gelso (2001)

Contents

Foreword ix

Preface xv

Acknowledgments xxi

Chapter 1 The Relational Imperative in EMDR 1

Chapter 2 The Therapeutic Relationship and Its Underlying Neurobiology 13

Chapter 3 Using EMDR Relationally in Daily Clinical Practice 27

Chapter 4 Phase 1: Client History Taking and Treatment Planning (Trauma Case Conceptualization) 47

Chapter 5 Phase 2: Client Preparation (Testing Affect Tolerance and Body Awareness) 65

Chapter 6 Phase 3: Assessment (Trauma Activation Sequence) 83

Chapter 7 Phase 4: Desensitization (Active Trauma Processing) 105

Chapter 8 Countertransference, Transference, and the Intersubjective 125

Chapter 9 The Relational Interweave and Other Active Therapeutic Strategies 165

Chapter 10   Phase 5 Through Phase 8: Installation
              (Linking to the Adaptive Perspective),
              the Body Scan (Intensive Body Awareness),
              Closure (Debriefing), and Reevaluation   191

Appendix A   Trauma, PTSD, and Complex PTSD   215

Appendix B   The EMDR International Association
              and the Definition of EMDR   221

Appendix C   Myths and Realities About EMDR   227

Appendix D   EMDR Clinical Applications
              for Diverse Clinical Populations
              © EMDR Institute, Inc.   233

Appendix E   Confusion Regarding Research on EMDR   237

Appendix F   Trauma Case Conceptualization Questionnaire   239

Appendix G   Clinician Self-Awareness Questionnaire   247

Appendix H   International Treatment Guidelines
              and EMDR Research   253

Appendix I   EMDR Clinician Resources:
              The Humanitarian Assistance Program   267

Glossary   271

References   275

Notes   285

Index   287

Foreword

Too many books are written from an "either/or" position. A major strength of this work is that the author is a sensitive, intelligent clinician who is an integrationist in the best sense of the word. Trained in psychoanalysis, gestalt, group, Ericksonian, family, and cognitive–behavioral therapies, Mr. Dworkin has incorporated EMDR into his sense of what is essential for effective psychotherapy. His insights into the importance of the therapeutic relationship are enhanced by 30 years of successful clinical practice with affiliations as diverse as the Mount Sinai School of Medicine and the Bronx VA Medical Center. In the 14 years since he learned EMDR, he has been able to answer for himself the following questions: "How important are empirically supported therapeutic procedures?" and "How important is the relationship?" The answers, we both agree, are that both are crucial. In short, neither can function to the best benefit of the client without the other.

In this text, Dworkin draws on his extensive clinical experience, the wisdom gleaned from the burgeoning field of neurobiology, and his understanding of the adaptive information processing model (Shapiro, 2001, 2002), which guides EMDR, to provide clinicians practicing any form of psychotherapy with a more thorough appreciation of the processes of clinical change and the dynamics of effective therapeutic relationships. He underscores and makes practical that which has been shown in extensive research: The importance of the therapeutic relationship cannot be dismissed from the realm of clinical practice (Norcross, 2002; Castonguay & Beutler, in press). Why indeed would one "separate the dancer from the dance" (Shapiro, 1994)? In addition, Dworkin illustrates how a thorough understanding and application of EMDR methodology is an important factor in substantial therapeutic change.

Clearly, psychotherapy should, whenever possible, be guided by solid research. Consequently, both the American Psychiatric Association (2004) and the Department of Veterans Affairs/Department of Defense (2004) practice guidelines now place EMDR in the highest category of effectiveness for the treatment of PTSD. As indicated in an extensive meta-analysis of the EMDR research literature (Maxfield & Hyer, 2002), fidelity of treatment predicts magnitude of treatment effects. The robust contribution of the therapeutic relationship to treatment outcome is likewise well established (Norcross, 2002; Castonguay & Beutler, in press). Moreover, an APA division of psychotherapy task force reviewed the extant research base and identified four relational elements that are demonstrably effective — the alliance, cohesion in group therapy, empathy, and goal consensus — and seven therapist relational elements that are probably effective — positive regard, congruence, feedback, repairing alliance ruptures, self-disclosure, management of countertransference, and quality (but not quantity) of relational interpretations (Norcross, Beutler, & Levant, 2005). Clearly, a thorough understanding and application of EMDR methodology, along with a sensitive and individualized use of the therapeutic relationship, will make for the best EMDR treatment and produce the greatest therapeutic effects. Indeed, it should seem self-evident that any therapeutic effect must be the result of an interaction of client, clinician, and method. In this volume, Dworkin demonstrates the practical application of these tenets.

An important contribution of this book is its emphasis on EMDR as a client-centered therapy that attends not only to symptom reduction but also to personal growth. Throughout the volume, Dworkin emphasizes the therapist–client relationship as an integral part of the healing dynamic. The importance of this aspect of psychotherapy cannot be overstated, given what I consider to be the inappropriate dismissal by some (see Norcross et al., 2005) of this relationship as mere "noise" akin to the placebo affect and the equally inappropriate dismissal of methods as somehow unimportant as long as the therapist is loving and well intentioned. For most practicing clinicians daily presented with the intense suffering of those people coming to them for aid, neither of these positions is tenable.

The human relationship is a sacred bond that joins the therapist and sufferer in a journey that may take them to the pits of Hell and back. The therapist may be the only one whom the patient trusts in his or her life. And it is the therapist's honest feedback, integrity, and presence as both model and mirror on which the patient must rely. When this foundation has been laid, then the use of empirically supported treatments can assist the patient to attain the most robust levels of personal health. As a field, we have been remiss in failing to honor this important foundation and equally lacking in our development of measures that chart the attainment of mental health, as opposed to the simple reduction of overt suffering. One hopes that a common treatment goal would be one of comprehensive personal growth, such as can best be attained by viewing the entire clinical picture. This text offers detailed case examples and transcripts to lead the reader through both complete and more circumscribed treatments, attained by the practical application of the principles of relational psychology, as well as by creative uses of EMDR. Clinicians at all levels of experience will find something to help them refine their practice.

So that readers not be confused, let me clarify that this volume does not involve a simple discussion of psychodynamic principles. While these principles may inform the practice of many clinicians, Dworkin clearly draws a distinction: "In all phases, EMDR is practiced as a means to an end, and the 'real' relationship is more important than the transference relationship." As he details in clinical examples the ways in which the relationship changes through the eight phases of EMDR therapy, he underscores the continued importance of clinician self-centering and self-awareness. To that end he provides clinicians with self-care exercises that they can use both during and after sessions, as well as a Clinician Self-Awareness Questionnaire. One of the hallmarks of EMDR therapy is that when the client is properly prepared, the targets appropriately accessed, and the intrinsic information-processing system stimulated, the client can transform even further than the clinician with respect to insight, consciousness, and adaptation. Many times clinicians have reported how much they have learned from their own clients' processing. However, the clinician sets the initial parameters. For more debilitated clients, clinicians serve as a model of health. It seems clear that the further along in our own development we are, the better for all concerned.

Another strength of the book is the honesty with which the author details treatment failures in order to illustrate his practical suggestions. He is able to show that "resistance," on the basis of which the clinician may dismiss the client as "noncompliant," is often a result of countertransferential issues, which are themselves borne of the clinician's own unprocessed material. With extended case examples, Dworkin goes phase by phase through treatment, illustrating when a neurobiological state of "co-regulation" supports therapeutic change, when it is punctured, and what steps the clinician can take: "When I notice that something internally is amiss, … I can go into a state of mindfulness where I 'just notice' my own reactions, use a compartmentalization strategy …, and then refocus on the client. It is my responsibility to undertake the difficult task of introspection in the moment." Besides detailing the use of self-regulating techniques for the clinician, Dworkin illustrates how the rupture can provide material for a "relational interweave" that can ultimately serve to enhance adaptive processing, as well as restore the needed therapeutic balance.

Ultimately, it is a pleasure to read a work that so beautifully complements the EMDR trainings by elucidating and expanding upon an aspect that has been sorely neglected. Although licensed clinicians are expected to know how to establish an effective and vital therapeutic relationship, this is not always the case. Further, regardless of how informed one might be in this regard, there is always room for improvement. In an engaging fashion, Dworkin opens the doors to his own clinical practice and shares important tools for the self-improvement of every clinician. For instance, in the appendix he offers his Trauma Case Conceptualization Questionnaire, the purpose of which is "to help the clinician develop an initial understanding of who the client is, what he or she is struggling with, and how the client and the client's struggles initially affect the clinician." Importantly, Dworkin also underscores our joint belief that EMDR therapy is one of equals, where the clinician joins the client on common ground to act as a facilitator of the process. This means paying attention to one's own state of being. Accordingly, in another appendix he offers the Clinician Self-Awareness Questionnaire and defines its utility:

> To assist in raising awareness of what old state-dependent memories may become activated in you, to assess what may be coming from you and what may be coming from the client, and to develop EMDR relational strategies. Sometimes problems occur in Phase 1 when the client shares information that evokes negative arousal, in Phase 2 when the client has trouble understanding the elements of preparation or wants to start processing trauma prematurely, or in Phase 3 when there is a problem structuring the assessment piece. Sometimes client information may not evoke negative arousal until Phase 4 when the client is actively processing. Often, clinicians' triggers are from old memories. These memories may be explicit or implicit (somatosensory). Noticing these moments in yourself may aid you in continuing productive processing.

Dworkin suggests: "Whenever an EMDR treatment session becomes problematic, consider this self-administered instrument when reflecting on this session." I agree.

Guided by the adaptive information processing model, the EMDR clinician may readily recognize that transference reactions and stumbling blocks in therapy are due to triggering the client's own unprocessed memories. Clients see the world in a certain way because of the emotions, beliefs, and physical sensations that arise when perceptions of the present link into their current memory network, and manifestations of the old stored material arise. What Dworkin so beautifully underscores throughout his narrative is the need for a sensitively attuned clinician who not only recognizes these attributes of the client, but also has the self-awareness and skills to self-modulate as well when unprocessed material causes a countertransference reaction or otherwise threatens to derail the therapeutic process. Ultimately, our shared belief is that a positive therapeutic relationship is an interactive engagement of two equals sharing an important and life-changing experience. Happily, this book elucidates both theory and practice.

Francine Shapiro, PhD
Senior Research Fellow
Mental Research Institute

References

American Psychiatric Association. (2004). *Practice guideline for the treatment of patients with acute stress disorder and posttraumatic stress disorder.* Arlington, VA: Author.

Castonguay, L. G., & Beutler, L. E. (Eds.). (in press). *Principles of therapeutic change that work.* New York: Oxford University Press.

Department of Veterans Affairs & Department of Defense. (2004). *VA/DoD clinical practice guideline for the management of post-traumatic stress.* Washington, DC: Author.

Maxfield, L., & Hyer, L. A. (2002). The relationship between efficacy and methodology in studies investigating EMDR treatment of PTSD. *J. Clinical Psychol., 58,* 23–41.

Norcross, J. C. (Ed.). (2002). *Psychotherapy relationships that work: Therapist contributions and responsiveness to patient needs.* New York: Oxford University Press.

Norcross, J. C., Beutler, L. E., & Levant, R. F. (Eds.). (2005). *Evidence-based practices in mental health: Debate and dialogue on the fundamental questions.* Washington, DC: American Psychological Association.

Shapiro, F. (1994). EMDR: In the eye of a paradigm shift. *Behavior Therapist, 17,* 153–158.

Shapiro, F. (2001). *Eye movement desensitization and reprocessing: Basic principles, protocols and procedures* (2nd ed.). New York: Guilford Press.

Shapiro, F. (Ed.). (2002). *EMDR as an integrative psychotherapy approach: Experts of diverse orientations explore the paradigm prism.* Washington, DC: American Psychological Association Books.

Preface

This book has been germinating in me for several years. It is a commentary on Eye Movement Desensitization and Reprocessing (EMDR), based on my observations from clinical practice, that amplifies the relational perspective to Francine Shapiro's standard methodology. During the last 14 years I have conducted more than 5,000 EMDR sessions. The patterns of response I have seen in my clients and the latest discoveries in the neurosciences, which support my conviction in the relational imperative, have prompted me to write this commentary.

I believe that the relational imperative is intrinsic to EMDR treatment. It has been there, but has not been fleshed out as such. Therefore, this book is a commentary on Dr. Shapiro's text, not a substitute for it. In certain circumstances I may make modifications to the process, based on my clinical judgment. I also suggest an additional explanation of the healing powers inherent in EMDR. The main theme of my book is that healing takes place when proper knowledge of the standard methodology is integrated into the context of the therapeutic relationship.

This relationship embodies special features that are considered "common factors" in psychotherapy integration language and have in it issues of the working alliance; specifically the collaborative working alliance which include Bordin's (1994) transtheoretical concepts of goals-tasks-bonds. In EMDR the emphasis is more heavily on the "real relationship" as a vehicle to helping clients use specific "techniques", rather than the relationship being the primary vehicle for the remediation of the problems our clients present. An example of the relationship as "change agent" would be in the psychodynamic therapies where interpretation of transference distortions would be of primary importance. Of current importance is how elements of the relationship are specific to the types of treatment, and the different populations that are being treated. Much activity in the research field is now devoted to matching the kinds of therapy to the kinds of problems clients present. How I use relational aspects in EMDR is one of the foci of my book.

My ideas, derived from clinical practice, integrate this attempt at bringing method and relationship together for the best outcomes to occur. As EMDR integrates aspects of many forms of psychotherapy, my emphasis is to explain how this phenomenon of relationship and method integrate as well. In my opinion, there is a zone of conditions in which productive trauma processing happens. It is somewhere between states of hyperarousal and hypoarousal in the client, and it can be greatly influenced by the clinician's refined attunement processes. Clinicians' attunement to the client's process is complicated. We enter into relation with the client, using our abilities to be in alignment and to resonate with his or her deepest wounds. In practicing competently, we need to be aware of these chronic states of hypoarousal and hyperarousal in some of our clients. It is my opinion that only when we can facilitate staying in this zone does the deepest healing occur. Clinicians facilitate this zone by being in a co-constructive relationship with our clients.

I will develop this thread throughout the book when viewing EMDR through the relational lens. This relational lens encompasses the main factors involved in EMDR treatment including the emphasis on the real relationship as opposed to transferential and countertransferential phenomenon being healing, the need to develop and maintain the collaborative working alliance throughout treatment, empathic attunement, positive regard, congruence, and feedback. Though they are discussed at times as independent entities, they are in fact so intertwined that it is the mature and seasoned clinician who can apply his judgment wisely to use these concepts well.

Earlier in my career, when I was working for the Bronx Veterans Administration Medical Center, I was considered a "therapist" who was treating a "patient." In my book I will refer to the "clinician" as the one who has the knowledge and the "client" as the one who actively participates in the healing process. I have trained myself to change my language, as I believe that these terms connote equality rather than hierarchy. Many quotes from existential humanists still use the old terms, but they embody the meanings of the relational field I identify with. The use of the terms *therapist* and *patient* by authors in the postmodern camp in no way implies that the old hierarchy exists in their thinking. Sometimes life teaches you lessons that need to be unlearned. My use of the terms *clinician* and *client* is for my own clarity, and serves as a reminder to me about the necessity of the coequal lens of the relational field.

Shapiro is a brilliant humanist, and EMDR was never intended as a strictly by-the-book treatment approach. She has always advocated that clinicians approach our clients with our love and the highest of intentions of individual and planetary healing. The message has been there from the beginning; I am only amplifying it. For everyone reading my book, please see the appendix on the Humanitarian Assistance Program (HAP), the not-for-profit arm of the EMDR Institute. This program sends EMDR clinicians to different places in this country, and throughout the world, training clinicians in EMDR. There is either a nominal fee or none. Developed by Shapiro its mission is to "give forward" to those who do not have the means to pay for training, so that they can give to their clients. It is in this way that the EMDR world makes its contribution to planetary healing. I'm proud to be a part of HAP.

My suggestions to EMDR are made to help broaden clinical thinking and to encourage other EMDR clinicians to use their best judgment when applying this methodology. I am not recommending modifications to the standard methodology; I am enhancing it through the lens of the practicing EMDR clinician who thinks and practices in relational ways. EMDR is a very powerful modality, and, if used incautiously, it can dramatically increase a client's pain instead of healing it. When I teach EMDR, which I have done since 1995, I do so according to Shapiro's textbook.

I believe that newcomers to EMDR need to learn the standard method properly and thoroughly, and then apply it systematically over many sessions with consultation from a senior EMDR clinician, such as one approved by the EMDR International Association. Clinicians may also become more proficient in EMDR by earning certification through the EMDR International Association, or EMDR Europe, depending on the continent you want to practice. EMDR is practiced throughout the world; there are different EMDR associations with their own requirements, such as EMDR Europe, which is a consortium of European countries. I respect the right of these organizations to decide how best to ensure the proper use of EMDR. I am writing from my viewpoint as a practitioner in the United States.

I am offering my ideas in a conversational manner as a way of relating to you, the reader. This is no accident. I am relating to you in a way that I hope you find engaging. I have also included much of standard EMDR methodological thinking. I do this because by offering it conversationally (along with some ways I think about the phases), I hope to approach you from a different perspective (relationally, of course!) so that I might deepen your understanding of this approach to healing trauma. I have carefully attempted to explain what I bring from my perspective.

Throughout this book, I also talk about what happens in clinicians' bodies. I cannot emphasize enough that our bodies are our greatest tool and our greatest liability. My clients affect me. I affect my clients. This is all part of being in conscious relationship with our clients. I have also included statements made to me by other EMDR clinicians in an attempt to demonstrate that these are not my opinions alone. To quote Ringo Starr, "I get by with a little help from my friends." I believe that it would be grandiose of me to take credit as the only EMDR clinician who believes this way. To my knowledge, I am the only clinician who has written a book on the therapeutic relationship and EMDR. To all other EMDR clinicians whom I have inadvertently left out, I offer my sincere apologies. When one tries to be inclusive there is a danger of slighting others who have made significant contributions.

EMDR is not just about trauma processing. It has eight phases, and checks and balances, to determine whether a client is presently ready to process trauma, or whether he needs some time developing internal resources to contain intense negative arousal. As a young man I was quite shy. When I transferred to Boston University in my junior year I made a great lifetime friend. On the weekends we would see movies that were shown in the basement of Myles Standish Hall, our dormitory. It was our first weekend, and the movie was "Casablanca." The character Humphrey Bogart played, Richard Blaine, became important to me. He had been a man whose heart was broken, but still managed to go on. The same was true for me at the time. He became my "alter ego" and feeling his internalized experience encouraged me to be brave and more social with women. How was I supposed to know that I had "installed" him as a resource? As I became fluent with EMDR methodology, and especially when Andrew Leeds and others first developed RDI and other resourcing strategies, I realized that I had been doing this my whole adult life (without the bilateral stimulation, of course). It is because of my earlier experience that I resonated with the idea that internal resources are crucial when in deep distress. In secure and continuous attachments these resources are already deeply ingrained. Though my childhood was generally happy, it had more than its share of challenging moments. Don and Elizabeth, whom I refer to, are real people whose loving presence resonates deeply in my soul. Humphrey Bogart died when I was seven. His "presence" lives inside of me as well. One of the beauties of resource work in EMDR is that these internalizations can come from many different places. Thanks for being there when I need you, "Bogie." The late Jerry Garcia of the Grateful Dead is another imaginal resource.

"The Case of Madeline," which appears throughout the book, is an example of clinical judgment used relationally. In it, I made a choice to suspend the positive cognition (PC) and the validity of cognition scale (VOC) from Phase 3 work. I did so only after attempting to go through the full procedural steps outline. I have noticed that in some higher functioning, intellectually defended clients, too much confusion can develop around what they want to believe about themselves when they may already be becoming activated or negatively aroused. Some become overconcerned about which numbers indicate that the VOC is more true or false. The confusion plays out when the clinician asks for the positive cognition, after a client of this type starts becoming activated.

What I found with Madeline is that she switched to analyzing what *I* was looking for. In doing so, she became deactivated, and this was problematic in the first trauma-processing protocol. I also understand the underpinnings of the PC and VOC: the need to see what direction the client wishes to go, the fact that PC gives them hope, and that the purpose is to assess the distance from episodic memory to semantic memory. With clients like Madeline, I have discovered that assisting them into state-dependent memory is sometimes more fully achieved without the PC and VOC in the third phase. I will have ascertained their general wished-for beliefs in Phase 1 and had them rate how true these positive beliefs feel to them in their beginning sessions with me.

I also always ask clients to say what they positively believe about themselves at the beginning of Phase 5 and to rate this belief with the VOC. The SUDS is a measure of state change; the VOC is a measure of trait change. I use the full basic procedural steps outline as a matter of good practice. The case of Madeline taught me many lessons in applying EMDR relationally, and crystallized my thinking about how the relational use of clinical judgment may affect EMDR practice on a case-by-case basis.

There is also a second reason why I emphasize the relational aspects of EMDR. There are clinicians who believe EMDR to be a manualized approach that one should not deviate from. My view is that one learns the methodology completely; then, and only then, if a clinician makes a judgment call based on the interactions with the client, he or she has a responsibility to state the reasoning behind it. What I have done in this book is just a case in point of a much larger issue. The practice of EMDR does not mean giving up one's therapeutic self, but rather understanding how method and relationship meld in their specific ways. In my opinion they cannot be separated. I encourage you to think conceptually and, when making judgment calls, to be able to back up your reasoning with clinical data. That is the bigger reason for my presenting the case of Madeline.

My intention in writing this book is to encourage the reader to think conceptually. For practicing EMDR clinicians who need further training in EMDR, I have given many suggestions of ways they may further develop their abilities. Any clinician who reads only this text or only Shapiro's *Eye Movement Desensitization and Reprocessing* (1995, 2001) and then uses EMDR on clients, in my opinion, does so unwisely.

I offer this work to enrich the reader's understanding of how I practice EMDR clinically. I have not conducted research to validate my opinions. This work is based on acute and repeated clinical observations of the many clients with whom I have had the privilege to work.

References

Bordin, E. S. (1994). Theory and Research on the therapeutic working alliance: New directions. In A. O. Howatch and L. S. Greenberg (Eds.), *The working alliance: Theory, research, and practice.* New York: Wiley.

Acknowledgments

I would first like to thank my wife, Laurie, and my sons, Matthew and Hal, for putting up with me during what must have seemed like an eternity to us all. Laurie, your continued love, support, and tolerance are the hallmark of why all who know us consider you a saint.

Next I would like to thank Francine Shapiro for developing and giving birth to EMDR, for putting up with my continued campaign to make the therapeutic relationship explicit in EMDR thinking, and for fully supporting my efforts. I share her vision to end the cycle of violence and honor her work in creating the Humanitarian Assistance Program.

As this book took a career to germinate in me, I want to acknowledge the gifted professionals who influenced me the most, the blessed memories of William Frederick Orr, Laura Perls, and Dayashakti; Thomas Horvath and Ken Davis of the Mount Sinai School of Medicine; Alex Gitterman, Rene Solomon, Irving Miller, and Bea Seitzman of the Columbia University School of Social Work; Dick Cornfield, Seth Fielding, Leah Davidson, and Rose Jacobs-Baskind at the Bronx VA Medical Center; Richy Lasky (the most relational Freudian I know), Marsha Pollack, and Willa Cobert of the Manhattan Institute for Psychoanalysis; Edith DeGannon-Szold; and Carl Bagnini.

A special thanks to Patti Levin, Ricky Greenwald, Robbie Dunton, Zona Scheiner, Bennet Wolper, and Phillip Dutton for helpful comments on my final manuscript. My thanks to George Zimmar and his staff at Routledge. Thanks to my editor Margo Silk Forrest for helping with the architecture of the book and rushing to meet deadlines; to Cindy Hyden for her valuable critiques and my editorial assistant, Lauren Mondello, for putting up with and then organizing my papers, and for her careful editing. Lucky is the publishing house that hires her.

I also wish to thank my New York EMDR facilitator buddies, Uri Bergmann, David Grand, Carol Forgash, Ruth Heber, Sandy Kaplan, Barbara Kourzan, Maudie Ritchie, Sandy Shapiro, Beverly Wright, and William Zangwill; our dear fellow facilitators from New Jersey, Victoria Britt and Sheila Bender (thanks, Sheila B., for those early days of brainstorming on transference, countertransference, and the intersubjective in EMDR methodology); Barbara Korzun, our fearless logistics coordinator from New Hope, Pennsylvania, and our New England "cousins," Kathy Davis, Leslie Weiss, Patti Levin, and Debbie Korn. Every time we facilitated, we shared valuable time and interesting discussions on EMDR methodology. All those Saturday night dinners were intellectually stimulating and fun. Victoria was always into something new.

I also thank my fellow board members (of the EMDR International Association), with whom it was a pleasure to serve: Jim Gach, Roy Kiessling, Celia Grand, Rosalie Thomas, Barb Hensley, Irene Giessel, Laura Steele, Wendy Freitag, Zona Scheiner, Andrew Leeds, Byron Perkins, Elizabeth Adams, Judith Boel, and Marilyn Schyler (whom I never got to place a bet with over whether the New York Jets would beat the Cincinnati Bengals in the AFC Championship — maybe next year, Marilyn). Good luck to Cocoa Garcia, Valerie Sheehan, Helen Huffington, and Ed Halsten. By the time this book is in print, you four will be seasoned veterans of the EMDRIA Board of Directors.

I have made many friends in the EMDR world who have been sources of inspiration and support to me: Robbie Dunton, Roger Solomon, Andrew Leeds, Gerald Puk, my whole New York gang, Jim Gach, Roy Kiessling, Celia Grand, Zona Scheiner and Bennett Wolper, Patti Levin, Ricky Greenwald, Deanny Laliotis and Dan Merlis, Nancy Smyth, Sue Rogers and Louise Maxfield, Howard Lipke, Byron Perkins, Curt Rouanzoin (the real "Bubba"), Jocelyn Shiromoto, Phil Manfield, Carol York, Ginger Gilson, Frankie Klaff, Carl Nickerson, Gene Schwartz, Eileen Freedland, Marsha Whisman, A.J. Popky, Terence and Darlene Wade, Larry Sine and Silke Vogelman-Sine, Elaine Alvarez, Marilyn Luber, Bill Solz, Jerry LaMangne, David Ogren, Peter Barasch (who first wrote to me and asked me, "Where's the book?" after reading some ideas I wrote on the EMDR discussion group), Tom Cloyd, and John Marquis (thanks to you and Helen's sons for permission to use her story). Also thanks to my friends in Canada, Judith Black and Louise Maranda, Judith Boel, and Heather Pearson, and those in Europe and around the world: Kerstin Bergh Johannesson, Anne Martinell-Vestin, and Reet Oras of Sweden; Richard Mitchell of Great Britain; Philip Dutton and Therese McGoldrick of Scotland; Michael Paterson of Northern Ireland; Arne Hoffman of

Germany; Udi Oren of Israel; Isabel Fernandez of Italy; Masaya Ichii of Japan; and Ad de Jongh and Joany Spierings of the Netherlands. We are truly blessed to be an international community of friends.

Special thank yous go to Gene Schwartz for his invaluable help in jogging my memory of the VA post-Vietnam era; Ricky Greenwald for his helpful guidance to a new author; Uri Bergmann, who consistently fielded the questions about the neurobiology of EMDR that I mercilessly and constantly threw at him; and all my students and consultees who challenged me to explain EMDR thoroughly.

There is one who is no longer with us whose influence through her writings and our talks encouraged me to think about the use of transference in EMDR: Liz Synker. Her chapter, "Into the Volcano," in Phil Manfield's case book, *Extending EMDR,* is the first example of this integrative thinking. Liz, know that you are loved and you are missed.

The EMDR International Association is lucky to have Scott Blech as our executive director. Scott, you "passed the audition." Gayla Turner, it has been an honor watching you grow into the fine associate director you are. My thanks to the whole staff at the EMDR International Association, who fielded incessant questions I threw at them. To a person, you have acted in the highest professional manner.

Thanks also to Christine Wilson, John Marquis, and Jim Gach for helping me launch the health care committee of the EMDR International Association, which Dave Wilson took from a task force and made a standing EMDRIA committee. Our struggles with the managed care world in gaining EMDR's acceptance were a monumental effort for four people. Thanks for hanging in. A special thanks also to two very special people, Scott and Jennifer Sade, for giving shelter and succor to a weary traveler at Casa Sade, a Ben Moshe Land Preserve. Another thanks of equal dimensions go to my two favorite inner guides whom I refer to throughout my text; Don Cornelius DSW, professor of Social Work at Molloy College, and Elizabeth Paulette Coughlin, writer, body worker, yoga instructor, and friend.

Finally, we should all have a guardian angel looking over our shoulder, supporting, encouraging, and critiquing our efforts. I am blessed to have as my guardian angel my spiritual sister, Sandra "Sam" Foster. Thanks, Sam.

CHAPTER 1

The Relational Imperative in EMDR

1.1 Introduction

Clinicians are happy to think that our professional experiences, theoretical knowledge, and clinical skills affect our clients' progress, but we are distinctly less comfortable admitting that our personal histories also play a role in the therapeutic process. Ever since Freud sat back in silence while patients lay on his couch talking about their troubles, some clinicians have preferred to see themselves as keen observers, wise counselors, and perhaps kind listeners, but definitely separate persons from the anguish that often is played out in their consulting rooms. While relational psychoanalysts have been correcting this issue for decades, there are those in the EMDR community who interpret "staying out of the way" as harkening back to being separate from the client.

Yet even in EMDR, which first took root in the soil of cognitive–behavioral therapy, who clinicians are — and how well we know ourselves — matters. And it matters deeply. In each of the eight phases of EMDR, relational issues play a vital role.

The therapeutic relationship is a critical aspect of EMDR; it has been assumed from the beginning that licensed mental health clinicians already have good understandings of the need to have this relationship in place in order to work with traumatized clients. The EMDR Institute's trainings were designed to teach the principles, protocols, and procedures of EMDR methodology within the context of the attuned relationship. My goal is to flesh out what has not been fully written about. The working alliance is an important part of the therapeutic relationship; it is necessary, but not sufficient for work with traumatized clients, as I will elaborate further in this chapter. Alliances are formed when people walk shoulder to shoulder toward a common goal. Relationships are formed when people stand face to face. An alliance is not a strong enough container for a traumatized client who comes to us short on trust, long on isolation, and knowing he will be asked to reveal and feel — perhaps for the first time, if he dissociated during the original trauma — the most terrible moments of his life. The client's degree of fear is identical to the degree of connectedness he needs with his therapist in order to feel safe.

This is because the essence of psychological trauma is sudden exposure to extreme danger, whether that danger is a tsunami, a rapist, or a raging parent. This terrifying experience causes victims of post-traumatic stress to negotiate their lives around feeling safe. They know they are vulnerable to extreme harm, so they isolate themselves out of fear of being harmed again and out of shame at their previous vulnerability. Many victims of interpersonal trauma believe — no, they *know* — they are bad people: They were to blame, after all, for what happened to them (or so they believe). This leads trauma victims to make faulty self-assessments in the present and to shut down their ability to respond appropriately to new situations if these situations stimulate the neural networks where their old pain is stored. Thus, to maintain their internal balance, many traumatized people defend against past pain by limiting their ability to feel in the present.

This is why, when an EMDR clinician establishes a therapeutic relationship with a trauma client, it is essential that he or she anchor that person in the present, in a safe relationship from the first session on, with emphasis on the real relationship, rather than the transferential one. (And this absolutely must occur before the client begins bilateral stimulation.) This anchoring is one of the two focal points for the dual attention essential to EMDR. (The other is the client's simultaneous concentration on a state-dependent memory that is held in a dysfunctionally excited state. I will go into detail about this later.) Active trauma work (phases 3–6 in EMDR methodology) can be successful only in an atmosphere of safety. When it is done in the context of a therapeutic relationship, the client no longer experiences himself or herself as alone with the horror. The pain can now be shared, and the activities necessary to begin accelerated information processing are laid down. The working alliance, with its emphasis on goals, tasks, and bonding, optimally creates the kind of safety between the two parties in which the work is to be done. This bond, however, will be subject to many potential ruptures that go beyond what an alliance can hold. Identifying potential ruptures, preparing for them or repairing them, and managing transference and countertransference are essential parts of the work in EMDR.

The relational imperative is what makes EMDR — despite appearances — a two-person psychology. To call EMDR a one-person psychology is a "straw man argument," as all psychotherapies are two-person events. However, some clinicians and researchers discuss EMDR from the perspective of method alone. Some clinicians and researchers disagree. They view EMDR as a one-person psychology, with the one person, of course, being the client. A one-person psychology works like this: The client comes in. The clinician takes the client's history and prepares the client for the procedure. The clinician tells the client what he or she needs to do; the clinician respects the client and builds an alliance. The client goes through the procedural steps, perhaps with a few blocks that need clearing up along the way, and improves. All is clean, crisp, and clear-cut.

This is not my interpretation of Shapiro's intent. EMDR will never be a one-person psychology as long as there are two people in the room. Even in the no-nonsense realm of physics, we know — thanks to the Heisenberg Uncertainty Principle — that the mere presence of an observer affects the results of the experiment that is being observed.

So it is with EMDR. Common sense, clinical experience, and hard science present convincing arguments that the presence of the clinician affects the traumatized client — and vice versa — and that these variables affect the progress of the therapy. There is simply no escaping the I–Thou nature of our work. Picture this scenario, which was given to me during my psychoanalytic training: A slender, 4'10" male behavioral therapist is about to meet a new client. When he hears the client's knock, he opens his door and is confronted by a man who is 6'5" and weighs 350 pounds. The therapist has an atavistic moment of pure terror, but he promptly pulls himself together when he sees that his new client has noticed his fearful reaction. The therapist steps back, swings open the door, and says, "Well, come in anyway!"

Bingo. In that moment, a one-person psychology — behaviorism — turns into a two-person psychology. We are human. We can't help but have an effect on each other, whether we intend to or not. The bottom line is, whenever two human hearts are beating in the same room, you have a two-person process, no matter how crisply you attend to principles, protocols, and procedures. And because it is a two-person process, it is relational.

Norcross (2002) states that, "We unanimously acknowledged the deep synergy between technique and relationship. They constantly shape and inform each other… the relationship does not exist apart from what the therapist does in terms of technique, and we cannot imagine any techniques that would not have some relational impact."

1.1.1 From Working Alliance to Therapeutic Relationship

The beginning of the therapeutic relationship starts with a good working alliance. This embodies a facilitation of the definition of the client's goals, an explicit understanding of the co-collaboration of the shared tasks between each party, and the different roles and responsibilities each commits to making. This makes for a positive bond, based upon the mental model of a good enough attachment relationship that the client hopefully enjoyed from infancy. With higher functioning clients, this alliance may take a session or two; with more disturbed clients who suffered from early forms of preoccupied, dismissive, disorganized, disoriented, and fearful attachments, it will take longer. The working alliance is only a part of the relationship in therapy, and it does not take the transference or countertransference phenomenon into account theoretically, though the beginnings of this phenomenon may begin at the onset of the first phone call from prospective client to clinician. This alliance may become strengthened or weakened by the shared agreement of tasks and goals, and how both client and clinician carry out these tasks together in their respective roles, based upon the kind of treatment approach the alliance is embedded in. Gelso and Hayes delineate three basic types of alliances; the nurturing alliance, in which the clinician is directive and supportive, insight-oriented, in which the clinician stimulates the client's self-understanding through the clinician's insight-oriented approach, and the collaborative alliance, which is marked as a joint venture between clinician and client working together on shared goals. In EMDR I believe that the collaborative alliance is what is developed as a prelude to, and as a continuation of the work throughout.

The working alliance goes by different names, but the variations should be seen as more similar than different. Horvath and Bedi (Shapiro, in press), found that the mean correlation across 89 studies between the "therapeutic alliance" and therapy outcome was 0.21, which they considered to be a modest but very robust association. The therapeutic alliance, which they refer to, embodies the quality and strength of the collaborative relationship between client and therapist, typically measured as agreement on therapeutic goals, consensus on treatment tasks, and a relationship bond (which has the same characteristics as the collaborative alliance).

Gelso and Hayes also point to the significance of the alliance being different in different phases of the work. In EMDR the importance of the alliance is there from the beginning, in Phase 1, when client and clinician develop an action plan with their roles and responsibilities spelled out. In Phase 2 its importance exists as the clinician continues to act as educator to the client of the process. In Phases 3–5, assessment, desensitization, and installation, the alliance is crucial, for here is where the some of the most daunting and challenging parts of the work occur in EMDR. These are the phases of active trauma work. Though of continued importance, the alliance may not be as crucial in Phases 6–8, during the body scan, closure, and re-evaluation, since the lion's share of detraumatizing and reprocessing will hopefully be completed. These are general statements, as each therapeutic encounter will have its own set of circumstances. It is from the starting point of the working alliance that all other aspects of the therapeutic relationship emerge.

1.1.2 The Adaptive Information Processing Model of EMDR

However, it is important first to note that EMDR is based on the adaptive information processing model, which posits that there is a self-healing quality in all humans and that it is the negative experiences in living that inhibit these innate neurobiological functions.

Shapiro states, "When someone experiences a severe psychological trauma, it appears that an imbalance may occur in the nervous system, caused perhaps by changes in neurotransmitters, adrenaline, and so forth. Due to this imbalance, the information processing system is unable to function optimally and the information acquired at the time of event, including images, sounds, affect, and physical sensations, is maintained neurologically in its disturbing state. Therefore, the original material, which is held in this distressing excitatory state-specific form, can be triggered by a variety of internal and external stimuli and may be expressed in the form of nightmares, flashbacks, and intrusive thoughts—the so-called positive symptoms of PTSD" (Shapiro, 2001, p. 31).

Howard Lipke, in his book *EMDR and Psychotherapy Integration*, describes information processing in generally easy terms. He states, "Information, usually in the form of sensation or perception, is taken in by a person, it interacts with the person, change occurs, and usually at some point there is an output of activity, such as language, or other behavior" (Lipke, 2000, p. 13). "The goal of information processing psychologies is to explain that when an event occurs in which the individual is stimulated, positively or negatively, there is an interaction between this state and other states of mind that are associated in the client's consciousness. As a result of this interaction, a series of evaluations occur in the brain prompting certain actions and behaviors." (Lipke, p. 13).

It is from that starting point that we may view Shapiro's idea of adaptive information processing. She states

> Specifically, there appears to be a neurological balance in a distinct physiological system that allows information to be processed to an

adaptive resolution. By adaptive resolution I mean that the connections to appropriate associations are made and that the experience is used constructively by the individual and is integrated into a positive emotional and cognitive schema.

The purpose of EMDR is to restore that neurological balance, so that information can be processed to an adaptive resolution. Where there is a trauma there is often dissociation.

1.2 State-Dependent Memory

Throughout this book I use the term *state-dependent memory* in a more limited way than might be generally accepted in academic psychology. In my way of explaining the different quantities of traumatic experience, I use this term to connote memories held in dysfunctional states where the visual, auditory, and sensory motor aspects are held by the brain in a way that is separated from semantic or autobiographical memory and that is not accessible to left-brain logical linear thinking. One of the great harms humans do to one another (and clinicians may do this inadvertently) is to try to talk others out of their "irrational" ways of experiencing aspects of their lives. Were it that straightforward, treatment might not be necessary for a great number of people. Take a moment and notice your own unpleasant experiences. How many times have you said to yourself, "Get over it," only to find yourself on the frustrating end of knowing that you are reacting irrationally but that you do not have the capacity to "snap out of it"? We risk retraumatizing ourselves and others through this misguided form of advice.

The brain works on the principle of association. People over 45 years of age, when they hear the phrase, "Winston tastes good," will automatically respond, "like a cigarette should." It seems that these associations become so embedded in the brain that extinction is a very difficult process.

1.3 Early History of Trauma Treatment

I was introduced to treating trauma in 1975 when as a young man of 24 I was hired by the Department of Psychiatry at the Bronx Veterans Administration Medical Center to be trained to help Vietnam veterans who were suffering as a result of their war experiences. The formal diagnosis of post-traumatic stress disorder (PTSD) would not be established until 1980, and at the time I was hired, it was common just to say that these men had been "dramatically affected," or were experiencing "post traumatic stress" by the war.

The outpatient mental health department where I worked was a hundred yards down the street from the building site for a new VA hospital. In digging the foundation, the builders had encountered a small problem. About 30 feet down, they hit solid rock. Their only recourse was dynamite. So several times a day, we would hear two short whistles, followed by a very loud BANG! and a long "all clear" whistle. Can you imagine what that was like for our combat veterans? We were told to instruct our clients carefully that they would be hearing these sounds and to reassure them that they would be all right. You can guess how effective that was. When the whistles blew and the dynamite roared, some ended up under my desk. Others went into flashbacks. It was clear that exposure to aspects of the trauma in the here and now could be retraumatizing, even in the presence of a safe enough relationship.

Looking back, it is shocking how little was known at the time about traumatic stress. Sometimes it seems as if even common sense was absent in the way we were trained to handle clients. In those days, many vets were applying for war-related disability benefits, and in order to screen out fraudulent claims, the VA hired consultants to teach us how to test for startle sensitivity, a classic sign of "shell shock." We were instructed that during our initial consultation we should casually walk behind the combat veteran and slap our hands together loudly to assess his startle sensitivity. I am surprised that I am alive to report this story. Those poor men must have jumped five feet. Many of them (after their heart rate had returned to normal) told me their initial impulse was to defend themselves — by killing me.

We were not successful in ameliorating the symptoms of PTSD in those days. Most vets were put on medication. Many had comorbid symptoms of depression or drug and alcohol abuse, as well as a severe sense of isolation from society. Arthur Egendorf, a Vietnam veteran himself, studied this population in the 1970s and found that the only place they were really comfortable was at the Vietnam veterans outreach centers just starting to be opened at the time. These men could only relate to and get a sense of community from their peers (Egendorf, 1985). Perhaps those peers provided a relational aspect that had been lacking elsewhere.

Twenty years later, having been trained in EMDR and become known for my success using it with clients, I got another wake-up call about the vital importance of the therapeutic relationship.

A well-respected colleague asked me to do a consultation with a high-functioning client who had a phobia that they had been unable to resolve. After an initial consultation with this business executive, whom I will call Dan, I agreed to use EMDR with him to resolve his fear of driving over rainy bridges. After we had completed our preliminary work and begun bilateral stimulation, Dan started to remember upsetting events from earlier in his life. Although EMDR is *not* a method of memory retrieval, any EMDR clinician can tell you that when you use a target memory to stimulate a memory network, other memories associated with the target can emerge. I had explained this possibility to Dan during Phase 2, the preparation phase, but he was still not prepared for the memory that came up. He became quite agitated, and we stopped doing the eye movements.

We then went through all the steps to close down processing and end our incomplete session. I made sure Dan was able to drive home and called him that night to check that he was okay. He said he was. In short I had fulfilled all the requirements of Phase 7, closure, and all the requirements of the collaborative alliance. At our next session, though, Dan read me the riot act. He was not here for anything but to cure his phobia, he declared vehemently. Under Dan's verbal assault, I found myself in an induced state of countertransference. I froze and was unable to manage my countertransferential reaction. Meekly, I complied with Dan's wishes, and we spent a few more unproductive sessions trying to relieve his phobia. After that he thanked me and said that he did feel a mild improvement. He returned to his primary clinician, who later confirmed my suspicion that Dan was simply acting compliant and had not achieved the desired result.

I realize now that I had not established a good enough relationship with Dan, either for his sake or mine. I had simply gotten the history of Dan's presenting problem from my colleague and begun with Dan by giving him a brief explanation of EMDR. After testing him for dissociation and completing the preparation and education work of Phase 2, I consulted with my colleague on my brief evaluation of Dan. Then, believing I understood Dan's case and had established an adequate treatment alliance with him, I proceeded with EMDR processing. As I have said, it was not a success. I had a powerful countertransference experience, and Dan was not "cured" of his phobia. Since then, I have learned how tricky it can be to establish a safe therapeutic *relationship* — not just an alliance — with a client whose primary relationship is with his own therapist.

That was the last referral I received from this clinician. It was an instructive moment in my professional career, one that reaffirmed what I had learned in many years of training in contemporary interpersonal psychoanalysis: The therapeutic relationship is an integral part of the successful practice of any type of psychotherapy. This includes EMDR. In fact, my interpretation is that Shapiro has written quite a bit about the therapeutic relationship, though without using that term. (Her discussion of it is subsumed under the concept of "good clinical judgment.") If clinicians are truly client-centered, then our actions are informed by what the client is experiencing in the here and now. (This is consistent with the experiential schools of psychotherapy.) A simple example of the client-centered approach is the clinically driven stop signal, which is explicitly taught to clients in Phase 2. The client can use the stop signal during processing to let the clinician know that he or she feels overwhelmed and needs to stop bilateral stimulation for the moment.

1.4 The Therapeutic Relationship

At this point, I want to say a word or two about what I mean when I use the term *therapeutic relationship*. There are many ways to define the therapeutic relationship, depending on what school of therapy you consult. However, I think Gelso and Hayes (1998) express it simply and accurately in their description of what happens in a therapy session: "In the midst of all this ... the clinician and client develop attitudes and feelings toward each other. These attitudes and feelings, along with the manner in which they are expressed, constitute the psychotherapy relationship" (p. 135).

I am also in agreement with Gelso's concept of the "real" relationship. With all due respect to the postmodern social constructivists who wisely question the nature of what is real, Gelso defines the real relationship as "genuineness, on the one hand, and realism on the other" (Gelso, 2002). He references the works of Carl Rogers in defining *genuineness*, and defines *realism* as that which "may be seen as the experiencing or perceiving of the other in ways that benefit him or her, rather than as projections of wished for or feared others" (Gelso, 2002). In my opinion, it is the real relationship that carries the healing path. Transference and countertransference will always be there, lurking to interrupt the process, but, as I will elaborate in Chapter 8, they are issues that can be dealt with in ways to promote healing as well.

The therapeutic relationship is used differently in the process of healing, depending on the type of therapy practiced. In this case, I would add one important caveat for EMDR. The psychotherapeutic relationship is the way in which both clinician and client negotiate these attitudes and feelings within the eight phases of EMDR treatment. In Phases 1 and 2, for example, the clinician acts as the psychological evaluator of the client's problems, the client's ability to work on them, and the possible strategies whereby the client can reach higher levels of functionality. During the active phases of trauma treatment, the clinician shifts from the role of expert to that of co-participant as the client–clinician relationship becomes central to facilitating the release of painful state-dependent memories.

The therapeutic relationship is present in all psychotherapies, whether one wants to acknowledge it or not. In their writings, Gelso and Hayes (1998, pp. 15–16) have suggested a useful way to contrast and compare different types of psychotherapy, by looking at the following four variables in the therapeutic relationship:

- Centrality: "the extent to which the client–therapist relationship is seen as the crucial change agent"
- Means–end: whether the therapeutic relationship is an end in itself or a means to an end
- Real–unreal: whether the real relationship or the transference relationship is of primary importance
- Power: the amount of power the therapist has compared to the client

For example, in the humanistic therapies, the importance of the therapeutic relationship as a change agent is high, the relationship is an end in itself, the "real" relationship is primary, and the therapist's power is low. In psychoanalytic practice, the importance of the relationship as a change agent is also high, but the relationship is seen as a means to an end, the transference relationship is primary, and the therapist's power is medium. Again by contrast, in cognitive–behavioral therapy, the importance of the relationship as a change agent is medium, the relationship is a means to an end, the "real" relationship is primary, and the therapist's power is high (Gelso and Hayes, 1998).

In EMDR, however, these four variables are not static; they change depending on the phase of the work. For example, in the preparatory phases (Phase 1 and Phase 2), the relationship's importance as a change agent is fairly low, and therapist's power is high. However, as the work proceeds to Phase 4 and the client begins to re-experience highly distressing state-dependent memories, the relationship's importance as a change agent increases. If the client does not feel safe with the therapist, he or she will be unable to continue processing when difficult memories and feelings emerge, as we saw in Dan's case. Also, at this point, the therapist's power has dropped from high to low, with the clinician staying out of the way as much as possible. In the later evaluative phases of EMDR, the therapist's power becomes high again. In all phases, EMDR is practiced as a means to an end, and the "real" relationship is more important than the transference relationship. There are a number of ways to describe the therapeutic relationship. I think that I was born a Rogerian. Unconditional positive regard, congruence, and empathy have always been in my blood.

Focusing on the real relationship between my client and myself has been a hallmark of my work. This does not blind me to the unavoidable realities of transference and countertransference. The risk of these is increased with traumatized individuals. In chapter 8, I will suggest ways of understanding and dealing with these issues within the EMDR framework, but for now I want to say that relational psychoanalytic thinking about them has great merit. In a sentence, it holds that the ways in which the traumatized client behaves in life will be played out in the treatment setting, and their effects on the clinician will impact treatment.

Many psychotherapy authors comment on the effects of the relationship on psychotherapy. Beutler and Harwood (2002) state that, "Patient, therapy, and relationship factors are shown to selectively add to the variance predicted in psychotherapy outcome studies" (pg. 25).

Kaslow (2002) discusses the therapeutic relationship as a co-construction between the clinician and the client, with emphasis on teamwork rather a hierarchical relationship. She asks early on in treatment,

> "(1) What do you hope to accomplish? (2) What are your goals for therapy? (3) What is the outcome you seek?" ... Then we co-construct the treatment plan that becomes the map for the implementation phase. This approach garners much greater involvement and participation than a more hierarchical relationship and approach does. (Kaslow, p. 87)

Kaslow also elaborates that she switches to the term *action plan,* as it represents a joint venture rather than a treatment of a client (which connotes hierarchy). I believe that this approach is consistent with the goals and objectives of EMDR and lays the best foundation for the work to follow.

Psychotherapy researchers Lisa Najavits and colleagues conclude that in treating substance abusers, the psychotherapeutic relationship counts, as do therapist factors, and their implicit theories of therapy (1994, 1997, and 2000). Jeger and colleagues (2004) investigated the role of therapist-patient interaction through action control theory, which states, "Action control theory describes a motivational behavior that occurs before the actual action. It can be assumed that a successful therapeutic treatment should be marked by an increasing motivational coherence toward therapeutic goals and intentions of the interaction partner" (p. 415). One of the results of their research suggests that "...the relationship between patient and therapist exerts a decisive influence on the regulation of the patient's readiness to change..." (p. 426).

Bohart (2002) agrees that healing, and productive thinking ("reprocessing") come as a result of this joint venture between two human beings involved in dialogic activities. His thesis supports the idea that the therapeutic relationship "supports productive client information processing." Respect, understanding the client's frame of reference, empathic listening; treating the client as an intelligent person of respect, capable of making their own informed decisions; and working in a collaborative coordinative way with the client are the hallmarks necessary in the therapeutic relationship. His position, citing the work of Dweck on task focus, resonates deeply with the EMDR position in its different tasks necessary to be accomplished in all of its eight phases.

He notes that the task-focused approach looks at "failure" as information, instead of personal inadequacy. Not every EMDR treatment session may produce the desired effects. Keeping an eye on the task, rather than the outcome, is something Bohart and EMDR agree upon, and in the end will enhance more possibility of succeeding. (I interpret the instruction we give to our clients in Phase 2, "sometimes the picture will change, and sometimes it won't ..." as more broadly stating that sometimes you (the client) will experience change and sometimes you won't; try not to judge it, as that may inhibit productive thinking. Bohart states that the task-focused person will step back and take a broader view. This seems to be a parallel to part of what EMDR aims for in "dual attention."

There is another crossover between the two positions when Bohart states that the task-focused client *"holds constructs tentatively, reserving judgment, while exploring and waiting for things to come clear instead of jumping to conclusions"* (italics are mine).

This is the hallmark of active trauma work that takes place in Phase 4: desensitization, with the effects of detraumatizing painful state dependent memories (desensitization), and reprocessing, which seems to be a neurobiological way of facilitating productive information processing. His position on letting go of the hierachical position of the expert who "does something" to the "intervened" client, and focusing on the co-collaboration of two persons having an intelligent dialogue also resonates and underscores the importance of the real relationship.

The power of the "real" therapeutic relationship to help heal traumatic wounding can be found in the very nature of interpersonal trauma: Human beings hurt each other, and human beings can help each other heal. (Or, as I heard it put at Kripalu, a yoga and meditation center in the Berkshire Mountains of western Massachusetts, "Community is stronger than will.") This calls for heart. But the heart is not the only part of our humanity that creates the relational imperative in EMDR. The brain plays a critical role too. Let us look now at how recent findings in the neurosciences can inform our work as trauma therapists doing EMDR in the context of a relationship.

CHAPTER 2

The Therapeutic Relationship and Its Underlying Neurobiology

2.1 Introduction

Although doing EMDR in the real world is very different from doing EMDR under research conditions, science still guides our approach in the consulting room. I mentioned earlier that hard science fully supports what common sense and clinical experience tell us about the relational imperative in EMDR. In fact, hard science supports the existence of a relational imperative in *all* modalities of psychotherapy. Neurobiologists have discovered that human beings are hard-wired to interact relationally. This means that we cannot avoid interacting relationally if we are interacting with another person. That is how our brains are organized (Schore, 1994, 2003a, 2003b; Siegel, 1999).

In the brilliant books *The Developing Mind,* by psychiatrist Daniel J. Siegel, and *Affect Regulation and the Origin of the Self,* by neuroscientist and developmental psychoanalyst Alan Schore, the authors describe how the brain of a newborn infant depends on interaction with other human beings in order to complete its development. "Human infants have profoundly underdeveloped brains," Siegel writes. "Maintaining proximity to their caregivers is essential, both for survival and for allowing their brains to use the mature states of the attachment figure to help them organize [Siegel is speaking literally] their own mental functioning" (1999, p. 149).

"The structure and function of the developing brain," Siegel continues, "are determined by how experiences, especially within interpersonal relationships, shape the … maturation of the nervous system" (1999). Schore describes the resonance that occurs in a good-enough attachment between the mother or caretaker and infant as a function of the neurological communication between both parties' right orbitofrontal cortices (Schore, 1994).

Siegel explains in detail the key brain functions that a newborn acquires from observing how the mother or primary caregiver interacts with him or her. The evolutionary goal of these functions, as we will see, is to ensure survival — in other words, safety. These are the very same functions that the client's brain — and yours — engage in when you are together in a therapy session, whether you are a Jungian analyst, a cognitive therapist, or an EMDR practitioner. Like many other neurological processes that go on behind the scenes in a client's mind, these are important for the clinician to understand.

First I will give some brief definitions and examples of these brain functions; then, we will look at how they played out during a specific EMDR session I had with a client. As you read, bear in mind that these functions are the basis for the way every one of us navigates every moment of our lives.

The orienting reflex — The orienting reflex is the brain's immediate (and automatic) reaction to a new sensory stimulus that attracts the person's attention, be it positive or negative. It is the brain's way of telling the whole system, "Pay attention! Something is happening here." In practice, the orienting response occurs when the client arrives at your office, takes off his or her coat, looks around, sits down, and chats a little before the work of the session begins.

Appraisal — Next, the appraisal centers in the brain (the orbitofrontal cortex, anterior cingulate, amygdala, and hippocampus) assign meaning to the new stimulus. They evaluate the incoming data (by consulting the mental models the brain has created based on past experiences, as explained in the next definition), and they determine whether what is happening is good, bad, or neutral. Based on this appraisal, the brain will decide either to move toward the new stimulus or to avoid it. Both internal and external factors play a role in this decision, and information about the social context (that is, the relationship between you and the client) directly affects it. Siegel points out that "without such a ... mechanism, stimuli from the outside world and internally generated states and representations would be equally welcome." The appraisal process is what the client is doing at the start of a session when the person thinks, "Can I trust you today? Are you too sleepy or distracted to pay attention? Do you still care about me? Do you remember what I told you last week?" Based on this appraisal of you, the client decides whether to tell you about the terrifying and embarrassing nightmare she or he had last night.

Mental models — Siegel aptly calls the brain an "anticipation machine" (1999, p. 30). Anticipating danger was how our ancestors survived. It is still how our brains work. The brain creates mental models that are generalizations from past experiences. These mental models are consulted when the brain appraises a new situation. They can even influence our actual perceptions, inclining us to see new situations in light of previous similar situations.

Arousal — Based on the appraisal (good, bad, or neutral) it has made, the brain directs the flow of energy through the system to prepare the rest of the brain and the body for action. The essential message of this arousal function is "Act!" This arousal is internal emotional arousal, as opposed to external physiological arousal from a stimulant such as caffeine or exercise. Emotional forms of arousal result from the brain's assigning an evaluated subjective meaning — positive or negative — to a stimulus. If the client appraises the clinician as genuinely interested, then positive arousal occurs, and the client begins a narrative, such as, "I've been thinking about what we've been working on, and I remembered that it was my older brother, not my father, who bullied me the most."

Attunement — The concept of attunement embodies both alignment and resonance. Attunement occurs when one person tunes in to another; that is, a person nonverbally perceives and feels the other's experience. When this occurs, the other person feels "felt." Attunement is very close to empathy. It creates an attachment bond between the two people involved. Attunement is "a profoundly important dimension of human experience," Siegel tells us (1999, p. 000). In practice, attunement is what happens when the clinician really "gets" what the client is feeling in the moment, and the client realizes it. Attunement is a requirement for successful EMDR. When something interferes with clinicians' attunement, we slip into what is called misattunement or malattunement.

State of mind — refers to the cluster of brain activity (and mental modules) at a given moment in time. This "moment" can be brief or extended, and states of mind can have various degrees of sharpness or blurriness to their boundaries across time. The repeated activation of states of mind as time goes by – over weeks, months, and years – into a specialized, goal-directed set of cohesive functional units is what we are going to call a "specialized self" or "self state" (Siegel, 1999, p. 230).

Resonance — Resonance is a very deep form of attunement. When a client tells you of a dream about being trapped between two tribes about to close in vicious battle, resonance has been achieved when you can hear in your own mind the war drums beating out their threats. "Mental state resonance," Siegel states, is when "two individual states are brought into alignment" and deep empathic attunement (Siegel, 1999, p. 70).

Co-regulation — Co-regulation is the back-and-forth process whereby each person allows the other to influence his or her state. The goal of co-regulation is usually alignment (see definition). In practice, co-regulation occurs when you and your client discuss what the focus of that day's session should be.

Alignment — Alignment takes place when the clinician directly attempts to match or anticipate the client's state. Alignment can also take place mutually, when each person moves toward the other's state. Whereas attunement is a requirement for successful EMDR therapy, alignment is not. Sometimes you and your client will be in alignment, sometimes you will not. For example, a client might ask you to look the other way while he or she talks about something the client feels ashamed of, and you feel the need to keep looking at the client to stay in attunement.

Response flexibility — As clinician and client engage in direct communication, they are doing more than just perceiving and interpreting the verbal and nonverbal signals between them. They are working toward the ultimate goal of good trauma treatment: the restoration of the client's response flexibility, that is, the ability to respond to new situations in appropriate ways, unhampered by the triggers or aftereffects of old trauma.

2.2 The Brain Functions in Therapy

Although the clinician will get clues to the client's state of mind from the client's orienting reflex, it is through the clinician's own appraisal, arousal, and attunement functions that he or she sets the stage for effective EMDR — or any other type of psychotherapy. Clinicians use these three brain functions on both the clients' processes and their own. Appraisal occurs when the clinician explicitly and implicitly observes and experiences the client and arrives at conclusions about what is going on for the client. The implicit nature of the clinician's ability to be clear internally, so as to be in attunement with the client, is one of the strongest neurobiological–relational tools in his or her arsenal. Ideally, the clinician's positive arousal moves him or her to work with the client. If so, the clinician opens his or her heart and seeks attunement with the client, allowing himself or herself to be affected by the client's feelings — literally to feel what the client is feeling. By nonverbally communicating this to the client, perhaps simply through the way the clinician looks at the client, the clinician sends the message that the client is understood in the deepest sense. The client feels "felt" by the clinician. It is this interpersonal field, elaborated by the two parties, that creates the safety necessary to engage in active trauma work.

In these transactions, the brain of one person and that of the other are influencing each other in a form of co-regulation. Siegel writes, "Co-regulation … allows minds to connect with each other. Co-regulation is the hallmark for the attunement of states. As adults we need not only to be understood and cared about, but to have another individual simultaneously experience a state similar to our own. With shared, collaborative experience, life can be filled with an integrating sense of connection and meaning" (Siegel, 1999, p. 22).

In reading Siegel's work, I am reminded of a situation that came up in my practice. It is an excellent example of attunement that illustrates how EMDR therapy can benefit from an awareness of the relational imperative dictated by our neurobiology.

A 41-year-old client was starting to work on a memory of his experience of being raised by a violent, alcoholic father who often beat him. He was in the third phase of our work, and we were about to set up a protocol to detraumatize this memory. His eyes filled with tears as he began to tell me of his most painful episode. He hadn't even given me the picture that was most disturbing. His hands trembled. My client's state of mind was both intense and consuming. As my client started speaking again, he concentrated on his father's positive attributes. His nonverbal signals shifted, as did his state of mind. He tried to compose himself with the rationalization to let the past be the past.

I could see my client had been flooded by implicit elements of his early experiences, activated in part by his recounting the story of his father's rages. Despite his diversion (into talking about his father's good traits and finding a rationalization for not dealing with his memories), I used my body's signals, which remained intensely negatively aroused, informing me in real relational terms to use my empathic attunement skills. I said, "I imagine it must be hard to tolerate remembering how painful those beatings were." The client responded, "You can't possibly imagine." Both of us experienced a momentary calming effect. I was now aligned with and attuned to my client. I said, "What is your oldest experience of your father's brutality to you?" After he'd had time to think this over, he told me of a memory when he was 9 years old and had left his bicycle in the driveway. His father arrived home drunk, ran over the bike, and came in screaming at him for his carelessness; he then beat the boy severely. Now not only had my client lost one of his most favorite possessions, but in addition, his mother criticized him. He was an only child. There was no one there to comfort him. My use of myself empathically brought him back into attunement. I asked, "Would you like to work on this memory today?" (This is a co-regulatory question.) The client, feeling "felt" and safe, responded, "All right." He had been too hyperaroused to begin working on this memory when he first started talking. He then used rationalization to defend himself, and then my attuned empathic connection to him helped enable us to come into a state of co-regulation.

But what might have happened if the client had seen something critical in my eyes or had had an old state-dependent memory and projected this critical response stance onto me? (This is my definition of transference in information processing terms.) His style might then have become submissive because he did not want to reenact with me the scene with his father that he was talking about. The developing abilities of maturing clinicians create sensitivity to their clients' signals. This sensitivity serves as the ground for perceiving both their own and the clients' states of mind, and it increases their awareness of their own and their clients' feelings. Empathic attunement means being able to open yourself to the client's feeling state while at the same time maintaining your own sense of self in the present. Problems arise when the signals sent by the client trigger the clinician's negative arousal and activate unforeseen and incomplete memory networks of his or her own.

This is my definition of countertransference, in the terminology of adaptive information processing. Unaware, I can get lost in the blur between "I and Thou" and may easily slip into misattunement. At these moments, the mutual process of co-regulation ceases to exist. When I notice that something internally is amiss, however, I can enter a state of mindfulness where I "just notice" my own reactions, use a compartmentalization strategy (see Chapter 8), and then refocus on the client. It is my responsibility to undertake the difficult task of introspection in the moment. (I will outline other preparation and containment strategies for the clinician in Chapter 8.) I sequence out what I said and what the client said. I may even recognize this moment as a source of deeper information about the client's issues. When I notice that my client is reacting to my state-dependent emotional arousal, and that his processing has become blocked, I may use that moment to devise a strategy for even deeper processing. This is a form of intervention I developed, which I call the relational interweave. I will give a detailed example of it later in this chapter and discuss it fully in Chapter 9.

No matter how faithful to the protocol I am, I may still become activated and get out of attunement with my client. Trauma expert Bessel van der Kolk, in his 1996 book *Traumatic Stress,* stated that "Working with people who have been traumatized confronts therapists as well as patients with intense emotional experiences; it forces them to explore the darkest corners of the mind and face the entire spectrum of human glory and degradation. Sooner or later, those experiences have the potential to overwhelm therapists" (van der Kolk, McFarlane, and Weisaeth p. 552).[1]

In misattunement we cease to be functional clinicians and are in danger of colluding in reenactments. Take, for example, the overly responsible clinician who is overinvested in his or her client, or the emotionally seductive client who forms an insecure dependency attachment to the clinician and stimulates the clinician by complimenting his or her perceptiveness and intuition. In such situations, complementary characteristics between the two parties may cause them to reengage in old dysfunctional patterns. These are examples also of implicitly broken connections in the working alliance due to these reenactments of the transference/countertransference matrices.

When I discussed my ideas for this book with Shapiro, she cautioned me to make clear distinctions between the two types of resonance that can occur in the clinician–client dyad: mental state resonance and the kind of resonance that may be a collusion with the client to avoid anxiety. For me, the critical issue to notice is whether any of my old schemas (self-defeating emotional patterns stemming from past negative experiences) are resonating with my client's schemas, and to listen carefully to my body's signals. For example, if the client defers to me because he or she has a defectiveness schema, and I am compensating for an incompetence/failure schema, his or her schema would resonate with mine, and therefore I might tell the client what I think he or she should do. When the client and I have mental state resonance between us, and the work is progressing, I am in a state of mindfulness and am attuned to my client.

While there may be less likelihood of the clinician's becoming activated by his state-dependent memory in EMDR therapy (thanks to all of its rational processes, procedures, and protocols), this phenomenon is rooted in the neurobiological. This is why I believe that it is impossible to separate the method from the clinician–client dyad.

Now let us look at these brain functions from an EMDR perspective. Clients appraise their clinicians based on the mental models they have developed because of their past experience with them or people who are generally like them (such as caregivers). Remember, the brain summarizes past experience and generalizes it into a mental model that will enable the person to anticipate and rapidly process new situations. Thus, for example, if a client had experiences of insecure attachment with his or her primary caregiver, the client is likely to be anxious or fearful at first around a clinician who reminds him or her implicitly of that caregiver. However, if the client resonates with a different mental model of a compassionate "other," he or she may be more amenable to connect with the clinician differently.

So, having implicitly "consulted" his or her mental models and appraised the clinician as caring, the client may then experience sufficient emotional dearousal, becoming calmed by the clinician's empathic use of self and the genuine invitation to be fully who he or she is in the clinician's presence. This invitation then facilitates a different state of mind where the client is able to reenter a memory safely and begin to process it productively. Now the clinician tunes in (attunement) and guides the client into the proper phase of EMDR. If the client is not ready — and says so — co-regulation is demonstrated, and collaborative communication continues, with a return to attunement as the clinician and client work together on stabilization strategies. When the client begins to journey through the perilous territory of the old trauma, the clinician demonstrates an attuned state by resonating with him or her. Let us see what this looks like in practice.

2.3 The Neurobiological Subtext of an EMDR Session

John, a 50-year-old telephone sales rep, has been working with me for four months. A married Jewish man, John decided to start treatment because of a chain of events that began when he reacted to his 15-year-old son's disrespectful behavior by striking him. John grew up in a very strict household with a domineering father who beat him severely and often. As a result, he made a vow to himself many years ago that he would never hit his children. So when he began to get angry at his son's disrespect, he first exploded and hit him, and then imploded and dissociated his rage instead and became depressed. He had trouble falling asleep, had intrusive and distressing recollections of the times when he was badly beaten as a child, and found himself avoiding any contact with his son.

When John first came in, he was riddled with guilt and suffering from severe anxiety. His strong negative belief was *I am a bad father*. We successfully completed Phases 1 and 2 and began active trauma work, using as a target memory the most severe beating he had at the hands of his father. After two sessions of trauma processing, John's Subjective Units of Disturbance (SUDS) level dropped from 9 to 3, and he was happy with the results of our work.

When John came to our next appointment, he said he needed to "just" talk. He told me he was embroiled with an irrational supervisor who, because of corporate demands to cut costs, ordered John to take an action he deemed unwise. The supervisor threatened him with sanctions in a menacing manner. John went to his union rep and filed a grievance. John told me he could see the connection between his father's beatings and his supervisor's threatening response.

As a youngster, John never had anyone to share his feelings with, and he said he needed a session to "just let some steam out." He had come in that day in a state of high negative arousal. John let me know that "the EMDR," as he called it, could help, and he would be willing to go back to active trauma work next time. For now, he needed "to vent." And that is what we did for the duration of the session. (By the way, "the EMDR" includes keeping a log each week of triggers for any other associational channels that may have been activated.)

Were we engaged in EMDR, or were we just talking? Of course, we were engaged in good EMDR practice! During the reevaluation, John needed to vent (actually, this is a good example of sharing associational channels that became activated during the week). Then we were able to talk about how our last processing session went, what he got from it, and what remained incomplete. John knew that his reaction to his supervisor was partially a function of old, unresolved trauma. He also knew that talking to his union rep (who was supportive) and filing a grievance were the proper procedures, but he was surprised that doing this had not mitigated his rage.

As John and I talked, we agreed that what had been activated most and what he re-associated to was his memory of being a lonely little 9-year-old boy who had just suffered the worst beating of his life and had no one to support him. Talking to the union rep and filing a grievance did not help because his state-dependent memory from childhood was held in a separate memory network and could not be linked with the present-day experience of receiving the support he needed. John and I agreed that we would start with this old memory next time and reprocess it. This, by the way, is a good example of using EMDR methodology relationally. In this case the collaborative communication between us helped us focus on a deeper level of wounding that we both believed needed attention. But it still was basic EMDR.

Let us look at the neurobiological underpinnings of this session. My initial appraisal of John that day was that he was in a state of high negative arousal. I was able to become empathically attuned to his pain. Furthermore, I was in alignment with him since I did not try to intrude my agenda of doing trauma processing with him that day. To do so would have constituted a moment of nonalignment: I would not have been resonating with his deepest needs. John set the tone for our co-regulation by making a specific request ("to vent"), and we proceeded in an atmosphere of safety. After John had let off steam, I used EMDR's floatback technique, (see Chapter 6) with him to elicit an old memory from when he was 9 and his mother was too busy with the laundry to comfort him after his father had given him the worst beating of his life. "Floatback," a technique developed by Cindy Browning and William Zangwill, is an adaptation of Jack Watkins' Affect Bridge, a hypnoanalytic technique that he wrote about first in 1971 and then again in 1997 in *Ego States: Theory and Therapy* (coauthored with his wife, Helen). The technique is used to help the client connect back to earlier neurologically similar memories.

In that moment, John remembered the lucky rabbit's foot he used to carry. It had given him such solace in childhood that he had kept it to that day. He asked if he could bring the rabbit's foot to our next session, when he would process the memory of being hurt and alone. Using an EMDR resourcing procedure called resource development and installation, developed by Andrew Leeds, we spent some time in session strengthening the resource of the rabbit's foot. In short, John had found a resource that could empower his containment skills so that we could desensitize this memory. (One clarification: When an EMDR clinician uses resourcing strategies for containment while doing active trauma processing, it is useful to return to the painful memory after it has been desensitized down to a zero, *without* the resource, and notice if any remnants of the trauma are still embedded in the memory. The same suggestion applies for clients who are initially treated with SSRIs or other psychotropic medications.)

Because I had response flexibility, I was able to go with John's needs — within the context of EMDR — and in this way lead him gently back to what was core for him now: not the beatings, but the accompanying isolation and lack of support. This is an example of how an associational channel of trauma — John's mother's refusal to comfort him — gets activated and then either "acted out" in the treatment or dealt with appropriately. The key to knowing I was on the right path was my "affective knowing" — that is, that my body *felt* connected to John and his pain. This connection then instructed me about the next target memory (age 9), which turned out to be the next issue to process as John found his readiness through talking over the memory with me. Our next session proved very productive. John was able to process his "mother issue" within the context of being severely beaten. Then, after having reprocessed this old trauma, he was ready to deal with the present-day referent. Now he could share his pain with me safely. This sequence of work empowered him, with the end of processing old trauma (the first stage of the "three-pronged protocol"), to return to the original issue (the "present-day referent" — the second prong of the three-prong protocol) that he had come in for: his rage at his

son's disrespectful behavior. This is just one example where understanding these neurobiological processes (in this case, my own implicit sensory motor awareness) can enhance active trauma work.

Siegel's and Schore's work demonstrates that clinicians make a mistake in EMDR when we try to separate the method from the relationship. Some clinicians with a cognitive–behavioral orientation might say that say it is the EMDR method more than the relationship that is healing to the client. But no matter what type of therapy the clinician is doing, the client's brain is built to interact with the clinician on an interpersonal level — even if the clinician is not aware of it. "The human brain, in its genes, is hard-wired to be social," Siegel told attendees at the 2001 EMDR International Association Annual Conference. "It is a social organ."

2.4 The Subtleties of Empathy

When Siegel talks about alignment, attunement, and mental state resonance, many clinicians may feel on familiar ground. Attunement is close to what Carl Rogers, writing 40-plus years ago in *On Becoming a Person*, called empathy. Rogers believed that being in this process (to him, empathy was a process, not a state) with a client was the most crucial aspect of the therapeutic relationship. To have empathy with another human being, he wrote, means

> entering the private perceptual world of the other; becoming sensitive, moment to moment, to the changing felt meanings which flow through this other person. It means temporarily living in the other's life, without making judgments, and sensing the meanings which the client may only be dimly aware of. (Rogers, 1980, p. 142)

Rogers also defied the powers that be in the psychoanalytic community by shifting the stance of the clinician from analytic neutrality to what he called "unconditional positive regard." Let me tell a story about Rogers' method; this comes from the pen of psycho-oncologist Rachel Naomi Remen, as told in her book *Kitchen Table Wisdom*:

> While I was still part of the Stanford faculty, I was one of a small group of traditional physicians and psychologists invited to a day-long master's class with Carl Rogers, a pioneering humanistic psychotherapist. I was young and proud of being an expert, sought after for my opinions and judgments. Rogers's approach to therapy, called Unconditional Positive Regard, seemed to me a deplorable

lowering of standards. Yet it was rumored that his therapeutic outcomes were little short of magical. I was curious and so I went.

Rogers was a deeply intuitive man, and as he spoke to us about
how he worked with his patients, he paused often to put into words
what he did instinctively and naturally. Very different from the
articulate and authoritative style of presentation I was used to at
the medical center. Could someone so seemingly hesitant have any
expertise at all? I doubted it. ...

Finally, Rogers offered us a demonstration of his approach. One
of the doctors in the class volunteered to act as his client and they
rearranged their chairs to sit opposite one another. As Rogers
turned toward him and was about to begin ... he stopped and
looked thoughtfully at his little band of experts, myself among
them. In the brief silence, I shifted impatiently in my chair. Then
Rogers began to speak. "Before every session, I take a moment to
remember my humanity," he told us. "There is no experience that
this man has that I cannot share with him, no fear that I cannot
understand, no suffering that I cannot care about, because I too am
human. No matter how deep his wound, he does not need to be
ashamed in front of me. I too am vulnerable." (1996, p. 215–217)

Rogers then did his demonstration with the doctor volunteer, the result of
which Remen describes this way:

In the safe climate of Rogers's total acceptance, he began to shed his
masks, hesitantly at first and then more and more easily. As each
mask fell, Rogers welcomed the one behind it unconditionally,
until finally we glimpsed the beauty of the doctor's naked face. I
doubt that even he himself had ever seen it before. (1996,
pp. 215–217)

Empathy, as it is traditionally defined, is taking the felt experience of the
other person into oneself and resonating with what that person is saying,
literally feeling what the person is feeling. This is distinct from sympathy,
in which one feels *for* someone who is in a painful situation. When I am
sympathetic toward someone I may feel sad or sorry for the person. But
when I resonate deeply with the other's pain (that is, when I feel the
person's feelings, not just feel for the person), that is empathy, or empathic
attunement. Forty years after Rogers' work, Siegel eloquently demonstrated the neurological substrates of what Rogers was teaching.

One of the outcomes of empathic attunement is that the traumatized
client feels deeply understood by the clinician. This enables the client to

feel safe enough to do active trauma work. As Judith Herman writes in her seminal work, *Trauma and Recovery*, "Traumatic events, once again shatter the sense of connection individual and community." Trauma victims feel like outcasts from society, both perforce and voluntarily. Whom can they trust, after all? Van der Kolk notes that "despite the human capacity to survive and adapt, traumatic experiences can alter people's psychological, biological and social equilibrium" (van der Kolk et al., 1996, p. 4).

Empathic attunement can safely recreate the client's feeling of belonging and bring him or her back into the communal fold through the dyad of client and clinician. When the clinician consciously chooses to be attuned, resonating, and in alignment with the client, the clinician holds the client with his or her eyes or in his or her soul. Thus the clinician is creating something greater than safety: the attachment necessary to optimize EMDR treatment. Making the choice to do this is a left-brain analytical process, yet empathic attunement itself is a right-brain affect-to-affect process, or, as Schore has shown, a right orbitofrontal connection of the clinician to the right orbitofrontal part of the client's brain, amplifying the attuned attachment.

Dr. Uri Bergmann, an EMDRIA-Approved Trainer and Consultant, and one of the most oft quoted clinicians on the neurobiology of EMDR, adds to the depth of understanding the neurobiological substrates of empathy and the intersubjective (Personal communication, Feb. 16, 2005). He states

> At the interface of the neurobiological and psychoanalytic literature it becomes apparent that the interactive transfer of affect between the right orbitofrontal cortices of both the other–infant and therapeutic dyads are extremely similar, and can, in both, be described as intersubjective relational fields. It is the clinician's right amygdala and right orbitofrontal cortex considered by LeDoux (1996, 2002) and Schore (1994, 2003a, 2003b) to be the predominant neural substrates of the unconscious cortex that is responsive to fluctuations in the emotional and unconscious communications of the client's amygdaloid and orbitifrontal cortices, facilitating his or her "oscillating attentiveness" to nonverbal behavioral and affective shifts in both himself and the patient. This generates the empathy that is imperative for the clinician's attunement and for the patient's unconscious knowledge that he or she had been understood. It also facilitates, as Schore (2003b) has described, a treatment focus on the identification and integration not of conscious mental states but of nonconscious psychobiological states of mind/body that underlie state-dependent affective, bodily, behavioral, and cognitive–memorial functions. At a neurobiological level,

given the right orbitofrontal cortex's direct connection to the ventral vagal complex (the main affect regulation engine of the brain-stem), these regulated emotional exchanges may very well trigger synchronized energy shifts in the client, just as they do in the infant, facilitating a more adaptive regulation of the emotion-processing orbitofrontal cortex and true trait-change. (Personal communication, March 15, 2005)

Even when I am empathically attuned to my client, however, I remain grounded in my own state of mind. This lessens the likelihood that I will become vicariously traumatized by the client's story. This is why it is critical that clinicians maintain who they are in the situation, even as they are taking the other's feelings into themselves. In saying this, I am disagreeing with Rogers. He states that being empathic means "laying aside not only your own views and values, but also in some sense laying aside yourself" (Rogers, 1980). I do not believe a human being can do this (as I wrote in the *Journal of Psychotherapy Integration* in 2003). Humans take ourselves with us wherever we go. Believing that we can lay aside both our conscious and unconscious selves is, to me, a fiction.

Empathic abilities are developed over time, and they can entail a measure of risk. Caution must be taken, even by the most mature, well-trained clinician. (I live outside New York City, and after the 9/11 crisis, there came a time when I could not tolerate hearing any more client narratives of seeing people holding hands and jumping to their deaths instead of being burned alive in the World Trade Center.) Because of the nature of the intersubjective — which is defined as two people having reciprocal influence on each other — trying to maintain an empathically attuned stance with a traumatized client is like walking through a minefield. When clinicians enter the world of someone like this, we are walking collaboratively into the minefield with them. The potential for our being triggered increases dramatically. This is why knowledge of transference and countertransference, as I define it in EMDR terms, is crucial to doing EMDR successfully. I will examine this topic in Chapter 8.

CHAPTER 3

Using EMDR Relationally in Daily Clinical Practice

3.1 Introduction

The difficulty some clinicians have in using EMDR comes partly from the necessity of paying attention to all the mechanistic aspects while at the same time creating a working alliance and real relationship with their clients. Some have voiced fears and concerns to me that if they were to become an "EMDR therapist," they would lose their therapeutic self with the client and become robotically fixated with the EMDR model. This was never the intention of the trainings.

Is EMDR a by-the-book treatment approach or an in-the-moment mindfulness experience? It is true that the standard methodology is quite dense, and there are many processes, procedures, and protocols to learn. Experiential clinicians are often turned off by the plethora of information that must be gathered and digested. In my opinion, however, this information is crucial to being able to be in the moment with the client. In addition, I have never been more in the moment than when I have established rapport with a new client, gone over the details, and gotten a good idea of the person I am dealing with. I believe that people want to be known. When they feel received, they open up to doing the healing work. Once the information gathering is done and we move into the active trauma work, I am a co-participant in the trauma processing. I continually scan my body for information on my client's state. I ask questions in the form of interweaves when my client gets stuck looping or shutting down. I can be fully myself with the knowledge that I am using a powerful and well-tested methodology to empower my client's brain to master his or her trauma.

In her 2002 paper, "EMDR: Adaptive Information Processing," Shapiro defines the successful treatment of experienced-based pathology as "clinician assisted." She views the client's brain as doing the healing, while the clinician provides the structure and the container in which it can heal. Shapiro's ideas about the role of the clinician are important. They have to do with the tasks on the clinician's part in the working alliance (spelled out in Phase 2). The piece that I add comes from Siegel's work on the neurobiology of interpersonal relations. Whenever two people are in a room together, one discussing or processing issues and the other facilitating the necessary mix of strategies for healing, their interactions, implicit and explicit, will be part and parcel of the work they are doing.

Seeing EMDR from this perspective shifts one's attention slightly. The best way I have seen it stated (in psychoanalytic circles) is by Stolorow and Atwood, who, in talking about the intersubjective nature of the work between clinician and client, call it the "empathic–introspective approach" (1997, p. 431– 449). These authors write

> If the notion of analytic neutrality grasped as a grandiose defensive illusion is to be given up and mourned, with what shall it be replaced? What is an alternative stance appropriate for the analytic situation recognized as a dyadic intersubjective system of reciprocal mutual influence, to which the organizing activities of both participants make ongoing, co-determining contributions? We have characterized this stance as one of empathic–introspective inquiry. (p. 441)

In this approach the clinician is in empathic attunement with the client and is continually using his or her awareness to notice his or her own inner reactions. This does not change the nature of EMDR's eight-phase structure. It introduces additional elements, beyond the working alliance, to be considered.

3.2 Overview of Treatment

3.2.1 Beginning Treatment

Many trauma clients have suffered through different forms of therapy without making the transformational shift out of their emotional pain. In fact, many have reported to me that they do not want to tell their life histories again because of how retraumatizing it is. Others choose EMDR treatment because they have heard it is a miracle cure; they want to begin by immediately bringing out an old memory that hurts them and to "start doing the eye movements." While my heart goes out to these suffering people, I know it is not yet time. In fact, I usually spend sufficient sessions forming an overall impression of the client and his or her case before I decide whether to go ahead with active trauma work or to do some stabilization first.

I always work relationally. I ask myself, how am I going to approach this individual? I consider the following: What does this person want from me? Does this client act in consonance with his or her stated wish? How much response flexibility does this person show? What is his or her genetic family history? Is the client functioning adequately in the spheres of love and work? What are this person's strengths? Which of these strengths are accessible? What core negative beliefs are blocking his or her path? What positive beliefs about himself or herself does the client want to resonate with when treatment is over? What is this person's capacity to safely release old memories? Then I decide the best way to proceed.

For example, Mandy is a 50-year-old dissociated woman who was severely depressed. She was clearly a client for whom the diagnosis DESNOS was appropriate. (DESNOS stands for Disorders of Extreme Stress, Not Otherwise Specified; see Appendix A for how this diagnosis is characterized.) Resource development and installation or other forms of resourcing had to come before active trauma work. DESNOS clients present many challenges and in my opinion need a prolonged period of stabilization before they proceed to the more active trauma-processing phases with which EMDR is most commonly associated. Mandy and I would consider trauma processing in the future. For now, the top priority was simply for her to come to feel safe with me.

Jeff is a 27-year-old dental student with severe unrelenting standards. He needed to be kinder to himself. He understood that active trauma work could tap into core issues for the purpose of healing them, but this was not the right time for that. He needed his "angels and guardians" (resources) to help him get through his last weeks of training. He had informed consent and made his decision. So we developed and installed internalizations of these protective figures before doing active trauma processing.

Carla is a 37-year-old artist, married for the second time, happily, with a grown son. She was physically challenged by an autoimmune disorder that she was taking excellent care of. Though she had had many traumas, she had already developed the ability to cope with her present-day living issues. Carla was ready to face her old state-dependent memories and proceed with active trauma work.

I also talk with my clients from the beginning about how the relationship may become a source of richness that can be used to promote healing. I explain that this consulting room is a place where the rules of communication are slightly different. While we may withhold certain reactions in daily life, here it is important for the client to be as honest with me as possible. Of course I explain that honest truth is something to be spoken without fear of reprisal (this is similar to Shapiro's comments on the necessity of "truth telling"). In doing so I am reinforcing the parameters of the collaborative working alliance. In life, saying that you are confused or hurt by what someone has or has not said may arouse the other person's defensiveness or hostility. In this room, I explain, honesty may bring us back into attunement and may signal to me a reaction that can inform us about something going on even more deeply, which may make healing a more complete experience. I also explain that I am human too. I may have reactions that come from my own unfinished work. When that happens I make a pledge to be as aware as I can of myself in relation to the work we are doing. I never promise that I will share what my personal issues are, but I let my client know that I will take responsibility for any personal issue that arises during treatment. I let my client know that I am grateful for these moments, even if they are difficult ones, because they may inform me of ways to use them in our work (as in the relational inter-weave).

I am truly grateful to clients when I become triggered. I am not alone in this view. Many clinicians realize that the true test of how we grow to be the best we can be lies in how we become aware of and handle these reactions. Living consciously in the consulting room fosters growth in both parties.

3.2.2 Implementing All Eight Phases of EMDR

In order to be in a successful relationship with a client, it is essential to learn and understand all eight phases of EMDR. I have heard legions of EMDR-trained clinicians talk about "the EMDR" as a function of Phase 3 through Phase 6 (assessment, desensitization, installation, and the body scan) — as though that was EMDR methodology, in spite of Shapiro's firm and numerous public statements that EMDR is a comprehensive eight-phase approach. Phase 3 through Phase 6 are the active trauma phases, and they are the ones that need the greatest amount of fidelity to Shapiro's method, but they do not constitute all of EMDR. Every single phase is important, or, as Shapiro stated in her 2004 Plenary (EMDRIA, 2004), EMDR begins the moment the client walks into the clinician's office.

For example, if the clinician skims over Phase 1 and Phase 2, moving directly to processing, he or she can actually do harm. Other times, the client will only make partial gains. Some clinicians start trauma processing in the first session without making a thorough evaluation of the client and the client's history. For example, a client came to see me about his fear of heights. He had been treated by an EMDR clinician who started him out with auditory tones. He made some good gains, but treatment did not follow EMDR methodology; in fact, the clinician never even took the client's history or established a firm therapeutic relationship. The client was discharged and told that he would always have some degree of discomfort. There was no attempt to apply the three-pronged approach of processing past trauma, then targeting present-day referents, and then installing a future template.

Without taking a thorough history of the client's presenting problem; learning the client's feeder memories (old traumatic memories that feed the intensity of the presenting problem), family history, and medical history; exploring his or her other past trauma; and assessing the client's present coping skills, the clinician is walking into the minefield with his or her eyes closed. To begin with, though it sounds simplistic, the clinician does not know the client yet. The two have not yet formed a working alliance, let alone a therapeutic relationship. Many clients have been hurt by thoughtless, selfish, or cruel people in their lives. Without carefully getting to know the client and testing his or her capacities for containment, the clinician could open a Pandora's box and thus — in the client's implicit memory system, at any rate — join the list of people who cannot be trusted.

3.2.3 The Individual Session

Since EMDR is not a cookie-cutter approach to treatment, it does not dictate that a client necessarily work on the trauma during each session, although that is the preferred approach. The treatment should be guided by the clinician's clinical judgment, which will be in large part based on knowledge of the client and on the relationship. What the client works on will be ecological to what is happening in his or her life. As long as the clinician thinks about how the client is processing the information he or she is receiving (in any arena of life) and identifies stuck points, those stuck points may be the targets of intervention that will allow them to get back on track with the process of detraumatizing old memories.

For example, Ray is a 56-year-old chiropractor in private practice. He initially requested treatment to deal with the effects of being an only child of Depression-era parents. Ray is married and has a 7-year-old daughter. His life with his wife has been less than ideal. After we had gone through the first phases of EMDR treatment, we began to set up a protocol for dealing with the sequeli of living with parents who had lived with a "Depression-era mentality."

During this time, Ray's wife began an extramarital affair. Ray found it necessary to shift out of trauma processing to deal with his reactions to this life crisis. He needed me to listen and give him support. He thanked me for offering resource development and installation strategies; he found my flexibility very useful in dealing with a current life situation. During this time he also received a part-time job offer in a more successful chiropractor's office. His life was too full of changes. Blindly continuing to process old painful memories would have complicated his present life unduly. It took Ray 4 months to make some necessary changes. After that, he declared himself ready to restart active trauma work, which he did quite successfully. Patti Levin, LICSW, PsyD; believes that one of therapy's major goals is to keep the client in a functional state as much as possible (personal communication, Feb. 3, 2005).

3.2.4 Clinical Judgment in EMDR

I have found that many new EMDR clinicians are unclear about whether they are following good EMDR practice if they deviate from the protocols. In EMDR methodology, good clinical judgment always takes precedence. Clinicians who are junior in the field may believe that in spite of external constraints, continuing the protocols will unlock the client's ability to deal with the current situation. These clinicians may even not listen to the client, but rather try to impose what they think is good EMDR practice. In reality, good EMDR practice is client-centered and therefore flexible to the demands of the client's life. While there are inherent practices in EMDR that amplify a person's resources, the client remains in charge. If a client wants to "just talk," he or she talks.

Although later I will look more closely at the role of the intersubjective in each of the eight phases of EMDR, I want to give you some highlights now. Next I will look at how relational aspects are used differently in EMDR than in other modalities and consider some of the barriers to doing relational EMDR. Finally, I will provide a preview of a new type of intervention I have developed called the relational interweave.

3.3 Relational Aspects in Each of the Eight Phases

The relationship between client and clinician begins even before Phase 1, when the client calls to make an appointment. We can expect that the person calling is full of pain and expectations (both positive and negative). As I have written elsewhere (Dworkin, 2003), the clinician listens to the client's voice and is affected, perhaps developing some beginning empathy, perhaps even being triggered by the client's tone of voice or what he or she says. The client hears the clinician's words and tone of voice, and accepts a time to come in for the initial consultation. The client is affected, perhaps with hope, perhaps with anxiety. Perhaps the client is triggered by the process and content of the phone call. Both clinician and client now begin to imagine what their first meeting may bring.

Then they meet, and Phase 1 begins. The clinician asks questions, the client talks, and the clinician listens. Now the relational field is becoming a fluid interpersonal experience. This phase sets the tone for treatment. In what manner does the clinician ask the questions? Is he or she simply gathering data, or does the clinician evince sincere interest? How are these questions received? Does the clinician have a sense that the client is being too guarded or too open? Does the clinician remind the client of anyone in his or her past? What about the clinician? Does the client remind him or her of anyone? Does either feel sexually attracted to the other? Turned off? Shocked? Empathic? Neutral? Judgmental? Already the client and clinician have moved through several cycles of appraisal, arousal, coregulation, and — one hopes — attunement.

During Phase 2, the clinician begins to explain how and why EMDR works. EMDR is far different from other therapies the client may have experienced, be they psychodynamic, cognitive–behavioral, hypnotherapy, or family therapy. There are many opportunities for client anxiety and misunderstanding here. Careful attunement to how the clinician relates his or her understandings of EMDR and how the client receives this introductory information is instrumental in assessing whether the client will be a willing partner or a wary participant. It is helpful to give the client a handout on EMDR or to direct him or her to appropriate Web sites (e.g., www.emdr.com and www.emdria.org).

Also in Phase 2, the clinician tests for affect tolerance. The client whose boundaries and defenses are weak may feel shame if he or she is not able to "perform" the way the clinician instructs. The clinician may be faced with a client who wants to move immediately into the trauma processing. What if the clinician judges that the client is not ready? Does the clinician feel guilty over disappointing the client? Does the clinician worry about losing the client and a source of income? Do they foolishly move ahead? Are both client and clinician ready for the role shifts they are about to embark on?

Phase 3 can be confusing to new clients. They wonder, what is a negative cognition, really? And why is this therapist asking me to put something I *used* to think in the present tense? The clinician may wonder, why can't this client come up with what she would rather believe about herself? Should I be helping her or would that be infantilizing her? All of these questions swing on the hinges of the relational.

Moving into the desensitization phase, Phase 4, things really get tricky between client and clinician. Does the client feel comfortable revealing what he or she is experiencing? Does the client block his or her processing to avoid revealing it? Is the clinician ready to experience the client's most disturbing memories? What happens if the client chokes or begins to vomit when re-experiencing an oral rape? Does the clinician become vicariously traumatized? Does the clinician dissociate? If so, does the client notice? If the client does notice, does he or she then tell the clinician, or is the client ashamed of being so disgusting that he or she made the clinician dissociate?

Clinicians are in a relational mode whether we remain quiet during processing or use an intervention like the cognitive interweave. This is important. Trauma begets shame and isolation. Community — including the dyadic community of clinician and client — begets healing. In Phase 4, the clinician is facilitating not just the brain's ability to resolve trauma, but its ability to resolve trauma while in a relational mode.

Many unforeseen variations may occur. Clinicians have reported using the standard protocol and interjecting nurturing words such as "Good" and "You're doing fine," only to find that these were the very words the client's perpetrator used during the abuse. What if the client not only projects onto the clinician (because of the particular words the clinician used), but also begins to respond to the clinician as though he or she really were the one responsible for triggering the client's pain? To whom is the client responding now? If triggered, the client may be responding to both the clinician and the person whom the clinician represents in his or her mind.

Now let us take the relational complexity a step further. Suppose that the way the client is presenting has triggered the clinician, and unbeknownst to the clinician, they are reenacting both of their old traumas. The client's traumatic need to stay isolated has triggered the clinician's traumatic need to "help," which has manifested by his or her being overly active in order to bring the client back into the process. Therapeutic attunement has been disrupted. What old, painful memory or set of memories has been neurally stimulated in the clinician? To whom is the clinician relating? It is possible that the clinician may be relating to the perpetrator energy stimulated in him or her because of old, unfinished interactions? What has the client said or done to elicit this response? Is the client aware that he or she has elicited this response? Does the client feel terrified at having done so? Gratified? You can see why I call this territory a minefield.

In Phase 5, the installation phase, the clinician may doubt what the client is reporting: Did his SUDS level really go down to 0, or does the client just want to avoid any further experience of the painful memory? Is the belief the client is installing ecologically valid? Is the client really ready for installation? If not, is the clinician aware that the client is not ready but relieved to be let off the hook? This relief would be about not having to plumb the depths of the client's despair empathically — that is hard work, especially if the clinician is suffering from vicarious traumatization or is in the depths of a countertransference experience. Does the clinician collude with the client to avoid experiencing any more stress by playing "Let's believe you're all better"?

During Phase 6, the body scan, the concerns become: What is it like for the client to experience a novel physical sensation? Do any old dissociated memories arise in consciousness? (See "The Case of Tricia," in Chapter 10.) Has the client been truthful in reporting a completed process? Does he or she still feel a body sensation but not report it so the clinician will feel successful? Does the clinician sense that something is not right? If so, does the clinician bring this up or instead collude with the client in a make-believe completion? What bodily sensations are occurring in the clinician? Might any of these be caused by attunement with an unfinished process of the client's?

In the closure phase, Phase 7, the client and clinician are deep into their relationship. If the session is complete, what good feelings are generated between them? What if the session is incomplete — does either feel disappointed? Defective? Critical of the other? Does the client get angry with the clinician over being left in an emotionally difficult place, even if the clinician closes down the session properly? (This is what happened in the case of "Dan.") Does the clinician become annoyed that the client was avoiding something that was obvious?

In Phase 8, reevaluation, the concerns are: What feelings arise in the clinician if the client has not been journaling? What if the client has called the clinician several times because of distress, nightmares, and the like? What if the client had these reactions and did not call, not wanting to bother the clinician? Why did the client choose not to call although he or she was informed of the right to do so if events during the week stirred up too much negative arousal?

Throughout each of the eight phases, the clinician is in relationship with the client. The clinician has empathy for the client. The clinician feels what the client feels, ideally without becoming lost in it. The clinician holds the container, and the client has the opportunity to re-experience the trauma in the company of someone who cares. It is my experience that a clinician who does not understand the true meaning of empathic attunement is not going to do very well with EMDR, even if he or she follows all the procedures and protocols precisely. That is why EMDR must be practiced from the heart: It is where empathy lives.

3.4 How Relational Aspects Are Used Differently in EMDR

To me, there is no question about whether the therapeutic relationship is an intrinsic part of EMDR's standard methodology. The question is, what is unique to the therapeutic relationship in EMDR as opposed to that in other types of psychotherapy?

First, reflective empathy and psychoanalytic interpretations are almost always contraindicated in EMDR. (One exception is the rare case when such activity constitutes a cognitive interweave, in which case the clinician's words serve specifically to link adaptive memory networks to dysfunctional ones.) The clinician can be relational with a client without using reflective empathy. "For full emotional communication, one person needs to allow his state of mind to be influenced by that of the other," Rogers wrote (1980, p. 142). In EMDR, however, unlike in Rogerian treatment, it is the function of the practitioner to keep the brain of the client in a state of adaptive information processing by staying out of the way as much as possible. This is rooted in the adaptive information processing model itself, which posits that under the right set of conditions, it is the client's brain or body that does the healing, not the therapist. Reflective and interpretive empathy is contraindicated as long as the "train keeps going down the tracks," as Shapiro so well puts it (Part 1, Institute training). It is unnecessary and may even be intrusive.

Psychodynamic therapies also use relational aspects to help heal trauma, but they do so in very different ways from EMDR. In EMDR, the primary focus is on healing traumatic memories. What transpires relationally between client and clinician is subsumed under this primary focus, although it still needs attending to. In addition, EMDR does not encourage the development of transference. When transferential reactions occur during the active trauma phases (assessment, desensitization, and installation), they can be a rich source of target material to be processed. (See Chapter 8 for detailed information on this.)

There are other differences in how the client–clinician relationship in EMDR differs from that of other therapies. In EMDR, the clinician's role is to assist the information processing abilities of the client's brain to do their own healing by reestablishing the excitatory–inhibitory balance. This is quite different from, for example, helping the client talk through past experiences and feelings in hopes that a cognitive and emotional shift will occur.

The interventions used in EMDR, which range from resource development and installation (discussed in Chapter 5) to active therapeutic strategies like the cognitive interweave (discussed in Chapter 9), are aimed solely at restoring the client's excitatory–inhibitory balance. The goal of the cognitive interweave, created by Shapiro, is to assist the client in Phase 4 when there are blocks in processing an old trauma, in order to get to the next step in the chain of adaptive information processing — to assist in the sequence of effecting a trait change. The particular intervention that the clinician offers always stays within the client's frame of reference. The clinician (through knowledge of who the client is and what the client is struggling with) uses the functional memory networks that the client already has in order to link to the dysfunctionally stored information. In this way the clinician uses empathic attunement to empower the client either to unblock the stuck process or to help contain overwhelmingly intense feelings. (The cognitive interweave must be used judiciously and only when adaptive information processing is blocked because of feeder memories or blocking beliefs.)

My relational–EMDR view of transference and countertransference phenomena, based on recent discoveries in the neurosciences, is quite different from the old analytic perspective of neutrality. Such neutrality is a myth. Traditional analytic views of the "blank screen" mentality have been disproved; modern relational analytic practitioners have known this for years. Stolorow and Atwood, in their 1997 paper, "Deconstructing the Myth of the Neutral Analyst: An Alternative From Intersubjective Systems Theory," effectively challenge the notion of clinician neutrality. They disagree with the analytic view that a clinician can remain objective in the face of the client's subjectivity: "Starting with the initial phone call, a multidimensional, non-linear system of reciprocal mutual influence develops and grows" (p. 431). They take the empathic/introspective approach to healing: empathy for the client, introspection for the clinician.

The clinician's maintaining empathic attunement throughout all eight phases of the EMDR protocol enables the deepest healing to occur. Research rightly concludes that three double sessions with EMDR clinicians can statistically lower the felt symptoms of PTSD (Wilson et al., 1995, p. 928), but the wisdom and empathy of the experienced EMDR clinician may be needed over a longer period of time to help dysregulated clients with complex trauma to reprocess their terrible experiences.

The questions that clinicians continually need to ask themselves are: Have I been successful in maintaining my empathically attuned position and my response flexibility? Has anything in me become triggered? Have I successfully attended to my own process? Has it gotten in the way? How? What corrective actions have I taken, in myself and with my clients, to ameliorate this condition? Have I looked back on a session and recognized a pattern of interactions that feels unfinished or interventions that I might have used better?

Things are definitely happening for the clinician, on both the professional and personal levels. There is no neutrality.

3.5 Potential Barriers to Relational Aspects of EMDR

If clinicians want to be attuned to their clients' experiences, we need to attend to three aspects of the relationship that too often are overlooked in the consulting room: use of a common language, gender issues, and cross-cultural issues.

3.5.1 A Common Language

Clinicians who are committed to establishing empathic attunement with clients learn to talk to them in their own words. We do not use the language of psychotherapy or even of EMDR at first. We do not immediately ask clients for a "negative cognition" or a "SUDS level." We do not talk about their experiences in our own idiosyncratic words, nor do we provide our own explanations of them. Instead, we listen to the clients' explanations. We enter their world and learn how they think and what words they use to describe their experiences. We develop a common language with them and apply it during the EMDR procedures.

3.5.2 Gender Issues in EMDR Treatment

When working with opposite-sex survivors of emotional, physical, and sexual abuse, clinicians must be extremely careful to observe appropriate boundaries. We also need to monitor our emotions continually to see what visceral sensations we experience and whether any old, painful memories of our own are being stimulated. I have never felt so stimulated that I could not work with a client, but I once consulted with a colleague on the possibility of being aroused sexually. With her help, I was able to ground myself and regain my "evenly hovering attention" with this particular client. I recommend that every clinician have a colleague with whom he or she feels safe to discuss issues of sexual arousal.

I once used a variation of eye movements in a session. The motion was diagonal, and I was unaware that my motions were directing my client's eyes to my private parts. She was kind enough to inform me. I immediately changed directions and became introspective, seeking an understanding of what might have been in my implicit memory system. I then did my own work to be able to return fully to empathic attunement.

3.5.3 Cross-Cultural Issues in EMDR

EMDR is now practiced all over the world. Clinicians of every color and creed assist and facilitate traumatized people to heal. However, subtle and not-so-subtle differences exist in the way EMDR is practiced in different cultures and in the way people of different cultures respond. As British and Italian colleagues Richard Mitchell and Isabel Fernandez have pointed out to me, a tear gathering in the eye of an Englishman may signify a huge abreaction, while the cries of an Italian mother may mean that her child has caught a cold. To give another example, Americans love using the pronoun *I,* but its use may be distasteful or forbidden in other cultures. These differences have profound implications for all EMDR clinicians. We now have Christian clinicians treating Jewish Rabbis, African American clinicians treating Japanese World War II internees, and German EMDR clinicians treating children of Holocaust victims.

Every clinician from every country needs to be sensitive to the differing customs and behaviors of the people he or she is treating. EMDR colleagues around the world, contacted via the Internet, can help clinicians to do that. Dr. Joany Spierings of the Netherlands, an EMDR teacher and consultant, has self-published a fine manual on this subject. (Spierings, J 1999 Multi-Culti EMDR)

3.6 The Relational Interweave: A New Intervention

How the clinician comes across will affect the client, which may then affect trauma processing. In EMDR, I acknowledge this relational aspect by using a variation of the cognitive interweave that I call the relational interweave. The relational interweave is based on my understanding and acceptance that I am part of my client's process. I own this role. Sometimes my client and I may struggle with similar blocking beliefs, and sometimes I may be activated by what my client is experiencing and momentarily lose my empathic attunement. This may open up a countertransferential moment, perhaps based on a state-dependent memory of mine. I usually detect this first through somatic awareness. Monitoring my bodily sensations may spontaneously bring up in me a dissociated memory that was stimulated by the client's style, tone, or bearing. How to share this awareness (but without content) and have the client process it — if it resonates — will be elaborated on in Chapter 9.

The relational interweave is the logical extension of an active relational intervention. Its purpose vis-à-vis the adaptive information processing model is to acknowledge that clinicians' fallibility as humans may sometimes affect our clients. This is the opposite of what happens in core trauma. There, responsibility is usually placed on the victim exclusively. The father who hits his son with a belt and then cries, "Now look what you've made me do!" is assigning full responsibility for the abuse to the boy. This is the stuff that irrational negative cognitions are made of.

3.7 Conceptualizing EMDR Treatment in Three Stages

I have found it useful to divide the phases of EMDR treatment into three easy-to-remember stages.

Stage 1: Evaluation and Preparation (Phase 1 and Phase 2)
Stage 2: Active Trauma Work (Phase 3 through Phase 6)
Stage 3: Closure and Reevaluation (Phase 7 and Phase 8)

I respect that this is Shapiro's work, and I wish only to complement, not to change, the essential aspects of the work. However, from my experience both practicing and teaching EMDR, I have observed that clinicians may not make proper use of Shapiro's concepts. To enhance learning EMDR, I use nicknames for the eight phases as a device to help my consultees better understand the focus of each phase.

Stage 1: Evaluation and Preparation
    Phase 1: Trauma Case Conceptualization (Client History Taking and Treatment Planning)
    Phase 2: Testing Affect Tolerance and Body Awareness (Client Preparation)
Stage 2: Active Trauma Work
    Phase 3: Trauma Activation Sequence (Assessment)
    Phase 4: Active Trauma Processing (Desensitization)
    Phase 5: Linking to the Adaptive Perspective (Installation)
    Phase 6: Intensive Body Awareness (The Body Scan)
Stage 3: Closure and Reevaluation
    Phase 7: Debriefing (Closure)
    Phase 8: Reevaluation: The Forgotten Phase (Reevaluation)

Adding the concepts of the intersubjective, as discussed by Stolorow and Atwood (1996), and the neurobiology of interpersonal relations, as Siegel so eloquently describes, only serves to enrich and broaden clinicians' understanding of EMDR practice and not to change the methodology.

In the chapters to come, I will discuss various refinements to EMDR based on my clinical experience. Along with these refinements, I will give an extended case history to demonstrate the intricacies and difficulties of an EMDR treatment that started out as an apparent case of simple PTSD and turned into longer-term psychotherapy, in which complex PTSD was uncovered and dealt with. This case example shows what it is like to practice EMDR relationally in the real world.

3.8 The Case of Madeline

In Chapter 2, I discussed the results of my history taking with Madeline. What follows is the description of her presenting problem, which she wrote as a journaling exercise at the beginning of treatment. I reproduce it here verbatim.

> After a wonderful 36½ years of a teaching career, I retired in January 1998, joining my husband who was already retired. We immediately put our beautiful home of 23 years on the market. We planned to go to live in North Carolina after having been there and in and around South Carolina and Georgia for many visits over several years. We had worked hard and planned well for our retirement lifestyle and abode. We spent a very hectic, busy year on the final preparations, sold our home and moved everything we owned to our destination in North Carolina. It was now March 1st of 1999. We had a lovely beginning to our new home state. On the 21st, we visited some community ("plantation" is the southern word for this) in which we were temporarily renting until we found and closed on a permanent residence. On the 22nd we delivered an application to a banker we had befriended. He planned to have our mortgage done in two to three weeks so we could close quickly on the place we had just found.
>
> On the 23rd, for some reason not remembered by my husband, Richard, or me, we crossed the border from North Carolina to South Carolina, perhaps on the way to the beach for shopping. It was a bright, somewhat cool day. At about 3 P.M., I was at the wheel of the car when we were T-boned by a 23-year-old male driver who was accompanied by his girlfriend. He had run a red light and was doing at least 60 mph — well over the speed limit. Richard and I never saw him coming as he struck us in the blind spot of the driver's door. He demolished our car and nearly killed us both, as we later learned.
>
> The police came with ambulances to rush us to the hospital. For the next 3–4 hours, the medical staff was very busy trying to save our lives. First, they had to cut us out of our car seats. I was squashed into 10 inches of space. My husband smashed his head, lacerated his ear and punctured a lung. The left side of his body was paralyzed, temporarily! He had to be intubated. Reconstruction surgery had to be done immediately on his left ear. Ultimately, he was unconscious for 10 days or so.

I was left with numerous traumatic physical injuries and unable to sit up or walk. Both my lungs were punctured. My liver and spleen were lacerated. My pelvis was broken. Ditto my left arm, a rib behind my collarbone, and cervix #2 (the "Hangman's Bone"). Additionally, the air bag smashed my left eye and charred my face from friction. Shattered glass left my head bruised, bumped, and bleeding. I had brief, cogent moments, but was primarily unconscious from extreme pain for 5 days. I was intubated with 10 tubes and catheterized, as well. Within 3 or 4 hours, a medical helicopter flew me to the trauma unit of a University Hospital, some 100 miles away from my husband. I was in the ICU for a week. The day I was removed from the ICU, I went into total respiratory failure. Luckily, the medical team brought me around and returned me to the ICU.

I believe on April 12, I was discharged to a rehabilitation hospital. On that same day, my husband, Richard, was also discharged to the same facility. It was the first time we had seen each other since the 23rd of March. According to family and friends, the first question Richard and I asked when conscious was how and where our counterpart was. The second question was: How is our son? Each of us had done this!

Richard's brothers Bill and Frank flew down, as did our only child Gabriel. Bill literally held and squeezed Richard's hands and massaged them, too, for days, hoping he would come to, fearing he would die. Gabriel ran back and forth to the two hospitals a hundred miles apart, spending a little more time with me as Richard had his brothers with him. Gabriel then came regularly to the rehab. Bill also came down again to visit us and brought a friend who is a lawyer. We were deluged with calls, gifts, cards, and letters from friends, family, and former colleagues and students. Three of my best friends came down to visit. One spent a week with us. Another visited repeatedly and accompanied us home to New York along with Bill.

We were so busy working hard and getting better, there was no time to worry or be upset or angry. We progressed and continued to progress, amazingly well. We are not physically scarred or maimed. We returned to New York to finish therapy and recuperating, both of which are still ongoing. It has been 7 months, 5 of which I wore a neck and body brace (a Minerva), and then a Philadelphia collar for 24 hours a day until cervix #2 finally healed totally — a wonderful surprise and a long, impatiently awaited day for the collar to come off. Richard is in a head injury program called Transitions, and I attend within the same system. But I still receive physical and occupational therapy.

I, who could not even sit at one point, finally made it to a wheelchair. Eventually, I became able to stand and walk, which I can do unaided and normally. My left arm has gone from painful and non-functioning to virtually normal. My neck is healing and improving steadily. I can drive now, but Richard is not, yet. We have both lost part of our sense of taste and we have both lost weight. Richard, a very intelligent, well-read, and highly educated man still struggles with an improving but impaired short-term memory and diminishing moods and sleepiness. I have no pain now and sleep fairly well. I was medicated earlier with oxycodone, a synthetic morphine used for pain. I gave this up in May. I had a great difficulty sleeping and most of the time spent the night lying wide awake or wheeling around in my chair till I could walk.

We are now renting a nice house in a nice neighborhood while we finish our rehab therapies and find a permanent home. Our son, Gabriel, is with us for this period (one year rental, done in June). He has been wonderful and has taken care of almost all matters, especially us! He had to leave his job because he spent so much time going south. Gabriel packed up the rental house down south, moved everything up north and into storage, found the rental, and researched and found both of our rehab therapy programs. We are now sending him to school for computers (his choice). It is an advanced program and a fine choice of careers awaits him when he graduates.

So why am I seeking Mr. Dworkin's help? Well, I am now well enough to think about other things besides physical therapy. I worried a lot about my husband's injuries and whether he would recover and be "his old self," the very special man I have loved and lived with for nearly 4 decades. For myself, I never doubted I would walk again, but I thought I would have problems from my broken neck, and I was almost certain my left arm would be crippled. I am tired of hearing how lucky we are to have recovered so well — if we were so lucky, we would not have had a horrible accident disrupt our lives this way. The man who caused the accident had no injuries and only a pittance for insurance. I am mad as hell about this, my worrying and my suffering, all of which stem from the accident he caused. I drive, but I am afraid this will happen again, and I have no control over it. Richard and I both feel we could not live through this again. I am even more frightened when I am a passenger than when I am a driver.

I feel I have been ripped out of my lovely life and been thrust into a nightmare. I have had to relinquish my independence and my control over my body and my affairs for almost 8 months! I have had seven address changes since February 1999, but no real home. I hate the rental house because Richard and I did not choose it. The fact that it is a pleasant house in a pleasant neighborhood means little because I feel homeless, sometimes helpless, and wish I were not here. We are living out of 310 boxes. For almost 3 months in the hospitals, we had no clothes, no money, nothing from home. Had it not been for our son, Bill, family, and friends helping us, we could not have made it. At the same time, I hated having everybody take care of our lives and affairs. Intellectually, I understand that it was necessary and we needed the help. Emotionally, I felt helpless, inadequate, and dependent — exactly the opposite of what I usually feel. I had no control over anything — and I do not like that. It made me feel worthless at times. Then I would feel depressed.

My husband and I have always been a dynamic duo and a great team. The accident seems to have taken that away, temporarily I hope. Physical recovery has been arduous, but it is a "piece of cake" compared to the emotional aspects of recovery. My husband cries — just like that. It is part of the head injury and has been diminishing — but still it is there! I have cried off and on for days at a time. Will we ever get our lives back to normal? Will I ever feel "happy" about the future? Can I be in a car without being scared of another accident — sometimes I become queasy from the fear. Sometimes I feel so alone because I have no one to talk to — I don't want to worry Richard or burden Gabriel. My closest friends are so thrilled about our apparent recovery and how good we look that I cannot tell them how bad we feel.

While our emotional state probably has improved, there is a way to go. Some days I wonder if I can make it and if Richard can too. Both of us have wished that we died in the accident on more than one occasion. I am tired of recuperating and having therapy, which will be ending in about 3 weeks, but what will I have to do when therapy ends? I'm tired of being grateful that I am recovering or that we might have died or that there are people worse off than me. I'm often angry or depressed and I worry about everything. If only the accident had not happened — but it did — and I need help in dealing with the aftereffects.

Madeline started treatment very insistent that we work specifically on the near-fatal car accident. She was crystal-clear: Other factors in her life were not relevant to her at this point. As we look at practicing EMDR relationally, phase by phase, we will follow Madeline's case to its surprising conclusion.

CHAPTER 4

Phase 1: Client History Taking and Treatment Planning (Trauma Case Conceptualization)

4.1 Developing an Atmosphere of Trust

While there is quite a lot of background and data to gather from the client during Phase 1, it is of equal importance that the clinician work on developing an atmosphere of trust. Several different forms of working alliances are used in psychotherapy: nurturing, insight-oriented, and collaborative (Gelso & Hayes, 1998, p. 45). I believe that the collaborative alliance is the correct focus in EMDR (even with fragile clients who seem to have great need for the clinician). I educate my clients from the start that EMDR therapy is a collaboration where our roles and responsibilities are spelled out. I make it quite clear that EMDR is not something I do to them. It is something I do *with* them.

This approach is crucial when working with survivors of trauma. Trauma is by definition an experience that is overwhelmingly noncollaborative and nonconsensual. Herman tells us,

> Trauma robs the victim of a sense of power and control; the guiding principle of recovery is to restore power and control to the survivor. … The first task of recovery is to establish the survivor's safety. This task takes precedence above all others, for no other therapeutic work can succeed if safety has not been adequately secured. (1994, p.159)

In Phase 1, establishing safety means being thorough. That can take time. Traumatized human beings are wary creatures: They need to be around the other person for a while before they feel comfortable. They need to have time to sniff out the therapist, so to speak, and to make their explicit and implicit assessments, neurobiological appraisals. This is why — unless emergency care is required (as in the emergency room protocol developed by EMDR clinician Gary Quinn) — I recommend taking at least three 90-min sessions to do Phase 1 and Phase 2. My average is some-where from three to six sessions. This does not apply to clients for whom a longer period of stabilization is necessary before beginning active trauma work. For those clients, it takes as long as it takes, period. I will talk about this in more detail in the next chapter.

The consensual approach to trauma treatment — which reassures the client and consciously activates the neurobiological states of co-regulation, alignment, and attunement — requires that the client be evaluated *and stabilized* before any active trauma work begins. Anything else can be a recipe for disaster.

4.2 Taking the Client's History

I use the phrase Trauma Case Conceptualization to describe the activities of Phase 1. There are two reasons for this. I am in agreement with Shapiro (Shapiro, 2001, Shapiro, 2002b); it has been my experience that most presenting problems that are not genetically based have trauma (experien-tial contributors) at their core. This could be something as recognizably traumatic as the sudden death of a loved one or an event as "minor" as being taunted by schoolmates in childhood. According to the adaptive information processing model, on which EMDR is based, a trauma is any experience that has interrupted the information-processing ability of the brain, not necessarily meeting the requirements of Category A in the DSM-4 nomenclature for PTSD. There are "small *t*" traumas such as not being invited to a birthday party, and "large *T*" traumas, such as Egendorf describes when he relates how some soldiers fighting in Vietnam had their faces pushed into the cut-up remains of a North Vietnamese soldier (Egendorf, 1985). The second reason I use this phrase is to stress the crucial importance of conceptualizing the client's case before treating it. For some clients, EMDR processing may be part of the treatment (action) plan, or it may be elaborated as the entire treatment action plan. Unfortu-nately, there are clinicians who do not have treatment (action) plans. Some do not conceptualize where the client is in treatment, and others do not make differential assessments about what kind of therapeutic experience is needed within the context of the therapeutic relationship. Practicing

EMDR competently requires the clinician to think through all of these issues.

Shapiro stresses the importance of taking a detailed client history before creating a treatment plan, and I fully agree. I have had many consultations with EMDR-trained clinicians who began presenting a client's trauma to me without including any more background than the person's gender. Another problem I have run into is that even if the history taking is done well, the client's case is not always conceptualized well. A trauma case conceptualization includes who the client is, the stressors in his or her life, the size and dimensions of old trauma, and how he or she perceives them. The astute clinician will also observe the client's capabilities and any self-referencing negative beliefs that may help or hinder functioning in the present. I have heard countless stories from clients who worked with EMDR clinicians who started bilateral stimulation in their first session. This is a Phase 3 and Phase 4 activity, and in many cases jumping ahead to it can cloud the "field" of the clinician–client dyad (if not end their collaborative work altogether).

It is this field of relationship that creates the context of trust necessary for trauma resolution. The content of the history taking questions and responses of this phase are important, of course, but the process of the beginning interactions of this dyad set the stage for how the client and clinician will create their relational field. Each appraises the other, and each makes subvocal assessments with or without concomitant senses of internal arousal. When the field is clear on both sides, an initial sense of trust and response flexibility emerges. For example, both accommodate each other as to the date and time of appointments, and each respects the other's rights in the therapy situation. This is the context necessary for trauma resolution to occur.

The first face-to-face meeting between clinician and client has another important aspect that will affect how well the work goes. That meeting is the start of an attachment relationship. Attachment relationships, as Siegel and Schore have pointed out, are crucial to the developing child not only because they protect him or her from danger but also because they enable the complete development of his or her brain. Attachment is based upon how well the child's primary caregiver was empathically attuned to the child, how nurturing the caregiver was, and whether the caregiver was able to set healthy boundaries with the child. Whatever the nature of the client's first attachment relationship — secure or insecure, organized or disorganized — it will likely be the foundation for the client's attachment relationship with the clinician.

All healthy adults manifest attachment. Siegel writes,

> Especially under times of stress, an adult will monitor the where-abouts of a few selected "attachment figures" and seek them out as sources of comfort, support, advice, and strength. For adults, such attachment figures may be mentors, close friends, or romantic partners. (1999, p. 68)

We can include clinicians on that list. Clinicians represent very significant attachment figures for our clients. Lest we wonder if an adult's need for comfort could create a bond as strong as attachment with another adult, consider what van der Kolk tells us:

> As primates, human beings are programmed to seek out others for soothing and regulation that they cannot provide for themselves … If comfort does not alleviate this distress, people keep looking for other means of relief. This relief may range from helplessly clinging to others, ingesting drugs or alcohol that alter the way they feel, or engaging in physical acts of purging or self-mutilation that cause shifts in their internal world. (2002, p. 63)

When humans are distressed, our need to receive support from others is so great that we can be driven to self-destructive extremes when it goes unmet. Bruce Perry, senior fellow of the Child Trauma Academy, addresses the importance of attachment in the infant–caretaker dyad when he states,

> For individuals fortunate enough to have an attentive, nurturing caregiver, eating as an infant (the time when the patterns of oropharangeal motor patterns related to eating are being built into the brain) becomes associated with eye contact, social intimacy, safety, calm, touch, cooing (e.g., Hatfield and Rapson, 1993). This wonderful, soothing, and interactive somatosensory bath that the nurturing caregiver provides literally organizes and "grows" the brain areas associated with attachment and emotional regulation. (Perry, 1999)

Thus the first meeting is a crucial one. The client brings the explicit and implicit effects of his or her trauma and attachment experiences, as well as a built-in neurobiological drive for relationship. It is a delicate situation, and one in which the clinician has the challenge of establishing a comfortable rapport with a stranger while simultaneously having to ask him or her quite a few personal and perhaps painful questions. It is a matter of both respect for the client and dedication to building a relationship to spend as much time as necessary on this phase.

To help guide clinicians in organizing the vast amount of information they need to gather in Phase 1, I have developed a Trauma Case Conceptualization Questionnaire (see Appendix C). Its purpose is to help the clinician develop an initial understanding of who the client is, what he or she is struggling with, and how the client and the client's struggles initially affect the clinician.

The first details in a thorough history are the age, gender, marital status, ethnicity, and cultural identification of the client. Also, what does the client do for a living, and what is his or her highest level of schooling? Does the client have a religious affiliation or a spiritual path? What is his or her current family system? What kinds of attachments does the client seem to make to significant figures? Ask, too, about the client's social support network, medical conditions, and current medications. Does the client have any obsessions or compulsions (including substance abuse)? Is there a history of mental health disturbance or trauma in the family of origin? I also ask myself how my body feels both during and after the initial session. Do I detect the beginnings of resonating with my client; does my body feel negatively aroused; what is that about? Sometimes my response may be informing me that I am sitting next to a volcano, or it may be telling me that my old stuff is getting activated.

Even at this point, the clinician now knows some important facts about the new client. This information provides an early lens into the client's world. Next, and equally important, is to elicit what made the client call for an appointment at this time. Has something happened recently, or is the issue an old one? Does the client have distressing symptoms for no apparent reason? It is vital to understand the symptom complex. If the client has a large trauma, does he or she show evidence of intrusive, avoidant, or hyperarousal symptoms of PTSD? Are there any anxiety, phobic, or depressive signs or symptoms? Are there any thought content or thought process disorders? All relevant diagnostic questions must be asked and answered to the clinician's satisfaction. Can you imagine not screening someone for a possible depression with suicidal ideation? It would be foolhardy to start active trauma work with someone with active suicidal ideation, unless a very well constructed care plan involving multiple supports and possible inpatient care is available. Without careful attention to Phase 1 activities, chances increase for problems to arise later.

There is another issue I want to touch lightly upon. Both the lay public and many mental health clinicians trained in Parts 1 and 2 of the EMDR Institute's programs have mistaken ideas about the potential for healing in EMDR. I have fielded many calls in which clinicians and clients alike, knowing my expertise, ask me to have a consultation with someone in emotional distress. There is a mistaken idea that clients can be treated immediately with the active phases of trauma work within very short periods of time. Some of these callers who are asking for help for themselves or their clients do not think about the potential downsides of beginning active trauma work when the client is not in a position to begin this part of the work. Many of the calls I receive are from people who have had chronic and persistent abuse throughout their lives and are affect dysregulated. Without an adequate period of preparation and stabilization, harm could occur. I have learned to inform potential clients and clinicians referring people for EMDR treatment with me immediately, in our first sessions but after making a thorough evaluation, about the necessary prerequisites before active trauma work can begin.

I mentioned that I wanted to touch lightly on this issue because the opposite reaction could occur as well. There are many potential clients whose life histories have been permeated with abuse from multiple perpetrators. However, this group of clients includes persons who, either through life experience or good prior therapeutic contacts, have the necessary skills to be ready to start active trauma work within a short period of time. Because they have had sufficient mastery, relational, or spiritual experiences, they have developed sufficient affect tolerance and affect regulation. This group includes the most rewarding people to deal with. Because of their developed abilities, they can contain intense painful experience in a manner that allows for deep healing to occur. The cases of Madeline, Janice, and Stephanie are examples of this kind of client. The point is that the clinician will not know until after completing a good enough evaluation.

4.3 Thinking in EMDR Terms

A wealth of useful information can be gleaned when the clinician thinks (to himself or herself) in EMDR terms, such as: What is the presenting problem? What are the worst memories that relate to this problem? (Any earlier memories that contribute to the problem are considered feeder memories.) What negative beliefs does the client hold (explicitly or implicitly)? Obviously, these are not the actual questions the clinician will ask. Rather, they are questions that may be answered in the course of the client's narrative. These memories and cognitions should be recorded immediately for possible use in Phase 3. One set of questions I always ask is, "What beliefs would you like to have about yourself when treatment is over? How far away from these beliefs do you currently feel?"

Even in Phase 1, the clinician needs to be thinking ahead constantly. Because a major criterion for screening a candidate for active trauma work in EMDR is the ability to tolerate high degrees of affective release, safety factors must be evaluated right from the start of a consultation. During history taking, the careful clinician will assess a client's history for the demonstrated ability to deal with strong emotions. For example, has the client successfully grieved the death of a close friend or family member? Has the client received criticism at work constructively?

In addition, although evaluating a client's ability to cope with high levels of emotional release is a Phase 2 task, the clinician can make an initial estimation during Phase 1. This can be done by asking the client to picture the worst part of what he or she went through and then asking how negatively the client judges himself or herself, noticing what emotions arise. EMDR veterans will readily recognize these questions as part of the procedural steps outline done in Phase 3. Asking this question in Phase 1, however, helps answer a number of important diagnostic questions: Does the client demonstrate sufficient ability to cooperate with the clinician? Is the client able to make the connection between the traumatic experience and negative self-belief? Does the client go numb or blank (negative forms of somatoform and psychoform dissociative states) when picturing the worst part? Does the client become flooded with emotion or have intrusive and distressing recollections (positive forms of somatoform and psychoform dissociative states; Nijenhuis, van der Hart, & Steele, 2002)?

Dissociation is a major risk in dealing with traumatized clients. To assess for this, Carlson and Putman's Dissociative Experience Scale (DES) is administered. It takes about 10 min to administer and covers most factors in dissociation. It is not a diagnostic scale, however; it is a screening tool. A high score does not mean the client has Dissociative Identity Disorder, but it does mean the clinician should be aware that dissociative symptoms are present.

The clinician also needs to assess how connected the person is to himself or herself. A client may score low on the DES but still have many issues that are not available to his or her conscious mind because they reside in implicit memory.

At this point, I recommend eliciting the desired positive beliefs and outcomes when treatment is completed. The clinician should rate how strongly the client believes he or she will be able to accomplish these outcomes. Having a working set of positive cognitions and their Validity of Cognition (VOC) ratings can be very useful in organizing an understanding of the complex human being who sits before the clinician with his or her traumas. I find that this information also helps in Phase 3, when a client seems to be stuck on the question, "When you see that picture in your mind's eye, what negative beliefs do you hold about yourself now?"

Asking about hoped-for outcomes this early on, as Kaslow suggests (2002, p. 90), is also a good reality check. Many times I have had to disabuse a potential client of the unrealistic expectation that EMDR can provide a "fix" in a couple of sessions. One prospective client likened the effects he wanted to those he had gotten at a New Age growth center. He wanted the profound change within a few sessions. This is also the point at which the clinician needs to learn what the client expects from him or her, realistically and otherwise.

Identifying all this information is not as straightforward as it may appear. Something the client says that seems insignificant at first may have much larger implications as treatment progresses. To pick up on such subtleties, I continually scan my body for clues that information the client is giving me may be more significant than either of us consciously realizes. This also helps prepare me for possible transferential and countertransferential reactions later.

This relates to another Phase 1 task: making (and noting) initial transferential and countertransferential observations. For example, what are the client's initial behaviors toward me? How open or guarded is the client during the first sessions? What might I intentionally or unintentionally stir up in this person? How do I react to the client, in general and in his or her presentation? Am I aware of any judgments the client is making about himself or herself and his or her presentation? Do I observe any evidence of my effect on the client?

Let me give you an example that embodies some common problems I hear about in my EMDR consulting work: insufficient knowledge of what information processing can and cannot do, incomplete history taking, and countertransference.

4.4 The Case of Walter

Walter, 37, is a married Jewish male with a son, age 12, and two twin daughters, age 8. His wife is a status-seeking woman who comes from "old money." Walter works as a sales rep for Nike, but has been living above his means so that his wife and her parents will accept him as one of their own. His father-in-law had given him the Nike connection. As the only child of two elderly parents who covertly wanted him to make their lives a success, Walter grew up with insecure and ambivalent attachments to his parents. He suffers from esophagitis and had chronic acid reflux before being started on Previcid by his gastroenterologist. Though Walter has a bachelor's degree in business administration, he finds even the most mundane business chores overwhelming. The reason was found when Walter was evaluated as having the symptoms of depression, specifically a loss of energy, interest, and motivation. Walter was also terrified of a presentation he was due to give the very next day after our first session. He was not prepared for it.

Walter presented himself as an anxious, needy man in crisis, and he expected a miracle to happen during that first session. After all, this is what he had heard EMDR does. This miracle would manifest as an increased ability to analyze and present data to the evaluators at Nike and would save his job. His desired belief was, "I am confident." His EMDR clinician got caught up in Walter's immediate problem, did not establish a firm collaborative working alliance, and missed the fact that Walter was not prepared with his facts. In essence there was no therapeutic relationship. The clinician, though well intended, only relied on the procedures and protocols of active trauma work in EMDR, and did so in an inaccurate way. He began targeting the most frightening scene (being at the presentation, trying to answer questions, and going blank). Walter's negative cognition was "I am a fraud." Fifteen minutes after bilateral stimulation began, Walter started having chest pains and ended up being hospitalized. Fortunately, he was found to have suffered a panic attack, not a heart attack.

Shapiro has made it clear that EMDR can alleviate suffering in an individual who has painful state-dependent memories but not in a client who has a reality-based reason for worrying about an immediate upcoming stressor. (In the latter case, however, EMDR could be used over time to reprocess an old trauma that resulted in the person's being a procrastinator.) In Walter's case, the clinician made two important mistakes. Not only did the clinician attempt to make EMDR do what it is not meant to do, he did not elicit enough client history from Walter to make an informed judgment about how to proceed. He did not inquire deeply enough into why Walter presented in this manner. This left Walter vulnerable to the triggering of partially dissociated, state-dependent memories before he had been evaluated for affect regulation. Walter became overwhelmingly stimulated during the sets and shut down without resolution. The risk of retraumatization must always be in the forefront of the clinician's mind as he or she gets to know a new client.

But Walter's clinician did not stop to ask an even more important question: Who is this client to me? Does he stir up any old state-dependent memories in me? (In Chapter 9, I will go into greater detail about the significance of this issue and suggest strategies for dealing with it.) Instead, the EMDR clinician took responsibility for treatment without thinking the issue through. In this case, the clinician's misjudgment was driven by an irrational need to believe that he could use EMDR to save Walter's career.

Here's an example of how misuse of the method and uninformed counter-transference can hurt a client. This assumption rested not only on an incomplete understanding of information processing but also on the clinician's own state-dependent memories and beliefs of inferiority. The clinician overcompensated for these implicit memories by proceeding with active trauma work in an attempt to heal Walter right away, which would make the clinician feel better about himself.

Apparently the clinician thought that this was a chance for him to fix someone with an immediate need. But EMDR therapists do not fix anyone. We facilitate. And we start our facilitation on the first day, when we evaluate the client. If the client is needy and wounded, we do not rush into doing bilateral stimulation. We know that education in mindfulness, distress management, emotional regulation, and interpersonal skills is needed before active trauma work can commence (Linehan, 1993).

"Clinician, heal thyself" sounds rather preachy, doesn't it? What might be better is simply to say that clinicians are all human and all subject to times when we are not aware of the activation of implicit traumatic memories. This clinician would have served Walter better if he had taken the time to help Walter develop anxiety-management and problem-solving strategies to cope with the next day's presentation, and then investigated what led to Walter's desperate need to be fixed. A fuller trauma case conceptualization would also have included issues of Walter's not being prepared to give his presentation and issues related to how Walter evaluated himself. The clinician would have been wise to establish which schemas Walter was most vulnerable to, which ones he was avoiding or overcompensating for, and how he had developed character traits to defend against these anxieties.

Schemas develop in childhood based on the interaction of a person's temperament with the hurtful experiences the child has with parents, siblings, and friends. A *schema* is a relatively enduring, dysfunctional trait that deals with the ways the client views the world. All people have schemas. Many have "unrelenting standards" schemas, which means roughly that humans usually are quite hard on themselves. This trait may develop in response to a stern parent's loving concern for the child to do well in school, or in overcompensation for an implicit schema of defectiveness being simultaneously defended against and acted out. A comprehensive discussion of schemas may be found in Jeffrey Young's works, *Cognitive Therapy for Personality Disorders: A Schema Focused Approach* (1990) and *Schema Therapy: A Practitioner's Guide* (Young, Klosko, & Weishaar, 1993), where he provides a comprehensive understanding of these issues. Young's Schema-Focused Questionnaire (available in his books) is extremely helpful in Phase 1 to help the clinician discern specific client vulnerabilities. For example, a client's attachment style can be evaluated to assess stability and make guesses about how the client may overtly or covertly relate to the clinician.

Here is an example. A client told me he "understood that his mother was having a tough time herself when he was little." He always gave and sacrificed, and she did not realize how wounded he felt. This subservient schema, reinforced with rationalization, was a defense against the pain of his wounding. As always when I notice something like this happening, I went into my "Columbo" routine. I scratched my head, uttered a few "humphs," then told my client I was confused. "Do you mean that you are not wounded because Mom had a drinking problem?" I asked. (I have found that Peter Falk's "Columbo" character usually is disarming enough that my client receives the information I give in a nondefensive manner).

"Of course I am wounded!" the client responded. So I talked with him about setting aside some of the judgments he had made so we could focus on his issues.

Dismantling a client's dysfunctional defenses and assisting him or her to develop better ways of coping is not an art form, but it does take a measure of creativity. Clinicians usually cannot allow the client's dysfunctional defenses to continue, especially when the client has developed enough affect tolerance to cope with them instead of being overwhelmed by them. Do you notice another overlap here? If I were asking the exact same question in Phase 4, desensitization, we would call it a cognitive interweave. Asking the question here in Phase 1, it might be considered a cognitive challenge. What does the relational have to do with a cognitive challenge? Isn't it important to challenge with sensitivity? Wouldn't you as clinician like to know how the client takes your feedback and your style? I use this information to test initial response flexibility. This little process helps me understand how to relate better to my client. When I get into trauma processing, this information is invaluable in maintaining empathetic attunement.

Of course, we cannot dismantle the client's dysfunctional defenses by bluntly confronting him or her. In the example above, I knew the client's prominent characteristics and schemas, so I knew the best way to intervene. Because he had to be right all the time and feel in control, I shaped my intervention in a way that would make him feel safe to open up. (Just in case you have never seen *Columbo*, no one ever feels threatened by Falk's character because of his ability to play the fool.)

It may take a session or two or three to get a good enough sense of all the significant issues a client needs to impart about the presenting problem before getting older relevant information. This is the interpersonal nature of the work. However, there is a reason why it is important to get the rest of this information (core negative beliefs, positive attributes) up front. When clinicians do this, they are acting in concert with the standard method, which seeks to gain all the information needed to help the client heal. When it is time to move into active trauma work in Phase 3 and Phase 4, this information will speed the process of healing. The clinician will feel the client's pain, and the client will not only have expressed the pain, he or she will have felt heard.

4.5 Seeking Feeder Memories and Self-Beliefs

I mentioned earlier that I try to think in EMDR terms right from Phase 1, and I make observations about components that are typically not identified until Phase 3. Let me say a little more about that. I find that when I search for feeder memories during Phase 1, I immediately ask for the negative beliefs a client holds about himself or herself, and I also ask for what the client would like to believe about himself or herself once treatment is over. For example, if I were the clinician treating Walter, I would ask what old memories led Walter to the distress he was in, and I would gather both existing and hoped-for beliefs right then and there. If identified now, these memories and beliefs can be used in Phase 2 when the clinician explains the principles of EMDR to the client to prepare for processing. Feeder memories are old state-dependent memories, thematically related to a similar problem, if not the presenting problem. An example of a feeder memory for Walter was when he missed the final shot in a championship game and saw the look of disappointment on his father's face. His negative belief was "I am a failure," and his wished-for belief was "I'm fine the way I am."

Accompanying these feeder memories are negative beliefs about the self. These negative cognitions can be captured by the astute clinician who listens for and hears these pieces of information, which the client usually utters spontaneously. In Walter's case, one of these was "I always fail," which translated to "I am a failure." This was his core negative belief. It ruled his life, and some eye movements made one day before an important professional presentation were not about to magically erase what was neurologically stuck, at least not before a number of evaluation and preparation sessions had been completed.

When the clinician does not pick up on the client's core negative belief, it is useful to ask, "And when this [the traumatic event] happened to you, what negative judgment did you make about yourself? Had you ever made that judgment about yourself before this traumatic event? If so, when? And how many incidents have there been like this?" More than one negative belief may emerge. Clustering these memories by their irrational beliefs ("I am a failure," "I am not loveable") will organize the client's thinking about himself or herself in EMDR terms.

One caution about this phase: Even when the clinician tries to take a careful history, the story elicited from the client at the beginning of treatment may turn out to be quite different from the history that unfolds during treatment. For one thing, bilateral stimulation promotes free association. This can trigger memories that were dissociated during the early phases of treatment. Another issue is that the client may not feel comfortable early on revealing information he or she is ashamed of.

In this phase, it is also important to understand how the client has tried to cope with stressors previously. Which strategies worked and which did not? What character traits does the client have? Is the client a hardy soul who has found ways to overcome experiences similar to the presenting problem? Or does the client become "needy" and reliant on "the experts" — individuals he or she deems more capable of finding solutions than the client?

This brings up a problem that can arise right at the start of treatment: the needy, wounded victim who begs the clinician to fix him or her with EMDR. This type is usually obvious to the seasoned clinician, but when a novice EMDR clinician is not prepared for it, the clinician may be convinced to start active trauma work before laying all the groundwork. To these novices I say good luck. There are also seasoned clinicians who for doubtful reasons have bought into this manipulation and begun active trauma work too early. This is not a problem about methodology; it is a problem about applying the methodology in the context of knowing the client. It is quite conceivable that in the here and now, the clinicians' state-dependent memories are being activated, and they are making treatment choices from a reactive position. I scan my body often for any sensory motor signals of dissonance or reactivity. As the French phenomenologist Merleau-Ponty wrote, "I know others through my own body" (1968, p. 186).

Another type of client who may present a problem early on is the one who has truly never thought of using the strengths he or she has developed. With a client like this, I do a slight role shift from psych evaluator to psych educator. This happens right in Phase 1. Clients of this type are usually quite a bit easier to deal with than the needy type. Once they "get it," they feel empowered and express gratitude for being shown their own capabilities.

In fact, I ask every client about his or her strengths, resources, and accomplishments. This knowledge can be used as a guide to what cognitive interweaves may be most acceptable to the client when processing gets stuck. This elicitation begins only after the client has clearly spelled out the narrative and the problems in living that have occurred as a result of the trauma that the client has come to heal. I ask my new clients what strengths they have brought to the table to be active partners in the healing process. If the client has initial problems answering this question, sometimes a simple, straightforward question such as, "What successes have you had in life, and how did you achieve them?" will prime the pump. Many clients have inner resources that they have not given themselves credit for. An extended period of resource work may not be necessary if the clinician asks the right questions. Clients need to have these resources, but they may be there already. Dr. Sandra "Sam" Foster states, "I am always concerned when there are not resources accounted for prior to beginning our work with clients, whoever they may be" (personal communication, April 14, 2004).

Based on the full appraisal of who this person is, what the person suffers from, and what the person's strengths and limitations are, I encourage my consultees and trainees to write themselves a story about who this person is and how the person strikes the clinician initially. In doing so, the clinician creates a picture that will continue to change based on the information that continues to arise, but at least the clinician will have created a good enough foundation for an initial working understanding. I have created for myself a comprehensive Trauma Case Conceptualization Questionnaire, which may be found in Appendix E. While it is time-consuming work, I find it most helpful in developing a full understanding of the clinical picture. I freely offer it to anyone who chooses to use it. What follows is a sample of a completed questionnaire.

4.6 Madeline: A Completed Trauma Case Conceptualization Questionnaire

1. Presenting problem(s) (include duration and length of problem; why treatment now?) *PTSD, secondary to near fatal car crash 3/99*
   Time in treatment *3 sessions*
   Most disturbing picture? *Seeing the car seconds before impact, and hearing the glass breaking*
   Core negative beliefs spoken spontaneously? *"I am going to die"*
   Somatosensory experience of the trauma? (also note the lack of feelings or sensations associated) *Goes into extreme fear state — Severe anxiety in the pit of the stomach; and muscle spasms in the back*
2. What strategies has the client used to deal with this current problem? *Has sought psychotherapeutic help to remedy this situation*

Age	59	Gender *F*	Ethnicity	*Jewish*	Marital status *Married*

Highest level of education   *M.S. in teaching*

Occupation   *Retired Teacher*

Religious affiliation   *None*

Spiritual path   *None*

Cultural identification   *Modern American Jew*

Current family system (including marital status) and social support system   *Married for 36 years to a man 10 years her senior; they have one child, a son, age 39; excellent relationship; has a well-developed social support network; has been estranged from brother and father for over 15 years. No contact whatsoever.*

Medical conditions (list)   *In physical therapy, finishing the end of a protocol; no lasting physical limitations from the auto accident. She has been very careful in taking care of herself all of her life. No medical conditions.*

Medications   *None*

Substance abuse or compulsive/obsession life patterns   *None*

DES Score   *3.1*

Genetic predispositions   *None noted*

What has worked? *Nothing; that's why she's willing to attempt psycho-therapy (would never have done so otherwise)*

What strategies have not worked, and why? *Avoids riding in cars, and is beginning to have a phobia of leaving her house except for medical appointments*

3. What old painful memories (feeder memories), especially of the original cause of the problem, if remembered, does this presenting problem stir up in the client? (List all relevant ones. Also list other traumas client has suffered.) Or can the client not recall or make connections to old traumas of the same type? Is this truly a single-incident trauma? *[Since Madeline would deal initially only with the presenting problem, she did not list any older traumas. They came up later in the processing. These are the parts of her experience that initially plagued her:]*

- Being behind the wheel or being a passenger.
- Heavy traffic and traffic noise.
- Flashing lights and sirens.
- Seeing a BMW or seeing a Honda Prelude (1992 and newer).
- Seeing an accident, either actual or reading about such in a newspaper or seeing pictures.
- Having trucks next to or behind her.
- Going over bridges.
- Driving in the rain or at night.
- Richard's symptoms: his moods and upsets, temper fragility and health concerns, lack of self-confidence; countenance and posture: sleepy, dour, dropping, shuffling, defeatist. The deliberateness with which he moves and does things. He has been very slow and quiet (e.g., he places each piece of flatware in sink carefully, one at a time, no noise; walks around the house and places his feet similarly). He has been inappropriately taciturn or loquacious. Does not answer questions or is indirect and placating. This all adding up to the fact that her "beloved lion has lost his roar."
- Being kept waiting.
- The incompetence or errors of others.
- Financial matters.
- Not being in charge of her life.

4. What are the core negative beliefs this client holds, and how do they apply to each of these traumatic memories? *[Madeline believed that]* "*I'm in danger," when she sees similar cars, or when she attempts to drive, "I'm going to die," when she remembers the accident, and "I can't stand it," when she thinks about Richard's emotional outbursts.*

5. What resources (including ego strengths, coping skills, self capacities) did the client use to attempt to deal with these old memories? *Madeline had a difficult early life that made her quite strong and resolute. Her beliefs were, "I can do anything I set my mind to" (within reason), "I can overcome obstacles," "I am capable."*

6. What psychoform and somatoform types of dissociative symptoms does client present with? *Madeline shows evidence of strongly numbing out the pain, worry, and despair that breaks through as crisis calls to me periodically.*

7. Clinician's assessment of client's ability to tolerate intense abreactive experience? *Adequate.* Rationale? *She's made it through some hard times and made a productive and accomplished life for herself. When prompted, she could access feelings and tolerate them.*

8. Clinician's assessment of client's body awareness? *Adequate.* Rationale? *Can feel tears in her eyes when sad, tension in her belly when anxious, and laughter in her chest.*

9. List general resources including ego strengths, coping skills, self capacities. *Intelligence, perseverance, and a belief that she can make her life better.*

10. Past treatment episodes and the diagnoses. *None*

11. Past responses to treatment both positive and negative. *N/A*

12. Past responses to previous clinicians and reasons why. *N/A*

13. How does the client initially appear to relate to you? *Guarded and controlling, though she cooperates when I explain the outline of EMDR. She says she will only deal with the problems the accident activated. (That's okay with me — she understands active trauma work and agrees to cooperate and free associate.)*

14. What old memories, negative cognitions, and feeling states does the client induce IN YOU? *She reminds me of a strict teacher I had in elementary school. I feel slightly activated and experience myself as being a little bit more vigilant than usual.*

15. Significant symptoms and defenses of client (also note how you are affected by these symptoms and defenses). *Actually, I'm amazed by both her and her husband. I have read their medical records, she is not exaggerating. "Failure to thrive" is not a term that is used lightly. It is used to connote the initial belief that the patient will not survive. She showed me pictures of herself in a body cast. Let her have her defenses, she's smart and independent — I'm fine letting her have her way as I think she has the right stuff to come around.*

16. What is the desired outcome of treatment? *Significant detraumatization, for instance, being able to travel around by car without distress. Being able to come to terms with her husband's brain damage.*

17. What are the desired positive cognitions at the start of treatment, and what are their current VOC ratings? *Positive cognition: I can cope with my life. VOC = 4*

18. Are there any current constraints to beginning active trauma work? *No*

19. Trauma case conceptualization summary (including possible transferential and countertransferential reactions)
This is a 59-year-old highly intelligent married woman and retired schoolteacher who presents with intrusive, avoidant, and hyperarousal symptoms of PTSD, secondary to the car accident that almost claimed her life and the life of her beloved husband. Though traumatized, she has an enormous range of abilities as attested both by her history and per-

sonal acknowledgment, "I have never let anything stop me, and I won't ever give up."

Her greatest trauma lies in the terror and grief she feels when noticing how her husband has changed since the accident. She has fantasies of running away when he cries, as he is subject to do, when he gets what he interprets as a signal from Madeline that he did something wrong. He also cries when he is alone and he does something that he believes Madeline will disapprove of (this perception is grossly distorted). They had a life that was rich in intellectual engagement. That meant that having differing points of view was part of their normal course of events, but now no matter how gently Madeline presents an idea, he will get activated. I observed this phenomenon happening numerous times in my office with the two of them.

Though she usually activates old state-dependent memories of mine relating to teachers in grade school, I will be aware of them and deal with them, when activated. I am impressed by her intelligence and motivation, and I feel happy to be of assistance.

Madeline has stated that she has been skeptical of psychotherapy and psychotherapists all her life, but is truly willing to engage because she was referred by a treasured friend who knew of my work, and she is at the point of despair.

As you may have noted, some of the information on Madeline's questionnaire comes from Phase 2, when I focused on her affect tolerance and body awareness skills. In the next chapter, I will describe the specific objectives of Phase 2 and then return to how Madeline fared as treatment progressed.

4.7 Conclusion

During Phase 1 and Phase 2, the clinician's role in the therapeutic relationship is that of expert, teacher, and evaluator. The client is being examined. This view of the relationship at this point may not sit well with experiential clinicians who want to let the information flow spontaneously. Many times clients, especially when they are new to psychotherapy, are heartened that the clinician takes an active interest. I want to reassure my experiential colleagues that during the active phases of trauma work, the dynamics and roles of the client–clinician dyad shift to co-participation, and the relational aspects become central to facilitating the release of the pain of state-dependent memory. This is the "Zen of EMDR." The implications of this shift and its logistics are covered in the next chapter.

CHAPTER 5

Phase 2: Client Preparation (Testing Affect Tolerance and Body Awareness)

5.1 Overview of Client Preparation

The most important assessment to be made in Phase 2 is: Can the client and clinician develop enough trust and affect tolerance to do active trauma work together? It is in this phase that the goal setting, division of tasks, and bonding of the collaborative working relationship need to gel. The clinician has made a preliminary appraisal of the state of the relationship based on the activities of Phase 1. Now, as EMDR treatment moves into Phase 2, the clinician continues to demonstrate unconditional positive regard and assess the client's trust level while explaining EMDR, testing bilateral stimulation, facilitating the Safe Place exercise, and doing stabilization work, when needed.

Bonding during Phase 2 must take into account both the client's and the clinician's initial take on one another. It is useful for the clinician to ask himself, "Are we on the same page as to the goals that the client wishes to attain?; are the tasks each of us need to perform clear?" Given the information the clinician has garnered during the history-taking, the clinician must ask, "Can I continue to be fully present when my client re-experiences his or her particular trauma, or are there factors that may be triggered in me that might interfere with this?"

Phase 2 opens with giving the client a non-technical explanation of how EMDR works, including adaptive information processing, and what the client can expect in terms of results. The way this explanation is received is crucial to the success of the therapy. Does the client truly understand what will happen? Or does the client only pretend to understand so as not to disappoint the clinician or so as to put the responsibility for success in the clinician's hands? If either is the case, problems may arise from the mutual role and task change from Phase 2 to Phase 3, with the dyad moving from a doctor–patient model to a collaborative model where roles and responsibilities are flexibly defined.

The clinician would be advised to look for possible dependency issues with low-functioning clients. Clinicians let their clients know that they will be there for them between sessions, but one of the problems clinicians encounter with low-functioning clients is their desire to have us be more than their clinician; many times they want us to be their friend. Some clinicians, in a mistaken though caring effort, will attempt to do more than what is usual and customary. The greatest problem here is that often the more the clinician does, the more the client wants. Part of the relational preparation for trauma work is the setting of good enough boundaries. Under no circumstances, even in the midst of urgent requests from the client or the client's relatives, should active trauma work begin until this relational piece is firmly established. Remember, part of a relationship is having the ability to say no (or "not yet"). Clinicians who find this to be a problem should seek out a senior clinician and do some work on their own state-dependent memories.

5.2 Explaining State-Dependent Memory

One of the most challenging aspects of this part of Phase 2 is giving an accurate and lucid definition of state-dependent memory to enable the client to understand why *then* (when the trauma happened) and *now* (the present-day experiencing of the state-dependent memory) are really one. It is very hard to break the linear-thinking left brain's insistence that now is now and then was then. So even though the client may acknowledge the concept and repeat the definition back to you, problems can arise during the procedural steps outline in Phase 3. When the clinician asks the client at that point, "When you see that picture in your mind's eye, what negative thoughts or cognitions do you hold about yourself *now?*" the client may still be confused because he or she is in a different state of mind than when the instructions were given.

I have found a user-friendly 21st-century way of explaining this concept. I ask my client if he or she can make CDs on the computer. If so, I ask the client to imagine copying the first Beatles album, "Meet the Beatles," onto a blank CD (for his or her own personal and private use, of course). Then I ask my client to imagine playing the copy he or she has just made in the here and now. With his or her co-participation, I ask my client to tell me the difference between the original and the copy in terms of the music, the lyrics, and how the songs make him or her feel. The client tells me there is no difference. I tell my client that the same is true with state-dependent memory.

5.3 Dual Attention

Dual attention is another issue that needs careful attention on a relational level. Shapiro's concept of the client as having "one foot in the consulting room, and one foot in state-dependent memory" is necessary for active trauma work. Think about this need for balance. There are two *nows*. There is the "here and now" and the "state-dependent now." When the client is only in the here and now, accelerated information processing is not occurring. When the client is only in the state-dependent now, he or she may experience flashbacks, flooding, and dissociation.

Dual attention has three important parts: First, it is about being internal and external simultaneously. Second, it is about being safe in the present (in the context of the relationship). Third, it is about accessing material and doing a focused (bilateral stimulation) task. The left brain needs to let the right brain know that it is safe in the here and now. The right brain needs to connect with the left brain, which is detached from the traumatic material. Talking over safety factors (stop signal, dual attention) in Phase 2, as well as using active coaching in Phase 4, when necessary, gives the left brain the grounding it needs to stay present, while the client is invited to activate right hemispheric traumatic memory. Having a safe therapeutic relationship firmly in place allows the traumatized client to enter safely into the dangerous inner world that he or she is experiencing *now*.

5.4 Bilateral Stimulation

The next step in Phase 2 is to test bilateral stimulation. It is important to do this with the client now, before he or she is holding traumatic memories in consciousness. (Prior to starting, I revisit the medical questions I asked during Phase 1, especially those related to problems with the eyes, such as a detached retina, or with the ears or nasal cavities.) I explain the three major types: eye movements, audio tones, and tactile stimulation. Then I have clients try out each form of stimulation while keeping in mind a neutral experience. This is a task-oriented event of the collaborative working alliance. I tell clients they can change from one form of stimulation to another anytime they wish. Remember, it is not only the modality that counts, but also how that modality is used in a co-participatory way by the client and clinician.

EMDR training, based upon research (Shapiro, 1989b), states that faster stimulation is usually better because faster seems to induce an episodic retrieval not found in slower stimulation. The initial research found that slower gave a desensitization effect but not necessarily the cognitive shifts. Sometimes rapid bilateral stimulation may induce such an intense response that the client may begin to dissociate, block, flood, or shut down. In part of every EMDR training, participants are instructed to notice their clients' nonverbal cues to help them select the number and speed of the sets. How many repetitions are best really depends upon how well the clinician is reading and relating to the client, and vice versa. When the client is abreacting safely, I may do hundreds of repetitions in one set. Shapiro originally suggested 24 to give an initial indication of whether information is processing or not. Sometimes I may do only 15, 10, or even fewer because of what I perceive happening in my client or what he or she is telling me. The key is to follow the nonverbals. This key goes beyond the working alliance and goes to the heart of how clinical judgment is used relationally.

5.4.1 A Relational View of Intermittent Bilateral Stimulation

How do I determine when to take breaks? I have found ways to make this decision in a co-regulatory manner. I explain that I will watch the way they are responding very carefully, and may suggest that they start processing material that they have accessed and experienced the stimulation of. As clients begin to process, I watch their nonverbal signals of sympathetic arousal and parasympathic dearousal very carefully. The easiest call to make is when a client begins and moves through an abreaction. When the wave of emotion crests and then subsides it's time for me to check in, because a desensitization effect has probably taken hold, and I need to hear how they are experiencing themselves. This informs me if the brain is processing information in a productive manner. If so, I get out of the way and support the process. If not, then it's time to intervene. I spell out my thinking to my client and get their input. Based upon each client's expressed preferences, and the methodology, we make an agreement, about how we are proceeding.

Sometimes clients are very quiet on the outside. I need to determine if I notice any nonverbals, such as tears, clenched jaws, tight shoulders, shallow breathing, or a change in the breathing pattern. These are my cues also. Sometimes I make agreements with my clients about signaling me when they are ready to take a break.

Restarting after a client reports back is complicated. The standard way is to hear their associations, and as long as desensitization or reprocessing is happening, stay out of the way. There are clients who will use talking as a way of diffusing affect. These clients will have a reaction, and then try to analyze it. When I read a defense coming in to close down productive processing, I instruct my client to notice their sensations in their body and start there. With these kinds of clients I actively attempt to keep them out of their heads and into their bodily experiences. Of course I do this with permission, and never go through a stop signal. The issue is to learn how to be relationally tuned into your client. This takes practice, and it takes a commitment to doing your own work. I use my body to sense the signals I get, and then use these signals, checking out with my client how accurate they believe me to be. I've got a good track record.

Bilateral stimulation is not used in a vacuum; it is performed interpersonally. Induced transferential reactions can occur when the EMDR clinician is more determined to do it the "right way" than to notice what is going on with the client in the moment. Testing different types of stimulation, their speed, and the duration of sets during Phase 2 gives the clinician a baseline from which he or she and the client may vary when they are in the middle of processing in Phase 4. Proper preparation limits how intensely this induced transference plays out in the latter phase.

Let me give you one word about self-care for the clinician. In the EMDR Institute trainings, participants are taught to lead bilateral stimulation by moving their hands back and forth. This is fine and dandy for training purposes, but any practicing EMDR clinician knows that to do this regularly in daily practice may result in muscle pain. I recommend using any one or more of the fine tools made for the EMDR community. A light bar for eye movements, bilateral audio beeps, bilateral tapes and CDs, and bilateral tactile devices are available. There are even novel computerized methods. Be kind to your body. This is strenuous work.

5.5 Orientation to Active Trauma Work

Next, I orient the client to the second stage of EMDR, active trauma work (Phase 3 through Phase 6). Gaining and maintaining my client's active participation in this process is for me one of the key indicators to successful treatment. I start by talking about our respective roles and telling the client that we are moving from a doctor–patient relationship to a collaborative one. I explain client safety factors, such as the stop signal, stress-management techniques, and between-session journaling. Then I describe the specific activities of active trauma work. I assure the client that I will actively be there if he or she floods or shuts down. I normalize any possible irrational responses that may arise during processing by explaining that these are merely the opening up of unforeseen memory networks. We discuss ways of handling them as well. I emphasize in language that my client can understand that there is a "zone" between hyperarousal and hypoarousal where productive processing takes place. This in no way means that I stop if I think the client is getting too upset. I let clients know that moving through an abreactive experience, if it happens, can be very healing. I let them know that they are in charge and that if they need to stop processing, I respect that decision.

I give specific instructions about what is to come during the active phases: "What we will be doing is a simple check on what you are experiencing. ... Sometimes things will change and sometimes they won't" (EMDR Part 1 Training Manual, 2004). By doing this I am actually instructing my clients on what will happen procedurally. What happens in the moment during trauma processing is avolitional. All the set-up work is done. Then it is time for pure experience.

I also show my humanness by admitting that despite my intention to be fully present, I may be "off" in an intervention or I may have one of my own state-dependent memories triggered. I invite my client always to challenge my perceptions if he or she has any disagreement or if something does not "sit right" with him or her. I explain that I continually scan myself mentally and on a sensory level for signs of triggering, and if they occur, I admit them to myself as soon as they come to awareness. Then I tell the client that when I have the sense that the triggering interferes with the flow of treatment, I deal with it accordingly. I let my client know that this is part of my responsibility in our collaborative work. All of these instructions are designed to help reinforce the nature of the alliance, but this last part speaks directly to the necessary bonding that is a prerequisite to successful active trauma processing.

Throughout this phase, the emphasis is on being client centered. For example, one night a client called me to talk about the length of the processing sessions. She was a bright, sophisticated woman, and we had met five or six times before the first processing session. My client informed me that she had been reflecting upon the upcoming processing sessions, and she had decided that because of the particular nature of her issues, an hour would be preferable to the usual 90-min session. She had thought this out with deliberation, so I agreed to work in this way. While 90 min is the suggested amount of time, it may not work for everyone, and the client has to be comfortable enough to talk frankly to the clinician. These introductory phases give us both the chance to make these calibrations.

During this stage, I also assess for secondary gain issues, and if they exist, my client and I develop strategies to counteract the possibility that these issues might block the treatment process.

Although affect tolerance will be tested during the Safe Place exercise, the clinician can also test for it now by asking the client to bring up a disturbing memory and just talk about it. When attuned and in alignment, the clinician can get a read on how strong the client's response is. If the client experiences resonance with the clinician at this time, the clinician gains another clue to the client's abilities. I do not force this. I simply offer it as an experience that we can use in codetermining readiness for active trauma work. It also sets the stage for active coaching, a relational strategy that will be elaborated in Chapter 9.

I highlight these relational issues not because they are so new or ground-breaking, but to explain to the relationally and experientially based practitioner that EMDR is far from a rigid, by-the-book treatment approach.

5.6 Creating a Safe Place or a Control Place

One of the important aspects of Phase 2 is to determine with the client whether he or she has sufficient affect tolerance to handle the distressing feelings that may come up during processing. (This procedure was originally developed by EMDR clinician Neal Daniels.) The Safe Place exercise helps the clinician to diagnose whether the client can develop his or her own sense of safety. It also enables the clinician to determine whether a client can engage in dual attention, because it asks the client to recreate the feeling of safety when experiencing a low level of distress. This part of Phase 2 must be handled with delicacy and care on the part of the clinician so as not to stir up what Aaron Beck has termed "evaluation anxieties" (Beck, 1985, pp. 146–164).

There is a cluster of clients for whom the Safe Place exercise will not be useful because they lack the ability to bring up the imagery necessary for the process. For this group, affect control techniques are helpful, and the clinician should evaluate their ability to shut down intense affect when they need to (such as at the end of an incomplete active trauma-processing session). Techniques such as controlled breathing and Jacobsonian muscle relaxation exercises are a good substitute. For those clients who can access imagery, I prefer to use the entire Safe Place exercise.

By using this exercise, clinicians are training their clients in the skills necessary to process their trauma. It is crucial that no client should begin active trauma work until he or she can successfully complete the Safe Place (or control place) exercise. There are eight steps in the Safe Place exercise. It is not my intention here to teach you this exercise. It is documented in Shapiro's first and second textbooks. I will, however, comment on the ways in which various parts of the exercise affect the client–clinician relationship.

The clinician starts the Safe Place exercise by asking the client, "Do you have a place where you can feel perfectly safe?" This could be a place the client has been, a place he or she could go, or a place in his or her imagination. If the client does not have a safe place or the clinician and client cannot develop one within a few minutes, the client is expressing how unsafe he or she feels inside. Relationally, the client is telling the clinician how vulnerable he or she is.

Sometimes the client is not certain what is being asked. It is fine to give some examples of a safe place, such as sitting on the beach or being with one's best friend. But do not choose the safe place for the client. That would defeat one of the diagnostic purposes. Also, you might choose a place that seems safe to you, but it might not feel safe to the client for personal reasons. For example, not everyone will choose a safe place that has a loving person in it. Remember, the aftereffects of trauma include isolation and shame. Some clients will feel safety only with a pet or in solitude. For example, Madeline's safe place was the womb. To her, it was a place that was pressure-free, stress-free, totally soothing, pleasant, warm, relaxing, and dreamy.

It is not uncommon for a client to choose the clinician's office as the safe place. This could be dicey (it is where the client will relive the trauma, which may be quite frightening at first), but it speaks to the importance of the therapeutic relationship. As long as attunement is not breached transferentially or countertransferentially, the client will feel a safe connection to the clinician. In some cases, this alone may be sufficient to create enough affect tolerance for processing to begin. By the way, try asking your clients about their safe place after treatment has been successfully concluded. It may surprise you to hear how fully they have reentered the community.

It is easy to work with a high-functioning person who has lots of access to safe places. Conversely, when the client is multiply traumatized and cannot find a safe place at all, the clinician must help stabilize him or her, possibly by using the strategy of resource development and installation, which I will discuss shortly. Most clients fall between these poles.

The second step in the Safe Place exercise is to have the client focus on and describe the feelings and emotions that the image evokes, and then to notice where he or she feels them in his or her body. This step helps the client ground the experience inside. Again, the astute clinician will be able to assess whether the client is capable of having a positive somatic experience or if the client is experiencing psychic numbing. I see this next step in the exercise as highly Rogerian. It is called enhancement, and it entails the clinician's use of his empathic attunement abilities to strengthen the client's safe place by speaking in a soothing tone and repeating the feelings and emotions that the client has described.

The clinician's repetition and the client's reception enhance not only the safe place but also the dyadic state of mind between the two, thus linking the client's positive feeling of the safe place to positive feelings toward the clinician.

The Safe Place exercise also gives the client a sample of dual attention. When the client first brings up the positive image, feelings, and sensations, he or she is moving into a different state of mind (albeit a positive one). That state of mind is usually about something outside the consulting room. Therefore, the client is learning to be in two places at once. The brilliance of the Safe Place exercise is that the client and clinician start with a positive dual experience; then the client shifts back and forth from a positive state of mind to a mildly disturbing state of mind, doing so with the empathic attunement of the clinician. Dual attention is what creates the balancing of two worlds that otherwise may have remained separated by blocks, or may even have collided. During this stage, the clinician orients the client to active trauma work and explains the role that he or she will play in keeping the client safely in both worlds.

Step 4 of the Safe Place exercise involves the client's first actual experience with bilateral stimulation. The clinician instructs the client to bring up the image of his safe place and to concentrate on the positive feelings and sensations it evokes, noting where he or she feels them bodily. Then the clinician applies a short set of 6 to 12 eye movements, auditory tones, or tactile stimuli. The client is then instructed to notice whether the feelings of safety improved. The clinician and client repeat this procedure a few times, continuing to notice whether the safe place remains safe or strengthens. This is a very strong interpersonal moment. The clinician is now actively applying a procedure to the client. How does the client perceive this process? Does the client actually feel safer? Is he or she telling the truth about how he or she feels? Does the client seem to relax or instead tense up? Is what the client reports congruent with what the clinician notices? How does the clinician deal with any perceived dissonance? These are just some of the interactions that make the Safe Place exercise one of the best ways I have found of forming a deeper bond with the client.

5.7 Sophie's Safe Place

Sophie is a 17-year-old junior in high school who was referred to me after her school social worker received reports that she had been missing classes and her grades were falling off. Sophie's mother brought her in. At the first session Sophie was guarded. Her parents were going through a divorce after having had many vicious verbal battles. Sophie has a brother, age 13. She thought he was a brat when he was younger, but they have recently established a solid relationship. They were helpful and supportive of each other when they heard their parents arguing. Sophie's grades used to be above average, and she has hopes of attending college. She also has a good enough circle of friends. She described her mother as overprotective and her father as cold and critical.

During Phase 1, I was able to tune into Sophie's dilemma and reflect that she was saddened and depressed by the impending breakup of her family. I also was able to talk with her about her being a young woman talking to a man. Sophie did not initially seem to have a problem with that, after her first guarded session. She said that she had male friends who were sympathetic to her dilemma and that talking to me was easier than she had imagined it would be. She was able to tell me of many painful occurrences when her mother and father argued in front of her and her brother. She also described instances when her father would be emotionally cruel to her when she did not perform up to his expectations.

During Phase 2, I explained that having a safe place to go to in one's mind could be a source of comfort at times of distress. The first image Sophie picked was of being in her room holding her teddy bear. Then she reflected that this was most helpful when hearing her parents fight. I explained that the best safe place would be one where she felt completely safe. She chose an image of a lake at the summer camp she attended: It is early morning, there is a mist on the lake, and a lone loon is lazily gliding by. She reported feeling a calming sensation deep in her abdomen. I repeated the scene and she reported enhancement. However, when I applied the first set of bilateral stimulation, I noticed that she became tense, held her breath, and tightened her shoulders. Even so, Sophie reported feeling a little calmer. I scratched my head because there was a mismatch between what Sophie was reporting and the reaction of her body. I asked if she could hear some feedback. She said that she was open to whatever I was going to say. I told her what I thought I noticed, and I asked her if my perception was accurate.

A sad little smile started around the corners of her mouth, and tears came to her eyes. Sophie admitted that she had started remembering being at the lake the morning after her first boyfriend at camp broke up with her. While the image was soothing at first, her spontaneous associations were painful. She had not remembered that incident until we began using bilateral stimulation. This information told me two things: First, she tightens up when she gets activated, and, second, she resisted reporting to me what she had truly experienced. Having gotten a good enough sense of Sophie, I wondered aloud if she had given me at first what she believed I wanted to hear so as not to evoke another experience of a man being critical of her. Sophie laughed and said, "Okay, you got me." I told her I appreciated her difficulty in being honest with a man old enough to be her father, and I promised her that if she could be straight with me, I would be as honest and gentle with her.

We then went back to finding a different image of a safe place. Sophie thought of being in her maternal grandmother's kitchen, watching and learning how to bake brownies. She loved the smells of the food and the kindness and gentleness of her grandmother. When we went through a series of bilateral stimulation, her feelings of calm and safety grew. (As a relational psychoanalyst, I could wonder if my gentleness activated a sense of safety, which Sophie then associated to a purely safe place. It is certainly possible but less important than the fact that she was able to access a safe place with my observation, feedback, and support.)

5.8 Completing the Safe Place Exercise

Step 5 in the Safe Place exercise is to find a cue word that mentally activates the safe place with its sights, sounds, and sensations. Sophie's cue word was *grandma*. After deciding on the cue word, we then did a few more sets of bilateral stimulation successfully. Step 6 is self-cuing. I instructed Sophie to bring up her cue word and notice what she experienced. She reported experiencing a state of calm. I pointed out to her that she had just learned a skill that she could use whenever she felt distressed by some life event. I told her that we could practice that now, and we moved into Step 7, where the client brings up a minor irritant and I cue him or her to return to the safe place. Sophie recalled an unfair homework assignment given to her by her English teacher over the past weekend. The negative feelings were irritability and tension in her hands. She imagined the moment the teacher gave the assignment, then I said "grandma," waited 10 seconds, and repeated the cue word. Sophie reported returning to her safe place. The final step in the Safe Place exercise is to have the client bring up a different minor disturbing image and use the cue word (self-cuing) to return to the safe place. Sophie was able to do that with ease. This final step is usually fairly easy to accomplish when the first steps are followed in order.

Returning to Madeline's case, she went through all steps of the Safe Place exercise and did very well. To strengthen her affect tolerance, I taught her mindfulness meditation and another form of meditation (Vipassana) that focuses on counting one's breath. Madeline also demonstrated sufficient body awareness skills and we moved quickly to Phase 3.

5.9 Improving Body Awareness and Reducing Tension

One method of improving body awareness and reducing tension is to make observations about body awareness during the Safe Place exercise. Another is to have the client bring up a disturbing image, self-scan his or her body for any physical reaction, and report to you what he or she has found. When negative somatoform dissociative responses, such as psychic numbing, are discovered, I offer techniques such as the gentler forms of yoga and meditation as ways to help the client return to the body.

I also teach mindfulness meditation to all of my clients and students. Mindfulness meditation, where the goal is to stay in the present moment, not only enables the client to be more fully in the body, but it is also a good way to explain what the client will be doing during trauma processing. Staying in the present moment is an essential element of dual attention. Like all the other awareness techniques, this is taught in the atmosphere of calm, gentle safety that is part and parcel of the therapeutic relationship.

There is also a Western stress-reduction technique I use for clients who have trouble getting into their bodies. It is an old method of muscle relaxation training developed by Arnold Jacobson in 1938 (Barlow & Craske, 1989). This procedure involves gently tensing different parts of the body, going from the feet to the head, for 10 sec at a time, then letting go for 20 sec. Noticing the difference between tension states and relaxation states helps to release tension, teaches coping strategies, and, most important, raises awareness of the body.

More important than any of these techniques themselves is the quality of the clinician–client relationship when they are using these techniques. I explain that body awareness comes of its own accord. We cannot force it; we can merely make space in our consciousness for it. The making of space is a volitional process. Experiencing a greater level of awareness is an avolitional experience. It is my belief that true processing of trauma takes place only avolitionally. To wit, we cannot make it happen. We can only allow it to happen. That is the "Zen" piece.

I explain the need for gentleness and self-compassion; without these we run the risk of hurting ourselves physically or emotionally. So much of the time humans complicate our lives by negatively judging ourselves for the negative arousal that we feel. Arousal is avolitional, and we can exercise little control over automatic reactions. Judging, however, is an internal action over which we can exert more control. In a way, judging actually reinforces the habituated avolitional response of negative arousal. Explaining this helps the client understand that negative arousal is a process that goes on without conscious intent. It also shows the client that while it is possible to defend against feeling negative arousal, it is not possible to release old pain without feeling it.

5.10 Resourcing Strategies

Based on my observations in Phase 1, the client's score on the DES, and my client's experience with the Safe Place exercise, I now make a determination about whether he or she needs resourcing work before going ahead with processing. Both the consensual model of trauma treatment and the need for a good therapeutic relationship necessitate my discussing my conclusions with the client. If I think he or she needs an elongated period of preparation (read: stabilization) work, I explain why. I always check my conclusions about whether to start active trauma work or to do more resourcing with the wishes and ideas of my client.

Some clients need a longer stabilization period that draws on different resourcing strategies. Without such work, the clinician will hit a block in treatment when both the clinician and the client recognize that he or she has problems in current-day functioning and that his or her coping skills need to be enhanced. Even then, not all clients can immediately engage in resourcing strategies, even resource development and installation (RDI). Using RDI requires the retrieval of a positive experience involving either mastery, a supportive relationship, or something that symbolizes strength and calm. Some people have such intense blocking beliefs that they are not able to retrieve *any* positive affective experiences. In these cases, the clinician will need to teach strategies for tolerating states of positive affect before moving to RDI.

Clients — especially those who have attachment disorders — need an extended period of resource strengthening in Phase 2. To address this, Andrew Leeds began in 1995 to develop RDI. Debbie Korn and Andrew Leeds published case studies in this area (Korn & Leeds, 2002), and RDI is now a standard part of EMDR methodology (Shapiro, 2001). Other EMDR-related innovations include the ego state work (or "states of mind", in information processing terms) of Forgash, Bergmann, Paulson-Inobe, and others (2000). Because RDI has a flexible structure, it is the creativity of the clinician who is using it that makes all the difference. The first step in RDI is to identify a current life difficulty. Then the client is instructed to think about the resources he or she needs to develop or strengthen to overcome this difficulty. There are three categories of resources that may be developed:

- Mastery resources: the client's own memory of a successful coping response and the good feelings related to it, or a physical stance or movement that embodies the ability to respond effectively.
- Relational resources: a memory of a positive role model (real or from a book, movie, and so forth) or a memory of a protective and loving person or pet.
- Symbolic resources: a memory of an object from nature, a spiritual or archetypal symbol or experience, a figure in a daydream, a totem animal, an image from artwork, a metaphor suggested by the clinician, even a piece of music that evokes a feeling of strength and calm. (For a full explanation of the procedure, see Shapiro, 2001, pp. 434–440.)

Another way to conceptualize containment is suggested by Marsha Lineham in her book *Dialectical Behavior Therapy* (Linehan, 1993). She suggests three categories of resources that clients can develop: emotional regulation skills, distress-management skills, and assertiveness skills (all of which she discusses under the rubric of mindfulness). Once one or more of these resources are developed, the clinician enhances each one by eliciting more information about it. For instance, if the client's resource is to walk in the woods behind his or her house, the clinician might ask: What sights do you see? What does the air smell like? How does your body feel?

After enhancing the resource, the clinician checks to see how capable the client feels to call upon that resource to help him or her when in distress. Leeds advises checking whether the client can hold this resource in consciousness without negative affects bleeding in. If the client cannot, he advises trying a different resource. Once resources have been developed, accessed, checked, and reflected, it is time to install them by using bilateral stimulation, just as one installs a positive cognition. This includes the use of the VOC to assess how fully the client can internalize the resource.

After the resource is fully installed, the clinician further empowers the client through the use of verbal or sensory cuing. A verbal cue might be, "Walk in the park." A sensory cue might be, "Let your shoulders relax," or "Notice the tension in your shoulders and allow them to relax." The final part of formal RDI is establishing a future template, wherein the clinician helps the client imagine himself or herself in a difficult present-day situation using the resource effectively. Last of all, I recommend that before beginning desensitization with a fragile client, the clinician should make sure the client has successful practice in using one or more of the new resources on current-day challenges.

Note that these resources may be installed specifically to deal with current life problems or certain schemas the client holds. Matching a resource with a maladaptive schema may make the client amenable to further intervention. (This is another reason that Jeffrey Young's Schema-Focused Questionnaire is so useful.) For instance, a very shy man with a vulnerability to harm schema, who needs masculine support to practice the assertiveness skills he has learned, might choose as a symbolic resource the character of the tough and savvy nightclub owner played by Humphrey Bogart in the movie *Casablanca.*

It is not only the low-functioning client who can benefit from RDI, however. I recently had an eye-opening experience with a variation on this technique when I traveled to Italy to work with one of the greats in the EMDR world, Sandra "Sam" Foster. Having received her doctorate at Stanford and studied with luminaries such as Albert Bandura and Paul Watzlawitz, Foster specializes in using EMDR for executive coaching and peak performance. This application (which she developed in concert with Jennifer Lendl) follows the standard method with a few modifications. My goal with Foster was to use her peak performance work to enhance my own skills as a therapist and writer.

Foster began by instructing me to bring up a number of "inner coaches and guides" who would be there to help me along the way if I got stuck. (These coaches and guides can be regarded as positive internalizations of good relationships one has had.) At first, being from the Bronx, I pooh-poohed this idea. I'm not pathological, I'm high functioning, right? So, I thought, let's get on with it! But Foster gently insisted: She would not proceed until I had done this. So I created two very powerful inner coaches: my friend Don Cornelius, DSW, a professor of social work at Molloy College on Long Island, and my dear spiritual friend Elizabeth Paulette Coughlin, a poet, writer, body worker, and yoga instructor. We went through a process of elaborating my coaches' qualities and enhancing them by using bilateral stimulation in the form of tapping. I was sure that I would not need to use these resources, but being positively disposed to Foster, I went along with the process.

My target was to write the best book that I could and to use my healing and teaching abilities at an optimal level. As we started envisioning and processing my target, a very interesting and informative event occurred. I started getting woozy and felt myself dissociating. Foster noticed this and instructed me to use my coaches. She made interventions like, "What would Don or Elizabeth say to you now?" I found this very calming and centering: I could feel their love and support. As I shifted into a more positive space, some amazing things happened. First, I started to remember a part of my life between the ages of 13 and 15 when my parents were having difficulties and I felt very alone. My hormonal development was delayed, which made me an easy target for my peers. I was scapegoated and called derogatory names. I have always had conscious knowledge of this time in my life, and I had worked on it in a number of psychotherapy sessions. I had not believed I was still troubled (i.e., traumatized) by the events of this period.

I was mistaken. For the first time in 30 years of growth work, I was able to make contact with these old, previously dissociated states of mind. The difference was that now I had my coaches and guides to support me. I cried for that young boy who felt so lost during those years. I had been given the message many times, "You're not too bright, but if you really work hard, maybe you can make something of yourself." So here I am in Italy in the year 2004, a successful 53-year-old man who still has buried trauma from 40 years ago inhibiting my ability. Issues of low self-esteem and body dysmorphic disorder were clearly evident. As I processed the pain of those state-dependent memories, I began to realize those negative messages were still dragging down my potential. I was amazed. What seemed to help tremendously were the positive messages I was getting from Don and Elizabeth (and my friend Debbie Korn, who spontaneously showed up in my imagination and did shiatsu on my back — with a very determined face) while Foster kept gently questioning me, using the equivalent of Shapiro's cognitive interweave.

Then another amazing event happened. After releasing the pain of this buried and dissociated trauma, we continued the tapping, and I found myself on the block where I live now, standing with Wayne Dyer. Puzzled, I looked at him and said, "Where did you come from?" He answered, "What does it matter? You've been listening to my audio and videotapes so long, I figured that I'd drop by to remind you that you are only limited by your self-limiting beliefs. Imagine the abundance you want, really imagine it, and you'll create it."

So another inner guide appeared spontaneously to help me continue my work. Now, Foster is very careful about who she does peak performance work with, and she will not work with someone who still has major trauma. In my case, even as high functioning as I am, I still had dissociated trauma. The presence of my inner guides (and Foster's special gifts) was crucial to my getting through this painful state-dependent cluster of memories.

This experience has influenced my general practice of EMDR so that during Phase 2, I ask my clients, no matter how high functioning, to identify inner guides and coaches to assist in doing the work, if necessary.

In neurophysiologic terms, I am facilitating the activation of positive memory networks to enhance the work and serve as a source of support for my client during difficult periods. What this seems to do is to strengthen affect tolerance so that painful state-dependent experiences will be more amenable to being processed by the brain. You see, it is all about relationships, both the kind you have in real life and those you have in books, audiotapes, and the like. (Thanks for being there, Wayne!)

Activating resources in the client — whether it is a fragile client, persistently traumatized as a young child, who is trying to cope with the challenges of everyday life, or a high-functioning individual in the process of self-actualization — is a useful modification that empowers clients to heal faster and more fully. Whatever resource is chosen, when the client has internalized it sufficiently, his or her sense of self strengthens. This is the goal of RDI: to prepare the ground so that the clinician and client can move from preparation and stabilization into Phase 3, the start of active trauma work.

5.11 Determining Readiness for EMDR Trauma Processing

Debbie Korn has introduced many important factors to be evaluated in making a determination of readiness for trauma processing, among them being

> Coping skills and adaptive, soft defenses
> Adequate affect (arousal) tolerance
> Capacity for self-regulation (auto and interactive)
> Accessible positive affect schemas, ego states, and resources
> Safe embodiment (versus dissociation, numbing)
> Object constancy and permanence
> Adequate "SELF," observing ego, internal boundaries, and ability to manage merging of states

Remember (says Debbie Korn): Neither diagnosis nor trauma history determines readiness for trauma processing or response to treatment. ("Determining readiness" appears on Slide 36 in her workshops.)

I have found that new EMDR clinicians are often hesitant to take the plunge into active trauma work. I remind them that the first two phases of EMDR treatment are specifically designed for the clinician to do "due diligence" so that he or she can make a solid diagnostic assessment and plan a sequence of treatment strategies to achieve the goals the clinician and client have agreed upon. If you have done your due diligence and created a good relationship with your client, there is less to worry about when you progress to trauma activation and processing.

CHAPTER 6

Phase 3: Assessment (Trauma Activation Sequence)

6.1 Overview of the Trauma Activation Sequence

The third phase, assessment, begins the second stage of EMDR treatment — active trauma work. The clinician has signed off on the client's readiness for processing, and the clinician and client are starting the phase that I refer to as the trauma activation sequence. Shapiro calls this phase "assessment," but most of the client assessment necessary before processing has been completed in Phase 1 and Phase 2. The only assessment remaining is to rate the intensity of the emotion connected to a particular memory and, if applicable, the truth of the positive cognition. I want to underline that although I have my own nicknames for the phases, I follow the procedural steps outline almost to a T.

What Phase 3 seems to do is to start the countdown to launching the client into state-dependent memory. In my experience, once the picture, negative cognition, emotion, and body sensation linked to the trauma have all been stimulated, the client often enters a spontaneously activated state. We will look more closely at the consequences of reframing Phase 3 as a launch sequence later in this chapter.

This stage is where I believe that the working alliance alone, even with good enough bonding, is not sufficient. Though we operate from the real relationship, the acceleration of information processing has profound effects on both participants. It is the responsibility of the clinician to be the wise moderator of both the client's and his own states of mind. The client is instructed into the nature of avolitional experience "just notice…", and in so doing has his hands full. It is our job not only to be proficient in the methodology, but also to monitor the reactions of each participant and intervene accordingly.

I think that Shapiro's conceptual insight about re-associating the picture, negative belief, emotion, and body sensation attached to a particular state-dependent memory constitutes a major contribution to the field. When we link these four key elements, we are directly accessing — and thus activating — neural networks that hold traumatic memories. We are collaborating with the client to enter a form of imaginary exposure to the traumatic elements of his or her memories.

Relational issues of trust and presence are intensified during active trauma work. A healthy attachment relationship creates a safe container in which the client can process frightening and painful memories. What is more, it provides a healing experience for clients who suffered trauma at the hands of other human beings.

As experienced EMDR clinicians know, the client's potential responses to imaginary exposure are so varied that the clinician must be comfortable going wherever the client needs to go. This willingness contributes to the client's bond with the clinician. Re-experiencing the past while being anchored in the present in a safe relationship with the clinician is the essence of dual attention. It is the clinician's job to maintain this collaborative and safe journey.

As I mentioned earlier, there is a critically important shift in roles that takes place at the beginning of Phase 3. Prior to that, the nature of the relationship between clinician and client is akin to that of doctor and patient. There is a disequilibrium in the relationship, an imbalance of power. This is not only a good thing, it is necessary. The client is in despair; he or she needs an expert who provides guidance and instruction. Clinicians do this in Phase 1 and Phase 2 by gathering data, testing the client's abilities, and instructing the client in what is to follow.

When the launch sequence begins, the situation changes. The truth is, the clinician knows where he or she and the client are starting and knows where they want to end up — with the client released from the traumas that haunt him or her — but the clinician does not know where or how things will reach that point. Thus, in Phase 3, the clinician switches to a co-participatory role. This changes the nature of the relationship. The clinician and client are now two people with different roles and responsibilities exploring the unknown together. It takes courage on both their parts. Doing EMDR relationally does not mean being touchy-feely or even the clinician's reflecting back insights to the client. It means that the clinician and client are partners on a journey. Together they will decide on which trauma to start with. Together they will open the doors to state-dependent memory.

6.2 The Power of the Procedural Steps

In this chapter, we will look at some of the pitfalls and best practices in following the procedural steps outline, which comprises Phase 3: selecting a target memory to reprocess, selecting the picture best represented by it, identifying the negative cognition, identifying the positive cognition and rating it by using the VOC scale, naming the emotion stimulated by the picture, getting a SUDS rating, and identifying the body sensation. I think the procedural steps are brilliantly conceived. They give the EMDR practitioner a tool to activate fully the client's targeted memory network, stimulating first the visual and then the auditory part of the cortex. From there, it is usually a straight shot to the underbelly of the traumatic experience: its related emotions and body sensations. This is a robust activation sequence that puts the client in a state of safe but highly negative arousal, making him or her fully ready for Phase Four.

Despite the effectiveness of the procedural steps, I have observed that some clinicians have problems with using them as Shapiro intended. A common concern is that their formal structure may prevent clinicians from empowering their clients and themselves to be in the here and now of the client's experience. Some of my colleagues who are experientially oriented seem to have the most difficulty with this. But the procedural steps do empower the client — they empower the information-processing ability of the client's brain to release old pain and reorganize the experience in a more adaptive way. This is the goal of the procedural steps, with their emphasis on which question to ask when. Understanding that this is the goal seems to be what makes a clinician successful in facilitating a client's fully processing a state-dependent memory.

My experience in 30 years of clinical practice is that most clients come into treatment with a presentation of what hurts them now. They want the clinician to help them make sense of what is happening to them now (and what happened in the past to cause it). This is a reasonable request, and most forms of psychotherapy are designed to do just that. In psychoanalysis, interpretations re-associate painful memories, interactions, and attachments through linking past relationships with present-day difficulties. In Rogerian treatment, the emphasis is on empathic reflection, which helps to clarify the client's deeper state of mind. During chair work in gestalt therapy or in ego state work, the "client" contacts another part of the self that either clarifies the dilemma or empowers him or her, and is thereby enabled to understand and resolve the dilemma. In Gendlin's focusing, the client develops a "felt sense," which is a "body sense of meaning," a way for the body to provide its own answers to experienced problems (Gendlin, 1981, 1996).

In EMDR clinicians empower their clients' brains to get unblocked, reorganize painful experience, and make sense of it. The theory of EMDR states, "The simultaneous focus on traumatic memory (and being grounded firmly in the safe present) may cause the activated system to process the dysfunctionally stored material" (Shapiro 2001, p. 33). Many EMDR clinicians say that when the client's state-dependent memory is processed by the brain, a feeling of empowerment generalizes to the whole person, and there are concomitant rises in self-esteem and functionality. This describes exactly what I have seen in my own clients.

Having come down solidly on the side of sticking to the procedural steps, I now must confess that in a few special cases I do not always include the positive cognition and VOC in Phase 3. I will explain in some detail why, with certain clients, I choose to defer getting to these two elements until Phase 4 has been completed.

6.3 Target Selection: Pitfalls and Best Practices

The first activity in the launch sequence is selecting the target from among the 10 worst memories that are linked to the presenting problem. These memories should have been elicited from the client in Phase 1. Although Shapiro has stressed the importance of linking the old target memory to the presenting problem, I have talked to too many clinicians who do not do this rigorously. Instead they simply ask which old memory the client wants to work on. The problem with this is that the clinician and client may end up targeting the client's state of mind that day, not the character trait the client came into therapy to address (and the old memories that started these traits). Targeting a state of mind will not ensure successful resolution of the presenting problem.

Another cause for concern is that after processing is underway, many EMDR clinicians will open a session by asking, "What old memory would you like to work on today?" So what is wrong with that? It sounds relational, doesn't it? The problem is that because we need to finish one protocol before moving on to the next, we cannot leave this decision entirely up to the client. Opening too many wounds at once, before finishing work on the original target memory, may cause flooding or shutting down. Instead the clinician needs to continue working on the first target and its associational channels until they are completely processed. That does not sound too relational, does it? But when experience shows that certain elements of a procedure need to be followed with fidelity because they create more safety and better outcomes, *that* is relational.

The goal for targeting a memory is to select from one of these two categories:

1. The oldest memory (of the worst and most painful memories elicited in Phase 1) that intensifies the problem(s) the client came in for. (Remember, it is not enough that the target memory be the oldest; it must also be associated with painful emotions and negative cognitions.)
2. The *worst* of those memories.

The client and clinician should decide together, in a co-participatory way (neurobiologically, this is co-regulation), which memory to target. If the client is unsure, I ask him or her to think of a related memory, then close his or her eyes, and do a quick body scan to determine what is most disturbing, using the SUDS Scale as a measure.

Although the oldest painful memory is usually targeted first in EMDR, it may not be the most accessible. It may carry implicit fears connected to other state-dependent memories. This may not be obvious to the client — or to the clinician. That is why starting with one of the oldest memories that hurts *now* seems to be a better choice. As I tell my clients (and it is something I have learned from years of experience), "It ain't gonna sing if it ain't got that zing!" And, it is only going to "zing" — hurt — when state-dependent memory is "singing."

Many times clients want to work on a present-day traumatic event. This may not be the wisest course of action. In 14 years of doing EMDR, I have seen that clients often get stuck and block during the next phase, when they actively process their traumatic memories. For example, a 42-year-old woman may walk into a session and want to work on her tough day at the office when her boss was irrationally on her back. Since I already know the client's history and her worst memories, and we have completed processing the memory we were working on, I recognize that this experience is similar to her childhood when she was often harshly and unfairly criticized by her alcoholic father. If this is the case, a possible strategy is to use a "floatback technique" (this is similar to Watkins and Watkins' [1997] affect bridge and is discussed in depth in the next chapter) to elicit the implicitly associated childhood memory of being harshly criticized. Once the client has processed the childhood feeder memory of her father's drunken irrationality and released her pain about it, we can more directly focus her attention on current-day referents to her childhood trauma. She might spontaneously develop a solution to her problem. If not, we can figure out together appropriate ways to deal with the situation with her boss, such as giving her assertiveness training. If not, we can then assess what is not finished in terms of other associated trauma.

It is vital to recognize that the interaction between client and clinician at this stage is as important as which memory is selected for processing.

If the clinician is not attuned, aligned, and resonating with the client in the moment, it will be much harder for the client to successfully process the trauma. Having an attuned heart and mind enables the client safely to open the door to hidden depths. One of the organizing principles of Phase 3 work is an affectively and cognitively shared agreement by both parties on where to begin. The clinician is the agreed-upon expert on methodology; the client is the agreed-upon expert on his or her life. Deciding where to start a protocol is a judgment call that you, the clinician, have input into, but that the client has the final say in. I believe that not just what you and your client decide to target, but *how* you work together to focus on the target memory, pictorial representation, and appropriate negative cognition is a good predictor of outcome. Relatively speaking, the clinician should instruct the client carefully on the proper procedures to follow (i.e., starting with the oldest memory), but once clinicians have given our instructions and rationale, I believe that we should respect our clients' wishes about which target memory to start with. Any exceptions must be spelled out very carefully and conceptually to the client so he or she understands them on an energetic and emotional level, as evidenced by somatosensory changes that are either noticeable to the clinician or reported by the client.

For example, suppose a 38-year-old male client has had a trauma-processing session about his father. The session was incomplete in that the client's SUDS level did not reach 0. However, definite progress was made. The starting SUDS was 9; the ending SUDS was 4. During closure the client remembers that there was a very important way in which his father let him down: by not attending any of the client's basketball games. In the next session, when client and clinician are in the reevaluation phase, the client states that he has made enough progress on this issue. Now he wants to work on his professional and future issues. His SUDS on the original issue in the following session is a 5. What judgment call needs to be made? It would appear that the client either has dissociated or wants to disassociate the painful affect related to his father's lack of love. The client's reaction to the previous session gives the astute clinician a roadmap of his psyche. Remember, this is the "Zen" of EMDR: "Be here *now.*" Clearly, to me, the starting point is the client's desire to avoid feeling the effects of active trauma work. I would suggest that clinician intervention is appropriate here.

Once the best target has been selected, the clinician asks the client what picture represents the worst part of the memory. This is to enable the client to have as clear a visual representation as possible in the hopes of potentiating the trauma activation sequence. Asking for the picture, however, is not an invitation to explore the meaning of the event. There are times when the client may want to say something more about a particular picture. But talking or telling stories at this point can actually defuse the pain of the memory. It is probably a method of implicit avoidance as well. In as gentle a way as possible, the clinician should guide the client back to the procedural steps.

How specific does the target image need to be? Must it be real, or can it be representative of a group of memories? How detailed should it be? Does a part of the picture trigger any other old trauma? If so, which part and what trauma? All the client and clinician really need is an image that is focused enough to start the activation sequence. It should be enough to answer the question, What old memory is being accessed and stimulated to activation by the procedural steps outline?

Often an EMDR consultee who is consulting with a more experienced colleague will present a session that "did not go well," meaning the client showed no — or little observable — shift in affect or insight. My experience is that this is often the result of the target image's being cloudy or vague and the clinician's struggling unsuccessfully to help the client be more specific. This is usually a sign of negative psychoform dissociation (cloudy image) and negative somatoform dissociation (lack of feeling, numbing). When material is not accessible enough, it should be a sign to both parties that more resourcing needs to be done, specifically on resources that will lower negative hyperarousal so the image and sensation can be present along with negative cognition. There are other times when the clinician is not clear about how to use the procedural steps outline properly. The antidote for this frustrating situation is to ask oneself, What are we working on? Clarity counts.

Here is an example. An EMDR clinician presented a case of insomnia. There was no target memory. The target picture was of the person in the present day having trouble sleeping. So there was no specific memory, just a symptom. And "the EMDR was not working." As we discussed the case, it also came out that the client, a combat veteran, was actively drinking. Clearly, the consultee's trauma case conceptualization had not been fully thought out. The client's insomnia was both a symptom of PTSD and the consequence of using alcohol abuse to wipe out the feeling states that PTSD stirred up. After the client had a period of sobriety and training in relapse prevention, a possible target would be the worst or earliest upsetting combat memory. The clinician had not thought through the task-centered need in the working alliance to do his due diligence.

The clearer the EMDR clinician is in the trauma case conceptualization, the more focused the target will be, and the better the chance for a successful and robust outcome. In general this case shows us that the clinician needs not to note the client's symptoms but to find out what painful memories, thoughts, and sensations those symptoms are connected to. This, of course, takes place *after* the client and clinician have addressed the client's need to attain sobriety. This may take a considerable amount of time. Then client and clinician, with relapse prevention strategies in place, can begin active trauma work safely. This is where having access to the *EMDR Chemical Dependency Treatment Manual* and A. J. Popky's DeTUR protocol is invaluable.

Once the target memory is chosen and the picture comes into focus, trauma activation begins. At the same time, the client is quite aware that he or she is sitting in my office with me, safe in present time. Being able to create this dual awareness of traumatic past and safe present is the foundation that will enable the client to process traumatic memories and release traumatic stress permanently.

6.4 Using Dreams as Target Images

A clinician who is working with a client who has already had at least one trauma-processing session should seriously consider targeting images that have come up in the client's postsession dreams. Processing stimulates many associational channels. In fact, this is the most important evidence that processing is continuing after the therapy session. When a client dreams after an EMDR session, the dream must be looked at as a serious contender for the next target to work on. Many times after a processing session, the client continues to "work" on the trauma avolitionally, which may stimulate more directed dream activation. This is why I ask my clients to keep dream journals in the days following bilateral stimulation. When a dream is brought to the next session, the client and I decide together whether there remains a sufficiently disturbing charge to the memory of the dream to justify targeting its most disturbing element. Such dreams give us a glimpse of what is being processed by the client's brain, as opposed to just his left-brain analytical function. If the client's dream reactivates his or her central nervous system — as evidenced by the disturbance felt when remembering it — we can see the nature of the traumatic stress the client is experiencing. This can give both client and clinician valuable information on what to activate and process next.

6.4.1 Jim's Dream

Jim is a 56-year-old man who served in Vietnam. He presented with severe agitation and overreactions to people and life events. He has been married for 22 years and has two teenage boys, ages 14 and 17. He reports being very hard on them, though he has not been abusive. Jim functions marginally in society. He works full-time running his own "Photo Mat" but says that the less contact he has with people the better. For a long time he was active in his local outreach center.

Jim is plagued by flashbacks of acts he judged as shameful, committed on the enemy during his years in Southeast Asia. He has been in EMDR treatment with me for 3 months, during which time I have assisted Jim to become more aware of being in his body and more able to tolerate intense affective experiences. We have been working on how scared, young, and alienated he felt being in a strange land with his life at stake every minute.

The initial target memory we worked on had to do with the first firefight Jim had been in. He remembered squatting in the bush with his rifle, scanning the trees and open spaces around him. The trails of tracers streaked through the nighttime sky. He heard mortar rounds whistling and booming, and he lost his nerve. The essential aspects of this memory were

Picture: being in the bush and crouching with his head between his legs, frozen in terror
Negative cognition: *I am a coward.*
Positive cognition: *I deserve to survive.*
VOC: 3
Emotion: shame
SUDS: 8
Body sensations: heart racing, gut clenched

Jim's first processing experience was generally positive. He had a fairly typical desensitizing event, and he reported an ending SUDS of 4, which he was quite pleased about. He also reported feeling calmer than he had in many years. We agreed that Jim would journal anything that came to his mind that had intense energy attached to it. That week he had the following dream:

I am standing in a forest. There are dangers lurking behind every tree and shrub. Suddenly I see a comrade who has been hit. I rush to save him. I cannot recognize the face, but he has an unmistakable mustache. I wake up feeling uneasy.

During the next session, he processed the dream. The essential aspects were

Picture: the mustache of his fallen comrade
Negative cognition: *I am powerless.*

Positive cognition: *I am powerful.*
VOC: 4
Emotion: terror
SUDS: 9
Body sensations: heart racing, gut clenched (Jim's body sensations were the same as in the earlier session. This is not always the case. I speculated that experiencing the same body sensations could be evidence of unfinished business along this central nervous system path.)

When Jim processed the dream, the mustache reminded him of a beloved old uncle who was a very masculine and nurturing figure in his young life, and whose support he had lost when he went to Vietnam. As he continued to process, he reported that he could start to feel his uncle's support, and he spontaneously said, "If my uncle Abe were here, he would give me solace." To his own surprise, he then said, "It sort of reminds me of your mustache, too." We processed this association next. A feeling of peace and self-forgiveness came over him, and he was overcome with a major abreaction as he actively mourned for that young soldier, scared out of his mind in the jungles of Southeast Asia. His ending SUDS that day was a 1.

6.5 The Negative Cognition

In the previous section, I discussed how specific the picture that goes with the targeted memory should be. The bottom line is that the picture needs to be detailed enough to cause activation of the associated negative cognitions, disturbing emotions, and body sensations. Once the picture has been identified, it is time to look at the negative judgment that the person has made about himself or herself as a result of the traumatic experience being targeted. Patterns of cognitions — derived from the history taking — may become clearer. For the client, one of the best ways to come up with a negative cognition is to state a long-held and long-hidden "truth" about himself or herself, related to the picture of the memory. If the clinician has established a solid relationship with the client, the client will feel safe enough to share this often shameful belief.

The negative cognition may be held in an age-dependent way. Consider how old the person was at the time of the trauma. Knowing this will give the clinician a clue about how much psychosocial development (with its attendant learning as well as neurological development) the client had achieved before the trauma. A typical negative cognition at the beginning of treatment for a client who was sexually abused as a young boy may be "I am to blame." For example, a young boy who is subjected to sodomy by a relative when he is 6 will not have the neurological development or life experience to "know" that he is not to blame.

Other things to look for include the theme(s) in the client's life that arose from this dysfunctionally stored memory. Does the client show signs of believing that he or she will never heal, for instance? Does the client believe he or she is "damaged goods"? Note whether the negative cognition varies. What is it *now* as opposed to then? If the memory is state specific, the evaluations, emotions, and sensations will be stored in episodic memory with linkages to the implicit memory networks.

We use the word *now* when asking the question, "What words go best with that picture (or incident) that express your negative belief about yourself *now?*" The word *now* has been a source of confusion to many clients when they begin EMDR treatment. The word is used because state-dependent memory is held in the present but is not acknowledged as such. As was discussed in Chapter 5, this point needs to be made to the client in Phase 2, with examples and explanations, as part of the orientation to active trauma work. It cannot be emphasized sufficiently that the client and clinician are working with state-dependent memory during the trauma-processing phase. It is also crucial to remember that, according to the adaptive information processing model, there is an inherent part of ourselves that strives toward self-healing. (This construct, based upon Shapiro's observation of the equivalent physiological process, states that the organism, when unfettered by traumatic blocks and genetic limitations, will transform to greater and greater levels of complexity.) "In this way," says Siegel, "living systems are open systems capable of responding and adapting to the environment." As Siegel defines the scope of his thesis, he says that he draws from a "variety of related theories," including the information-processing theories of "parallel distributed processing" or "connectionism" (1999, p. 215).

An important point must be made here. The negative cognition will largely depend on what state dependent memory network was activated, so a variety of responses can be expected. The most important thing to notice is how the client has become activated. For example, do tears fill the client's eyes? For a client with blocking beliefs about letting go, I suggest closely watching the jaws and the breathing. A tight jaw and shallow breath are indicators of activation. Changes in breathing patterns are especially important indicators for clients who present with panic disorder. Every clinician treating panic-disordered clients should take the time to learn about breathing physiology.

Determining the negative cognition is not as easy as it may sound, even if the client appears to understand the concepts and demonstrate them as well. A client in Phase 2 may have demonstrated an understanding of the principle of linking the picture of the traumatic event with a negative self-belief. But in Phase 3, the client may block upon hearing the word *now* when you ask, "What words go best with the picture and express your belief about yourself *now?*" Many clients reply by asking, "Do you mean how I feel now?" (There is general cloudiness in everyday language about the distinction between thoughts and feeling states.) Other clients will ask, "Do you mean do I still believe this irrational belief?" (Of course, the answer is that the person still does believe it — but not with the thinking left brain. The client believes it because it is still deeply imprinted in the traumatic memory.) It is this deep imprinting that thwarts response flexibility in traumatized humans. Many clients seem to have habituated to partitioning their outer and inner worlds into the sharply divided *now* and *then*. In state-dependent memory there is no little neurobiological *then*, it is still *now*.

When this occurs, the clinician, as educator, needs to clarify four points for the client:

1. The client is finding a *belief*, not a feeling.
2. This belief, although it is part of state-dependent memory, is happening right now in a number of old circuits in the brain.
3. We say "now" because we are speaking to those circuits. We need to reroute them to the present day in order to work on them.
4. From a relational point of view, the clinician acknowledges the difficulty of asking the client to accept the clinician's language, instead of staying with the client's own. I have found that when I explain this duality (and use copying a CD on the computer as a metaphor), clients usually are able to "get" it. Still, I need to remember that my client is filled with negative arousal so that my explanations may be difficult to encode and to retrieve.

Once these points have been explained, the clinician again asks the client to bring up the most disturbing picture and to notice what negative self-beliefs he or she has in relation to it. If necessary, the clinician can help the client formulate a negative cognition based on his or her spontaneous utterances during history taking. These core negative self-judgments are also embedded in the client's worst memories, and as the clinician listens to the client's stories and observe his or her body language, schemas (such as vulnerability to harm or unrelenting standards) will become clear. The demand characteristics around which the client has organized his or her life will come into view. (Young's Schema-Focused Questionnaire is excellent at pinpointing where the client is at risk in this regard.) Then the clinician can consider this question: Of the schemas observed during the history taking, which negative self-judgment strikes both me and my client as the most representative of this emotional pattern?

The degree to which the client is unable, after an adequate period of preparation, spontaneously to articulate a self-referencing negative belief may signal not just dissociation but also the degree to which he or she is apt to have further dissociative experiences during processing. Given that dissociation occurs on a continuum, a client who needs little clinician assistance in determining a negative cognition is likely to have only a mild dissociative reaction during processing, and vice versa.

If I judge that dissociation is the reason why the client seems unable to re-associate the target picture with a negative self-belief, I presume that he or she has already become activated and that activation has caused him or her to dissociate. (This can happen even with people who have low scores on the DES.) In this case, I use the negative cognition question as a diagnostic tool to discover what has been too much for the client to handle. I do not believe that clients shut down, become confused or distracted, or use diversion explicitly. Trying to link the earliest or worst picture and its related negative cognition may have sparked a distressing feeling state, re-associating the client to the traumatic experience too intensely and causing an activation of dissociative defenses. Remember, the original trauma may have been accompanied by partial or full-blown dissociation.

This situation does not rule out doing active trauma work. However, it must be noted, understood, and taken into consideration as the clinician continuously evaluates the client's readiness throughout the launch sequence. It is important to keep making this evaluation in the moment, because it may be at odds with the clinician's overall evaluation of the client's readiness to do active trauma work. In Phase 2, the client may have gone through all eight steps of the Safe Place exercise, but he or she needs to feel safe now, at the start of re-experiencing the trauma. In case of interpersonal trauma, there was often no choice but to dissociate, or so the immature brain of the developing child decided at the time. In choosing to re-experience the trauma, there is a price to pay. The client may experience a fully activated neurobiological state and abreact the trauma before becoming desensitized to it. (This is a point where the positive cognition serves as a valuable resource for hope. It gives initial direction and reminds the client that he or she is bigger than the "psychopathology.") This is also the time when the clinician may be the strongest resource the client has when they are in a state of mental state resonance.

If a client cannot articulate a negative cognition, yet the clinician still believes he or she is ready for EMDR, the clinician can bring out the list of generic negative cognitions in Shapiro's first book and ask the client which statement resonates the most or "feels most true." (This may be akin to Perry's example of "feeding" the client).

As discussed earlier, the clinician serves as the container for the client during trauma work. When a clinician shows a client the list of generic negative cognitions, for example, he or she is helping that client be in an organized, secure, attached relationship with the clinician. In fact, one of the chief goals of practicing EMDR relationally is to enable the client to have an organized, secure attachment relationship with the clinician — in contrast to the disorganized insecure attachments the client most likely had in childhood.

6.6 The Positive Cognition and VOC

Shapiro states,

> Once the negative cognition is identified, the positive cognition should be developed. The positive cognition is a verbalization of the desired state (a self-belief that is a distillation of the positive affects) and is generally a 180-degree shift from the negative cognition. It is an empowering self-assessment incorporating the same theme or personal issue as the negative cognition. (2001, p. 136)

The positive cognition gives hope and direction to the client, and implies that the person is larger than the "pathology."

When clients state long-held and long-hidden secrets about themselves that they associate with the worst picture from the traumatic incident, they are opening up visual and auditory channels sequentially. It is my experience, in many cases, that when these two channels are opened up and activated, it means "the train has left the station," as Shapiro puts it. When this is clearly the case, I may diverge from the procedural steps outline by postponing getting the positive cognition and VOC at this juncture. (Remember, I made a list of the client's positive cognitions during history taking, and I will elicit them again at the end of Phase 4.) I may omit the positive cognition in Phase 3 only after observing how my client processes — thus, I never omit it during the first protocol — and only when the client is already activated into state-dependent memory and has shown signs in the first protocol that the positive cognition and VOC cause deactivation. Then, in my best judgment, I deem it unwise to interrupt for fear of lowering arousal and slowing down the process.

In these cases I ask what emotion was sparked when the picture and negative cognitions were linked. I ask the client to rate it quickly on the

SUDS Scale. Then I ask about body sensations. Next, the moment the client is able to name the part of the body where he or she feels signs of increased negative arousal, I begin bilateral stimulation. Remember, though, that during Phase 1, trauma case conceptualization, I spend a good deal of time asking clients where they want to be and what they want to believe about themselves when the treatment is over.

Since my experience has taught me that some clients are already starting to become activated by this time, I interpret Phase 3 as the trauma activation sequence. I understand from Shapiro that the term *assessment* is used to connote a phase where a traumatic memory can be broken down into its component parts and some of those parts measured. This is in keeping with the scientific method. Measuring the distress level of the client via self-ratings that are taken before and after processing certainly seems like a sound idea. It also is a left-brain function, and, because of that, bilateral stimulation should follow, so we — clinician and client — want measurable starting points. The picture and negative cognition are right-brain activities, the positive cognition and VOC are left-brain, the SUDS level is both, and identifying the activated part of the body is a whole-brain task. However, I have found on occasion that stopping to ask for the positive cognition and VOC can interfere with the attunement I have established with my client by interrupting the activation of the memory network where the trauma is stored.

Giving a specific case example is probably the best way to illustrate this. Ira is a 52-year-old laborer who lays ceramic floors. He has two teenage sons from his first marriage and has been married to his second wife for 4 years. Ira and his ex-wife have maintained a civil attitude since his divorce 10 years ago. When they were married, Ira used to go out several times a week to the bar to "have a few with the boys." After the divorce, Ira started attending Alcoholics Anonymous, and he has been sober for 9 years. He was born Jewish but does not identify himself with any organized religion.

When Ira was 12, he was having the traditional shaving cream fight that boys have on Halloween. He and his friends were doing this in the park near his house. A gang of Irish boys from another neighborhood showed up. His friends ran away, but Ira froze. The boys asked him if he was Jewish. He said yes. Then the boys beat him up and poured prune juice over him.

Ira entered treatment when his 12-year-old son started being a bully at school. Ira's temper had gotten the best of him, and he had humiliated his son in front of other children. Ira saw that his rage was way out of proportion to the situation. Realizing that he had to address this issue, he sought treatment and was referred to me.

Phase 1 and Phase 2 took us 5 weeks to complete as Ira's insurance coverage only allowed for single sessions. When we began Phase 3, Ira chose to work on the memory of the Halloween beating. His DES rating was low. The picture he chose was being surrounded by the gang while the biggest boy asked him in a threatening voice if he was Jewish. His negative cognition was *I'm helpless.* At this point, tears welled up and Ira started to shake softly.

We moved on to the positive cognition. I asked Ira, "When you bring up that picture, what would you like to believe about yourself *now?* He paused and then said, "I'd like to believe that it never happened." Now, during our orientation to trauma work in Phase 2, we had carefully gone over examples of positive cognitions and discussed how magical wishes would not help information processing. But Ira's traumatic re-arousal was so great that his brain's retrieval abilities were temporarily diminished, and he experienced being overwhelmed. He was unable to access his knowledge of how to formulate an appropriate positive cognition. After we talked together a bit, Ira stated a new positive cognition: *I can take care of myself.* This took about 2 minutes.

Then I asked, "When you think about that picture, how do those words, 'I can take care of myself,' feel to you now on a scale of 1 to 7, where 1 is completely false and 7 is completely true?" Ira replied, "Do you mean can I take care of myself now?" I guided him back to the protocol and asked him to link the target memory with the positive cognition and rate how true the positive words felt when he connected them to the target memory. He paused and scratched his head. Eventually he looked up and said, "I guess about a 5."

Next I asked Ira to go back to the target memory and connect it with the negative cognition (*I'm helpless*) and notice what emotions came up. He shrugged his shoulders. The tears were gone from his eyes and he had stopped shaking. He told me he did not feel much at all.

I think you can see my dilemma. Asking him to choose a target memory, a picture, and a negative cognition had "started the train down the track." The associative channels in his brain were opening up. He was feeling sad and frightened, as evidenced by his tears and shaking. But when I asked Ira to formulate a positive cognition and give it a VOC rating, I was, in effect, asking him to put on the brakes, jump the right-brain track, and go into an analytical, left-brain mode. When he followed my instructions, he first had difficulty coming up with an appropriate positive cognition, and then he was tripped up by the wording of my request for the VOC. He may also, as other clients have told me, have been confused by using a scale that works in the opposite way to the

SUDS Scale and across a different range of numbers (1 to 7 instead of 0 to 10). Since this was our first active trauma-processing session, it was necessary to bring in the positive cognition and VOC. In future protocols, leaving this part out proved useful when Ira again became activated by linking the picture with his negative cognition.

6.7 Postponing the Positive Cognition and VOC

Shapiro explains in her first book that asking for the positive cognition and VOC at this point in Phase 3 offers the client an alternative to the negative self-belief he or she holds. She posits that this alternative "serves as a light at the end of the tunnel. This factor may inspire the client with courage and commitment to treatment born of the belief that an alternative is indeed possible" (1995, p. 141). It may also clarify the direction the client desires to go, and by rating it the clinician gets a sense of how far away from the preferred belief the client is.

Although there are times when this is a compelling argument, there are also times — as in Ira's case and others like his — when I have seen the positive cognition and VOC take clients out of the experience and into their heads to think about what they would rather believe. This is problematic enough, but the fact that clinicians get rather wordy when we ask for the positive cognition and VOC compounds the problem. (Many clients have asked me, "Which number is totally true and which is totally false?")

So first we get wordy, and then we introduce a second analytic question involving a new scale for measuring it. And we are doing this directly after having begun to stimulate a painful memory. The result in certain cases is to take the client out of state-dependent memory just as he or she is entering it. I believe that Shapiro probably intended that the client would re-associate the adaptive belief (the positive cognition) with his picture of the trauma, thus seeing that he or she is larger than the pathology. But asking for the positive cognition and VOC seems to distract some highly intellectualized clients and stall the activation process — thus reinforcing just the opposite of what was intended: The distraction may in and of itself cause a small dissociative (negative somatoform) effect, which may inhibit a client from reentering the traumatic state-dependent memory.

Since the picture and negative cognition are still in the client's working memory, it seems to make more sense — under certain conditions — to continue stimulating the memory in preparation for the trauma processing in Phase 4. These conditions relate to where the client is on a continuum ranging from hardiness to fragility. By "hardy," I mean having a well-developed ability to tolerate affect. (Ira was toward the hardy end of the continuum.) The hardier the client, the less concerned I am about suspending the activation process to get a positive cognition and VOC. The more fragile a client is, the less likely I am to leave it out. For them it serves as an excellent resource of hope. That is why clinicians try to not let clients have a VOC of 1. It is usually too far a leap for them, and therefore it provides another way of expressing hopelessness. For some clients, distracting them from the neurologically stimulated memory closes them down to the experiential nature of EMDR processing. It may also inadvertently interfere with the synergy that exists between an attuned and aligned clinician and the client.

I am not advocating the elimination of the positive cognition and VOC. I simply believe, from my clinical experience, that there are certain times when it better serves the client to postpone asking for these items until the beginning of Phase 5, when there is a moment of rest, even of celebration. Every EMDR clinician and client will recognize the wonderment and joy that spontaneously occur when a traumatic memory has been desensitized.

With the sole exception of postponing the positive cognition and VOC in certain circumstances, I rigorously follow the procedural steps outline, and I recommend that all EMDR practitioners do so. Clinicians ought to be so familiar with it that we can recite it in our sleep. It is an excellent way of organizing the data held in different parts of the brain that are needed for adaptive information processing. This is a preparation of another type. By asking the questions in the procedural steps outline, the clinician stimulates multiple brain centers, brain circuitry, and chemical and electrical reactions. Often this is enough to open a portal into state-dependent memory. The clinician and client are now time travelers together. The train is rolling out of the station, full speed ahead into the past.

6.8 Naming the Related Emotions

The next part of the launch sequence is to ask the client to link the picture and negative cognition. I phrase it this way: "When you see X (the image), and you link it with Y (the negative cognition), what emotions spark in you right now?" (I use the word *spark* as it relates to the notion of kindling points.) The client usually has little difficulty naming the emotion he or she feels, and I have the client rate it on the SUDS Scale.

Clinicians need to pay close attention when the client insists that trauma exists but assigns a low SUDS level to his or her emotion about it. This may be due to psychic numbing in parts of a particular memory network. This means, according to the structural model of dissociation, that the client is in a negative somatoform state, which may remain frozen unless it is directly addressed. Deciding whether to address it before proceeding is an in-the-moment judgment call the clinician must make.

When the SUDS rating seems to be artificially low, I usually ask the client about it. My goal is to "wake up" any split-off parts by sending the message that I am giving space for his or her feelings to be heard. An artificially low SUDS is often caused by hidden blocking beliefs. I try to flush out these blocking beliefs by asking clients what they believe about themselves in the moment.

6.9 Tuning in to Body Sensation and Concluding the Launch Sequence

The final step in Phase 3 is to ask where in the body the client feels the emotion(s) he or she has named. The clinician should have tested the client on body awareness skills during Phase 2. If the client demonstrated those skills but is inhibited during the part of Phase 3 pertaining to body sensation, it is likely that negative somatoform dissociation has occurred. Although other experts may say to go ahead with processing using the channels that are open (picture, negative cognition, and emotion) and hope for body sensations to become apparent later, I recommend having the client do a quick body scan to notice *any* physical sensation present (whether linked to the target memory or not) before proceeding to Phase 4. This idea comes from Gestalt therapy, focusing, and other body-oriented therapies. Awareness concentrated on the sensory motor channel may awaken a small but vital link in this sequence.

Traumatic stress lives in the body, and it is the body that clinicians are most concerned about addressing. When there is negative somatoform dissociation, our concern for awakening body sensation is even more compelling. We want to test for accessibility. Many times, feeling states are not very deeply numbed, and with visual and auditory cuing and gentle and compassionate instruction from a safe person (the clinician), feeling states do start to appear. In fact, giving the client permission to feel whatever body sensation is present can be enough to activate the sensory motor aspects of the memory and enable the client to notice the body sensation associated to the memory. The first volume of the old textbook *Gestalt Therapy* by Perls, Hefferline, and Goodman (1951) contains a series of awareness exercises that may assist in "waking up" the body.

When the client names the parts of the body that are activated by the old trauma, client and clinician are off and running. Phase 4, desensitization (or active trauma processing, as I frame it) begins. When processing starts, thinking stops, and the client is in a supercharged free-association state where anything related to the original incident can arise. The "Zen" of

EMDR is about to begin. I will leave further discussion of this to the next chapter. All that need be said now is that we have been launched by the trauma activation sequence of Phase 3. The metaphorical rubber band has been pulled back as far as it can go, and we have been shot into the timeless dimensions of state-dependent memories.

6.10 Increasing Trust

The depth of what can occur when clinician and client activate old trauma memory networks should not be underestimated. The clinician can be greatly affected by what is to follow. Whether the clinician is dealing with a woman who was repeatedly raped by multiple members of her family or a client who witnessed the horror of people holding hands and jumping to their deaths from the burning towers of the World Trade Center, the effect on the clinician can be enormous. These effects are eloquently described by Pearlman and Saakvitne in their textbook *Trauma and the Therapist: Countertransference and Vicarious Traumatization in Psychotherapy with Incest Survivors* (1995). I will discuss vicarious traumatization and countertransference thoroughly in Chapter 8 and Chapter 9. For now, I want to suggest that as the clinician and client finish Phase 3 work and prepare to enter Phase 4 activities, clinicians silently say, in the spirit of healing, words such as, "I agree to voluntarily enter this dimension in time with you, stay empathically attuned to you, and hold a safe space for you to process your past." In doing so I am committing to being authentic and present with whatever comes up. I take responsibility for times that I may be challenged to remain present, and I develop strategies to stay aware.

Letting the client see, within appropriate therapeutic boundaries, the clinician's empathic attunement and resonance with his or her experience allows the client to see the clinician as not just competent but also vulnerable and caring. For the client, this is something that is felt more than cognitively experienced. This is a vital aspect of doing EMDR relationally. I remember a discussion I once heard about the respected psychoanalyst Charles Brenner, who was a traditional Freudian. Someone asked one of Brenner's students and analysands, "He doesn't *say* anything. How do you know he cares?" The student replied, "He holds you with his eyes." So even back then and even in orthodox Freudian psychoanalysis, the relational aspect was present in its contextual form.

For the client to experience his clinician as both vulnerable and strong creates the climate for trust to deepen. The client knows from the deep confidence of the experienced clinician that he or she has been down this road before and will be an active companion and guide. The essential relational piece here is that the client no longer experiences himself or herself as alone with the horror. It can now be shared, and because it is being shared in the context of adaptive information processing, the client feels safe to release the traumatic stress. I believe that these interpersonal conditions allow the client avolitionally to open more deeply in Phase 4 work and process old wounding safely while the clinician holds a safe space — even a sacred space — in which he or she can do the healing work. This is wonderment full of surprises, twists, and turns, as you will see in the next chapter.

CHAPTER 7

Phase 4: Desensitization (Active Trauma Processing)

7.1 Overview of Active Trauma Processing

Phase 4 is what EMDR was best known for at first: "moving your fingers in front of someone's eyes" and "magically erasing" negative feelings and beliefs. To the serious practitioner of EMDR, this is laughable. It is also a bit frightening. I have been told about nonclinicians who, having heard about EMDR, have actually used it as a party game. I cannot stress how much potential harm and havoc this can wreak on an unsuspecting person — and it does no good to the reputation of EMDR. I want to stress that what Shapiro developed is a multimodal and multiphasic approach to healing the traumatized client. Anyone who persists in thinking that EMDR is all about bilateral stimulation is either woefully misinformed or malicious.

What really happens in Phase 4, which Shapiro calls desensitization and I interpret as active trauma processing, is that the client starts the often painful process of desensitizing one or more memories that have haunted him or her — sometimes for a good part of his or her life. The client may go into a deep experiential mode, which puts him or her in an extremely vulnerable position. I am a co-participant, always at the client's side during this healing journey. As such, I empathically open myself to my client's traumatic experience and with my client create an atmosphere of established mental state resonance. I bear witness. This creates a special kind of deep empathic attunement while simultaneously allowing me to take care of myself in the moment of deep attachment that is often one of the most powerful factors, for me, in a client's healing.

EMDR is not for the faint-of-heart clinician. It is also not for the voyeuristic clinician who wishes to effect intense abreactive experiences in the client for his or her own implicit needs. Many body-centered events may occur for the client during active trauma work. It is not uncommon for the client to have deep, moving, emotional experiences, feelings that may have been trapped in his or her body for 25 years or more. For instance, the death of a beloved parent, partner, or pet may never have been grieved because of familial or cultural considerations. This grief and anguish continue in a "state-specific excitatory form" (Shapiro, 2001, p. 31). Hence, anything that activates associational channels to such losses will arouse these feelings. The client, given the opportunity of a safe, empathic environment (because of a positive therapeutic relationship) and a good enough understanding of how EMDR works, may begin to allow himself or herself to experience fully those feelings of anguish and grief. I have had the experience of being the first person with whom a client could share his or her inner experiences. This is an honor. Releases such as this, however, can sometimes come out in ways that are difficult to witness. Other times, only small observable changes will occur, but a day or two later the client may feel a shift or transition in thought and feeling. Examples of the difficult ones to witness are wild sobbing, screaming, choking, trembling, and other bodily expressions. Abreaction comes in many forms. (I have plastic liners in all the wastebaskets in my consulting room. I will spare you the graphic details; let's just say that it is wise to be prepared.)

Remember, too, that the client's pain will have an effect on the clinician. In some cases, it may enhance our empathic capacities. In others, it may activate old state-dependent memories of our own. We risk what Pearlman and Saakvitne call vicarious traumatization (1995) and Figley calls compassion fatigue (2002). In a manner of speaking, the clinician provides affect containment by giving the client a sense of community. Also, by being the object to which one half of the client's dual attention is directed, the clinician provides a great amount of support, even when saying very little, perhaps just "That's right" or "You're doing fine." We may say little, but it is our presence in the here and now that is powerful but at times assaultive or draining for us. The way I think about it is that as we become vicariously traumatized, we begin to suffer from compassion fatigue.

Since the clinician may be saying very little, this phase can highly relational without being highly verbal. Thus, I think the best way of highlighting the relational aspects of trauma processing is through sharing some of my cases.

7.2 The Case of Madeline, Continued

Madeline was one of the many clients I see who want to get started processing as soon as possible. We had completed Phase 1 and Phase 2 in three very successful 90-min sessions. She had decided upon using auditory stimulation, and her first memory was understandably the car accident. She would work on nothing else initially. She competently repeated back the instructions I gave her about Phase 3 and Phase 4 work.

It was during my first trauma-processing session with Madeline that I became convinced that processing can be derailed when the client becomes entangled in trying to figure out a positive cognition and VOC. Though I had noticed this kind of event in sessions with other clients, this particular experience altered my thinking conceptually.

For Madeline's memory of the car accident, the components were

Picture: car crashing into her
Negative cognition: *I am going to die.*
Positive cognition: *It's over, I am safe.*
VOC: 7

A seven? "But wait," I said. "You see the car crashing into you, and you hear the words that you are going to die, and just a moment ago I saw tears well up in your eyes. Then when I asked you what you'd rather believe, you said, 'It's over and I'm safe,' and you rated that as completely believing it."

"But you said what do I want to believe *now?*" Madeline replied.

"When you see the picture of the car smashing into you and you hear the sound of crunching metal, what would you rather believe about yourself?" I repeated.

"It's over, and I'm safe," she said.

"How true do those words seem to you now, as you experience the car crashing into you?"

"You mean you want me to experience what I believed then?"

By this time, Madeline had become deactivated, and her tears were gone. I explained state-dependent memory again. It was not a question of intelligence. Madeline is one of the most intelligent people I have ever had the pleasure of working with.

Finally, we settled on the following:

Picture: car crashing into her
Negative cognition: *I am going to die.*
Positive cognition: *I am safe, it's over.*
VOC: 1 (I realized that a VOC of 1 was problematic, but decided that this was the best we could do for the moment.)

Emotion: anxiety
SUDS: 7
Body: heart beating fast, breath shallow, fingers tense

At the end of this first session, Madeline felt agitation as she envisioned Richard lying in the car after the accident. She experienced herself wishing that it hadn't happened. Her ending SUDS was a 7.

This was a seminal moment in my EMDR experience. I realized that what was so elusive for Madeline had been captured and then partially lost during the part of the procedural steps outline when we were talking about the positive cognition and VOC. When Madeline came in next time, she reported that she had experienced little positive affect. She said that her first EMDR experience was not a positive one and asked (in her own words) if I could eliminate the positive cognition and the VOC from her target memory but keep the remainder of the procedural steps. I agreed to this variation. So now the components were

Picture: seeing Richard in the crashed car
Negative cognition: *I am helpless.*
Emotion: terror and fear
SUDS: 7
Body: chest tightening and shallow breathing

Madeline processed deeper feelings of horror and terror, and screamed a little, with lots of pain around Richard's mental state. By the end of the session, she was spent, but her SUDS was a 3. When she arrived at our next session she reported driving over a bridge in the rain without distress to pick up her husband from his physical therapy and cognitive-retraining sessions. It took three sessions to process this first target memory. Madeline had no trouble with any present-day referents, and not only could she run the movie of herself driving, she had already successfully done it.

7.3 Using a Blocking Belief as a Sub-protocol

The next target that Madeline and I worked on was her being in the hospital, helpless and severely injured. Here the components were

Picture: being in multiple casts in her hospital bed
Negative cognition: *I am trapped.*
Emotion: terror and sadness
SUDS: 6
Body: gut, chest, arms, throat

It was during this processing that we ran into a blocking belief. Although Madeline had had a number of intense trauma-processing sessions and had even screamed, she had not shed any tears. When tears started welling up during this protocol she swallowed them back down. She experienced herself as having a lot of negative self-judgments that made her choke back all the tears she kept locked inside. Madeline was clear that she was not ready to continue processing at the moment. As we dialogued, she voiced a deep blocking belief: *I am weak if I cry*. The standard way these blocking beliefs are usually processed is by adding a cognitive interweave and just starting another set once the client's train is back on the tracks. A cognitive interweave is an adaptive suggestion to link into the blocked process. An example of an interweave I used was, "I'm confused, are you saying that only weak people cry?" That intervention did not link to an adaptive connection. Then I asked, "What if this was your child, or your best friend — would they be weak if they cried?" In most cases, this intervention seems to do the trick, but in this case I tried a few interweaves without success. To me, working relationally means using my best judgment to vary my responses, even if that means a deviation from a standard procedure.

When blocking beliefs like this arise, and cognitive interweaves do not seem to enable productive information processing, it can sometimes be useful to "float back" to earlier memories to process their origins related to the core trauma. I have learned that a sub-protocol (my term) is a useful manner of focusing on older state-dependent memories. When I asked Madeline to identify and target her blocking belief about crying, she said that crying is a sign of weakness. I asked her how she learned this belief, and she was confounded. Then I had her hold the belief, *I am weak if I cry*, and notice what she felt in her body. She said there was a tightening in her chest and tension in her arms and legs.

One of the ways I like to do the floatback technique is as follows: I have the client imagine a scene that is congruent with a calm experience. In Madeline's case, I had her envision standing on a mountaintop in late spring with the sun shining, gently warming her. From there she could see a whole vista of mountains and valleys covered with trees. I then had her imagine calling her mountaintop "the mountain of the present." I asked her to pick one of the other mountains, about 200 yd away, and we would call that "the mountain of the past." Next I asked Madeline to imagine a big wrought-iron bridge with foundations sunk deep into the earth that connected these two mountains.

I suggested that she begin her journey across this bridge thinking the words, "I am weak if I cry," and holding the sensations of tightening in her chest and tension in her arms and legs. I asked her not to try to remember anything, but just to notice what old memories floated back into her mind. I let her know that I would give her as much time to cross this bridge as she needed, and that I would sit in respectful silence while she completed her process. About 15 sec into her journey, Madeline's eyes opened, her jaw dropped, and she uttered the words, "Oh, my God!" (An interesting choice of words for an atheist, I thought.)

She reported to me that a very old memory had come into her mind. She was 3 years old and her brother was 1. They shared a room. One afternoon, Madeline's baby brother began crying uncontrollably in his crib. She was in her own crib and tried to climb out to comfort him, but got trapped between the top of her crib and her dresser. Her head was stuck in such a way that all she could see was the parquet floor. She cried out for her mother, who (unbeknownst to Madeline) was down the street visiting neighbors. Her mother did not come. Madeline realized that she had to focus all her energy on holding on between the crib and the dresser. She could not climb back into her crib, and she could not just let herself drop. The floor looked too far away; she knew she would die if she fell. Her brother's crying continued unabated, and Madeline could remember feeling angry at him for making this moment even more difficult.

We decided to develop a sub-protocol to release the trauma that was the source of her blocking belief that crying was a sign of weakness. (While we could have just processed the memory that came up while using the float-back technique, Madeline's propensity for analyzing was too intense at that point in treatment, and I decided that some additional structuring via the procedural steps outline would enable her to get back into the process.) The elements were

> Picture: holding on between the crib and the dresser, looking down at the floor
> Negative cognition: *I am trapped.*
> Emotion: terror and sadness
> SUDS: 10
> Body: tightness in the chest, arms, and legs

Notice the similarity between these components and the previous ones. Madeline's negative cognition, emotions, and body sensations were nearly identical to those representing the hospital trauma that she had been unable to process. This was a very significant moment in Madeline's treatment. Up until this point, she had been adamant that she would only deal with issues related to her car accident and its sequeli. But having now had some positive experiences in processing trauma, she was more open to taking a wider view of what experiences may have been trapped inside her.

Madeline was quite surprised by the result of her floatback experience. I gently explained to her that often associated channels of trauma that are held in separate memory networks are connected through core negative belief systems and body sensations. She had noticed the similarities as well. The result was that in one double session, Madeline was able to release the pain of being trapped between the dresser and the crib, and she also remembered her mother rushing back into the room and grabbing her just as she was losing her strength. She remembers bursting into tears at that moment and hearing her mother say, "Now, now, big girls don't cry."

Torrents of tears poured forth as Madeline felt the feelings of the helpless little girl locked inside her who was trapped and terrified of dying. We were able to desensitize that memory down to a SUDS of 0. However, because this was a sub-protocol of her hospital trauma, I asked her to continue working and to re-access the original incident. Madeline again remembered seeing herself in the hospital bed with casts and bandages all over her. Now there was no need to continue the rest of the procedural steps; Madeline's awareness had shifted, and anything more than returning to the target might have caused her to become deactivated, so we just started with the image. During the next two double sessions, Madeline successfully processed the trauma of being helplessly trapped in her hospital bed.

7.4 Using EMDR With More Than One Member of a Family

One reason this moment became so important in Madeline's treatment was that she realized that some of her husband's emotional instability might be caused not just by his minimal brain damage, but by old trauma as well.

Richard had been the oldest of five children. When he was 7, his father, a railroad engineer, whom he loved very much, had been called to work unexpectedly very early in the morning. On his father's drive to the train yards, he was killed in a car accident. Being the oldest, Richard was told that he was now the man of the family and was responsible for caring for his brothers and sisters. To that day, Richard had never grieved his father's death. Madeline encouraged Richard to engage in this process. Richard was 69 at the time. Having been trained to be a leader at the age of 7, Richard had used this experience productively to become a leader in civic and educational activities during his entire life. Now, the smallest thing would send him into a tailspin.

I consulted Richard's neurologist, who said that the brain injury could not account for the depth of emotion that Richard experienced avolitionally. I explained EMDR to the neurologist and asked if he thought that this could be harmful to Richard in any way. The neurologist, though skeptical, said that he did not believe it would affect Richard one way or another. "But try it if you think it is going to help," he said. Richard had accompanied Madeline to many of her sessions and had heard me explain the process of EMDR to her. When Madeline told Richard she believed that his unresolved grief over his father's death was playing a role in his problems now, he agreed to do some trauma processing.

I took Richard through all the requirements of Phase 1 and Phase 2. Richard, like Madeline, is a person of superior intellect and had led a high-functioning life until the accident. In Phase 2, he was able to shift into places of safety inside himself and demonstrate self-soothing techniques. His DES score was negligible. I judged him to have sufficient affect tolerance, so we moved into active trauma work. The components of his first memory were

Picture: being awakened by his mother and told his father was dead
Negative cognition: *I can't stand it.*
Positive cognition: *I can survive.*
VOC: 3
Emotion: grief
SUDS: 9
Body: all over

When we began bilateral stimulation, Richard first had many recollections of the scene of the accident and then spontaneously accessed many precious memories of his relationship with his father. Over the next three double sessions, we detraumatized his grief over losing his dad so young.

In further sessions, we targeted other aspects of his grief: being victimized by a sadistic aunt who came to "help," his mother's inability to take charge of the family effectively, and his loss of his childhood. With this old trauma healed and the use of medication prescribed by a competent neurologist, Richard's incidents of suddenly crying like a little boy — which had been diagnosed as due to his head injury — diminished over time.

Now, my psychodynamic colleagues may take a dim view of my working with both members of a couple. This is not an easy task. But I have found that if a couple has a solid relationship, and both members have been subjected to the same trauma, treating both of them during the same time period (though in different sessions) is quite effective. There is only a mild danger of a splitting phenomenon occurring in such cases. When this does happen, it is usually because one or both members have a secret that they have not shared with me. I have learned to explain this danger to the couple before engaging in EMDR with couples.

7.5 The Stop Signal and Intermittent Debriefing

EMDR processing can be extremely challenging for the client, even though he or she is in charge and can use the stop signal, learned in Phase 2, whenever trauma processing becomes too intense. When this happens, the client can go to his or her safe place, engage in clinician-led guided imagery, or debrief with the clinician. The ability of the client to stop the process at will is relevant not only during a session but between sessions as well. Many EMDR clinicians whom I have consulted with are under the mistaken notion that they are not "doing EMDR correctly" if during reevaluation at the beginning of the next session, the client requests an extended period of talking, which may take up the entire session. As long as the clinician's judgment is that the client is having a necessary debriefing experience and is not using talk as a method of avoidance, this activity is appropriate. The clinician should keep the content and tone of the client's associations uppermost in mind when making this assessment, while also recognizing what other associational channels may have been activated. There is an important distinction between reporting out experience, and starting a monologue that deactivates the client's experience. The clinician should consider whether the client might have blocking beliefs impeding the work or, instead, needs to talk out issues as a means of consolidation, elaborating other connected channels, or stabilization.

Although there are methods for stabilizing clients, even in Phase 4 work (i.e., resourcing of different kinds), sometimes a client needs to talk. Affect tolerance varies among clients, and pushing someone to continue trauma processing when he or she asks for a break can have harmful effects. Working relationally, I am always sensitive to the limit of the client's affect tolerance.

7.6 Clinician, Know Thyself — and Thy Methodology

Clinical experience indicates that it is best to allow the neurophysiological processes that have been jumpstarted to do the healing. As Shapiro puts it, as long as the train is moving down the tracks, the clinician should stay out of the way and let the client's brain do the work. This is very empowering to the client and very validating. It is also an amazing experience to behold.

In and of itself, the experience of safely releasing one's state-dependent memories in an atmosphere of support and compassion is very healing. But that is not the end of the story. Many times I have seen clients spontaneously link to the adaptive perspective, coming to far different conclusions about the traumas they suffered without my intervention. These are awe-inspiring moments. They make all of the preparation work worthwhile.

The clinician's self-knowledge is as crucial in Phase 4 as it is earlier in treatment. While the client is processing, the clinician has to be continually aware of anything else that is occupying his or her own mind. Is the clinician fully present? Is the client's abreaction affecting him or her? If so, how? Is one of his or her own state-dependent memories being activated? (This situation will be covered in detail in Chapter 8.) Is the client's trauma so horrific that the clinician is becoming vicariously traumatized? Knowing how clients react to the protocol and knowing oneself will help the clinician tell when he or she is being triggered. When misattunement occurs, trauma processing may become corrupted by either client or clinician, and it is time for more active therapeutic strategies. By *corrupted*, I mean that the process goes off track, with the client flooding or shutting down. Even when all the preparatory work is done carefully, the clinician cannot know what is in the client's Pandora's Box. Once that box has been opened via the procedural steps and bilateral stimulation, the clinician sometimes just has to hang on for the ride.

Another issue is that no matter how much I prepare them, I find that most of my clients still attempt to direct their thoughts and make something happen during processing. I guess that is part of human nature. When they experience difficulties, I assure them that this is common. (I mention this as a possibility during the preparation phase.) I then guide them back to a place of just noticing. Now that the train is moving down the tracks, they are the passengers watching and experiencing the scenery from the safe vantage point of being in my office. I use the expression "tick-tock-time" to differentiate the *now* of the literal present from the *now* of state-dependent memory. Once they "get" it and let go, processing usually proceeds.

Clinicians can corrupt the process in two ways. First, they may become activated by their own unfinished work. In that case, admitting that something got in the way and processing the client's reactions through a relational interweave will usually get things back on track. I will discuss this further in Chapter 9. For now, suffice it to say: How many trauma victims have you known who had the good fortune to have their perpetrator realize in the middle of an unconscionable act that he or she was doing something wrong and immediately stop and make amends?

Second, the clinician can corrupt the process through faulty judgment or insufficient knowledge of EMDR. The clinician may feel the need to break into the client's abreaction and comfort him or her, or feel the need to say something to show how insightful he or she is. I do not know the extent to which this happens, but I do know that it does. An ethical clinician, realizing this error, will seek an Approved Consultant (a title conferred on an EMDR clinician by the EMDR International Association who has met certain rigorous requirements) for further training. (This title is relevant to those practicing mainly in the United States and Canada.) However, once the EMDR clinician has become proficient in the methodology, the clinician's issues are the source of most difficulties.

EMDR clinician Bennet Wolpert (personal communication, Dec. 14, 2004) states

> After many years of doing clinical consultation (in EMDR), it is remarkable how infrequently it is simply lack of technical ability that hampers the experienced (EMDR) clinician. The problems are more likely to be found in the demand characteristics of the relational context between them. In this moment of encounter, where the therapist has 'reacted TO the client' the problem is revealed and so is the potential solution. That is, if the clinician can access their internal processes. For it is in these moments that a therapist has the greatest opportunity to create both the most powerful and meaningful interventions. It is in this contextual space that the therapist truly 'knows the client' and themselves because they have allowed themselves to be acted upon, and have experienced their own personal reactions to the clients emotional intensity and pain. This moment is the essence of psychotherapy.

7.7 Active Therapeutic Strategies

When a client is flooded or shuts down, the clinician needs to intervene. At these times, a small cognitive interweave, linking a more adaptive way of thinking to a dysfunctional state of mind, may be all that is necessary to get the client back on track. Take, for example, a client who was sexually abused as a child and is struggling around the issue of responsibility. The clinician might intervene with a statement such as, "What if it were your child who was abused? Would you blame her?" At other times the client may not be able to take in a verbal intervention and may need instead to temporarily stop processing. (In Phase 2, clinicians teach the client the stop signal and the understanding that the client is ultimately the one in control.) When this happens, there are EMDR procedures to assist the client in coming out of a hyperaroused state. This may consist of helping the client go to his or her safe place or using resource techniques to help the client strengthen his or her containment ability. The client may also need help calling upon resources if he or she has temporarily forgotten them in the moment of flooding. Thanks to having done a thorough trauma case conceptualization for each client, I have a pretty good idea of what the person's resources are.

On the other hand, a client who gives the stop signal may need to spend the remainder of the session debriefing. When shifting back and forth between talking and processing with the client's full consent (and without subservient schemas), the clinician needs to do just the right amount of nudging, allowing, and holding a safe space for the client to heal. This is the dance of attunement, alignment, and resonance that is so sacred to the therapeutic relationship, as I see it applied to EMDR — and to the healing process.

In Chapter 8, I will extensively discuss the active therapeutic strategies. For now, please note that these strategies are designed for use in Phase 4. They range from Shapiro's cognitive interweave to the therapeutic interweaves described in Gilson and Kaplan's manual (2000) and may include any other intervention that results in linking a dysfunctional memory network with an adaptive one.

7.8 Active Coaching

I have interpreted Shapiro's instruction to "stay out the way" as meaning that while clinicians are facilitating processing, our first obligation is to let the client's brain do the healing. Reflective empathy or analytic interpretation may take the client out of the process and make him or her more dependent on us for solutions and answers. I agree. Additionally, Shapiro advises that clinicians intersperse short comments like, "Good, you're doing fine" to support the client's processing. There are clients for whom processing is a challenge, yet they can be coached to continue down the tracks of healing.

Active coaching is similar to Shapiro's instructions in her treatment manual for "nurturing through." While training in a spiritual and experiential method of healing at Kripalu, a yoga and meditation center in the Berkshire Mountains of Massachusetts, with Don and Elizabeth, I learned to actively coach my clients through rough moments of their processes. My gentle verbal presence and support seems to help many clients to stay in their processes rather than "jump off the train." When the client's emotional response starts to rise to a crescendo, they may be taken aback by how intensely they feel themselves. This may be so new to them after years of talk therapy that it may startle them. When I see this phenomenon happening, I will coach the client's process, adding more verbal interventions to support this healing experience. Remember, I have checked and "signed off" on their containment abilities, first by examining their history for affect regulation and also by taking them through the Safe Place exercise.

For these clients, I become their strongest container during moments of intense abreactive experience.

I have learned through experience to notice when clients who are beginning to abreact may need more than just interspersed comments of support. I will identify (to myself) these moments and begin to become more verbally active, supporting their processes. (I learned to do this during an intensive training experience, also at Kripalu, taught by a former Hindu renunciate, Dayashakti. Her training is called Wave Work, and I studied again with Don and Elizabeth, my two chief inner guides.) Take, for example, a client whose jaw is quivering; I might say, "Just notice your jaw, breathe, it is safe to feel what you feel," and so on. I have found that this style of working enables my clients who may have blocking beliefs and feeder memories to continue directly processing their feeling states. I do not get in the way of the process; I support it. As clients' abreactive experiences amplify, they may become worried about experiencing deep emotional release. Continuing to give support in this way gives them an external resource that they trust, enabling them to complete the process.

Marla, a 60-year-old child care worker, came to treatment because of issues relating to her retirement. She had been taught by her parents always to be productive and to work for social justice. However, she was also taught, verbally and nonverbally, to put aside her own feelings for the sake of other people. Whenever she focused on herself, her parents would become very stern and critical. Growing up in rough neighborhoods and rough times, it was a challenging to her when she was confronted by bullies or gangs. When she came home after difficult confrontations with other children, her parents were not there for her emotionally, and she learned to either shut down or become aggressive. As she processed old memories of being beaten by members of a female gang, she began to abreact. Tears welled up in her eyes, she began to hold her breath, and she tightened her lips. Noticing her body's reactions and knowing her beliefs about releasing emotion, I gently intervened, attempting to address her reactions (not her content) empathically. I used phrases like, "Just notice how you are holding your breath; let the breath come in and out, no holding; you're doing fine; it is safe to feel what you feel in your body; I'm right here for you." These verbalizations were clinician-assisted ways of encouraging her to stay with her process rather than jump off the train. My coaching seemed to help her contain and be present as she experienced her emotions of sadness for the little girl within her who never had a chance to cry over these old painful memories. As she experienced my compassionate coaching, she began, for the first time in her life, to let go and sob deeply. From this point on, her ability to have different kinds of emotional experiences began to grow. Over the next few sessions, she had many productive releases, enabling her to come to peace about entering a new stage of her life.

7.9 External Constraints

It would be nice if life just let us do our work. Unfortunately, external circumstances too numerous to mention crop up, and whether to continue active trauma work needs to be thought through with the client. When a college student has a final in 2 days, when a client has just found out that a family member is ill, or when a person is moving to a different location are not the times to go into high gear with trauma processing. This comes directly from Shapiro. When clients want to process heavy trauma right before an important event, I usually tell them that I do not do active trauma processing with a tax accountant on April 1st. This metaphor usually makes it clear that I am not infantilizing them, but I am taking the responsibility of directing treatment. How I inform my client is as important as the judgment call I make. I will give a case example to demonstrate the complex thinking that needs to go into each judgment call an EMDR clinician must make, in a co-participatory way, with a client. Clinicians make treatment decisions in the moment, with theory and experience as our guides.

Paul, a 32-year-old electrical engineer, came to treatment for the release of traumatic memories relating to harsh punishments his mother gave him as a child. During the middle of the work, in Phase 4, he learned that a patent on a project he was working on was coming up for review. Paul needed all the support he could get to focus on the task at hand. Continuing to process his mother's harsh criticisms and punishments would have hurt his ability to focus during this period on finishing his project. (In addition, focusing on this present-day task would have interfered with his ability to "time travel" into the past to work on his trauma.) Paul and I both believed that it would be a wiser choice to shift into a problem-solving mode for the 2 weeks it would take to complete his project. After the patent application had been reviewed, we resumed active trauma work.

7.10 Working Experientially in a Coparticipatory Manner

Because I work relationally and experientially, I am prepared to go wherever the client's processing leads. Having done my own growth work over 30 years, I have the ability to contain a client's deep, deep pain by staying in empathic attunement. I believe that clinicians who have not done their growth work will be at a disadvantage in assisting their clients when the horrors of childhood abuse surface during processing. I believe that clinicians hold our clients' traumas in our own bodies, and if we have not done sufficient growth work and healing, we are less available to our clients and more apt to have countertransferential reactions and vicarious traumatization and to suffer from compassion fatigue. This ability, developed over time, goes beyond the parameters of the collaborative working alliance. It means staying authentic in the real relationship, and any ruptures of empathic attunement are usually functions of countertransference phenomenon, or the effects of vicarious traumatization (compassion fatigue).

Even when we are on our own healing paths, our bodies are at risk. Think of any time you have been desensitizing a client from a painful memory and you became sleepy. It happens to many of us, especially with our more disturbed clients or when a client's process influences and activates our own state-dependent memories. Desensitizing deep trauma calls on all of my skills and abilities. I would like to give you an example now. This was a case I was privileged to be part of earlier in my career, which helped me learn to be flexible from session to session, as well as during sessions.

7.11 Deep Abreactive Experience: "Into the Abyss"

This is a full case example of one of the most deeply moving EMDR experiences I have been part of.

Stephanie is a 43-year-old mother of three children ranging in age from 7 to 14. She described her marriage as a good solid partnership, and her only complaint was wanting her husband, Steve, to be a little more psychologically minded. Stephanie had her master's degree in hospital administration and was director of the task force for the homeless in her community. The focus of her work was to strengthen social systems, encourage healthy lifestyles, and improve the quality of life for children. She worked part-time, during school hours, so she could spend plenty of time with her children, as she regarded motherhood as her primary occupation. She also had holidays and summers off.

Stephanie had been raised as a Catholic, but she was not currently practicing. She had a strong social support network and had good relationships with five of her six surviving siblings (all female). Her only brother died tragically of a pulmonary embolism. Stephanie is the sixth of seven in birth order. She had numerous medical problems at the time I saw her, but she had obtained medical clearance to do EMDR work. Her younger sister, Ruth, referred Stephanie to me after successfully completing her own EMDR treatment with me. Ruth, Stephanie, and all their sisters had been sexually violated multiple times by multiple perpetrators in their home and neighborhood.

Stephanie traveled from out of town and stayed with Ruth while she was in treatment with me. She had come with her children, and her husband was to join them later during the visit. She had a very clear intention for herself in treatment and wanted to work on specific dreams that haunted her nightly. Before arriving, Stephanie wrote me a very moving letter. Here is an excerpt from that letter:

> Ruth is going to help me arrange care for my children while I am working with you so that I will have the freedom to work each day as long as necessary. Ruth has explained to me some of her sessions with you that have included periods of journaling until I have resolved or can deal with issues that have been raised by your style of counseling. I don't know any counselors in Boise that work in this style.
>
> I am anxious to meet you and experience your style of counseling. I can tell from Ruth that it is effective. However, I am not a novice at therapy, and the thought of dragging up more of my past isn't pleasant or even appealing. I am doing this to put some faded skeletons in my memory closet *in their proper place* [italics mine] and to enhance my family life. It is hard to be a happy loving parent or spouse when ungrounded fears and reactions, as well as nightmares, plague you. I have come a very long way since my discovery of the term "adult child of an alcoholic." My family life is very good, and my husband is a loving, kind, and gentle man. My life today is drastically different than the life I was raised in, and I'm proud of that. My children are loved and cared for well. However, there are ghosts that are keeping me from having the life that I want, and I have decided that it is time to confront them.

This introductory letter, along with my initial evaluation, confirmed to me that this was a woman who had suffered deeply as a child and young adult. She also impressed me as someone who had done much healing work for a number of years. Yet she was still haunted by the ghosts and dreams of her childhood.

After completing Phase 1 and Phase 2 (her DES was low at 7.5, and she had completed her Safe Place exercise successfully), I felt that we had developed enough trust so that the working alliance and the therapeutic relationship had taken root, and believed it was time to begin the second stage of EMDR treatment: active trauma work.

Stephanie had memories of being vaginally, orally, and anally raped. With the help and guidance of many clinicians and healers over a period of 25 years, she had been able to overcome much of her pain and dysfunction resulting from complex PTSD. However, she still had more work to do. For the past 30 years, she had the same nightmare every single night.

She dreamed that she was at the top of the stairs (or sometimes in the kitchen) in the house she grew up in, and she was being chased by a monster or a stranger. She tried to run for her life down the stairs, but her legs felt like lead, and she could not get away. She was knocked down. It felt as if bones had been broken. She kept getting up and trying to fight back. Just before she was going to be killed, she woke up, drenched in sweat and the bedcovers in disarray. Her husband bore scars and black and blue marks from Stephanie's nightly battle with this demon.

Stephanie came to me with the skepticism common back then (1995) that some "silly" hand waving in front of her eyes could ever "erase" the misery of her traumatic nightmares. It was only having witnessed a dramatic shift in her beloved sister Ruth that had gotten her to my office. Our sessions doing Phase 1 lasted for a while. During the history taking, Stephanie recounted every act of abuse she had experienced from her father, her brother, her grandfather, her neighbor, and her first husband. In addition to sexual trauma, there was physical trauma. She had even been thrown out of the house by her first husband and had to live in her car for weeks in the bitter cold. I listened to her in awe at her courage to survive.

Also during Phase 1, Stephanie challenged me about my credentials and my ability to deal with the devastation she had suffered. She had always been treated by women, and she did not have much faith that a male clinician could understand or feel sufficiently empathic to be of service. Again, it was only Ruth's faith in me and the results she had seen from our work together that gave Stephanie any cause for hope. I experienced myself in empathic attunement to this poor woman's plight and her doubt that she could be assisted by a man. (That has never been one of my "buttons.") I was more concerned about getting a good history, asking good questions, and getting a good enough feel for who this person sitting in front of me was.

By this time, I was not only on the faculty of the EMDR Institute but also a graduate of an excellent training program in interpersonal psychoanalysis (at the Manhattan Institute of Psychoanalysis). What also helped was that during the 1980s I had worked in hospitals, taught consultation psychiatry on the faculty of the Mount Sinai School of Medicine, and served as director of mental health consultation services at the Bronx Veterans Administration Medical Center.

Stephanie and I survived our initial sessions and had made a deep enough connection; we were ready to begin the second stage of the work. The target was the dream of the monster chasing her and threatening her life. She knew that it related to the sexual abuse she had suffered as a child. Here is the trauma activation sequence:

Picture: I am at the top of the stairs in my nightmare and a monster is trying to kill me.
Negative cognition: *I am going to die.*
Positive cognition: *I am a survivor.*
VOC: 2
Emotion: terror
SUDS: 8
Body: all over

Stephanie initially processed a series of pictures of her childhood; then she started to relive one day when she was 4. She was in her parents' room being raped orally and vaginally by both her father and her grandfather; she had almost choked to death. In that moment she made what seemed to be a pedestrian comment: "This is what my dream is about." But there was nothing pedestrian about the surprise she exhibited. "Of course it is! Why didn't I make that connection before?"

Over the next few sessions, Stephanie had deep abreactive experiences interspersed with periods of calm and consolidation. She remembered the graphic details and was amazed at the clarity of the pictures that flashed through her mind: seeing her grandfather pulling his zipper down, her father holding her down and shoving his penis deep into her throat. Stephanie was exhausted after each double session.

Then, as the pictures got sharper, she started to have a gag reflex. I was prepared for what might occur. I also counseled Stephanie to come to session on an empty stomach. At a pivotal moment during the next session, she put up her hand in a stop sign. We dialogued, and Stephanie expressed concern about fully re-experiencing this all-too-real nightmare. She was afraid she might choke to death or go crazy. I suggested we get medical clearance again; having worked in hospitals, I tend to be very careful with my clients' bodies. Stephanie called her physician, who assured her that she would not choke to death. At the same time I asked her for permission to consult an EMDR colleague. I contacted one of the local trainers (William Zangwill), who was kind enough to give me his support and good advice on various containment strategies to help Stephanie get through this challenging part of her treatment.

In the next session, Stephanie told me the reason for her fears: She had had a near-death experience during one of these rapes. She started to lose consciousness and then left her body and watched what was happening to her from the ceiling of the room.

This was our sixth session of trauma processing; we called it "Into the Abyss." Stephanie started with this picture: *I see my father's penis coming toward me while I am being pinned down to the bed.* During processing Stephanie avolitionally reexperienced choking to death. Her hands were on her throat, her head was thrown back, and her face was beet red. Her mouth was wide open, and she was alternating between choking and crying hysterically. She found herself gasping for air. I supported her verbally, reminding her that I was with her and she was here with me in my office. She occasionally signaled to me that she heard me through her terror.

Then came a 15-min period when all she was doing was choking. (We were using audio stimulation.) Do you know how long those minutes were? They were probably the longest 15 minutes of my life. That moment remains the deepest level of trauma release I have ever witnessed. As Stephanie started to come out of her choking episode, she remembered another dissociated part of her memory: Her father had told her that he would sew her mouth closed if she told anyone. She remembered being in a state of shock. Then her father and grandfather slapped her "awake" and dressed her. She had to go downstairs to help her sisters make dinner because her mother worked two jobs (her father did not work).

We spent time grounding and debriefing. Stephanie's SUDS level was 3. I asked her what prevented it from being 0. She said she felt very sad for herself as that little girl. When our session ended, she was stable enough to drive to her sister's house. She called me that night to say she was still stable, though she expressed amazement at the depth of the details that had flooded back to her. In her words, "I was there again, and I was out of my body again."

I saw Stephanie for her next double session the next day. We made it safe for her to reenter the experience again. I reminded her that she could stop at any time and that I was fully here for her for whatever she needed. It has been my experience that with higher-functioning clients who have been traumatized, the strength of the therapeutic relationship allows the greatest part of affect tolerance while they are processing the unspeakable.

When we began this time, Stephanie started to sob for the deeply wounded little girl who was subjected to such immeasurable cruelty. By the end of the session, she told me she was okay. Her SUDS level was 0. Then I checked her initial positive cognition (*I survived*) and its VOC, which was 7. After a few more sets, we were assured that her positive cognition was strong and her body scan was clean, and we closed down the session. We finished with the remaining old memories and the present day issues that emerged — her reticence about talking to her husband on issues that deeply affected her. She realized that though she loved him and wished him to be a bit more psychologically minded, it was her fear of emotional intimacy that had prevented her from reaching out more deeply. We completed the three-pronged protocol by having her imagine being safe having deeper conversations with her husband and processing this issue. Fortunately he was in town and very willing to come in for a few marital sessions where Stephanie practiced talking more deeply with him. Though he struggled a bit, he was able with some minimal coaching to open up to her in a way he had never had. Then they practiced on their own for a week, and we completed the three-pronged protocol.

After some termination sessions, Stephanie and her family went home. She sent me a thank you in the form of an orange-flavored tea called "Market Spice," which I drink to this day. Over the years, Stephanie has consulted me on other matters when she has been back to her sister's for visits. What continues to astound both of us (and her husband as well) is that she has never had that nightmare again, she has regained the ability to get good enough measures of sleep, and she no longer has startle sensitivity. This has been sustained through the 9 years since we first worked together.

I will now go more deeply into the relational aspects of the desensitization phase of active trauma processing before moving on to Phase 5 through Phase 8. I will also cover issues of transference, countertransference, and the intersubjective in all eight phases, vicarious traumatization, active relational strategies, and self-care for the clinician.

CHAPTER 8

Countertransference, Transference, and the Intersubjective

8.1 Defining Countertransference

Relational issues are endemic to treatment of all kinds. How the clinician uses these relational issues in conjunction with the technical aspects of EMDR methodology accounts for much of the difference in treatment outcomes. Relational issues, including countertransference and transference, are active in all eight phases. In this chapter, I will explain how to notice them and make in-the-moment decisions about dealing with them. Why start with countertransference? My reasoning is simple. When I can take care of my issues, I'm more available to be present with my client. I define countertransference as the activation of state-dependent memories in me, stimulated by something about the client, not limited to his "transference" to me. I also consider this state-dependent activation "information" rather than psychopathology, as I believe that we do ourselves no service by calling our unresolved issues "pathological." It becomes too value-laden.

There has long been debate on the definition of countertransference. According to Hayes in *The Inner World of the Psychotherapist*, Freud's classical view was that countertransference is "the analyst's unconscious, conflict based reactions in response to the patient's transference." Hayes goes on to explain that the totalistic view, taken by Heiman in 1950 and Little in 1951 and expanded on by modern-day relational analysts, held that countertransference is "all therapist reactions to a client, whether conscious or unconscious, conflict based or reality based, in response to transference or some other material" (2004).

However, I consider the classical view too confining. Besides, it interpreted countertransference as a product of the clinician's "pathology," a concept to be avoided at all costs. The totalistic view, on the other hand, I experience as too all-encompassing, especially in that it labels the clinician's use of self as countertransference. I disagree with this notion. Another line of reasoning suggests that countertransference may be a clue to what the patient is struggling with on a deeper level (Wachtel, 1977). Hayes writes, "Common to these various conceptions of countertransference is the idea that therapists must understand what clients are eliciting from them and not act impulsively on countertransference feelings. Rather, they must respond thoughtfully and intentionally" (2004, p. 22).

Hayes continues

> A third definition of countertransference known as the integrative conceptualization (Gelso and Hayes, 2002) emerged from existing dissatisfaction with both perspectives. Drawing on the work of Blanck and Blanck (1979) ... countertransference is defined as therapist reactions to clients that are based on therapists' unresolved conflicts (Gelso and Hayes, 1998; Hayes and Gelso, 2001). This definition is less narrow than Freud's classical perspective in that countertransference may be conscious or unconscious and in response to transference and other phenomena. Nonetheless, unlike the totalistic definition, it clearly locates the source of the therapist's reactions as residing within the therapist. This encourages therapists to take responsibility for their reactions, identify the intrapsychic origins of their reactions, and attempt to understand and manage them. (2004, p. 23)

I find Hayes' conceptualization most helpful when I think about relational issues within the context of EMDR.

Thus, I define transference in information-processing terms as the activation of state-dependent memories directed toward the clinician. And while I agree with the integrative view of countertransference, I define it as the activation of state-dependent memories in the clinician that have been sparked by the client, intentionally or not. I make different interventions depending on the source of this activation. For example, if I am triggered, but I believe that the client was simply reporting an experience, I compartmentalize my reaction (I will discuss this later) and use the empathic or introspective approach (developed by Stolorow and Atwood, 1996) to understand my issue. I do not mention this to the client unless it appears to have interfered with our work. When I believe that my reaction to the client is based on his communication about me, I ask him or her. The manner in which I do this depends on the phase of treatment we are in.

8.2 The Clinician's Use of Self

One of my reasons for agreeing with Hayes' view on countertransference is that there are times when I scan my body and notice that I am clear and present. Sometimes I am activated in a positive and empathic manner, thus informing myself of what may be missing in the client's presentation. Someone from the totalistic camp might say this is countertransference as well. However, in the clinical example of the neurobiological subtext of EMDR session given in Chapter 2 (John, a 50-year-old telephone sales rep), my client's hyperaroused state at the beginning of the next session informed me, on a body level, about his profound state of aloneness. By using my body's reaction, I was able make an empathic connection to his pain and, through dialoguing, to bring us back into attunement and inform us of the next link in the chain (his mother's not being there for him after the worst beating of his life). I do not consider my reaction countertransference but rather a productive use of self through my body awareness.

8.3 A Way of Working with Transferential and Countertransferential Issues

Before examining the depth of complexity and nonlinearity in the inter-subjective, let me give some examples of working with transference and countertransference issues. I also will discuss a case I mentioned briefly in Chapter 1, in which I failed to extricate myself from a countertransferential bind and its consequences.

When a client seems to have a reaction to me that pertains to the work of Phase 4, desensitization (this is where the fur flies, transferentially and countertransferentially), I ask him or her to notice that reaction, and I suggest that we focus on it while applying bilateral stimulation. Usually, in a few sets the client starts to associate back to the true origin of the pain. This point was first written about by Liz Snyker in Philip Manfield's first case book, *Extending EMDR*, in the article titled "The Invisible Volcano: Overcoming Denial of Rage" (1998). Snyker states,

> Combining a psychodynamic method with EMDR involves intro-
> ducing transference issues into the EMDR session. I have found
> EMDR particularly useful in this regard. I shift the focus of the session
> temporarily, and I become the EMDR target along with whatever

negative cognitions and feelings may be linked. After several sets of eye movements the client's focus usually shifts from me to the source material I represent. (p. 92)

8.4 The Case of George

George, a 32-year-old dentist, was referred to me for communication problems with his fiancée. Because of ACOA (adult child of an alcoholic) issues in his background, he had blocked off all the pain of his traumatic memories by becoming emotionally controlling, using strong intellectual defenses. He said he was willing to engage in treatment so he could have a better relationship, but he doubted there were any real issues left to deal with. He believed that he had solved them.

When I suggested EMDR to George to process the pain of his "remaining ACOA issues," he was triggered, implicitly thinking I was trying to control him. He was not aware of this, nor was I. When we reached Phase 3 and Phase 4, George chose what seemed to be a painful memory. We worked on it.

> Memory: seeing his father in a drunken rage, and George protecting his younger siblings
> Picture: father is screaming at his mother
> N.C.: *I'm powerless*
> P.C.: *I can deal with this problem*
> V.O.C: 3
> Emotion: anger
> SUDS: 5
> Body: chest

The next session, he came in and said in a faltering voice, as if something were stuck in his throat, "I've got to be honest with you. I didn't get much out of the last session. Maybe it was a poor choice of memories, or maybe things are no longer bothering me."

I realized that the phrase "I've got to be honest," said with the nonverbal cues I observed, was loaded with multiple transferential meanings. Now, if this had been an analytic session, I would have self-reflected and inquired into what might have been getting stirred up in him because of how I was reacting to him. We would then have gone through a detailed inquiry, where I might or might not have shared some of what I experienced.

Instead, I reflected silently on what might have transpired between us. I thought that we might have been stuck around the issue of control — George needing to block his feelings, and I needing to push my (EMDR) agenda. Here there seemed to have been a rupture of the working alliance inducing a transferential reaction in George. As a way of managing this rupture, I wondered aloud about making a slight alteration to the protocol, and I thought to myself about using a cognitive interweave of safety in a questioning manner. I chose safety because I believed that George's need to control was his way of protecting himself against implicitly felt danger in experiencing me as the abusive parent.

I asked George if it would be okay with him to imagine being completely honest with me while feeling safe. He thought he could experiment with that, so we did a set of bilateral stimulation. He began laughing heartily. His next set of associations had to do with how he had needed to be dishonest with his father whenever he felt pushed into a corner. I said, "Go with that," and out came many painful recollections and tears relating to the distress he had been defending against. Noticing his negative arousal in relation to our work, I took a chance and had George process his conflict (indicated by a sound like something was stuck in his throat when he said, "I've got to be honest with you"). The result was similar to most transferential reactions that occur in Phase 4. The client returned to a coregulated state with me. What had happened between us was partly a result of the old mental models that were activated by the flow of energy between us.

At other times when I notice that I have been triggered and that processing has been inhibited as a result of my reaction, I acknowledge this and ask the client if he or she noticed my reaction. (I always educate clients during the second phase of the work about the possibility of this happening.) I acknowledge that something had been triggered in me. I almost always do not share the content. I do not believe this is necessary. What is necessary is that the client experiences me as fallible. Then I ask him or her to process this moment. This usually opens up primary core trauma, where there was no resolution, when a similar event occurred. In essence, I am inviting my client to let the present be different from the past. I call this a relational interweave (to be discussed fully in Chapter 9), a variant of a cognitive interweave, and it usually brings us back on track.

8.5 The Death of Toto: Processing a Countertransferential Moment

Michael, a 29-year-old single male client of Irish background, was referred to me for pet bereavement. He was unable to release his grief over the death of his 16-year-old dog, Toto, who had seen him — and loved him — through many hard times. The client's blocking belief was, *I'm a sissy, and I'm betraying Toto's memory if I let go and grieve.* Michael presented with the signs and symptoms of acute depression; there were no other major mental status problems. He still lived at home. He had good relations with his brothers and a strained but respectful relationship with his mother. He also had a good circle of friends. He was gainfully employed, following in his father's footsteps as a fireman. Though Michael had no previous history of alcoholism, he had been binge drinking for 2 weeks following Toto's death. His EAP referred him to me for trauma work. The EAP clinician had screened him carefully for any signs of systematic alcohol or drug use and found Michael's binging to be specific to this situation.

Knowing a client's history always helps. Remember standard EMDR methodology for Phase 1: Always get a solid history — know who you are dealing with. I discovered in my history taking that Michael's family of origin had negative beliefs about releasing emotion. When Michael was little, anytime he cried, he was shamed. He was told that only sissies cry. (Here is the root of an unacknowledged blocking belief.) He had grown up in a working-class family, the oldest of five brothers. His father had been killed in the line of duty when Michael was 12; his mother was of "lace curtain" Irish descent and had been constantly told by her critical parents that she had married beneath her "station." As a result, when Michael's father died, his maternal grandparents refused to do anything to help. His mother had always maintained that a stiff upper lip could get you through anything. To her, letting your feelings show was a mark of weakness, and therefore shameful.

Toto came on the scene less than a year after Michael's father died, and the little dog became a constant source of solace for the boy. Toto's death 16 years later reopened the more painful wound of the death of Michael's beloved father.

By the time we completed Phase 1 and Phase 2, Michael had been sober for 4 weeks. We had made a no drinking, no drugging pact, and his job would have been in jeopardy if the EAP had found he was drinking. Michael's identification with his father was strong; the idea that he might lose his job was disincentive in itself to keep him sober. He had remarked to me that he would just have to grin and bear it (a strong family trait). Michael, like many of my trauma clients, wished to work on his current problems. He listened to my explanation of why and how he might benefit from working on earlier issues and acknowledged this as reasonable — but not for him. He was steadfast. No floatback for him! We started processing with the following:

Picture: holding Toto as the veterinarian put him to sleep
Negative cognition: *I am powerless.*
Positive cognition: *I can learn to live with my losses.*
VOC: 3

Emotion: sadness and grief
SUDS : 3
Body: heart

Initial processing brought almost no change. I had not expected it would. Michael's starting SUDS of just 3 was a dead giveaway, but in the moment my clinical judgment had been to let him do things "the proper way," a phrase he used that referred to his mother's teachings (his old mental models), not my instructions. (Here again I made a judgment call. Instead of trying to aid Michael in "waking up his body," I believed that this was all the affect he could admit to currently.) Michael's transference had to do with perceiving in me a critical parent's demand that he do things "the proper way." This was projected onto me, implicitly, as a demand that he keep "a stiff upper lip." Even as compassionate as I am, I started to feel a tightness in my chest and a little impatient with Michael's looping.

When I did some rapid internal processing on my impatience, I realized that Michael had perceived it subtly and that it led to his shutting down. I may have implicitly triggered Michael's old state-dependent memories of parental messages, even if the content of my impatience was different. My countertransference had to do with wanting Michael to get on with his grieving, as a defense against my implicit annoyance about his wanting to do things his way. I was now in a misattuned state of mind. My staying in this mind-set was not helping Michael continue processing. I had controlling parents and could get triggered when I was not the one in charge (my old mental models), especially when I believed that the other person's way would not work. Since I also had abandonment issues, however, I was likely to be compliant at first.

I made a comment wondering what had shut Michael down. He was unsure, so I wondered aloud if he had noticed anything in our relationship change when this happened. (I also wondered to myself if his shutting down might be linked to my feeling impatient.) Michael said that he had felt something coming from me but could not put his finger on it. He thought I was upset with him for doing something wrong. I let him know that I had just become aware of my reaction, and that my triggered feeling was my issue, not his. I told him that although we had disagreed on where to start our processing, I truly believed that he was just being himself. I said that this was all I could reasonably expect from him, and that my reaction came from my history. It did not have to do with him.

At this point, I experienced myself as returning to a state of empathic attunement, and I offered Michael an interweave. He was open to it. I asked him, using the interweave of choice, "Let's pretend that you could experience taking all the time you needed to deal with your grief in your own way that feels right for you." Then we did bilateral stimulation. This interweave gave Michael the message, within the context of our relationship, that the present is different from the past. It gave him a conscious moment to recognize that he can react in a different way that may be more natural to him. This intervention opened a portal to his being able to experience and express his grieving openly, safely, and without shame. During the next set Michael spontaneously began to cry fiercely over his father's death. Over the next two double sessions, he released and resolved his grief over both the losses of his father and his beloved dog. He no longer held the blocking belief that only sissies cry. Upon terminating, he thanked me and said that it felt like a huge weight had been lifted off him. He had also realized that he felt oppressed living in his mother's house and was making plans to move out. (This was evidence of Michael's increased response flexibility.)

I am echoing a viewpoint written on by Gelso and Hayes in their chapter, "The Management of Countertransference" (Norcross, 2002), when they state, "An area that has not been addressed by researchers but that must continually be addressed in clinical practice is how the therapist should deal with CT that has in fact been acted out in the work—that is, with mistakes therapists make due to having their unresolved conflicts stirred up. It is important for the therapist to understand that indeed he or she was acting out personal conflicts; in addition, some research (Hill et al., 1996) points to the value of therapists admitting that a mistake was made and that the therapists' conflicts were the source. Therapists need not go into detail about just what those problems were, for we suggest that doing so more often than not serves the therapist's needs more than the patient's. Yet a simple admission does appear to befit the work and diminish potential impasses" (pg. 280). I am suggesting an approach that remediates a countertransference phenomenon while keeping in the methodology of EMDR.

Not recognizing this phenomenon, on either party's part, may prove disastrous to the work. Several years ago, a clinician wrote me the story of when he worked with an EMDR clinician who yawned at a difficult moment in his processing. The EMDR clinician did not remark on it, even though the client stopped processing. The client was not able to continue to retrieve the pain of his state-dependent memory. He also terminated treatment, he wrote, because he could not have a good enough relationship with the clinician after that. It appears that the client had a state-dependent reaction, based, probably, on an abandonment schema. It is quite possible that the clinician simply had not had a good night's sleep. It is also possible that his yawn was a means of leaving a moment that became too distressing for him. In any case, the moment and the therapy came to a halt, and a valuable opportunity for bonding on a deeper level (by the clinician's admitting his own humanity) was lost.

Yawning while a client is processing something painful is an obvious example, but many more subtle events happen between a client and a clinician that block further processing. Without recognition and repair of these events (through use of a relational interweave), the chances of healing are diminished — no matter how faithful the clinician is to the protocol.

8.6 An Exercise for Affect Attunement

I teach this exercise to all my consultees and to attendees at EMDR conferences. You might want to do the actions suggested as you read along.

First I ask each person to bring to mind the memory of a disturbing session with a client that did not go well. I ask my listeners to choose a picture that represents the worst part of that session and then, keeping the picture in mind, to notice the negative self-referencing belief they hold about themselves. (Is this starting to sound familiar?) After taking them through their feeling states and body sensations, I ask them to open their eyes, take a cleansing breath, and write down what they noticed.

In the second part of this exercise, I have them remember the same memory with its same components, but from the client's point of view. This relational strategy assists clinicians in developing awareness of the intersubjective issues that can occur during and after a session.

Here is an example: A clinician came to me for consultation on a case where he was stuck. The client's presenting problem was a marital issue; his wife was critical of his not being aggressive enough in his job and not going after promotions that would bring the family more money. This problem had its roots in a dysfunctional relationship with his mother. The target memory was of his mother's harsh criticism of his study habits and grades. The sticking point was that the client, an angry man in a passive way, was being criticized by both parties. The sticking point happened when the client shut down after the beginning of processing this memory.

The clinician held the picture of the client shutting down. The clinician's negative cognition was, "I'm not good enough," and his emotion was shame. The clinician was then instructed to imagine the same picture from the client's perspective. I had the clinician remember the client's negative cognition; he responded, "I can't stand it." The clinician then became aware that his client's emotion was anger. The clinician immediately realized that he had been caught up in a countertransferential moment where he believed he was not using EMDR correctly because of implicit memories of having been verbally abused by his angry father. He had missed how his client's anger at his mother had shut the client down into a passive and resistant state. I wondered aloud to the consultee if using a "what if" interweave, such as, "What if you imagine that it's all right to feel anger at your mother safely?" The consultee was able to use this new awareness to help the client become unstuck, and processing continued very well. The consultee then realized that he needed to do more work on his own fear of his father's anger, and I sent him to an EMDR clinician whose work I trusted.

8.7 Transference and Countertransference, Phase by Phase

8.7.1 Phase 1: Client History Taking and Treatment Planning (Trauma Case Conceptualization)

In this phase, the clinician determines whether the client will benefit from EMDR and creates an action plan. The clinician begins by asking the client about specific traumas associated to the presenting problem. Although the client expects to be asked these kinds of questions, and the clinician has made it clear the client does not have to answer until he or she is ready, the very act of asking for traumatic memories may activate memory networks with painful emotions. Even with the instruction that the client can choose not to disclose until he or she is ready, the client may experience the clinician as intrusive, judgmental, overly analytical, or, on the other hand, understanding. And the clinician may react with fear, shame, hurt, or gratitude. This may occur in any type of psychotherapy, but it is especially necessary to be mindful of it in EMDR because of the nature of trauma treatment.

Though the clinician and client are only in Phase 1, and the clinician has not yet explained EMDR, many clients will have been informed by friends, books, or articles about the strong reactions people have to EMDR processing. This can cause anticipatory anxiety during the initial phases of treatment. Many hopes and magical wishes may surface, with the client expecting EMDR to provide healing overnight (as in the case of Walter). Alternatively, the client may be very skeptical. And then there are the clients who have low expectations of success, having seen several clinicians before, none of whom helped them to release their pain and process their memories, and those who simply believe that psychotherapy is for weaklings (as in the case of Madeline).

The client's hopes and wishes must be carefully attended to. Embedded in them are state-dependent memories that are potentially transferential. What happens if I start experiencing my client's fears and doubts while he or she is hypervigilantly attuned to my reactions? What if I am activated by my own old state-dependent memories? Clients' state-dependent memories may become activated by what they think they observed, possibly setting off a chain reaction of transferential and countertransferential events. This is why EMDR trainers strongly suggest that newcomers to the method start using it with clients they know well, who do not have major dissociative disorders and who like to try out new methods their clinicians have learned.

In Phase 1, the clinician must accurately assess the physical health of the client. Consultation with the client's doctor is often advised. Not doing so in the face of significant health issues could simply be the clinician's countertransferential wish to do more than he or she is capable of doing. This can inadvertently create problems. Undiscovered health issues may arise in treatment and create transferential or countertransferential reactions. A clinician once told me about a case he was working on. He had done everything correctly; I had carefully assessed his work. Shortly after the session, the client had a seizure. The clinician stated that "the client had not told me about his condition because he had heard that EMDR is not done with epileptics" (this is not the case; there is no indication that EMDR has adverse effects for people with epilepsy). There was no way of knowing that this might happen. The seizure may or may not have been precipitated by the work. The clinician had done due diligence in every aspect of the history taking and preparation. But due to countertransferential issues of feeling betrayed by the client's omission and being vicariously traumatized by EMDR's "power," the clinician never used EMDR again.

Also during this phase, symptoms such as flashbacks, intrusive thoughts, and other manifestations of PTSD must be thoroughly evaluated. The client's current triggers and their duration, frequency, timing, location, and other characteristics must be assessed. In a rush on the part of both client and clinician to alleviate suffering, many important details can be missed. Again, this may lead to negative outcomes. Remember, transferential demands such as "Cure me" will be strong and may activate painful memory networks in the clinician. It is crucial that the clinician understand the importance of history taking and not rush into active trauma treatment in an implicit effort to avoid or act out grandiose countertransference issues of being a "magical healer." Rushing ahead to Phase 4 is especially a temptation when informed clients enter treatment specifically to use EMDR. The client's transferential state of mind may stimulate a clinician's state-dependent memories based on dysfunctional patterns of subservience or defensive grandiosity and push the clinician to relieve the client's suffering as quickly as possible. Ironically, these corresponding countertransferential states of mind and dysfunctional reactions (such as skipping details during the history taking) may inhibit the healing process and — worse — result in both client and clinician feeling traumatized.

There are relational advantages to sticking to the protocol. The clinician can ascertain the client's negative cognitions simply by listening; during history taking these negative cognitions can provide clues to possible transferential themes in the client, and induced countertransferential states in the clinician. For example, the cognition "No one understands what I'm going through" is a common theme that can trigger a counter-transferential state of wishing to be the one person who can "heal" this long-suffering soul. This alone may create a sense of urgency in the EMDR clinician who then may neglect vital issues in the history taking and estab-lishing of the alliance goals and tasks, thus rushing prematurely into active trauma work. This may trigger a state of implicit collusion when the clini-cian becomes anxious (due to a defectiveness schema about failing to per-form EMDR's "magic" immediately), and the client's wish for this pain to be magically gotten rid of.

Empathic attunement must begin in Phase1, not when the client is deep in an abreaction mode in Phase 4. These potential issues must be identi-fied as quickly as possible so that the clinician does not act in a way that will actually be a defense against the client. In a best-case scenario, on the other hand, this time could mark the beginning of a deeper empathic state of resonance with the client's struggle.

Negative transference based on, for example, a client's defectiveness schema manifested during history taking, may stimulate negative counter-transference in the clinician, perhaps due to old mental models connected to maladaptive schemas of unrelenting standards. For example, although it is standard EMDR procedure to target the oldest memories first, the cli-ent's wishes are equally important. The client may be right about what he or she needs. If the clinician believes otherwise, then the clinician can reit-erate the EMDR protocol that was discussed in Phase 2 and again offer the client the choice of where to begin the next round of processing. Often cli-ents want to work on current-day matters because these are what are pressing. That is fine.

When the client needs to have a lot of control due to schemas such as vulnerability to harm or entitlement, he or she will usually not get far. His or her transferential reaction to authority will dictate that he or she con-tinue defending and blocking. The client may implicitly resist the free-associational part of bilateral stimulation, since that would mean exposing vulnerable state-dependent memories that have been long disso-ciated. And that is fine, too. This is simply another opportunity to review

EMDR procedure gently, give the rationale behind it, and then wonder if it might be difficult for the client to have experiences that are out of his or her control. When this awareness is present in me, I am usually able to restimulate mental state resonance. In practicing this way I am limiting potential ruptures in the working alliance. I share what I am experiencing from the client empathically, and this provides an opening for us safely to deepen our super system (Siegel, 1999) or super state of mind (meaning the "melding of my state of mind with that of the client"), which may enable the client to re-associate to dissociated states that have heretofore blocked the processing.

Trauma processing may not be the treatment of choice for every client, or at least not right away. The client's freedom to say no — or not yet — and to give reasons may stir up transferential issues of abandonment or defectiveness. This moment may resonate negatively with state-dependent memories of traumas where the client was told he or she was inadequate by a significant attachment figure. In addition, being able to say no comfortably, without guilt, is a challenge for some clinicians. Saying no may stimulate vulnerability to harm or subservient schemas in them. Woe is the clinician who says yes even though the client's current-day functioning is sufficiently impaired that a longer stabilization phase is needed. This can lead to disaster during trauma processing.

Too often clinicians are inadequately informed about the standard method of EMDR, or they are grandiose in their assessment of their ability to heal their clients. These are their own learning or countertransferential problems, stimulated by the client. Some clinicians have inappropriate defectiveness schemas and need to prove their worth, so they implicitly compensate for feelings and irrational beliefs about their own inadequacy. More than one clinician has told me that he or she does not follow the standard protocol because he or she "knows better." Others have said they do not want to be "told what to do" by the EMDR methodology. This last remark strikes me as a negative transferential reaction to EMDR. If active trauma work is initiated without a comprehensive history, the clinician is either not familiar enough with the method or is acting out his or her own needs.

The initial history taking may go smoothly with more highly functioning clients with limited trauma. The client who has had more disturbed early attachment patterns may react very emotionally to being asked questions and revealing "private matters." He or she may have felt disappointed or betrayed in the past when telling the story. What is more, there is always the possibility of retraumatization when the client tells the story. At highest risk are clients whose dissociative symptoms take the form of flashbacks (positive psychoform dissociation); psychological amnesias (negative psychoform dissociation); physical pain that cannot be explained (positive somatoform dissociation); or psychic numbing, the inability to feel the effects of unresolved trauma in their bodies. In my experience, this last form of dissociation (negative somatoform dissociation) is the most common. Many times these experiences are specific to the treatment situation. Several clients have told me that they were aware of feeling certain sensations when thinking about their trauma on the way to a session but could not retrieve (a function of the right orbitofrontal cortex) those same sensations in my presence. These kinds of transferential manifestations must be addressed with tact, sensitivity, and good timing. They provide a clue that state-dependent memories have become activated by the clinician's presence. That is fine. When this process is understood by both parties, it becomes "grist for the mill."

A potential client came for his first session. He had been bullied in school and developed a vulnerability to harm schema. He remembered feeling very sad on the way to my office. However, when he arrived, he stated that while he could remember the details of the experience, he had become numb to his sadness. I asked him what might help him feel safe experiencing this sadness. He replied, "Time. I don't know you, and I don't trust you yet." I accepted his need to defend himself, and we explored his issue around safety. Staying with him in this process allowed him to associate to many times when caretakers were not there for him when he needed them. The worst memory of this type was of his father's reaction when he told him of being bullied. Instead of nurturing him adequately, his father shamed him, saying that he was not a man and had better become one pretty quickly or he would have a life of being a coward. So I asked the client gently which part of this memory hurt the most. He burst into tears, remarking that it was his father's criticism. He realized that he had implicitly projected that memory onto me. Once we cleared the field between us (making a past–present duality), we deepened our mental state resonance.

Clinicians themselves may be triggered right in the first session by the feelings and beliefs that their clients' stories present and activate in them. Present constraints on a client because of the trauma can induce in the clinician rescue fantasies or angry reactions to the abusers. Whenever I take a history, I tune in carefully to my own physical sensations as I hear the material presented.

I am also on the lookout for the client's need to please or my own dysfunctional need to be very, very wise in that session. Many times clients have informed me that they knew I was the right clinician for them when they heard the sound of my voice on the phone and experienced my razor-sharp intuition. When I hear this, I immediately ask what the client believes he or she will experience when I make my first mistake. This usually shocks the client, but it also sets the tone appropriately: There are two fallible human beings in the room.

Transferential characteristics can manifest because of insufficient trust, a high susceptibility to demand characteristics, or a desire to avoid further painful material. Because of these, some clients (as with Michael in the case of "The Death of Toto") will inaccurately report a lower level of distress than they actually feel. This may be a transferential assessment of the clinician's capabilities, or it may reflect the state-dependent fear that the client will experience more harm. Sometimes, though, it is not dysfunctional memory; sometimes the client might be right. The client may implicitly be reading something in the clinician that is "off." Clinicians should be aware of this possibility as well. Not every reaction is transferential.

The interpersonal field is ripe for reactive responses from both client and clinician. Clinicians need to be keenly attuned to their own and their clients' appraisals and negative arousals. These are important clues! This is critical even in Phase 1. (Remember, information processing goes on during the waking and sleeping moments of every person with a brain.) In addition, EMDR clinicians need to be careful in monitoring our reactions to the traumatic events our clients recount. We need to be aware whether any of the content or the manner of presentation is triggering us. (I will discuss this in more detail later.) Another hazard stems from either failing to assess for affect tolerance or misjudging it. This can potentiate negative transference, putting the clinician at risk of countertransferential reactions ranging from believing he or she is incompetent to feeling shame and doubt. This is especially common in clinicians who have unrelenting schemas.

While I believe that clinicians should be on call 24/7 for clients going through the active trauma phases of EMDR, this does not mean that we should take responsibility for keeping them stable. If we buy into the idea that we should, I suggest that the client has demonstrated transferential dependency needs that have resulted in the countertransferential reaction of self-sacrifice. Clinicians may implicitly act out their own state-dependent memories relating to dependency by being too available in an attempt to take care of their clients. That is why RDI and teaching other resourcing techniques to clients is so important. These will limit the client's pathological dependency on the clinician by giving the compassionate message that the clinician believes the client is capable of learning to master his or her difficult emotional states. Some of my clients are not happy with my stance. They want me to provide the answers. I give them the old adage, "Feed a person a fish, you feed them for a day; teach a person to fish, you feed them for a lifetime." Those clients not willing to practice EMDR resourcing strategies are violating agreements that they have made when we set up the collaborative working alliance. I remind them. Some get back on the train, learn, and practice. Others decide that I'm not the "right train" for them. I don't consider this a breach of the alliance, but rather a deeper level of desire that manifests after the initial high of creating the working alliance. This is why I continue to say that while the alliance is necessary, it remains insufficient in working with traumatized clients. It is living with them in the moment-to-moment experience of their pain and how they and I deal with it that constitutes the full expression of the therapeutic relationship in EMDR.

Earlier, in the chapter on Phase 1, I discussed asking the client to describe times in the past when he or she had used self-control techniques. The importance of obtaining this information cannot be overstated. If the client can honestly give examples of self-control, then moments of misattunement may be diminished. This is because the client has the ability to acknowledge that he or she is the one who is responsible for containing his or her emotions during trauma processing (while the clinician is responsible for facilitating the processing).

Having a strong working alliance and therapeutic relationship may also limit moments of misattunement because the more mature aspects of the client's personality have been engaged successfully, and the clinician and client will have become stronger allies. I do not mean to imply that transferential and countertransferential reactions will not occur. They will. However, there will be a point of reference to return to in reminding the client about what role each participant plays in EMDR treatment. With this reminder, transferential reactions can be clarified more easily, since the clinician can rule out the possibility that the client does not understand the treatment process.

8.7.2 Phase 2: Client Preparation (Testing Affect Tolerance and Body Awareness)

During Phase 2, the clinician educates the client on EMDR and continues to make diagnostic evaluations about how ready the client is to do the work. This includes use of the Safe Place exercise to assess the client's ability to move from a level of comfort to a level of disturbance and back again. Some clinicians have transferential reactions to Shapiro, to one of their EMDR trainers or facilitators, or to the EMDR training itself, and think this part of client preparation is overkill. I refer clinicians who think so to Maxfield and Hyer's 2002 paper on the fact that fidelity to the protocol brings the most robust results. In addition, if the client does not fully understand the EMDR process and what he or she might experience, this can set the stage for magical expectations or confusion about what is expected and what to be prepared for.

Imagine this scenario:

> The clinician takes a thorough history and decides that the client has adequate affect tolerance. The clinician then, without preparing the client, instructs the client to put on the headphones and think about his or her darkest memory, his or her negative self-referencing belief, his or her emotion, and so forth. The client could have a miraculous outcome, or shut down, or go into a major abreaction without understanding that this was a possibility. Imagine the plethora of transferential reactions the client could have — and the plethora of countertransferential reactions these reactions might trigger in the grandiose, careless, or ignorant clinician.

The client may, explicitly or implicitly, wish to have his or her problems surgically removed by the clinician (the phrase I hear clients use is "I want to have my bad memories erased"). The clinician may respond with his or her own magical thinking, which is usually a defense against defectiveness schemas based on state-dependent memories. The research shows that a single traumatic memory can be reprocessed in three 90-min sessions. The Wilson study and its 15-month follow-up study show that three sessions of active trauma reduce the symptoms of PTSD to the point where they no longer meet the DSM criterion. Furthermore, the second study demonstrates that the positive results of EMDR held in 84% of clients, and these clients no longer had the diagnosis of PTSD (Wilson, Becker, & Tinker, 1995, 1997). Many studies corroborate this conclusion. This does not mean that clients will not still have other problems to work on.

Uri Bergmann and David Grand (two colleagues with whom I trained to become EMDR Institute facilitators) have worked with Long Island railroad engineers who became traumatized when individuals committed suicide by throwing themselves in front of the trains, and Grand reports excellent results of their work (1999). EMDR has greatly helped these unfortunate engineers.

When Colin Ferguson killed six people and injured 19 on one of these trains in 1993, one of my clients was on that train. My client was in the fourth car; the people were being killed in the third car. My client went into a freeze state as she helplessly watched people run to safety. As Mr. Ferguson was reloading his gun, right before entering the railroad car my client was in, she reported watching her life flash before her eyes, knowing she would never see her husband and children again. It was only the intervention of three brave men who overpowered Ferguson that saved my client's life. She called me that night in a state of hysteria. I saw her the next morning, and in three 45-min sessions we completely detraumatized her from the experience.

Being in therapy is hard work, and it can be very frustrating. Many clients run out of patience. Their transferential demands may stem from the failures of early attachment figures to help them become prepared for life. The countertransference of their clinicians may be in response to the clinicians' own unmet needs being projected onto the client, with the implicit hope that if the clinicians can cure their clients, their clients' successes will cure them in turn. Preparation for life takes time; there are many tasks that must be successfully accomplished in order for a person to live successfully. Phase 2 mimics the many issues in this arena, issues that may not have been resolved for either the client or the clinician (but mostly for the client). How does the client prepare? Does he or she ask questions, do independent reading about EMDR, and speak to friends who have had EMDR treatment? Or does the client simply submit himself or herself to the expert for healing?

Although Shapiro makes a strong argument for client empowerment and responsibility, some traumatized clients may hear and acknowledge the instructions in Phase 2 but lack the ability to put them into practice. Prodding these clients with the questions in the DES (in Phase 1), the instructions in the Safe Place exercise, and other challenges may reveal untapped layers of developmental conflict that had not been diagnosed. This discovery may annoy or turn off certain clinicians because of all the procedures that are necessary in Phase 2. But you know what? That's just too bad. Maxfield and Hyer (2002) proved conclusively that success in the practice of EMDR is causally related to fidelity (faithfulness) to the standard method. I am simply underlining this. So have some transference to me. Knock yourself out. But follow the standard procedures and protocols. My purpose in writing this book is to flesh out what is I believe is intrinsic to the model, but I want you to be clear about what is Shapiro (i.e., validated by research) and what is my opinion based on clinical experience. I have spelled out the collaborative working alliance, added the intersubjective from Stolorow and Atwood (1992, 1994, 1996, 1997) and the neurobiology of interpersonal relations, as Siegel and Schore have elucidated it in their books (Schore, 1994, 2003a, b, Siegel, 1999), to offer a deeper understanding of what it is like to practice EMDR competently. Yes, in my own practice I add a variation or two, but when I do so I am always thinking conceptually about a particular client's specific issues.

Testing forms of bilateral stimulation is also a necessary part of Phase 2. The EMDR clinician's manner of introducing and testing each form of bilateral stimulation with the client will have a relational effect. Activations of state-dependent memories in either party need not interfere if the clinician is sensitive to the client's needs here. (For instance, if I am treating a sexually abused woman, and she wants to test tactile stimulation, I will either use the TheraTappers or put a pillow on her knees so as to limit the possibility of my retraumatizing her.) For a detailed discussion of this topic, see Chapter 5.

The last issue in Phase 2, but certainly one of the most significant, is holding a safe, even sacred space in which the client can do his or her work. This means staying sensitive to the fear the client may anticipate feeling when he or she brings up and processes painful trauma. By addressing these fears compassionately, the clinician will strengthen both the working alliance and therapeutic relationship. Although this is addressed in Shapiro's first book, I make note of its importance here because it is best to cover all possible transference and countertransference issues that may interrupt empathic attunement during processing. Clients want to know if the clinician will really be there (as opposed to being grossed out and deciding to think about something else) when they are in the throes of a very painful abreaction. The clinician's response to the client influences the psychotherapeutic space in many ways. If you always start with the conscious intention to keep an open heart that pledges safety and compassion (i.e., to have unconditional positive regard), you will be less likely to be taken by surprise during processing and to become activated by the client's pain.

8.7.3 Phase 3: Assessment (The Trauma Activation Sequence)

During Phase 3, the client and clinician determine the target memory (or memories) and its components. This may not be a difficult process, depending on the circumstance of the trauma, but misunderstandings and resistances can arise. After all, who wants to experience pain? Also, what the heck do you mean by "now"? (Remember Madeline?) Even when the client has been adequately prepared during Phase 2, he or she is in a radically different state of mind now. The client is being invited to activate extremely painful state-dependent memories and to amplify the emotions and irrational beliefs attached to them. The clinician must double-check that the client understands what state-dependent memory is. Yes, the client successfully completed Phase 2 last week, but is he or she really ready *today* to go into unknown territory? The client may have false expectations of what will happen in session, or external constraints may have cropped up since the previous session.

Most clients want their clinicians to think well of them. Their implicit blocking beliefs may manifest transferentially by inhibiting the client's self-knowledge. Even for clients who are less focused on gaining the clinician's approval, selecting a painful picture may be very difficult. It may engender fear or shame and trigger painful reactions he or she may not wish to become aware of, let alone share. Next comes choosing appropriate negative and positive cognitions, an area fraught with difficulty for both client and clinician. Blocking beliefs may inhibit the choice of an appropriate set of cognitions. This is why the clinician must understand the model before even thinking about transferential and countertransferential issues. The clinician may be faced with the daunting task of assisting the client to articulate these cognitions. Negative cognitions (which I believe are endemic to trauma: think of how many survivors of childhood sexual abuse or combat veterans have survivor guilt) often stimulate other painful memories, and blocking beliefs may arise as a defense against having to think about these negative cognitions (for example, a blocking belief may be: *If I admit to my survivor guilt or my avolitional sexual arousal during the abuse, it means I am bad*). Thinking about these self-beliefs may be so painful for the client that the clinician may have a countertransferential reaction and unconsciously collude with the client to skip this crucial piece of the launch sequence. When this happens, the clinician is setting the client up for incomplete processing.

With the positive and negative cognitions chosen, the client and clinician are still not safely through the potential minefield of Phase 3 yet. Linking the picture and the negative cognition may immediately trigger the client into an abreactive experience that may be extremely difficult for both clinician and client. When the client starts showing emotion, this may stimulate negative beliefs that he or she transferentially projects onto the clinician. Client statements such as "I'm sorry" are manifestations of transference that indicate the client thinks he or she has been bad, has done the protocol wrong, or is personally inadequate. My advice is to have the client complete at least one full protocol before targeting the transferential remark. After completion of a protocol, it may then be useful to target the next transferential remark directly and process it immediately. This may bring the client to a deeper level of understanding what old trauma the apology represents, since what is happening in the moment may be a reenactment of an older traumatic memory. In addition, the clinician needs to scan his or her own mind and body to determine if he or she has been triggered by the client's transference.

8.7.3.1 The Case of Sally

Sally is a 44-year-old divorced receptionist with three children. She came into treatment because of anxiety attacks secondary to being a single parent. She had divorced her husband because he had been severely verbally abusive to both her and the children. Sally's first target was her husband's cruelty. These were the components of the first memory:

Picture: her husband verbally assaulting her
Negative cognition: *I am bad.*
Positive cognition: *I am fine the way I am.*
VOC: 3
Emotion: shame
SUDS: 7
Body: stomach and chest

Sally got a lot of relief from her first three EMDR sessions and successfully detraumatized this memory. I had informed her that it is usually wiser to work on the oldest trauma first, but she was quite adamant about working on the more recent abuse issue first. The second memory Sally chose to work on was of her father's verbal abuse when she did not understand her math homework. He had had grown irritated with her when trying to explain it.

The picture that Sally associated with this memory was of her father scolding her. However, when we moved to selecting the negative cognition, Sally began to block and could not articulate one. I gave her some suggestions and showed her a negative and positive cognition worksheet. She still could not come up with anything that felt right and began to apologize to me profusely. Her eyes were with brimming with tears. I suggested that she just link the picture of her father scolding her with her current feelings and sensations, as well as her apologizing to me, and that we begin bilateral stimulation.

When Sally did this, she started associating to a much deeper issue related to her mother. She remembered that her mother would question her and induce doubt anytime Sally made a decision. Thus, by processing her transference, Sally was able to start reprocessing old memories of indecisiveness that had been induced by her mother's chronic doubting of her. By processing the transference, I was able to assist Sally to access her old state-dependent memories, whereas trying to inform her of the standard way was met with resistance. In this case, the resistance turned out to be Sally's defense against doing things some other way than what she wanted, because it would have stirred up the doubts in herself that her mother ingrained in her.

What if, on the other hand, I had been triggered by the client's painful apology in a way that I found uncomfortable? Suppose for the sake of argument that I stopped her and made her identify the other components of the trauma. Might I have been acting sadistically, inflicting more pain on her? Let us take a hypothetical case.

8.7.3.2 The Case of Laurie

Laurie, a 21-year-old college student majoring in English, comes to treatment because the peer pressure in her dorm is making her feel inadequate. Everyone except Laurie is smoking marijuana. Laurie's parents raised her very strictly and had threatened to disown her was she ever to drink alcohol, smoke, or use drugs. In the area where Laurie grew up, most people in her age group experimented or became addicted to substances. Laurie knows that this is not her path, but as a result she is being ridiculed and scapegoated by the other girls in her dorm.

In taking Laurie's history, I learn that she had been ridiculed by her second-grade teacher for being a poor speller, and the whole class had made fun of her. Let us suppose I had a similar scapegoating experience when I was young. I know how bad it can feel, and I really want Laurie to get over this problem. No need for a floatback here, I think — I see what is going on. So I simply observe to Laurie that what is happening in her dorm is similar to what happened in second grade. Laurie immediately sees the connection and agrees. We decide to work on the second-grade trauma, using the picture of her seeing her second-grade classmates calling her stupid and the negative cognition *I am stupid.*

At this point Laurie starts to cry, but I have not yet gotten the positive cognition, VOC, and other components of the trauma. So I ask her what she would rather believe. She answers in an agitated voice, "I don't know!"

I say, "That's okay," and hand her the sheet with possible positive and negative cognitions. By now, she is sobbing. But I know I have to adhere to the procedural steps outline, so I keep pressing her. "Laurie," I say, "you are more than your psychopathology."

"I know, I know," she says, "but I can't come up with one."

Well, I think, we can't proceed with desensitization until we finish this phase.

In essence, I have just implicitly reinforced her negative belief about believing she is stupid and reenacted her second-grade experience, exacerbating it and therefore making it more intense. I am not aware that I identify with Laurie's second-grade teacher. I do not remember when I got a 33 out of 100 on a math quiz in third grade and the class laughed at me. I am only aware that I am doing EMDR "right." The problem, I think, is that Laurie is not cooperating. I am unaware of my sadism toward her. (The client is always cooperating; we just have to know how to read his or her communication.)

These two examples illustrate the complexity of making treatment decisions in the moment. The clinician needs to base these decisions on his or her combined knowledge of clinical procedures and best practices, the client's character style, the client's transferential reaction, and the clinician's own countertransferential reaction.

Now let us consider a different problem. What if the client reports a SUDS of 8 but is not aware of where he or she feels this distress in the body. Many clinicians, including Shapiro, myself, and many others have stated that sensory awareness is crucial in EMDR processing because it helps the client to "get into" his or her body. What if the clinician instructs the client to start processing without his or her sensory awareness? It is possible that the visual and auditory channels would be open and that some work could be accomplished, but I have found it more likely that this kind of client will block and shut down. Then there is the risk of a failure experience where both the clinician and client may be triggered. What if the clinician were to believe, in spite of what Shapiro and others say (that the client need not share the graphic details of the memories in order to process them), that the client must report old, gory details? To whom is the clinician having a transferential reaction? Is some old voyeuristic issue coming up for the clinician, or is he or she just not following good practice? It gets complex, doesn't it? When in doubt, always follow your best clinical judgment and your analysis of what is going on in the therapeutic relationship.

8.7.4 Phase 4: Desensitization (Active Trauma Processing)

Phase 4 has the most potential for intense transferential and countertransferential problems. Stimulating state-dependent memory usually triggers intense levels of feeling. For clients who have been in talk therapy for years, these moments will be especially challenging. The urge to talk or explain may be particularly strong as an implicit avoidance pattern, which was a dysfunctionally learned response to overwhelmingly painful feeling states. Even when the client has had proper guidance and instruction in Phase 2 and Phase 3, he or she could transferentially experience the clinician as the perpetrator who is once again causing pain. In response to this transference, some clinicians become activated into a state-dependent memory dealing with, for example, a loss of identity, or they evaluate the client's reaction as an imposition on how the clinician works. This is countertransference by the clinician to the client. Since by definition transference is the activation of old state-dependent memories, the clinician is now treating his client from a reactive state. Gone is attunement. Gone is the stability of the therapeutic relationship.

What other effect could adaptive information processing have on the clinician? Information moves very quickly: Could an avalanche of abreaction frighten the clinician and activate his or her old state-dependent memories? Yes, this can happen as well. Can the bearing or tone of the client affect the clinician? The answer is obviously yes. When it does, the client can become flooded with many negative emotions and irrational beliefs, as well as other associated dysfunctionally stored memories. I had this experience early in my EMDR career.

8.7.4.1 Clinical Example: "Fear of Rainy Bridges"

Even with a good understanding of the process, problems may arise and solutions may not be found. Let us revisit the case of Dan, bringing our new understanding of the relational piece to it.

Early in my EMDR career, I was detraumatizing a client from a bridge phobia that seemingly had its roots in some rough rides he had taken when there was rain while going over bridges. Dan was a quite successful businessman involved in many charitable organizations. He had a strong sense of self-importance but masked it with a veneer of being a very nice person. He saw the use of therapy to cure his phobia as akin to having a dermatologist remove a skin growth. During desensitization, he began to remember being a small child and having a life-threatening illness, a memory that had not surfaced during the history taking. Dan was quite disturbed and needed to stop processing. I used standard methods to close down an incomplete session, including soft, relaxing imagery and a safe place. I made sure he was all right and capable of driving. I called him later that night to see how he was doing. At the time he told me he was okay.

Dan came to his next session extremely upset with me. He reported having criticized his staff very harshly. He said that this was not like him. He thought it was the result of his EMDR session, but he could not say why. To my mind, his transferential reaction had to do with losing control. This was related to his childhood illness, his bridge phobia, and other impulses he had kept in check. I was triggered by his reaction, however, and by my knowledge that an important clinician (who was not EMDR-trained) had referred him to me. I needed to do well for both Dan and that clinician. Both secretly intimidated me. My countertransferential reactions had to do with being stimulated around issues of not being good enough, doing something wrong, being thought poorly of, and fearing that my reputation would suffer. (I always had to be my parent's perfect child. Dan was older than me, and his superior bearing frightened me — but being a tough kid from the Bronx, I was not going to admit it, even to myself.) I tried to clarify with Dan how I was to blame for the harsh criticism he had made. I asked him about his understanding of EMDR, about his ability to control what happened in session, about how I closed the session down and made sure he was okay to drive, and about my call to him that night. While one could say that I was just reminding him of the good practice procedures I followed, my coming from a reactive state is the key to understanding that I was having a countertransference experience and acting out defensively. (I lost my empathic attunement with Dan and his pain, and my countertransference blocked it from ever returning!) His responses were quite dismissive. He stated that he could not talk to me that night because his wife had been nearby and he did not want to upset her. He also said that I had not prepared him for other possible consequences of the work, such as what happened the next day at work.

Dan came in for three more sessions. He acted as the perfect gentleman. He made it clear that he would only deal with driving on rainy bridges and the fear associated with it. Again I was triggered. I knew that his negative cognition, *I am out of control*, was quite pervasive and that the restriction he put on our work would make our efforts pointless. I offered to develop coping strategies that might help him deal with issues around his impulses in the present. Again he was quite dismissive. He had come to deal with a bridge phobia, and by God, that was what he was going to deal with. Those three sessions were acts of futility on both our parts.

At the end of the third session, Dan thanked me and said he had driven over some bridges in the rain with some improvement. He then terminated treatment. I believe that he was acting out the role of a good, compliant client. Countertransferentially I was acting out the role of the chastised little boy who had done his work inappropriately. I did not believe that he had gained much relief, and the referring clinician corroborated this.

EMDR clinician Zona Scheiner related to me her views on how growth-producing these countertransferential moments can be (Personal communication, Dec. 14, 2004). She states

> The more experience I have as a therapist, the more grateful I am to those clients who have frustrated, angered, hurt, and disappointed me. They have been the stimulants for my own growth — the mirrors into my own dark places and shadows. When I've allowed myself to enter into those places, the riches have been available to both myself and to my clients. Countertransference has become less a flaw that needs to be eliminated and more an opportunity for connection and growth.

8.7.4.2 Processing Blocking Beliefs

Clinicians new to EMDR may think that the greatest resistance will come up during the first protocol, but that has not always been my experience. Rather, resistance may come up after the client has processed a memory that really hurts or leaves him or her feeling exposed and vulnerable, even though the memory was processed down to a SUDS of 0 and the VOC rating for the positive cognition was 7. I have found that during the second protocol, the now "wise and seasoned" EMDR client, knowing what is coming, may become implicitly resistant because he or she does not want to go through another cycle of pain.

I suggest that the clinician look for the blocking beliefs the client may have in response to feeling pain, such as, "I can't stand this pain," and trace them back to their origins. I would suggest that this be the next target memory to process. Otherwise such resistance can set up transferential and countertransferential reactions. Anger, irritation, frustration, impatience, unacknowledged fears, and other unfinished business may arise in the clinician. The client experiences transferential manifestations as fears, shame-based cognitions, and the like. It is not unusual for a client to limit or diminish the intensity of the trauma even when he or she has been prepared according to standard procedure. Another good strategy here is to invite the client to process his or her reaction to you about stirring this pain up, since it is quite possible that another associated memory network may become activated, with the clinician as perpetrator.

As I mentioned earlier, most clients want their clinicians to think well of them. This concern can manifest in compliance driven by the client's need or desire to please. Clinicians see this in clients who go through a protocol and convince themselves that they have detraumatized the old memory. They block out any discordant sensations in the body, and they leave the session appearing grateful and happy. Have you seen this happen in your consulting room? How did you react when you saw the client next and discovered that treatment effects were not holding?

8.7.5 Phase 5: Installation (Linking to the Adaptive Perspective)

In Phase 5 and Phase 6 I have noticed that transferential and countertransferential reactions are lessened, but they are not completely absent. This phase serves to enhance the positive cognition and to link it specifically to the original traumatic event. Since all of the information should have shifted during processing, the positive cognition is checked for both applicability and validity. By asking the client what he or she believes about himself or herself now in relation to the original incident and having the client rate the belief using the VOC, the clinician is checking to see if the client really has finished the work.

Though it happens infrequently, when clients cannot come up with a positive belief about themselves or the VOC remains less than 7, but they say they have detraumatized the memory, I know they are fleeing from having any more painful experiences. If I did not challenge these clients, I would be colluding countertransferentially in their flight. This usually means that transferentially they are feeling unsafe experiencing what is inside of them with me. So instead of going ahead with processing and using the stop signal when the pain gets too big, they may act in ways that are designed to keep me at a distance. If I let them succeed in this, I am indirectly telling them that I cannot tolerate what is coming up for them, thus reinforcing a negative self-belief they have, such as *I can't handle it.*

8.7.6 Phase 6: Body Scan (Intensive Body Awareness)

In Phase 6 the client holds the positive cognition and the original incident together and scans his or her body for any sensations. Negative sensations usually indicate unprocessed trauma; positive sensations usually indicate continued productive information processing. Although negative transferential acting out can occur (i.e., the client denies feeling any negative sensations), it has been my experience that this rarely happens. Usually by Phase 6 the client and I are on the same page. We have used many checks and balances along the way to ensure that he or she knows this is just another way to make sure all the processing is done. By this time, our collaboration is firmly cemented, and a joyful communion between us is usually the rule of the day.

8.7.7 Phase 7: Closure (Debriefing)

There are two types of closure: complete and incomplete. When a client and I complete a protocol, we have a "felt sense" (Gendlin, 1981, 1996) of closure. This usually creates a stronger bond; one might call it positive transference (meaning, positive memory networks are formed or existing ones are amplified). The only caution I give to EMDR practitioners for this phase is to be humble. Before congratulating themselves, they should wait and see if treatment effects hold over time. Otherwise they risk becoming overconfident and believing they are more competent than they actually are. This can be very dangerous for their clients.

Incomplete closure, which I find more common, is a horse of a different color. What if the client does not seem to get any benefit from processing, or even ends by feeling worse than when he or she started? Imagine all the negative beliefs the clinician and client may hold about themselves then. Imagine all the negative judgments the client may make about the clinician and about EMDR. The field is ripe for transferential and countertransferential blame. Obviously, this is a worst-case scenario. There are many different outcomes possible in an incomplete session. What if the client goes from a SUDS of 9 to a SUDS of 3 and says this is enough? The clinician — especially if he or she has an unrelenting schema — may judge himself or herself incompetent and react with disappointment. When this happens, it is useful to get consultation. Going from a 9 to a 3 is fabulous, even though it means there is more work to be done. If the clinician countertransferentially transmits disappointment to the client, explicitly or implicitly, he or she may induce a negative transferential reaction in the client, such as *I'm not good enough.*

8.7.8 Phase 8: Reevaluation

As I mentioned above, treatment effects do not always hold. The reasons are too numerous to mention, but I will point out a few. During days following processing, associational channels may have been stimulated that were not obvious to either party during the session. This may cause a return of symptoms. The client may withhold this information as to avoid displeasing the clinician. A clinician whose self-esteem rests upon success rather than competence may not even ask about the past week for (unconscious) fear of stirring up "finished" work. The truth is, the work is done when it is done. Asking how the client's week went and what associations came up as a result of processing is simply a way to make sure treatment is progressing effectively. Not to do so endangers any progress the client has made.

Not asking these questions at the beginning of Phase 8 is either poor practice or a form of countertransference (such as, "I know better than Shapiro") that will come and bite the clinician later, when a client who has become reactivated either leaves treatment because it is not effective or continues to re-experience symptoms. This, in turn, can lead to a transferential negative belief of not being good enough. The reemergence of symptoms may lead to the same countertransferential belief in the clinician. In reality, all the reemergence of symptoms means is that there is more work to be done. Any negative self-judgments are simply activations of the clinician's state-dependent memory. This point cannot be stressed sufficiently. It is all about learning, not magic. The best advice is to keep following the client's process. For an example from my consulting, a consultee had a negative belief about herself because she was not getting the same results other clinicians claim to get in one session. This consultee was competent. Her state-dependent memories of inadequacy were being activated by these questionable reports.

8.8 The Intersubjective

Having established that a two-person psychology is at work in EMDR, I want to discuss the concept of nonlinearity. This term indicates that a small event (such as a cognitive interweave) may create a large event (such as linking an adaptive memory network to a dysfunctional one, with a rather intense abreaction. It may also indicate that multiple reactions and interactions (both internally and interpersonally) are occurring at the same time between the two parties in the room. Hundreds of billions of neurons in each person, organized into multiple neural networks that are stimulated simultaneously and sequentially, are continuously in a situation where they may be activated. These sets of neural activations are nonlinear. In other words, "A causes B" is not even a close approximation to what actually happens between two people in any situation, much less a treatment situation.

The psychoanalytic concept of isolation of minds has been debunked by Stolorow and Atwood in their book *Contexts of Being* (1992) and by Siegel in his chapter on states of mind (1999). Compare the thinking of psychoanalysts Stolorow and Atwood with the ideas of developmental neurobiologist Siegel. In *Contexts of Being*, the authors state

> Intersubjectivity theory is a field theory or systems theory in that it seeks to comprehend psychological phenomena not as products of isolated intrapsychic mechanisms, but forming at the interface of reciprocally interacting subjectivities. ... It is not the isolated individual mind, we have argued, but the larger system created by the mutual interplay between subjective worlds of patient and analyst ... that constitutes the proper domain of psychoanalytic inquiry. From this perspective, the concept of an individual mind or psyche is itself a psychological product of crystallizing from within a nexus of intersubjective relatedness and serving psychological functions. (p. 1)

In *The Developing Mind*, Siegel describes the neurobiological substrates of this nonlinear phenomenon when he states

> Our review of complex systems and the example of how attachment experiences shape patterns of self-regulation raises the issues of how two individuals come to function as a dyadic system. ... Consider this view. The mind of one person, A, organizes itself on the basis of internal and external constraints. Internal constraints are determined by constitutional features and experience. External constraints include signals sent from others in the environment. Person B is in a relationship with A. A perceives signals sent from B, and A's system responds by altering its state. Two immediate effects are (1.) that A's state shifts as a function of B's state (or at least B's signals), and (2.) that A sends signals back to B. B in turn responds to A's signals with at least these two alterations, and contingent communication is established. ... So what's new about this view?

What's new is that patterns of A's response to B, and B's response to A can begin to shape the states that are created in both A and B. A and B come to function as a super system, AB. One can no longer reduce the interactions of A and B to the subcomponents A and B; AB is an irreducible system. Systems theory provides a hierarchical understanding of interpersonal relationships. For some people, sharing an "interpersonal state" is one of the most rewarding experiences in human life. For others, such dyadic states are occasionally welcome, but a hefty dose of isolation is preferred to the feeling of "disappearance" that such an AB state may create. Still others long for such a union but feel they can never truly achieve it. Even when they are "almost in it," they fear it will disappear; that very fear can itself destroy the dyadic experience.

Is this just another way of talking about the different attachment patterns? Certainly the attachment approaches may represent variations on the fundamental, "I–thou" theme. There are selves, others, and their relationships together. But systems theory offers us a perspective and vocabulary on the constraints that help the system organize itself. These internal and external factors provide a new framework for understanding how one mind joins with others to form a larger functional system. (1999, pp. 231–232)

Those who see EMDR as a linear, mechanistic method would be well advised to study the convergent theories of intersubjective psychoanalysis and developmental neurobiology to understand the fallacy of their reasoning. All we can do is be faithful to the EMDR protocols with their many diagnostic checkpoints to ensure that we have been as thorough as possible in desensitizing and processing traumatic events in the lives of our clients. As they say, "The proof of the pudding is in the eating." Wilson, Becker, and Tinker demonstrated this in their 15-month follow-up to their research on the effectiveness of EMDR. After 15 months, they found that 84% of clients experienced treatment effects holding, with the clients no longer experiencing the symptoms of PTSD. When a happy event such as this is reported, we can be relatively sure that this nonlinearity of being human has not interfered with healing (1997).

8.9 Vicarious Traumatization and Compassion Fatigue

Laurie Anne Pearlman and Karen W. Saakvitne, in their book, *Trauma and the Therapist*, discuss vicarious traumatization. This term refers to the cumulative negative transformative effect on the clinician of working with survivors of traumatic life events. As Siegel shows, clinicians are hard-wired to be affected by clients' narratives. When we open ourselves in attuned empathy to our client's suffering, believe me, we pay a price. As a result of this exposure to the reality of frightening, cruel, and terrible events in the world, we are changed.

Charles Figley, editor of the journal *Traumatology,* terms this phenomenon *compassion fatigue.* He states that it closely parallels clients' PTSD reactions, but in this case the clinicians are the recipients. Figley notes that trauma workers are more prone to compassion fatigue,

> especially therapists — who work with traumatized people on a regular basis. ... There are four additional reasons why trauma therapists are especially vulnerable to compassion fatigue:
>
> i. Empathy is a major resource for trauma workers to help the traumatized.
> ii. Most trauma workers have experienced some traumatic event in their lives.
> iii. Unresolved trauma of the worker will be activated by reports of similar trauma in clients.
> iv. Children's trauma is also provocative for therapists. (1995, pp. 15–16)

Figley has also correctly broadened his conceptualizations to include how families are affected when one of their members is traumatized. In my mind, vicarious traumatization is the act that takes place when clinicians are affected by our clients' pain. *Compassion fatigue* seems to be an excellent way of describing our reactions to the cumulation of empathically resonating with the traumatic affects of our clients. The traumatic material we are exposed to includes graphic descriptions of violent events, vivid illustrations of people's cruelty to one another, and involvement in trauma-related interactions either as a participant or bystander. It also includes being a helpless witness to past events and present reenactments. We do not blame our clients for our vicarious traumatization (unless we are implicitly activated into a countertransferential moment). Rather, we understand that it is an occupational hazard, a side-effect of doing trauma therapy.

Our clients' vivid and sometimes explicit descriptions of their brutal victimizations are the biggest contributors to clinicians' vicarious traumatization and resulting compassion fatigue. Although it is often essential to a client's healing to share specific traumatic images, clinicians may carry these images away from the consulting room with us, and they can suddenly appear, unbidden, as clearly as our own internal images. In order to share our clients' journeys to reclaim their truths, their minds, and their bodies, we must be open. I believe that without our having this commitment, our clients cannot commit themselves fully to treatment. Yet our empathy is a source of our vulnerability to emotional pain and scarring. We cannot protect ourselves from knowing about the atrocities that happened, and we cannot protect our clients from what they have already experienced. This often puts us in the position of experiencing ourselves as helpless witnesses to trauma, a position that is itself traumatic. Our helplessness is all the more painful when we see our clients locked in repetitive, self-destructive reenactments during the therapy.

Figley (2002) has edited a book titled *Treating Compassion Fatigue* in which researchers report self-help and programmatic ideas to empower the client to release this kind of traumatization. Some of the researchers' suggestions involve humor, stress-management, and self-soothing techniques. In addition, in conjunction with Dr. Shapiro, I have developed ways specific to EMDR to deal with difficult situations that arise or may arise in session; you will find these ideas in this chapter under the subheading of self-care. Additionally, Ricky Greenwald, founder of the Child Trauma Institute, devotes a chapter to self-care in his soon-to-be-published *Child Trauma Handbook: A Guide for Helping Trauma-Exposed Children and Adolescents* (2005).

Exposure to and participation in these reenactments is an additional, independent contributor to vicarious traumatization. Reenactments sometimes take the form of witnessing our clients' self-destructive behaviors but being unable to protect them. Reenactments also include interactions in which clients unconsciously set themselves up to feel victimized, rejected, or abandoned by the clinician; the clinician unwittingly repeats abusive or neglectful behaviors with the client; or the client takes the role of perpetrator, treating the clinician in a sadistic way that is a reflection of the client's traumatic childhood, as I unwittingly did in the case of Janice (described in Chapter 9).

Finally, any major trauma inevitably involves loss — the loss of loved ones, of dreams, of innocence, of childhood, of an undiminished body and mind. After a trauma, nothing is the same. This profound loss of the familiar is a hallmark of trauma. As clinicians we confront this reality daily and thus must daily face the potential for such loss in our own lives and in the lives of those we love. Trauma therapy assaults our belief that we are safe and in control of our lives.

Pearlman and Saakvitne speak eloquently to this issue and its relation to countertransference. Vicarious traumatization may activate countertransferential reactions, as they point out in this passage:

One antidote to these unconscious processes of countertransference and vicarious traumatization is the judicious use of countertransference disclosure. When a therapist recognizes and
understands his countertransference, there is an opportunity to
examine an interactive process at work in the therapy by naming
the countertransference in the context of the therapeutic relationship. This interpersonal framework provides the grounding that
helps contain the therapist's response to the therapy, and allows the
potential for therapeutic working through. Countertransference
disclosure requires thoughtfulness, and when framed in a relational, non-blaming way, invites further acknowledgement and
deepening of the therapeutic relationship. (1995, p. 321)

Pearlman and Saakvitne's writings helped prompt my thinking on the
relational interweave. There are some technical differences based on
method, however. In Phase 4 (desensitization) of EMDR, I am "in the
moment" in an accelerated mode. I have found that I do not have to have
worked out my countertransference before noting that a moment of it may
have occurred. Noting that the process has stalled, asking the client to
notice what he or she has just experienced between us, and owning my
part in this event seems to bring the client back to an attuned mode where
co-regulation is reestablished. Then, through processing that intersubjective moment, deeper levels of processing may be accessible.

Pearlman and Saakvitne also discuss how vicarious traumatization carries
a social cost. They write

Many people become clinicians because they are hopeful about
humanity and the possibility for a better world. Unaddressed vicarious traumatization manifests in cynicism and despairs and results
in a loss to society both of that hope and the positive actions it
fuels. This loss can be experienced by our clients as we at times join
them in their despair; by our friends and families when we no
longer interject optimism, joy, and love into our shared pursuits;
and by the larger systems in which we were once active as change
agents and which we may now leave, in disillusionment and resig-
nation. (p. 33)

For a personal example, I experienced vicarious traumatization when
I worked with victims of 9/11. On one particular day, I had seen many clients, five of whom had witnessed people jumping from one of the two
towers, holding hands, choosing to die instantly rather than be burnt
to death. After hearing the story for the fifth time that day, I was spent. So

I went to a trusted EMDR colleague to do my own work and become detraumatized. This one was too big for me to try to do on my own. If we do not take care of ourselves, the stimulation of vicarious traumatization will put us at risk for countertransferential reactions.

One can deal best with vicarious traumatization in session by being present and having a slight sense of detachment (by "detachment," I mean staying in a state of "witness consciousness"). Knowing one's own limits is crucial in order for productive work to follow. Sometimes clinicians may show our vicarious traumatization involuntarily by wincing at something the client recounts, or by dissociating. When this happens, it is useful to have a talisman, spiritual object, good-luck piece, or other personally significant object to reground yourself. I have many throughout my office. My most important resource is a picture of the late Jerry Garcia, looking at me over his shades and saying, "Dude, you are doing your best for your client." If vicarious traumatization does come across intersubjectively and blocks processing, the clinician should own up to it and perhaps offer a relational interweave.

One of a clinician's greatest and most necessary tools, empathic attunement, is also one of our greatest liabilities. Remember Carl Rogers' third stage of empathy, opening up and taking the client into ourselves? When it comes to vicarious traumatization, we may temporarily be unable to do this, with the result that the client no longer feels "felt" by us. When we are not conscious of it, vicarious traumatization can also lead to reenactments of our own old trauma. When this happens, community is lost. Instead we react to the client as the "too busy parent," or we become aggressive in our work to help the client "get over it already!" These reenactments usually take the form of old interpersonal interactions because we are now in a reactive mode and are reacting to the projective identification made on us. Harry Stack Sullivan, the great American interpersonal psychoanalyst, coined the term *malevolent transformation* (1953) to describe the activities that go on in session when the work function of treatment diminishes and client and clinician are responding to each other in a reactive mode. (Old state memories are being reenacted in both, in some complementary manner.)

Pearlman and Saakvitne emphasize the importance of having supervision while working with traumatized clients (1995). They focus on the importance of the therapeutic relationship and its parallel process in supervision. Those clinicians who are seasoned trauma therapists resonate with this approach. In addition to having a supervisor you respect and trust, I recommend using the self-regulation strategies of preparation and compartmentalization to fortify yourself and protect yourself against vicarious traumatization. I describe these below, using EMDR methodological terms. Mastering these skills will enable you to be at your best when anticipating and living through potentially traumatizing moments with your clients.

8.10 Self-Regulation Skills for EMDR Clinicians

8.10.1 Preparation

The best way to deal with countertransference is to become aware of it before it interferes with the work. Clinicians' being fully prepared for seeing the client, experiencing his or her personality, and hearing his or her issues goes a long way toward preventing our own old, unfinished memories from getting triggered. As I get ready for a client session, I begin by taking out the client's chart and reviewing my notes. I take the time to scan my body, noticing my feelings and beliefs in the moment about my client and about myself. I remember how our past sessions have flowed, and I think about what opportunities and problems may arise. I also picture my client and notice my feeling state and any negative self-referencing beliefs that may come up.

I am acutely aware of my inner reactions to my various clients. These range from feeling like I am welcoming an old friend for tea to experiencing anticipatory empathy or a sense of purpose. (EMDR strikes a rich chord in me because Shapiro's mission is to end the cycle of violence. Practicing EMDR is my way of joining with like-minded colleagues to help heal our traumatized planet.) There are darker moments I may face as I prepare to see a client. Sometimes I experience myself as "not getting it," meaning that I feel I have lost my sense of collaborative communication with the client. When I notice this, I ask myself: What I am missing? Am I triggered by something that happened in the last session or in recent sessions? Is there something about my client that I do not like? If so, where is that coming from?

When I picture my client and use elements of the procedural steps outline, I am often surprised to feel a surge of anxiety in my chest and abdomen. I take this as evidence of my own negative self-referencing beliefs. My usual ones are the garden-variety negative beliefs many of us hold. For instance, the negative cognitions I most commonly discern are *I am inadequate, I am a faker,* and *I am incompetent.* When this occurs, I usually "float back" to an older unfinished piece of work, and then put on my headphones and do some audio processing. Often this will quickly clear the issue for me, and I can decide whether this work was sufficient to put me back on track with my client or whether I need to seek consultation from a trusted colleague. (Clinicians — of whatever school — who have not done at least five years of their own growth work would be well advised not even to try to do any work like this on themselves, by themselves. I have been doing my own growth work for some 35 years.)

One of two major events usually occurs when I do this. I may discover something in the way I am experiencing my client that was triggered by previous patterns of dysfunctional interactions I have had. This discovery may lead me to realize that I am not "getting it." Suppose I am working with a hypoaroused client who does not seem to get triggered into any kind of state-dependent memory and just shuts down. In this case, I may discover that I have been feeling frustrated but am unable to recognize my part in this process.

One option I have is to educate myself. I may consult some of my textbooks or call a colleague for a consultation. For me, new learning is always welcome, especially when it sheds light on something I must be missing. At other times, I may find that there is an underlying theme in the "flow of states" between myself and my client. This information may be helpful in my understanding the deeper issues embedded in the client's verbal and nonverbal messages. The questions for me are then twofold: Why was I missing this message? And what old issues have come up for me that my body knows, but my consciousness does not? When an old issue has come up, I mentally review a piece of the client's previous processing session and determine what may be activating me. Sometimes the client has inadvertently stimulated some of my "old stuff."

Other times I discover my client has been reacting transferentially, implicitly trying to get my attention, but I was not cognitively aware of it. My body usually gives me clues. When I think about a client's problems and the way I am dealing with them, I may find myself having similar problems. Again, I view these occurrences as opportunities for me to grow rather than as evidence of any psychopathology.

Here is an example of how I helped a consultee work with his process. He had been working with Walter, and Walter had been displeased that my consultee would not immediately begin trauma processing. He had let Walter have his way, and the result was that Walter went to the hospital with chest pains. My consultee's first memory had the following components:

Picture: Walter looking unhappy when I initially said that I would not start active trauma processing
Negative cognition: *I am defective.*
Emotion: shame
Body: abdomen

Having triggered him, I have him erase Walter's image and just meditate on "I'm defective" and the feeling of shame, with auditory processing.

He told me a story: "I relate back to when a popular kid wanted me to push some gum he had put on top of a kid's hair in the movies. The kid was in front of me. I couldn't do it, and 'earned' the scorn of the popular kid." My consultee learned a valuable lesson that day (and survived being traumatized by causing Walter to go to the hospital with chest pains).

I want to reiterate that I do not recommend clinicians attempt the self-stimulation that I do unless they have already done years of their own work. Younger clinicians or those going through a rough time in their lives would do better to work with consultation groups of other EMDR clinicians who have proven their worth as friends and colleagues.

8.10.2 Compartmentalization

When I find myself triggered by anything during a session in a way that interferes with the flow of states of mind between my client and me, I follow a series of internal steps in the moment to return to a state of centeredness. (This countertransference often takes place during the Phase 4 work of desensitization.) I offer these steps as a guide rather than a hard and fast set of rules. I call the technique *compartmentalization.*

For an example, suppose my client is angry with me for not showing enough concern for him. I listen as nonjudgmentally as possible. I make an intervention, but the client refuses my interventions and stays in a hyperaroused state. This triggers my defectiveness schemas.

I notice a discomforting sense of arousal in my body, and I experience an internal interruption in the flow of collaborative communication. I am acutely aware that I need to determine whether my being triggered appears to have interrupted the client's work. If so, the following strategy is not appropriate; instead, a relational interweave is called for (see Chapter 9).

First, I take a cleansing breath and bring to mind of one of my safe places or consult my inner coaches and guides, asking them for advice. I feel the comfort of my safe place or listen to what my coaches and guides have to say.

Next, I press my left big toe into the floor, then my right big toe, simultaneously keeping in mind the words of my guides or my feeling of comfort. The toe pressing simulates tapping. I have found that using bilateral stimulation at this point centers me and returns me fully to the present.

I take note of what triggered me, and I work on it after the session is over, using techniques similar to those I use in preparing for a session. Then I record what happened in my psychotherapy notes, and I review the client's chart, problems, flow of progress, and fixation points.

Here is an actual example of a session where I used the compartmentalization process. Dick is a 56-year-old divorced man who works as an accountant. He came to me for EMDR treatment on his old issues of having been verbally abused. His current-day referent was the legal separation procured by his wife, Lynn, which left no room for negotiation. After 20 years of marriage, she had had enough of his verbal abuse of her and their 18-year-old daughter.

Dick's approach to treatment was similar to his approach to most issues in his life. He was impatient, wanting me to "move my fingers" and make the pain go away. He started off rather intensely and expressed feelings of disappointment and anger when I informed him of the multiphasic nature of EMDR work. Although he seemed to tolerate the boundary for the first two sessions (while I gathered history, developed a case conceptualization, and prepared him for processing), he remained fixated on the belief that once again he was going to "get screwed." (I did not do a good enough job in developing the collaborative alliance; he gave it lip service, but that was all.) Up to this point, I had experienced myself as feeling challenged but not triggered. Dick got through the Safe Place exercise, though with some difficulty. His DES score was low (an 8). I finished prepping him, and we started Phase 3 work in the next session.

Dick had trouble with the idea of the two nows. His verbiage and left-brain thinking interfered with his entry into state-dependent memory. He was the youngest of five children and had always perceived himself as "getting the short end of the stick." Now, as we were about to start active trauma work, he flinched and started accusing me of making this process too confusing for him. He said, "You therapists just want to make the process longer so you can get more money out of us." At this point I felt a tightening in my gut, and I noticed that my patience was wearing thin. I had the impulse to strike out verbally at him.

I consulted my inner coaches Don and Elizabeth, who told me to calm down and just notice what old memories might be getting triggered in me. I could not come up with anything in the moment, so Elizabeth suggested that I imagine myself at Kripalu, a place that Elizabeth, Don, and I visit frequently and where I experience a sense of spirituality and peace. I have learned to use EMDR Safe Place and RDI strategies on myself, and I apply them even when I am in session. My self-cuing word is "mountains."

Once I activated my resources, I found myself calming down and was able to bring my sense of calm spirituality back with me into the consulting room, and to separate the past from the present. This is the compartmentalization part.

Finding myself back in a state of attunement, I then asked Dick to notice if he had any old memories connected to getting "screwed" (his word). Up came a memory of when he was 7 and he was denied the chance to do something with his siblings at a resort because he was too young and frail to take part. With this awareness, he was able to return to a co-regulated relationship with me where collaborative communication resumed. He productively processed this memory. With this first protocol under our belts, our relationship strengthened, and Dick was able to continue doing his work.

After the session, I went back to the tightening in my gut. As I let my awareness wash over me, I noticed that the words *He's being unfair to me* came up. I asked myself, "Mark, when you hear the words *He's being unfair to me*, what negative self-referencing beliefs do you hold about yourself?" The words *I am a failure* came up. I then linked those words with the picture of Dick and with the tightened sensation in my gut. I realized that I had dissociated shame attached to this episode. Using floatback, I came upon a state-dependent memory of an old trauma with my father, who at times was quite demanding. In this case, I was able to do my own work and become re-centered.

CHAPTER 9

The Relational Interweave and Other Active Therapeutic Strategies

9.1 The Need for Intervention Strategies

The decision whether to stay out of the way during EMDR processing or employ an intervention strategy should be based on the clinician's assessment of whether the adaptive information process is progressing. When there is a block, the clinician should carefully examine, internally, aspects of the therapeutic relationship such as the flow of energy between client and clinician (as Carl Rogers, Robert Stolorow, George Atwood and Dan Siegel elucidate). When the client has been activated and the clinician maintains empathic attunement, issues such as transferential blocks, dissociative experiences of the client (in the moment), blocking beliefs, and feeder memories must be dealt with in order for active trauma work to continue to completion.

Breaks in empathic attunement come in two flavors, psychoanalytically speaking: transference and countertransference. This concept is a logical extension of standard EMDR methodology that blends Siegel's neurobiological concepts with Stolorow and Atwood's psychoanalytic theory on the therapeutic relationship.

It would be wonderful if the use of EMDR's standard protocol allowed us consistently to stay out of the way while a client is desensitizing state-dependent memories. This does happen, of course, especially with cases of noncomplex PTSD, but it is not always the norm. Instead, associational channels in the client's brain become stimulated and often cause him or her to block or flood during processing.

Remember, during Phase 4, desensitization, the client is responding avolitionally, not trying to direct his or her thoughts but allowing whatever comes up to come into awareness. Because of this, issues or memories with too much state-specific excitatory energy can inhibit the stimulation of adaptive memory networks. When this happens, the dysfunctional memories can get refrozen into state-dependent forms. This inhibits the brain's function — an accelerated state of productive trauma processing — and its ability to link to a more adaptive perspective becomes inhibited. No matter what kind of intervention the clinician makes, its purpose is to enable the client's brain to regain its ability to make a connection from a dysfunctional state to a more adaptive state.

9.2 The Cognitive Interweave

The first active strategy Shapiro created is the cognitive interweave, which is designed to be used when the clinician observes that processing is blocked, the client is looping, and desensitization has stalled. It was developed for use with more highly disturbed and fragmented clients. The clinician makes a cognitive interweave by offering an appropriate statement that will link more adaptive ways of thinking to the client's maladaptive memory.

For example, a client was a newly married woman who had been beaten by her alcoholic husband. Because of elements in her past, she developed a sense of overresponsibility and blamed herself for not being able to stop her husband's beatings. A cognitive interweave that would be effective for this client might be, "I'm confused. Are you saying that a 120-pound woman should be able to defend herself against a raging 200-pound drunk?"

A therapeutic connection the client, along with adding new information, can often make this important link to a more adaptive way of expressing one's self. Its purpose is to add the next link in the chain that is necessary to effect permanent trait changes in the client. As soon as the clinician sees a glimmer of understanding, he or she begins another set of bilateral stimulation.

Shapiro used the term *cognitive* to indicate that spoken words were used to assist the client's brain in making this linkage (personal communication, April 2, 2000). The term *interweave* is used because in this strategy the clinician offers a statement (sometimes posed as a question) that therapeutically weaves together the appropriate neural networks and associations (Shapiro, 2001, p. 249). The cognitive interweave has been a very useful addition to Shapiro's original conceptualization.

Shapiro distinguishes three types of interweaves: responsibility, safety, and choice. A responsibility interweave was used in the preceding example. Here is another example: An incest survivor blames herself for becoming aroused during the abuse and shuts down during processing. Her clinician might say, "I'm confused. What if this happened to your child? Would you blame her?"

For an example of a safety interweave, suppose an adult male client is so flooded with state-dependent memories that he loses track of present time and is overwhelmed with fear of a bully who constantly beat him up when he was a child. A safety interweave might be, "He's dead, he can't hurt you now."

A choice interweave would be appropriate when a client was coerced into doing something he or she knew was wrong, and the guilt is getting in the way of healing. The clinician would say something like, "Would you do the same thing now?"

Responsibility, safety, and choice are three plateaus where clients may become stuck because of insufficient information that either needs to be introduced or is already there but is not linked to. These are not the only appropriate circumstances for an interweave. An interweave is a technique that links in the next bits of information, mimics spontaneous processing, is used to jump-start information processing, and is viewed as a short channel that allows the client to go back and process the target memory without prodding.

"Fitting the intervention to the client" (Shapiro, 2001, p. 261) is a perfect expression of the relational in EMDR. Shapiro states, "If EMDR is properly applied (without major demand characteristics) and if the information offered by the clinician is accurate, a new perspective will be assimilated." (Shapiro 2001, p. 261). In order for this new perspective to be assimilated, there must be no major demand characteristics applied. I read Shapiro as instructing the clinician to know the client and be able, through the relationship, to craft an interweave that stays within the attunement of the dyadic relationship. She goes on to state that if the new information is inaccurate, the client will simply reject it. By giving the client this latitude, the clinician is gauging how much in attunement he or she continues to be with the client. Allowing for the fallibility of the clinician, I read Shapiro as implicitly stating that there will be times when the client and clinician will be out of attunement, and that by not pushing the "correct interweave" (the one that the clinician thinks is right), the clinician keeps the client at the center of the process. This makes for the possibility of being out of alignment. When this happens, the client will not resonate with the clinician's intervention.

The cognitive interweave is not the strategy of choice for all cases of blocked processing, by any means. Gilson and Kaplan, in their manual *The Therapeutic Interweave in EMDR* (2000), note that Shapiro cautions that many other factors can contribute to blocked processing. Some of these are

- Insufficient preparation of either or both the client and the clinician
- Incorrect use of the EMDR method
- Lack of safety
- Insufficient affect tolerance
- Secondary gain or feared loss
- Current life challenges
- Feeder memories
- Blocking beliefs
- Fear

All of these difficulties must either be corrected or dealt with in the treatment plan before the clinician uses the cognitive interweave or any other therapeutic strategy.

In recent years, Gilson and Kaplan have added many other interweave strategies. They define the therapeutic interweave as a means of assisting in a curative (trait change) manner by "weaving together, mixing, blending, fusing … interlacing strands" (2000, p. 4). In this way Gilson and Kaplan are expanding on the possibilities of positive outcomes. They suggest using the term *therapeutic*, as it is a "more inclusive" term. I read this as an expansion of the cognitive interweave concept, with the goal of effecting trait change. They state, "While the Therapeutic Interweave incorporates aspects of the cognitive interweave (thoughts, conceptual activity, and/or verbalizations), it also brings to mind essential categories of nonverbal or verbal interventions" (p. 4). These intervention categories include supportive, sensory, affective, body awareness, experiential, spiritual, and humorous strategies. It is critical to link the kind of interweave strategy with the characteristics of the client and what he or she is stuck on. An example of a spiritual and humorous interweave (Shapiro's category of metaphorical interweave), useful with people of spirit who cannot see what is right in front of them, is the story of the religious man caught in a terrible flood. First he refuses to be helped by the Red Cross, and then by the Coast Guard, declaring that he believes in God and God will save him. The floodwaters continue to rise, and he drowns. When he meets his maker, he is mad! He demands an explanation from the Almighty, who responds, "Who do you think sent the Red Cross and the Coast Guard?"

Understanding Young's schema categories is helpful when using interweaves. For example, if you know your client struggles with an unrelenting schema in his or her looping, a strategy to help the client "get off the hook" might be useful. Alternately, when the client has a vulnerability to harm schema, a safety interweave might be appropriate.

9.3 The Relational Interweave

All of these types of interweaves are sound strategies. However, there are times when processing is blocked by something that happens between the client and clinician. I have observed many instances, both in my own practice and in those of EMDR clinicians in consultation with me, when processing breaks down as the result of misattunement. I have developed a type of interpersonal intervention to deal with these transference and countertransference phenomena, which I call the relational interweave.

In a relational interweave, four main things happen:

1. The clinician uses himself or herself (his or her body) as a barometer of interpersonal interaction.
2. The clinician becomes aware of the reciprocal mutual influence between the client and himself or herself.
3. The clinician notices his or her contribution to the block in processing.
4. The clinician crafts an intervention through which he or she takes rational responsibility for his or her own reaction to the client.

An important aspect of the relational interweave is that it brings more safety into the relationship. When people are traumatized, their sense of safety is gone. Something terrible has happened to them, often at the hands of another person who takes no responsibility for the harm he or she has caused. In the traumatized person, this event activates a mental model about interpersonal experiences being unsafe. Even with a solid therapeutic relationship, moments of misattunement may occur because of a countertransferential activation. I believe that when this happens, the client's mental model of interpersonal danger becomes implicitly activated. In the original trauma, not only was the victim left wounded and vulnerable, he or she was all alone. You can see why, if the clinician does not act with awareness and congruence and take rational responsibility for his or her part in the client's blocked processing, the chance of retraumatization is high.

A key foundational piece of the relational intervention is Carl Rogers' concept of congruence. Rogers describes congruence as occurring "when the psychotherapist is what he is … genuine and without 'front' or façade, openly being the feelings and attitudes which at that moment are flowing in him" (1961, p. 61).

Another foundational piece is the separation of the past from the present. The relational interweave, by defining the moment intersubjectively, gives the client a solid experience of the present as being categorically different from the past. In the present, the person who "harmed" the client is taking responsibility for his or her actions. (The client's perpetrator may have said, "You made me do that!") In the present, the client is not alone and isolated. The clinician is fully present and is taking responsibility for his or her share in the problem. When the client can differentiate the past from the present, he or she feels safer to release old pain. This can open the door to a return to empathic attunement and productive processing.

A relational interweave is called for when a state-dependent memory has been activated in the clinician, is noticed by the client on some level, and appears to have temporarily stalled the work. When the clinician is triggered, a diminishing of empathic attunement and mental state resonance occurs. This may not be evident to either party. However, the clinician can usually detect activation of state-dependent memories on a sensory motor level. I train my consultees to scan their bodies continually during client sessions for any clues that an event like this might be happening.

Let me diverge for a moment to say that the incredibly rich subject of clinicians' somatic phenomena during client sessions is beginning to be studied. Robert Shaw, author of *The Embodied Psychotherapist* (2003), states in a recent article in *Psychotherapy Research* that, according to his study, "psychotherapy is an inherently embodied process" (2004, p. 271). "Therapist body experience … is invaluable information relating to the intersubjective space between therapist and client," he adds (2004, p. 271). Many in our field have examined the role of the body in psychotherapy, but the focus has nearly always been on the client's bodily experience. "The therapist's body," Shaw remarks, "is largely absent, as though there is only one body in the consulting room. (2004, p. 272)"

The neurobiological findings of Siegel have shown that the neurobiology of the clinician is a vital part of the process. EMDR is a two-person psychology, because humans' brains are hard-wired to interact relationally, and our brains are part of our bodies. EMDR is as much a two-body psychology as it is a two-person psychology. As French philosopher Maurice Merleau-Ponty, whose work has informed Shaw's research, wrote, "It is through my body that I understand other people" (Shaw, 2004, p. 272).

To return to the relational interweave, when the clinician perceives that something in his or her body feels "off," it is useful (but not necessary in the therapeutic moment) to try to notice what old memory may have been activated and caused the countertransference. What is also useful, in the moment, is to find a negative self-belief, such as *I can't stand this*. The next step is to determine whether the countertransference is purely your own "stuff" or is actually an empathic link to an implicit conflict or trauma in the client. Paul Wachtel has suggested this in his seminal work, *Psychoanalysis and Behavior Therapy: Toward an Integration* (1977). He is not alone; many others in the relational psychoanalytic community have written about the potential uses of countertransference.

Whether a memory or negative self-referencing belief appears (or not), the clinician will make an empathic statement (or initiate a short discussion) about what he or she believes just transpired between himself or herself and the client. The clinician takes rational responsibility for his or her part in it (without necessarily sharing the content of his or her state-dependent memory) and invites the client to process what just occurred interpersonally. This is followed by one or more sets of bilateral stimulation.

The following is a case in point, where I did retrieve an old memory in the moment. Judicious sharing of my process led to the client's ability to accept the interweave, which unblocked her processing.

9.3.1 The Case of Kristin

A 17-year-old woman named Kristin was referred to me for trauma work. She had been driving her car on a major thoroughfare when a drug addict stumbled out into the street. She did not see him quickly enough and hit him while going 40 mph. He was killed. There was an official inquiry, and the young woman was exonerated of all wrongdoing.

Two months after the crash, Kristin still had intrusive and distressing recollections of the accident, nightmares, and a strong reluctance to talk about the event. She could not drive down the road where the fatal accident occurred. She could not remember incidents immediately before and after the crash. She also had difficulty sleeping, could not concentrate on her studies, and had developed a pronounced startle response.

Kristin was an honors student at a local college and had always been clean and sober. She was the older of two children from an intact marriage. Her parents had been quite strict with her. Her father often made critical remarks, even though her grades averaged 96% and she had been in all high-honors classes in high school. Kristin had a good circle of friends and had dated sporadically. She had no psychiatric history.

Kristin was tearful and depressed on initial presentation, though she was well-oriented, well-dressed, and well-mannered; everything else in her mental status was within normal limits. She could not talk about the crash for the first session. She was able to give a coherent history, however, including a history of how she had learned to drive (her mother taught her). Until the accident, she had considered herself a competent driver. I felt compassion for this young woman and her plight.

Kristin said that she could never forgive herself, even though she had been found innocent of any wrongdoing. I asked her if it would be okay to remember the incident and at the same time release her pain. She was very reluctant, saying that she did not deserve to feel anything but pain, because a man had died and she was responsible. (I made note of this statement as a potential blocking belief to be worked on during desensitization.) I was not aware of being triggered by her refusal to release her pain at that point.

She was, however, willing to consider any therapeutic intervention that might have a chance of relieving her distress, even though she had doubts that anything could help. She especially doubted a method that sounded as weird (her word) as EMDR. But Kristin's psychology professor was a colleague of mine who knew about EMDR and had referred her to me. She trusted her professor and was willing to give EMDR a try.

We went through Phase 1 and Phase 2 with little difficulty. Kristin acquired a good enough working understanding of EMDR and went through the Safe Place exercise with no trouble. All elements of client preparation had been addressed. In Phase 3, we settled on the following components:

Picture: the drug addict crashing into the windshield
Negative cognition: *I am to blame.*
Positive cognition: *I did the best I could.*
VOC: 2
Emotions: guilt and shame
SUDS: 8
Body sensations: heart and gut

We moved on to Phase 4, but the initial processing showed little effect. I tried longer sets, a change of direction, and different methods of bilateral stimulation, but all proved ineffective. I then tried the cognitive interweave of responsibility: "Whose responsibility was it that this man was using drugs?" I asked. "It doesn't matter," she replied. "The man died." I attempted other interweaves as well. They were unsuccessful. While Kristin was (apparently) resisting my efforts to release her from responsibility for the drug addict's death, I started to feel a growing discomfort in my abdomen. This was my first indication that something was triggering me. As I sat with this feeling, I recognized that it came from an implicit identification with Kristin's unrelenting standards, and a similar blocking belief.

It was at that moment that a memory came back to me. I was 8 years old and riding my bike. A little girl came out of nowhere; she crossed my path, and I hit her. She fell to the ground and started bleeding from the head. Her mother picked her up, cursed at me, and ran across the street to the neighborhood doctor.

When I recalled this memory, I realized that I had never forgiven myself for running into the little girl. I also realized that while I was asking Kristin to forgive herself for running into someone and harming him, I was being triggered by a similar memory in which I had never been able to forgive myself. I wondered silently if I was communicating to her the dissonance between what I was saying and what I was experiencing internally, and thus contributing to her block in the session.

At first I had believed that Kristin's refusal to process the event was her transferential way of punishing both herself and me. Despite having made a verbal attempt to assist in releasing her from her pain, I now saw that I might have caused her transferentially to experience me as a punitive parent, since I was implicitly experiencing the punitive parent in myself. I had also believed that Kristin's refusal had been a way of punishing me for "lying" to her: She could not believe an adult could authentically offer compassion for such a "crime." That was when my memory from age 8 came back to me, and I realized that Kristin and I had similar blocking beliefs. With this realization, I was able to feel genuine empathy for her (and myself as well). I also knew that we had to deal with this blocking belief before we could continue to detraumatize her.

I said, "Gee, I guess I got a little tight when you said that it didn't matter because a man died. I guess I had a reaction." (In this case, as with almost all, it was not necessary for me to share my old memory — and I am not sure I would have shared it, even if it were necessary. One must be judicious in what one reveals.) Then I talked patiently with Kristin about the standards we had both set for ourselves. She appeared surprised and moved that a clinician could struggle with a similar issue. Her blocking belief, *I am responsible because a man died,* became more open to modification.

Having woven in this relational piece, I tried a variation on the question I had asked previously: "If your best friend had been in a similar situation, how would you treat her?" Kristin was stymied. I continued, "What if you knew a way to help, would your friend let you try?"

"Of course," Kristin said.

This gave me the opening to return to the cognitive interweave of responsibility that I had tried before. I instructed her to imagine asking her friend the following question: "Whose responsibility was it for this drug addict to be using drugs?"

This time she responded, "His."

I said, "Go with that," and from there it was not hard to detraumatize her.

Sometimes true empathy can move mountains.

When clinicians shift their attention from an exclusive focus on the client, in EMDR, to a more complex view of the therapeutic relationship, they move into the fertile intersubjective field of the therapeutic process. To focus on the therapeutic relationship requires that we examine our subjectivity. The relational space of the psychotherapy is shaped by what we bring to it, specifically our personal history, feelings, attitudes, defenses, implicit processes, conscious reactions, body awarenesses, and behaviors. All of these inform and are reflected in our countertransference.

9.3.2 Step-by-Step Review

A brief summary of a possible sequence of events in a relational interweave is as follows:

1. When processing is stuck, see if you notice any personal discomfort or negative arousal.
2. Check in with yourself to identify what was activated in you, such as an old memory or a blocking belief similar to your client's.
3. Bring your awareness of your part in the misattunement fully into your consciousness.
4. Ask your client if he or she noticed whether anything happened between the two of you right before processing was blocked.
5. Clear the air (relationally and within yourself) by acknowledging that you experienced an in-the-moment trigger and became activated. Sometimes, as in Kristin's case, a short discussion of a similarity between the two of you (such as unrelenting standards) may be useful. Sometimes just acknowledging to the client that an internal event happened for you is sufficient. Under no circumstances that I can think of would it have been useful to share my activated state-dependent memory of having hit a little girl with my bicycle.
6. Develop a relational interweave that restimulates processing, without necessarily sharing the content of what you discovered in yourself.
7. Get out of the way and begin bilateral stimulation again.

9.4 Linking Countertransference to Vicarious Traumatization

Pearlman and Saakvitne have written about the causal connection between implicitly defending against vicarious traumatization and countertransference (1995, p. 322). Imagine this scenario: You are in Phase 3, the trauma activation sequence, with a client with whom you have done active trauma work before. Your client is describing a particularly horrific experience of childhood abuse. You know what is coming (since this was one of the worst memories listed), and you brace yourself to listen. After a few minutes, you start to feel sleepy (even though you had a good night's sleep). Your mind has seemingly gone into hibernation. You are now dissociated from your client and from yourself. As you notice your inner departure from the relationship, you can acknowledge your feelings to yourself — perhaps you were feeling dread, revulsion, or anger — and your wish not to hear or even know about this painful experience of your client's. Using a compartmentalization strategy as described at the end of Chapter 8 could be sufficient to give you the inner awareness to allow you to reenter your body and the session.

What if your client has noticed and says that you spaced out at a critical moment, and he or she feels hurt and abandoned? You can acknowledge that you indeed spaced out and are back. It is possible that your countertransference response may have mirrored the responses of others who were unable to listen to the client's problem. Imagine suggesting to the client that the two of you start active trauma processing with his or her recognition of your spacing out. As the client processes this event and his or her feelings about it, the therapeutic relationship may very well move into confronting deeper material. Thus, your "mistake" — when handled appropriately by telling the truth and taking responsibility — can become the launching pad for potentiating and processing even more deeply stored disturbing memories. Since this was not the first time someone had not listened to the client, it provides an opportunity to create safety around the old issue. And with safety, processing may associate to older memories. I believe my viewpoint to be quite close to Perlmann and Saakvitne's, only adapted to an EMDR methodology.

Wachtel suggests that

> countertransference reactions could be used to inform us of what the client may be experiencing on more subtle levels. … If one is continually questioning one's motives and actions [as in my monitoring of my somatic reactions] and checking as well to see how what is surmised from within the session compared to what goes on outside, there is also much opportunity to correct and verify one's view and considerably enhance understanding of the patient and his or her difficulties." (Wachtel, 1977, p. 141)

Gelso and Hayes agree that countertransference can be used productively. Learning to use the Clinician Self-Awareness Questionnaire that I have created (see Appendix F) may help you gain insight into these mechanisms. I will warn you, however, that this strategy is very tricky: How do you know that the client's utterances are connected to your activation?

Here is a short example. A client is processing the traumas of being bullied and abused by persons the client perceives as members of another race. While the clinician is affectively attuned, the client utters a racial slur. The clinician has a visible countertransferential moment of distaste. The client observes it and shuts down. The clinician asks what happened. The client acknowledges seeing what appeared to the client as disapproval in the clinician's demeanor. The clinician admits that when the client used the slur, it touched a sore spot. The clinician validates the client's pain and admits that it is hard to hear a racial slur, because that kind of generalization has its roots in trauma.

As long as the client can hear that the clinician feels his or her pain, the clinician can then process this interpersonal moment. What sometimes happens in this situation is that the client starts processing this moment (the one right after clearing the air), and other old state-dependent memories connected to deeper levels of abuse arise (such as being beaten by a parent). Many other results may occur that may not promote productive processing, so let the reader beware!

9.5 Processing Transference Resistance

Occasionally during the treatment of trauma, clients need to talk instead of process during certain sessions. This often happens at the beginning of a session after one in which they processed a major trauma. Although I have noted clients' occasional need to use the next session to debrief from a particularly intense session and take note of other activated associational channels, there are times when this phenomenon appears to be based on an unacknowledged blocking belief that may not be recognized as a manifestation of a transferential reaction. While the reasons why this might happen are as varied as our clients, these resistances are based on the surfacing of dissociated memory networks that are intolerable to the individual but not acknowledged as such.

During the desensitization phase, other material may be stimulated that neither the clinician nor the client is aware of. This material may be projected onto the clinician in a way that appears irrational, because the clinician cannot see a connection to what the client is actually struggling with. Psychoanalysis has an excellent way of explaining this phenomenon. While the client may be aware of positive feelings toward the therapist, there may be a subtler awareness that signals the client to resist processing because something dangerous may occur.

The clinician may not be explicitly perceived as the source of this danger. Yet I would suggest that because of stimulated but still implicit material, the client projects onto the clinician those negative qualities that he or she experienced with other people in his or her life who actually were abusive.

9.6 The Case of Madeline, Continued

As I have stated, at the beginning of treatment, Madeline had made it clear what she did — and did not — want to work on. I recognized that she was telling me that there were past traumas in her life and that she was not ready to deal with them. Respecting her wishes, I carefully went through the first two phases and began the standard protocol for dealing with the trauma of a car accident. Madeline experienced a great amount of relief during desensitization and was able to overcome her fears about driving.

During treatment, Madeline was in excruciating pain over what seemed to be permanent changes in her beloved mate. The example I gave (Chapter 7, p. 112) about sub-protocols shows how intricately memory networks are woven together; yet at the same time some associated networks may be dissociated from consciousness. Madeline was 3 years old when she was left alone with her 1-year-old brother. His uncontrollable crying was one of the core memories that continued to plague her in her present-day relationship with Richard. Even though we thought that we had "completely" reprocessed it, a different theme emerged, relative to being caught off guard.

(The quotation marks around the word *completely* indicate a common phenomenon in EMDR treatment. The target memory might appear finished, meaning it has a SUDS of 0, a VOC of 7, and a clean body scan, but the three-pronged approach may still have dormant associated memory networks that may become activated either in treatment or by current and future life events. This does not equate to failure or misapplication of the protocols; it simply means that other stimuli may activate these channels, calling for more work to be done. Clinicians not familiar with this process may have their failure schemas activated. Keeping in mind that this only really means that there is more work to be done will help clinicians to feel more at ease in dealing with this phenomenon, as I will point out in a clinical example later.)

Madeline's early traumatic memory had many similarities to the problem with Richard. In both cases, she had managed to hold on by means of almost superhuman strength and determination. Although the original event probably saved her when she was struggling for her life after the accident, it now inflamed the current-day precipitant.

Now the situation is this: The man who is the love of her life is not able to overcome his "spells." She feels powerless to help him. Because such feelings are unacceptable to her, she begins to fantasize about running away or committing suicide. She recognizes the irrationality of these thoughts but feels completely trapped by them.

I suggested that perhaps the old trauma when she was caught between her crib and her dresser might be continuing to contribute to her irrational thinking. She was able to grasp the connection, and we returned to reprocessing the crib trauma. During desensitization she began to abreact and released more pain. By the end of the first session of this protocol, her SUDS was a 3.

Madeline arrived at her next session happy that she had done more productive work. She attempted to engage me in talking about some current-life events that troubled her. I asked her how her processing session went from last week, but she insisted on continuing to dialogue. I began to feel more and more uneasy. My body was informing me that there was something going on in Madeline that she was implicitly avoiding. I tried to bring her back to her unfinished work. She resisted. We were now out of alignment and misattuned, and coming dangerously near to a rupture in the working alliance.

Although I was acting in concert with proper methodology, I recognized that I was reacting countertransferentially, based on my own unfinished memories about being controlled by an older woman. I also saw that Madeline and I had become involved in an intersubjective power struggle where I was experiencing her as my controlling mother (my old mental model), and she was implicitly appraising me as another perpetrator. This was our "old stuff." I had a sense that the theme of being caught off guard was being played out in her resistance to continuing to process, but I thought that it would be wiser to address what was happening between us in the moment.

I wondered how to reengage Madeline's interest in processing the rest of her old trauma. I asked her to notice what seemed to be going on between us. She was insightful and said, "You're trying to make me do what I don't want to do, just like my father and brother did." I agreed that I was trying to do just that (return to attunement) and admitted that something more than just following the EMDR protocol might be going on for me. I added that, knowing this, I was once again fully present.

I asked Madeline if it would be all right to process what had just happened between us. She agreed (we returned to co-regulation). We did a set of bilateral stimulation. What came up for her were all the times her father and brother had caught her off guard, and how she had sworn never to let anyone catch her off guard again. We did another set of bilateral stimulation. Madeline said she was surprised that the feeling of being caught off guard had come up at all, because she had been assertive her whole adult life and had made the judicious decision to stop all communication with her father and brother. I replied, "Go with that," and we did another set.

Madeline immediately remembered a telephone call 22 years ago when her brother was mean and vicious to her. She was stunned by this recollection and how it came out of the blue. We continued to process. As she began to release the pain of this old trauma, Madeline spontaneously realized that her transferential projection (these were not her words, naturally) onto me was a reenactment of how vulnerable and off guard she had been when her brother's call came 22 years ago.

She also realized that there were a host of traumatic memories associated with both her father and her brother that remained unprocessed, and that the only man she had ever fully trusted in her life had been her husband — whom she almost lost completely, and who was now incapable of releasing his spells. These spells seemed to "come out of the blue," catching her off guard again. Further, Madeline had implicitly experienced me as the enemy and was not going to let her guard down. This situation had now been detoxified, and we returned to a co-regulated state of mind. She was able to release the pain of being wounded by her brother, for whom she had almost lost her life in the crib trauma, and the pain of his phone call.

Having reprocessed these old traumas, she was able to learn to tolerate her husband's painful spells without being retraumatized. Her thoughts of running away or killing herself vanished completely.

What does this case example have to teach clinicians? First, many old traumas can be hidden in the transference/countertransference matrices. Second, by identifying this process, especially his or her own countertransference reaction, the EMDR clinician may quickly conceptualize the problem both in relational and state-dependent terms and intervene by using a relational strategy. This can take the client right back to the source of the problem, which in this case was a transference resistance to proceeding with working on the crib trauma, because embedded in this trauma was a dissociated memory network of her brother's phone call.

It is extremely important for clinicians to follow the process and not to try to shorten it. Any transference interpretation would have been much less effective in remediating this block. By my identifying my countertransference, relating it to the client's transference, and then setting up a protocol to process the transference, the client's earlier traumas resurfaced by themselves and could be successfully reprocessed. This led to Madeline's developing the ability to tolerate her husband's spells, since they were now unlinked from the old traumas.

9.7 Minimizing Ruptures to the Working Alliance

The clinician new to EMDR might believe that dogmatic adherence to the method requires doing everything possible to make the client process unmetabolized memories. I have a slightly different take. My job is to inform, challenge, and facilitate. When I have fulfilled these requirements, I leave it to my client to decide what to do. My philosophy goes to the issue of "informed consent." I learned the importance of going over risk/benefit issues with my clients. Once I do this, I strongly believe it is the client's right to choose, even if I think they are making a poor choice. I tell them and leave the door open to their doing more work next session or during the next treatment episode.

Gerry is a 57-year-old teacher who was divorced with two children, ages 23 and 20. He had processed a memory of his parents' divorce and its effect on him. He believed that he was finished (his SUDS was 0, his VOC was 7). However, Gerry felt a slight discomfort in his chest. He chose to ignore it, saying it must have been from the chili dog he had eaten a few hours before. He thanked me for all the good work we had done. He refused my offer to process the discomfort in his chest, no less proceed with the three-pronged approach. He was done, and he terminated treatment. A few months later Gerry called asking for another session. The holiday season had come and gone, and his daughter had refused to spend time with him. She said that she could not forgive him for divorcing her mother for another woman. Gerry realized that his vague chest discomfort during the body scan had been his body's way of telling him that he still had remorse over the actions that led to hurting his daughter (this was his unacknowledged heartache over losing his connection with his daughter). He returned for a treatment episode to clear that channel, and to finish his work.

9.8 Repairing Ruptures to the Collaborative Working Alliance

Start by being clear that both you and the client have agreed about goals and respective tasks necessary to acheieve those goals. Then the question becomes, What happened? Research has shown that a typical relational pattern played out in the working alliance goes from high, in the beginning when hope has been instilled by a definition of goals and tasks. There can be no guarantee of success, but this certainly raises the chances, ergo, "hope." Then during the middle parts of treatment, the alliance, though still usually present, drops a bit due to the nature of this part of the work.

At times the nature of the work becomes daunting. The client is suffering. I am affected. I struggle with the best strategy I can offer; the client reacts negatively, but does not verbalize this.

It is necessary to keep the agreement about shared goals and and agreed-upon tasks that each would perform. Equally, it is crucial to "take the pulse of the therapy": Is there productive work going on? (a Phase 8 activity). Are each one of us collaborating on specific tasks? Problems may arise out of a not good enough understanding of EMDR methodology. An example would be when a clinician tries to push his or her agenda on the client, forgetting the golden rule in EMDR: "It's client-centered." The clinician may be anxious to use his or her EMDR skills in the Active Trauma Processing phases of the work. The client may not be ready. He or she may need more resourcing. One resource he or she may need to develop may be an assertive set of strategies to say, "Not Yet"! Reading the client is paramount; then resonating with whatever EMDR strategy is appropriate will help repair the rupture. Here is an easy example of an EMDR clinician wanting to "help the client" rather than take the time to read the signals his client is sending.

(TH) John – Let's start processing your old traumas.
(CL) Mary – I am not ready to, but I can't say this out loud.

Reading these signals correctly is a part of the essence of EMDR being "client-centered." Intruding active trauma work on a client who does not believe and feel they is an example of a possible breach. In "Repairing Alliance Ruptures," Safran, Muran, Samstag, and Stevens (in Norcross, 2002) have done research in this area. They draw these conclusions: Be aware of your client's negative feelings and recognize that the group that is most at risk to be non-assertive in admitting to and constructively dealing with negativity will also be at risk for rupture. Clients who truly do not understand what they are getting into are at risk to have a possible rupture.They suggest that a way of affecting positive change in repairing this rupture is by identifying its origins and manifestations. Open and frank dialogue; reiterating what both have agreed to; and an evaluation of where they are when this ruptures threatens the integrity of the treatment relationship, may be called for.

9.9 Processing Transference Directly

It is important to remember that in the context of EMDR, transference is defined as the activation of the client's state-dependent memories displaced onto the clinician, while countertransference is the activation of the clinician's state-dependent memories, wittingly or unwittingly triggered by the client. The clinician who senses a transferential moment with a client in Phase 4 or Phase 8 could, if it is contextually sound, use the transferential statement to start trauma processing.

This strategy is somewhat delicate. The therapeutic relationship must be sound, and it is wise for the client to have completed at least one protocol so he or she is familiar with the process of EMDR. When these preconditions have been met, and when the clinician is able to notice the transferential statement (and to be certain that it has not activated any state-dependent memories in himself or herself), he or she can instruct the client to just notice the statement, feel it in his or her body, and begin bilateral stimulation.

An example of this kind of situation would be when a client reports during Phase 4 that "nothing happened" and then apologizes for this. I instruct a client who does this to feel the apology in his or her body and invite him or her to notice what happens during a set of bilateral stimulation. Processing this moment will usually reveal shame-based defectiveness schemas with their accompanying old traumas.

This is a personal observation of an intervention I have made, used, and taught time and again. It has not yet been subjected to scientific scrutiny.

9.10 Dealing with Transference/Countertransference Binds

A number of years ago, I recognized a pattern that occasionally occurred between my clients and me, where their state-dependent activations triggered mine. I pondered this relational impasse. It seemed to me that to remain congruent, I needed to communicate my awareness of the problem. When I did, I noticed a positive response from my clients. If I thought through the patterns of misattunement and returned to attunement, my clients appeared genuinely appreciative of my admitting that my own stuff had been activated. They did not ask about the details, nor would I have shared them. What I noticed was that my actions seemed to bring us back into attunement because we had processed the client's awareness of misattunement and I had accepted responsibility for my part. This was the beginning of my thinking about the relational interweave.

9.10.1 The Case of Janice

Janice is a 32-year-old yoga instructor. She is single and lives independently. She was raised Methodist and now follows Eastern spiritual traditions. There is currently no significant other in her life, though she has had long-term positive relationships. Janice has been in treatment for 3 months. Her presenting problems were persistent anxiety and a feeling of burnout.

"Here I am running this health center, and I'm running myself into the ground," she told me.

Janice was born in a southern city and came to New York as an 18-year-old runaway. She describes her parents as constantly fighting. Janice said her father was a corporate executive who seemed rather jovial to the outside world but in reality was a rageful and dominating man who worked and drank constantly and beat his five children (of whom Janice was the fourth). She reported that her mother would abandon the children when this happened. She further describes her mother as a proper southern woman who taught her children manners but was never close to them. Nor were any of the children close to each other. They all went to private schools so that they would not have to associate with "those other kinds of people," as her mother put it. Janice also said that her father blamed everyone else for his misfortunes when the stockholders of the company he worked for blamed him for corporate losses.

Janice had used marijuana and alcohol throughout her early 20s but stopped after getting a DWI at age 24. She realized that she had been abusing these substances to soothe her feelings of anxiety and depression. She also met the criterion for PTSD but had not been aware that her nightmares, intrusive thoughts, avoidance behaviors, hypervigilance, and startle sensitivity were any great shakes. In place of drugs and alcohol, she had developed an Eastern spiritual practice and attended yoga and meditation classes. This is where she met a former client of mine, who became her friend and referred her to me. Janice was 31 when she was referred, and by this time had developed herself from working as a teller at a branch of a large bank to owning and operating a yoga studio with holistic-healing modalities.

During Phase 1, Janice presented as shy and withdrawn. She had great difficulty trusting that I would be fair and honest with her. She kept referring to how her father always seemed to be so decent and likeable at first to others who met him. She did not come out and say it, but the impression was clear that because of her old mental models she expected me to turn on her at any time. Janice's state of mind was always aggressive, sometimes in a taunting manner, though I was not aware of feeling triggered or offended. This was my first acknowledgment (to myself) that Janice had a negative transferential reaction to me. Though I took no interpersonal action, I noted that implicitly there was a trauma issue. It was very hard for Janice even to give me her history. It was only her friend's confidence in me that gave her some degree of trust in me.

Phase 1 lasted for six sessions. Even though Janice was mistrustful of me, I was not aware of any of my state-dependent memories being activated. I even told her that I valued her not trusting me initially since she had gotten such a raw deal from her father. It was then that she asked me for an explanation of EMDR. I believe that my empathy for her state of mind freed her a bit at this point. I took it to mean that an alliance was forming.

Phase 2 took three sessions. Janice was an exceptionally intelligent woman, whose intellect far exceeded her formal education (she was a high school graduate), but she continually challenged my explanation of EMDR, asking for proof of how it worked. Her state of mind had become aggressive, and she asked her questions in a taunting manner. I began to have a primary process fantasy that she was actually daring me to hit her. I felt a little activated and tucked away this information (also) for our future work. Seeing that I was not behaviorally activated, Janice eventually grew more willing and agreeable to accept my explanations as we talked over the current information I had on EMDR treatment effects. It was during the Safe Place exercise that our therapeutic relationship became stronger and our working alliance truly took hold.

Janice's safe place was in the living room of her apartment with her cat, Sandy, purring on her lap. As we moved through all eight stages of the Safe Place exercise, she went from being quizzical to nearly joyful. Janice stated that this was the first time since running away at 18 that she had the experience of feeling safe and calm. Her hostile, guarded manner seemed to slip away. She was able to tell me her cue word and to use that cue word to bring up her safe place on her own. She was also able to shift to a mildly distressing incident and, without assistance, return to her safe place fully. We went through the rest of Phase 2 without incident and were ready to move into Phase 3. (Sometimes the act of successfully going through the Safe Place experience or RDI creates new and positive memory networks that may strengthen the therapeutic relationship, enabling the clinician and client to be in a coregulated state.) Her DES was 5.7.

By this time, Janice had a good enough understanding of EMDR and had written down her 10 worst memories. She wished to start on memories associated with her mother's abandonment of her. (At this point I was not aware that her taunting manner during Phase 2 had had — and was still having — an effect on me.) The components of the first target memory were

Picture: seeing her mother leave the room when her father would get verbally abusive to John, her oldest brother
Negative cognition: *I am helpless.*
Positive cognition: *I can take care of myself.*
VOC: 3
Emotion: rage, shame, and sadness
SUDS: 8
Body: gut, heart, and arms

Using the standard EMDR protocol, we were able to detraumatize many painful memories relating to Janice's mother's abandonment of her and her siblings. The work proceeded very well until we began to work on setting up protocols to detraumatize her painful memories relating to her father's physical and emotional abuse of her brothers, her sister, and herself.

Up to this point in treatment, we had done excellent work together. Many of the desensitization sessions were quite intense, and Janice had extreme abreactive releases. During debriefing, she reported that she felt supported and safe with me during these times. We were both in states of mind that allowed for continued empathic attunement. (My state-dependent activation in response to her taunting manner was still not in my awareness. I had dissociated it by numbing and forgetting.) On a functional level she was even able to contact her mother and recreate a decent enough relationship, recognizing that her mother did the best she could. This surprised and delighted Janice. It is a good example of improved response flexibility. Our working alliance seemed positive and quite strong, and I was unaware of the possibility that other state-dependent memories were active in me.

When we began to talk about detraumatizing her painful memories about her father, Janice became quite resistant. She knew she had blocking beliefs but could not put into words what they were. She knew that her wounding was quite deep and she would probably experience unpleasant feelings when she processed it. However, since she had already been able to experience deep emotional pain, release it, and develop a relationship with her mother, her resistance was quite perplexing. (Talk about clinician denial?!)

As I probed, she admitted fearing that she would become angry with me because I was a man and we were exploring something very painful that related to an early male figure in her life. (I was still unaware of being in an activated state, but I now wonder if she had picked up on it, and her fear was either an empathic response or a perception that she might be in danger from me.) As we continued to explore her negative transference, Janice admitted that she feared both that she might see me as being judgmental of her and that the work would become too painful and cause her to quit therapy. I remember feeling tightness in my chest. (My learning experience with Janice was what taught me to do continuous body scans on myself during sessions with clients.) Now it was her taunting manner and her "lack of faith in me" (my problem) that triggered me again.

I suggested that we set up a protocol where she would see me being too probing and see herself growing rageful at me. (i.e., processing the transference directly). She asked why. I said that many times these blocks are important cues to the client about deeper issues. She agreed to try this. I asked her what her negative cognition might be and she answered, "I can't stand it." Her positive cognition was "I can tolerate my feelings." Her VOC was 3. When she linked the picture of me probing with her negative belief, her emotions were rage and shame. Her SUDS was 6. She felt a tightening in her stomach and pain in her shoulders.

Within a few sets, Janice's negative transference to me subsided; her SUDS reduced to 0, and her VOC was 7. She was now aware that her feelings were directly related to her father and had "nothing" to do with me, and she was able to make a distinction between how her father reacted to her anger and how I did. After this protocol concluded, I realized (when I reviewed our session) that I had had an angry reaction to what I perceived as her lack of faith in me. So now I was still triggered from her taunting, as well as from this last reaction to her.

We then set up our first protocol to detraumatize a memory of her father beating her. The components were

Picture: her father hitting her with a book
Negative cognition: *I am to blame.*
Positive cognition: *I am innocent.*
VOC: 2
Emotions: rage, sadness, guilt, and shame
SUDS: 8
Body: eyes getting watery, heart beating faster

We began to desensitize this memory. Although we had always used auditory bilateral stimulation, I suggested we try tapping, rationalizing that this was a superior way of using EMDR for this kind of problem. Though Janice initially agreed, she reported that I was tapping too hard, and it was interruptive to her processing. I realized then that I had implicitly reacted to her taunting and "lack of faith" in me in Phase 2. It immediately became clear to me that here I was, a man hitting a woman. I was reenacting the very abuse that we were trying to detraumatize. I did not know the content of the state-dependent memory that had been activated in me, but clearly some of my old stuff was in the way. I acknowledged to Janice that I had been having an experience from my own past. She was grateful that I was being honest and congruent with her. I asked her if she could choose to notice the last pattern of reactions between us. She agreed.

We switched back to the audio box and continued processing. What happened next surprised both of us. Janice began to realize that her father was a product of his early environment, which was in an undeveloped area of the world, and that he could not change. It was not her fault. She became quite sad for him and for herself. With this realization, processing continued smoothly. Later, after desensitization, I would reflect to myself and realize that Janice's taunting had reminded me of when I was a small, undersized boy in junior high school and a girl named Judy, who was tall, big-boned, and muscular, taunted me after having beaten me in an arm-wrestling match. I also realized that Janice's "lack of faith" was my old stuff too. I had been told as a child that I was not bright, but if I tried really hard I could make something of myself. It interests me that by using my awareness abilities flexibly, I was able to notice these dissociated trauma memories.

9.10.2 Projective Identification

It was Melanie Klein, I believe, who first developed the concept of projective identification, where the client projects onto the clinician split-off parts of himself or herself and then acts toward the clinician as though it were the clinician who had the problem. The situation then becomes a reenactment of the client's old core trauma. Janice's provocations about all men being brutal hit a nerve in me that was part of my own state-dependent or unfinished business and caused me, unaware, to act out in session, completing the cycle. However, when she responded that this method of bilateral stimulation was not useful, I recognized my own unwitting participation in her dilemma. By the use of my own self-awareness, I was able to take responsibility and be congruent with her. This allowed us to get back on track. This may seem a minor point, yet admitting one's own human fallibility can be one of the greatest gifts clinicians can give our clients: It allows them to accept their own humanness as well. This brings them into an adaptive state of mind, opening them to see that the present is different from the past.

Phase 5, installation (linking to the adaptive perspective), went smoothly for Janice. Her positive cognition remained "I am innocent," with the VOC starting at 6 (at the beginning of the phase) and going to 7. Janice was surprised and pleased. She expressed her gratitude toward me. I was feeling enjoyment that I had remembered an earlier memory that had been previously held in an unreachable state. I actually felt myself center more.

Phase 6, the body scan (intensive body awareness), seemed to be unremarkable except for a feeling of excitement in Janice's tummy. We did a few sets of audio stimulation. A transformation occurred, and Janice spontaneously started thinking about changes to make in her yoga center. She knew she was ready to delegate responsibility. She reported this sensation as growing stronger at first, and then settling into a nice calm state. I think this was her body's acknowledgment of her emotional transformation through a physiological release of residual held tension.

Janice had a feeling of elation during the debriefing phase at our success in overcoming a difficult hurdle. We talked about my tapping during the desensitization phase. Janice remarked that this was unusual because we had always used audio tones before. I told her that I had gotten caught up in something in my head and was not acting consciously. (There did not seem to be any productive reason to share the specific issues of my countertransference; simply admitting that I was off in my handling of the situation seemed to be sufficient. It also did not seem necessary to explore her feelings about this since we had surmounted the obstacle and moved on). The point to be made here is that what matters most is not our reactions, but what we what we do with our reactions.

The reevaluation phase was unremarkable. Janice had kept her log, and it showed thoughtful questions about what influences her father had had to live through. It also showed more processing and the beginning feelings of forgiveness for him. Her issues about other instances of beatings were our next targets. Her positive cognition was significant: She spontaneously came up with "I am learning to forgive him," further evidence of continuing response flexibility.

After reprocessing all her old traumas, we then processed the present day referent of her exhausting herself in the yoga studio, thus never having time for a relationship. What was remarkable was that another short channel opened up. This had to do with an implicit identification with her father's workaholism and her implicit fears of being a "failure" like he was. This issue of hers was reprocessed quickly as she could spontaneously make a past–present separation of her being different, and acting differently than her father, now that she had completed most of her work. We installed the future template of her delegating responsibilities, and I had her practice this shift for two sessions, while she became more comfortably social. Once she had completed these activities we were ready for termination.

9.11 An Important Empathic Interweave

I would be remiss if I were to give you the impression that I am the only clinician in the EMDR world who uses himself to promote productive adaptive information processing. Jerry Lamangne, LCSW, a student of Diana Fosha and her accelerated experiential dynamic psychotherapy, related the following vignette.

A client was looping around an issue of defectiveness. Nothing seemed to be moving this fixated, irrational belief. Jerry had a solid and positive therapeutic relationship with the client and was clearly in empathic attunement with him. He also felt profound compassion for him. Jerry asked the client what he noticed when he looked directly at Jerry. The client reported that he could feel Jerry's compassion. This helped him make a present/past distinction, using positive transference and Jerry's integrity (Jerry would not have had the client do this unless he was clear in himself that he held the client and his abilities in high esteem). The client was moved by this moment of mental state resonance, and he shifted. Jerry then assisted the client to process this new information, and the client took further steps to healing.

While Jerry also named this intervention a relational interweave, I think of it more as an important empathic interweave. (Whichever term works for you is fine with me.) What ties both kinds of interventions together is the use of the therapeutic relationship to link a functional, adaptive neural network to a dysfunctional one and thus enable a return to productive trauma processing. Our use of self can positively affect the outcome of treatment.

Phase 5 Through Phase 8: Installation (Linking to the Adaptive Perspective), the Body Scan (Intensive Body Awareness), Closure (Debriefing), and Reevaluation

10.1 Completing Phase 4

So, are we done yet? No, but we are getting there. Even though the client has hypothetically released all the pain of his or her trauma, he or she has not fully integrated a more adaptive way of regarding what happened. This is a very important moment for client and clinician. Before proceeding to Phase 5, installation, which I term *integrating the adaptive perspective,* the clinician must be sure that the client really has released all his or her old pain. In my practice, this is another case where I use myself as a barometer. When the client informs me that his or her SUDS is 0, and I have a clean body scan of my own, I am apt to think that the client really has finished the Phase 4 work. If, however, I sense any discomfort in my body, then I take the introspective approach and focus on my inner sensations. Sometimes I may realize that the discomfort is a state-dependent memory activated in me, and that the client really is done. In that case, it is time to move on to Phase 5, and I will take care of what has been activated in me later, on my own time.

Another common occurrence toward the end of Phase 4 is my sensing that the client needs more healing than he or she wants for himself or herself. For example, a 35-year-old man named Chuck had just finished working on a cluster of memories dealing with his father's physical and emotional abuse. We accessed the original incident and processed it. It was clean: His

SUDS was 0. Then I accessed all known associational channels, such as his memory of his father yelling at him while they were at Yankee Stadium, and we processed this channel. Afterward, Chuck said it was clean. I didn't buy it. I may not have had a reason I could put my hands on, but something in his presentation was off. How did I know? I can't say for sure, but when I scan my body and I am clear about not being activated, I use my body as a barometer. Using my body reactions is in keeping with Shaw's concept of the "lived body paradigm" (2003). What do I do when I sense something is incomplete? My guideline is, when in doubt, talk it out. So Chuck and I did, and he told me that my judgment was off. Maybe I was, maybe I wasn't. Without overwhelming data to support my hunch, I went with his assessment. I knew that I would have another checkpoint in Phase 6.

In Chuck's case, I was not off. As it turned out, he had residual tension in his toes, which he became aware of during the body scan. When we processed this sensory motor experience, a dissociated memory came into his consciousness, having to do with his father's humiliation of Chuck's sister on the evening of her prom. Chuck remembered standing there as a help-less 5-year-old, digging his toes into the carpet as his father instructed his sister's prom date on "proper etiquette," telling the boy that if he found that he had had sex with his daughter, he would kill him. How did I know that Chuck was not really done with this cluster of memories? I am still not sure, but what I am sure of is that I have done enough of my own growth work to trust my bodily reactions, and in this case my gut felt uneasy.

10.2 Entering Phase 5

Now is the time in treatment when I ask if the positive cognition that the client and I started with still fits. I have found in over half my cases that the positive cognition shifts. Shapiro writes,

> After initial processing has been achieved — with the accessed tar-get emerging at no greater than a SUDS rating of 0 or 1 — the installation phase begins. Installation concentrates primarily on the full integration of a positive self-assessment with the targeted infor-mation. This phase is used to enhance the positive cognition and to link it specifically with the original target issue or event. Since all of the information should have shifted during processing, the positive cognition is checked for both applicability and current validity. (2001, p. 160)

One of the biggest strengths of using the standard methodology during active trauma work is that it provides for repeated checks on whether the client has actually made progress in releasing the pain of state-dependent memories. I check to make sure that the SUDS is 0 (this is always my goal, unless it is impossible ecologically, as in a case where a parent loses a child or a combat veteran kills someone in battle and carries the burden of his action throughout his life), and I check that the VOC is 5 or above. I usually will challenge my client (by asking, "What prevents it from being a 7?") if the VOC is not at least 6. The reason is simple. During 14 years of EMDR practice, I have found that a VOC of 5 or less is usually an indication of an untapped associational channel related to the traumatic event. Alternatively, it could point to the client's holding a blocking belief related to the traumatic situation.

Chuck's experience of his father yelling at him at Yankee Stadium happened much later than his initial physical trauma. In this case, the client may be in a state of mind that is unrelated to the older trauma because a different developmental epoch is not accessible. An example of this would be when a client says something like "I believe I'm all clear" but does not have any memories of a significant part of his or her childhood due to negative psychoform dissociation. In situations like this, Shapiro's systematic checks and balances will provide the clinician with pertinent information on more work to be done.

Many novice EMDR clinicians have reported to me that they must be doing something wrong when the VOC is 5 or less, even though their fidelity to the method is high. I simply let them know that this is part of the human condition. We can only follow the method and notice what occurs next. Empowering my consultees to be in the moment without harsh self-judgment helps them continue to follow the client's process until the client truly is finished. When a simple explanation is insufficient, I will ask the consultee to reflect on what state-dependent memories might be being stirred up in him or her at the moment. When asked respectfully, the consultee is empowered to search himself or herself for internal blocks that thwart him or her from becoming even more effective. I then teach the consultee preparation and compartmentalization strategies.

10.3 Madeline's Case, Continued

The initial installation phase of Madeline's crib trauma was challenging (this was before we revisited it in relation to her feeling caught off guard by Richard's spells). Her positive cognition[1] was "I am a survivor" and her VOC was stuck at 5. You may remember that I postponed getting the PC and VOC from Madeline in Phase 3 of one of the protocols because her verbal and analytic abilities completely deactivated her. However, I always include the PC and VOC at the beginning of Phase 5. I asked, "What prevents your positive cognition from being a 7?" At first she was unsure. Then she said, "That's as good as it's going to get." At this point I noticed my gut speaking to me; my body was not accepting Madeline's statement. I asked her to review the crib trauma in all its aspects. Still she could find nothing that bothered her. I probed more, and she began defending her mother's absence from the house that day by saying, "She was sitting outside the apartment building with neighbors."

That gave me a clue. I wondered if Madeline had implicit abandonment issues related to her mother. Now, a good psychoanalyst might be tempted to continue to explore this area of her "psyche." I find exploring the psyche to be of lesser value. Instead, using the clues from my body and the wisdom of the EMDR standard methodology, I had Madeline process what she had just told me. In this moment I was not abandoning her; I was in empathic attunement with her. Madeline began associating to an old swimming memory. She was afraid of the water. Her mother coaxed her to try swimming in the deep end of the pool while she held her afloat. Suddenly Madeline flinched. "My mother let go of me. I thought I was going to drown," she said. Then tears rolled down her face as she remembered her mother's last days. She had been attentive to her mother's needs, while her father and brother were not.

Madeline realized that she had a blocking belief that prevented retrieval: *I'm a bad person if I say anything bad about my mother.* This belief was tied to her still-fixated unrelenting standards schema, as well as her genuine love for her mother. She then processed this awareness, and spontaneously the more adaptive states of mind linked in. Madeline said that she had made a superhuman effort to keep her mother comfortable during her last days. With this awareness she was able to allow that her mother was human and meant well. She also realized that she could have feelings and criticisms about her mother's being less than perfect. Processing this piece led Madeline to the realization that she could still be a good person and be less than perfect. From here she was able to process this associational channel to a SUDS of 0. I then asked about her positive cognition. She changed it from "I'm a survivor" to "I am a good enough person." (For a person with an unrelenting standards schema and an abandonment schema, this positive cognition hit a home run.) Her VOC was now a full 7, and it became 7+ after three sets of installing her positive cognition.

When the client's VOC is 6 or when the client's VOC is lower than a 6, the instruction is to link the positive cognition to the original event. Shapiro instructs clinicians to be general in asking this question, rather than repeating the memory or the initial picture, because a more pertinent image may have emerged spontaneously. I am in agreement with this. The clinician then instructs the client to hold the original incident together with the current positive cognition, and a few short sets of bilateral stimulation are applied. Suffice it to say, this appears to amplify the positive cognition and feeling state (similar to what happens to the client in the Safe Place exercise in Phase 2). In the majority of cases that I have handled or consulted on, the client will usually have a VOC of 6 or higher when trauma processing is completed down to a SUDS of 0. What usually follows is a strengthening of the adaptive position.

I have found that a certain pattern continues to repeat itself at the end of Phase 4 and the beginning of Phase 5. This pattern is the client's recognition of what he or she believes to be true now that state-dependent memories are no longer interfering with his or her thought processes. This is the adaptive perspective emerging, and it usually happens spontaneously. When it does not, I review my trauma case conceptualization form with my client and ask if the positive cognitions the client stated that he or she wished to believe about himself or herself still fit.

Although this is the same question that participants at EMDR trainings are instructed to ask the client, there are two basic differences: First, I ask for the positive cognitions up front in Phase 1, and by doing so avoid interfering with the client's entry into state-dependent memory during the trauma launch sequence when verbal defenses or confusion about the protocol may interfere with the launch. Second, the client's positive cognition shifts just as often from the desired self-belief he or she articulated during Phase 1 as it does from a desired self-belief presented during Phase 3.

Many times my client and I discover that the information was there all along, held separately in another memory network that was too weak to connect to the state-dependent memories stored dysfunctionally. This is what happened in Mary's case. Mary was 47 years old, with three children, ages 15, 12, and 9, and a doctorate in education. Mary grew up with fairly insecure attachments and without a good enough sense of herself. When her husband left her for another woman after a marriage of 19 years, Mary was devastated. She berated herself for not being smart enough or pretty enough. Her husband had been a salesman with a good deal of charm and had cheated on Mary throughout their marriage. After Mary finished Phase 4, she spontaneously said, "I am a good enough person. I'm smart, and I'm pretty, and I deserve to love and be loved." This was different from the positive cognition Mary had started with. So how did she come to this realization?

It was there all the time. In fact, she had admitted it several times during our history taking sessions. Mary cried in despair during those times because what her rational left brain knew to be true could not be felt by her emotional right brain. The release of her painful state-dependent memories allowed her to make this connection spontaneously and ener-getically. The same was true of Stephanie, who was raped by her father and grandfather in her family home. She knew when we began treatment that her life was good, and that she was safe. But after the removal of the pain of her traumas, she stopped having nightmares and could fully feel and experience her aliveness.

Many times a client will go through the storms of trauma processing and come to new realizations. In the case of Janice, she recognized that it was her need to control everything that went on in her yoga studio that was preventing her from having the time to make a commitment to a rela-tionship. She realized that her need to control was an implicitly driven trauma trait based on her need to avoid her father's beatings. In the case of George, he recognized that he could be honest and straightforward with people because not everyone was like his verbally abusive father.

10.4 Increased Functionality: Proof of Reprocessing

It is not enough for a client to have a healing shift in session, even if it lasts for a few days afterward. The proof of the pudding is in the eating. In EMDR our goal is that the client's ability to live in the world not only improves but remains improved. Having a positive belief with a VOC of 7 is nice. Having that VOC remain a 7 during the reevaluation at the start of the following session is very nice. Having a permanent change in a charac-ter trait to one that is more adaptive and allows for a more robust life is more than very nice. It is proof of increased response flexibility, and it marks the end point of EMDR treatment. All along the way, throughout the eight phases, the clinician continues diagnostically to check the work. At the end of Phase 5, we rejoice with the client for having surmounted internal obstacles to living a full life. This rejoicing should not be confused with believing that the job is complete. All we have done up to this point is to have been successful in detraumatizing a painful memory. We cannot yet be sure that the improvement is permanent.

This is a crucial point. Please do not confuse progress with magic. The wise EMDR clinician remains circumspect, continually checking and rechecking, both during and in between sessions, waiting to see if treat-ment effects hold. Remember, Madeline and I thought that we had finished with her crib trauma, only to find that there were other associated memory networks that had been dissociated until a present-day event, Richard's spells, activated them. Phase 6, the next part of EMDR treat-ment, adds a check on bodily sensations present when the new cognition is held in mind. Here the client and clinician have another chance to assess whether unprocessed trauma remains.

10.5 Phase 6: Listening to the Body

So many trauma survivors have lost touch with their bodies that pain is the only sensation they recognize. So says David R. Hubbard, Jr., in his foreword to Gay and Katherine Hendricks' *At the Speed of Life: A New Approach to Change in Body-Centered Therapy* (1993). There is a good reason for this. In his seminal paper from the neurosciences, "The Body Keeps the Score," van der Kolk supports the notion that the body holds old traumas (1994). Full healing requires that the body release its painful state-dependent memories.

Paying attention to the body of the client is not a new idea at all. Fritz Perls wrote about this in 1951 in his book *Gestalt Therapy* (Perls, Hefferline, & Goodman, 1951). One of the exercises he regularly had his clients perform was oriented to body awareness. In Part 1 of his book, he gave clear instructions on techniques of body awareness. His instructions read

> Concentrate on your "body" sensation as a whole. Let your attention wander through every part of your body. How much of yourself can you feel? To what degree and with what accuracy and clarity does your body — and thus you — exist? Notice pains, aches and twinges ordinarily ignored. What muscular tension can you feel? Attending to them, permit them to continue and do not attempt prematurely to relax them. Try to shape their precise limits. Notice your skin sensations. Can you feel your body as a whole? Can you feel where your head is in relation to your torso? Where are your genitals? Where is your chest? Your limbs? (p. 86)

In EMDR we assist our clients to become aware of their body sensations throughout the eight phases.

The purpose of Phase 6 is to investigate whether any trauma remains in the body so it, too, can be processed. This phase is a diagnostic relational check as well. Shapiro's instructions to the client for this phase are as follows:

> Close your eyes and keep in mind the original memory and the positive cognition. Then bring your attention to the different parts of your body, starting with your head and working downward. Any place you find any tension, tightness, or unusual sensation, tell me. (2001, p. 162)

I go through the same process as my client and notice if my body informs me of any memory networks that have become activated in me. If there are any, I go into an introspective mode to discover what is coming up for me. When it is my own old stuff, unrelated to the client's trauma, I take note of it so I can work on it later. There are times, though, when I recognize an associated channel of the client's that has not been explicitly dealt with. When this happens, but the client has reported no disturbance, I bring up that incident as a gentle challenge. It has been my experience that if the channel actually has been processed implicitly, the client will just shrug. When the client becomes reactivated (which is usually apparent on a sensory motor level), we both know we have more work to do. The client may not always want to keep processing. That is his or her right, although I do inform the client that unprocessed memories could cause continued problems in the present.

According to the standard methodology, when the client reports any sensations, he or she is instructed to open his or her eyes, and a short set of bilateral stimulation is done. Sometimes what arises is the unconscious holding of residual tension, even though the trauma work seems to be done. When the situation is as straightforward as that, the tension seems to dissolve quickly. I am not sure why that is, but I believe that implicit processing continues and is potentiated with a few short sets.

There are also times when the client notices positive sensations during the body scan, as in the case of Janice. Her pleasant sensations indicated that she felt excitement at the thought of no longer having to control everything at work and from believing that she could now have a relationship. In this case, a few shorts sets of bilateral stimulation seemed to strengthen her adaptive associations.

However, there are times when doing the body scan provides client and clinician with evidence of untapped associational channels of trauma that have been dissociated from consciousness. This is why Phase 6 is crucial. It is another of EMDR's excellent checks and balances, as I first learned when I was still relatively new to EMDR. Let me share a startling vignette from those days that informed and strengthened the way I practice EMDR.

10.6 The Case of Tricia

Tricia was a 42-year-old health care worker with an adopted daughter. She came to treatment because of problems in her marriage. It became evident during history taking that Tricia's problems began very early in life with profound issues of abuse and neglect. Both her parents were alcoholics and irresponsible with Tricia and her siblings. As an adult, Tricia was clean and sober, and she went to church every Sunday. She had no medical problems. This was her first treatment experience. We went through Phase 1 and Phase 2 in three sessions. Tricia's safe place was by an altar at her church. She scored 5 on her DES. There were no contraindications to moving immediately to Phase 3 work.

Tricia chose to work on a memory of being 13 years old and having to line up every Sunday morning with her siblings to be questioned harshly by their father on their homework assignments. Tricia trembled at the thought of being called on and scrutinized during these inquisitions. These were the components:

> Picture: standing against the wall, seeing her father's angry face, and smelling the alcohol coming from his pores
> Negative cognition: *I am stupid.*
> Positive cognition: *I'm fine just as I am.*
> VOC: 3
> Emotion: fear
> SUDS: 7
> Body: pit of stomach

Many memories and associations to her father's harsh ways surfaced. Tricia also had a number of abreactive experiences. After a few processing sessions, she seemed to be finished. Her SUDS was 0. Her positive cognition had changed to "I am an intelligent woman." Phase 5 work seemed uneventful. Her beginning VOC was 6, and after a few sets of bilateral stimulation, it went to 7.

During the body scan Tricia noticed a pinching sensation in her right shoulder. She was so happy with her progress that she initially dismissed this sensation and was ready to move to Phase 7. I let Tricia know that something did not feel right about allowing the pinching in her shoulder to go unprocessed. Fortunately, she and I had had a deep treatment experience of almost continuous mental state resonance, so I was able to convince her to go along with the process. We did a set of bilateral stimulation.

It was a good thing that I had been faithful to the protocol. Tears immediately started streaming down Tricia's face. A dissociated memory had come back. She was 4 years old. She had awoken at 3 a.m. and was unable to fall back to sleep. When she went to her parents' bedroom, it was empty. Tricia then turned on the lights and searched for her parents. She discovered that she was alone in the house with her two younger siblings. She was petrified but was able to keep her wits about her. Her grandparents lived close by and babysat for the children regularly. Their telephone number was written on a sheet on the refrigerator. Tricia called her grandparents, crying out for help. They immediately realized what had happened. Her grandmother drove right over to the house to comfort Tricia. Her grandfather went to the bar where he knew his son and daughter-in-law would be drinking. He raised holy hell with them, and they were quite embarrassed despite being drunk. The grandfather drove Tricia's parents home, then he and Tricia's grandmother left. Tricia's father was enraged at her. He grabbed her by her right shoulder and pinched it — right where she noticed the residual tension during her body scan.

Tricia and I processed this and a few other dissociated memories attached to it that emerged at this part of the treatment, until they all had SUDS of 0. We then reinstalled her positive cognition, "I am an intelligent woman" (and a very smart little girl, I thought). Her VOC started at 7 and became, in Tricia's words, a 7+. Now when we repeated her body scan, it was clean. She had fully reprocessed her traumas. Was my reaction a countertransferential moment? I would say no, though the totalistic camp might disagree. My body is where I live, as Shaw reminds us. When I am clear, it is my most important ally. My body awareness informs me when something is going on, and it does not always have to be an activation of my old state-dependent memories. That is why I believe that Gelso and Hayes' conception of integrative countertransference is superior to both the classical and the totalistic views of countertransference. My body awarenesses are ways in which I can productively use myself as a barometer of what may be going on beneath the layers of conscious awareness.

This very valuable lesson taught me to coach my clients during trauma processing to "feel what that feels like in your body." Time and time again I have found that going to the sensations in the client's body (as long as good enough boundaries have been established in the therapeutic relationship) will yield even deeper levels of trauma. These can be reprocessed on the spot.

10.7 Phase 7: Closure (Debriefing)

I interpret Phase 7 as debriefing. To me, this term captures the thrust of this phase and highlights some of its actions. I have had more incomplete processing sessions in my practice than complete ones. EMDR is suggested as a 90-min procedure. Due to logistics, insurance, and scheduling problems, however, my clients and I sometimes do 45- or 60-min sessions. Although a traumatic memory may be fully processed during this abbreviated time, often I have to move from Phase 4 directly to Phase 7 in order to close down an incomplete session. When a session is incomplete, it is not appropriate to go through Phase 5 and Phase 6. (I wish I had a nickel for every time a consultee reported on an incomplete session, only to add, "The SUDS was 3, the VOC a 4, and the body scan revealed lots of activations.") The only exception to this is when the client remains in a state of negative arousal. In this case, one strategy is to develop a bridging positive cognition (a Phase 5 task), such as "I am learning to cope with my feelings." I then install that positive statement as a resource for the client to use between sessions. It is important to note that this bridging cognition must be in concert with the client's consciousness.

I have also experienced clients' reactions to unfinished sessions. They vary from, "Boy, this was a great experience" to "Not much happened, I guess this method isn't for me." In the former situation, I first rejoice with my client and validate his or her progress. Then I ask what prevents the SUDS from being 0. This question usually prompts my client to think about the work that remains. The latter situation is a bit more challenging. When I was less experienced in EMDR, I would feel anxiety in my gut, and my defectiveness schemas became activated. Now I have learned to stay centered and spend time reviewing the session with my client. We may find that there has been productive processing going on, but it actually made the client feel more uncomfort.

In these cases I explain again that activating painful memory networks may cause a temporary shift into greater discomfort. When this has occurred, asking the client to go to his or her safe place or using another form of soothing guided imagery enables him or her to get back on an even keel. I also emphasize the importance of journaling during the week, either by using the "TICES" format (T = trigger, I = image, C = cognition, E = emotion, S = sensations; recommended by Shapiro, 2001, p. 429) or sometimes the SUDS rating. It is an excellent way of staying in an EMDR format. There are other methods of staying aware. In this age of technology, I invite clients to email me their thoughts during the week. It takes no time for me to download their email and reply that I received it. That is all that I do in response, other than let them know that we will talk about it at the beginning of our next session. Some clinicians may find this procedure intrusive. I do not, but I would not recommend using it unless you are comfortable with it. I have found that clients feel a stronger connection to me outside of session. This connection becomes even more important while engaging in the active trauma-processing phases of EMDR. With my more dysfunctionally regulated clients, I usually will set a limit of two emails per week. This group of clients has the potential to abuse the privilege. Setting a clear boundary with them lets them know I am here for them, but only to a certain point. I also will instruct them to do homework assignments to strengthen their containment skills. So I give a little, and I require that they do their own work outside of session.

I have learned over the years that the suggestions I make for enhancing my clients' here-and-now experiences and safely closing down state-dependent memories must be offered gently. I have also found that common instructions, such as journaling, are enhanced through the use of structured questions:

1. What was the most important part of the session for you?
2. What was the most challenging part?
3. What lessons did you learn from today's session?
4. What action are you willing to take this week to honor your new learnings?

These questions also seem to concretize what they have gained and help focus them on the next steps they need to take on their own behalf.

10.8 Phase 8: Reevaluation

I often call Phase 8 "the forgotten phase." I have mentioned earlier that for treatment effects to be as robust as possible, all eight phases are necessary (Maxfield & Hyer, 2002). Do not skip this phase! Reevaluation takes place at the beginning of every session that follows a trauma-processing session. It provides important information to the clinician and reestablishes alignment — and hopefully attunement — with the client. The first question to ask, after saying hello, is, "What came up for you this week?" It is crucial to get an initial take on the client's state of mind in relation to what was processed and to find out what external events occurred or are coming up.

This is the first of the three goals of Phase 8. The next is to determine whether treatment effects have held during the week (and whether the client has noticed gains). Sometimes asking the client about what he or she has noticed since the previous session elicits the response, "I don't really remember what we worked on." This can indicate the presence of dissociation, which in certain circumstances leads me to be initially cautious. The clinician should ask himself or herself what the client might be explicitly avoiding or what implicit processes might be going on that he or she is truly unaware of.

Because I usually use the eye scan, audio scan, or TheraTapper when doing Phase 4, my hands are free to record what the client is saying or doing. (I stop this activity if I feel that I am alienating the client, or he or she seems to need closer coaching during a rather fragile time.) This means that when a client says he or she cannot remember what we worked on in the last session, I can read it back to him or her. Most clients seem genuinely grateful that I have paid such close attention. Doing this also gives me a read on the client's current state of mind. If I begin reading my notes and the client stops me, saying, "Oh yes, I remember now," I can segue into asking what comes into his or her mind *now* that represents the target memory. In this way, processing can recommence swiftly and effortlessly. If, however, I read back the last session and the client has only partial or no memory of it, I must consider whether a more serious underlying dissociative disorder has been stimulated, which we would need to deal with first. This can be the case even after I have done my due diligence by using the DES screening questionnaire during Phase 2.

It is also vital to ask the client directly, "Tell me what it was like to share the experience you had last week with me now." In the previous session, an experience happened that affected both the client and clinician. The client needs to be invited to share how that was for him or her. For instance, a common response from clients is, "I was amazed that I could feel your presence and your coaching, and feel so safe with such horrible memories." This is usually a very gratifying experience, because sometimes the feedback will be critical, such as the comment I mentioned earlier from a female client who told me, "I got distracted by your diagonal movements with your arm. When it came down it was right over your private parts."

When a client has a criticism, it is important for both the client and clinician that the clinician listen and validate that he or she heard and is affected by the feedback. Clients are often on target. I thank them for what they have shared with me, and I adjust and become introspective. There are times when a client and I are having different experiences. I always start by validating that I have taken to heart what he or she is saying. There are also times when I have a different point of view. I ask permission to share it. If permission is given, I do.

It often happens that a client experiences himself or herself as stuck and thinks the process is not working. I may tell the client that although he or she did not show signs of dissociation during the preparation period, he or she dissociated when associating to the very first time, for example, his or her father had to be hospitalized psychiatrically. I let the client know that the process of dissociating to a very specific topic shows how intensely he or she was affected by it. If the client accepts this new information, we have gained a common understanding of his or her process, and our relationship is strengthened. From here we can go right back to processing, or we can spend some time working on resources to be developed or installed to assist the client with processing this part of the memory. Once we have been successful in stabilizing the client's awareness of the present–past duality, trauma processing may again begin.

I have found that clients usually have little trouble, especially when prompted, in giving feedback at the beginning of the next session. This important moment offers them the opportunity to let the clinician know what did not feel good intersubjectively. For example, the client might say, "Your coaching seemed to distract me, even though I knew you meant well and you saw me suffering." This allows me to fine-tune my relationship with the client during our next trauma-processing session.

Conversely, when I ask for feedback, clients are implicitly given encouragement to ask me how I experienced them. When there has been a successful session (whether it was complete or not), I can validate their experience and help with integration by saying something like, "I experienced myself deeply resonating with your processing." This validation empowers clients to go more deeply into their experience.

There are times when I will respond to a client's request for feedback with observations such as, "I noticed that your jaw was quivering as you were processing the memory of your mother slapping you in the face. My impression was that you were on the edge of a major release, but held on. This is what I sensed when I saw your jaw quivering." If I am not accurate, my client will simply shrug it off. When I am accurate, he or she usually appreciates my attunement. Often the client experiences rearousal. When this happens, we usually just start there. I will say something like, "Just notice your jaw quivering and allow a feeling of safety to be present. Nod when you get that." When the client nods, we have a combination of activation of state-dependent memories and interpersonal affect tolerance. Beginning bilateral stimulation in that moment restarts the brain's processing abilities on a deeper level.

When re-arousal has not been triggered by our discussion, but processing was incomplete the week before, the client and clinician must decide where to start processing again. It is especially important to keep in mind that EMDR calls for finishing one protocol before starting another. (If the client's associations to the previous week's work take you far afield, write them down as work to be done later; do not restart processing with them.) I take the client back into state-dependent memory by asking, "When you bring up the original incident, what do you get now?" This is one exception to the general rule of EMDR being client-centered. Here I am jumping out of my co-participatory role and sharing my expertise, explaining that experience has taught me that it is better to do things in a certain order.

If, however, the clinician has done his or her due diligence, and the client still wishes to start somewhere other than with the unfinished protocol, the clinician would be wise to avoid a potential rupture to the working alliance and instead to go where the client wants. Sometimes the wisdom of the client is superior, and the client may end up reprocessing something even more important in the moment. At other times, clients may become flooded because of how many old memories have been activated but not fully processed. When this happens, I help them ground themselves, and we discuss again the need to finish one protocol before starting the next.

This experience usually helps the client see the wisdom of following EMDR methodology.

10.9 Flexibility in the Methodology

One of the reasons why we talk about a treatment plan (or action plan) in EMDR is to differentiate who is coming for symptom relief and who is coming for comprehensive treatment. The difference may be seen by comparing a client of 9/11 to a person with many past traumas who wants to release and reprocess old state-dependent memories. However, clients may start in one place and finish someplace else. Working on a seemingly compartmentalized problem may re-associate with deeper partially dissociated material. This is the nature of free association (in analytic terms) or activation of associated memory networks (in information-processing terms). Protocols have been developed especially to compartmentalize certain problems. By charting where a client starts and where he or she progresses to, the clinician will continue to get clues to deeper patterns of response. This is one of the reasons that Jeffrey Young's Schema-Focused Questionnaire is so useful. It helps clinicians draw a nonbiographical sketch that we will eventually flesh out with specific memories attached to the client's schemas.

The use of EMDR in trauma processing helps to make the implicit explicit. When a client has reprocessed state-dependent memories, these memories transform into declarative memories. The client has released state-dependent sensations and is on the healing path. Think about this. To be on the healing path is no small accomplishment. For EMDR to enable a client to accomplish this task is magnificent.

There are also different ways of dealing with similar sorts of problems. Not every problem presented in an EMDR session will require the same strategies to facilitate healing. Take the example of dealing with blocking beliefs such as Madeline and Michael had. With Madeline, cognitive interweaves did not seem to effect a positive shift, so I enabled her to floatback to the original trauma, set up a protocol (because of how deactivated she could become), and process the old memory. Michael had a very similar blocking belief, but in his case I became triggered because he was not doing what I wanted him to do (grieve the death of Toto). In his case, I had a countertransferential moment that contributed to shutting down the processing. By using a relational interweave, we were able to regain a state of co-regulation. From that point he was able to see me differently from other authority figures in his life (i.e., his mother), and that awareness allowed him to release his blocking belief and let go of the pain of both losses (his father and Toto).

One of the messages I am trying to convey is that it is important to think about how different clients will affect us, and that knowing the relationship issues and developing different strategies will lead more readily to healing than to believe that EMDR is supposed to be followed "religiously" and "by the book." Know the methodology, and don't ever stop being yourself as a clinician. Many novice EMDR clinicians believe that they somehow have to give up their identities. You don't. There are as many paths to travel as there are clients to treat, and rational improvisation is the hallmark of a good relational EMDR clinician. (This does not imply that anything goes! Getting a history, preparing the client, setting up the target memories, processing them, installing positive cognitions, and doing a body scan, closure, and reevaluation are all necessary, as is using the three-pronged protocol.) No reasonable EMDR clinician would prescribe a Procrustean bed for himself or herself and the client to lie upon. This is where the interpersonal and intersubjective come in. A well-established therapeutic relationship is the primary vehicle for successful treatment. How EMDR is introduced and practiced must be within the parameters of the therapeutic relationship.

This relationship takes a few sessions to establish, since a client is likely to test the clinician, explicitly and implicitly, in a variety of ways. Horvath and Bedi found (in Norcross, 2002) in synthesizing the research state, "that there is evidence indicating that establishing a strong alliance early in therapy is important. Alliance measured between the third to fifth session has proven to be a consistent predictor of final therapy outcome" (p. 55). Clients appear to feel safe when the clinician is empathically attuned to them and offers some ideas about how they might use their time together. My clients bring their problems and agree to pay me for my time. I bring myself, with all my years of experience and training. I set rules about missed sessions and other boundary issues. I do not promise that I will see someone for the trauma-processing phases of EMDR. I promise that I will see the person for a consultation, which is usually a double session. I am known for practicing EMDR, so many callers ask for it specifically. I politely tell them that we will have to decide together which way to work, depending on what they want to work on.

Actually, when I think about it, all clients come to the clinician because they are stuck over something in their lives — so why not introduce these ideas in the initial sessions, as the relationship is being established? Why not ask about negative self-referencing beliefs in the first session? The answers will be indicators of the client's ability to self-reflect. (Clients who completely externalize their problems will not be able to do trauma processing initially.) My experience is that clients are happy to tell the clinician what their troubles are. And I am happy to be their guide and companion as they heal their problems and discover that they can live fuller, more authentic lives than they had ever imagined. In fact, I am more than happy. I am honored by their trust in me.

Even though I advise EMDR clinicians to be as thorough as possible, clients do end treatment before all the work is done. My best advice to the clinician is not to lose heart. When the work has been good, all that is needed are one or two sessions to sum up what you believe has been accomplished and what work may still be left to do. I have encountered clinicians who will fight their clients and call their desire to leave treatment "resistance." This may be so, but to me it is irrelevant. Clients have the right to be resistant. My obligation is subsumed under the doctrine of informed consent. In this case, informed consent means sharing my best analysis of the risks and benefits of stopping treatment at this time. Even when clients decide to terminate prematurely, I can live with it. I have done my job. I may be right in thinking they need to do more work, or I may not. The client has the right to make the final decision.

10.10 Staying in Charge

Bear in mind that if the client becomes disorganized or impulse-ridden, starting where he or she wants to can open a can of worms. Over time, the client may perceive that he or she is (inappropriately) directing treatment. I do not let that happen. It is my responsibility to uphold the parameters; my client has the obligation, which he or she consented to, to stay on task. With disorganized or impulsive clients, I try to remind them of my recommendation to do some resourcing work to stabilize themselves before returning to active trauma work and completing the unfinished protocol. Sometimes a short resourcing process may be sufficient, and the client will return to the original target. At other times, I have found it beneficial to target the difference of opinion between us (when I recommend starting in one place and the client wants to start in another). The process between us may parallel an old, unresolved power-struggle trauma the client had with a primary caregiver, for example. This time, though, the "caregiver" has shown a willingness to let the client make the decision and learn from it. Thus we have not only stayed out of a power struggle, we have made the implicit distinction for the client between the past and the present. This is another example of the relational within EMDR methodology.

The only times I step in firmly and take charge are when I see possible dangers to continuing active trauma work. An example would be when a recovering alcoholic, well into a sobriety program, processes an old painful memory and relapses. I learned this lesson during the early '90s when a client processed an old abandonment issue regarding her primary caretakers. She seemed to tolerate the processing well and had a deeply moving experience. However during the week that followed, she had a flood of associated memories and started drinking again. This experience led her to enter an outpatient rehabilitation program. This was before I learned A. J. Popky's DeTUR protocol (the acronym stands for Desensitization of Triggers and Urge Reprocessing) and studied the *EMDR Chemical Dependency Treatment Manual* (Vogelmann-Sine, Sine, Smyth, & Popky, 1998).

Then there are times when a client may want to keep processing the trauma in the next session, and the clinician thinks it unwise. In these cases, the clinician has an obligation to explain his or her reasoning and ask for the client's feedback. Doing this demonstrates the law of informed consent in the moment (meaning that risk–benefit issues can be addressed cooperatively).

For instance, if my client has a job interview later on the day of a session and has been in the process of desensitizing a major trauma, it is not wise to proceed with active trauma work during that session. The client will want to be at his or her best for the interview, and trauma work can definitely be draining. Preparing the client for this kind of situation should be done during Phase 2, so that expectations have been set. Honoring the relational does not mean that clinicians accede to every request that clients make. It means that we have an obligation to use our best judgment and to compassionately inform clients of our thinking. Do not fool yourself into thinking that being relational means accepting anything the client wants. At the end of the day, the client is in charge of his or her life, but the clinician is in charge of treatment and the treatment decisions he or she makes.

This point was beautifully driven home in an episode of one of my favorite TV shows, *The West Wing*. In this episode, President Bartlett had not been able to sleep for four nights. A psychiatrist (played by Adam Arkin) was called to the White House to evaluate the president's problem. At the end of a 2-hour consultation, the psychiatrist terminated the interview. The president stopped him, saying that they would be finished when *he* said they were finished. Arkin's response was something to the effect that the president could use some assistance, but that they had completed an important part of the work. He clearly took charge. Though it is a TV show, it accurately portrayed the need for the professional to be in charge of the treatment process. (As it turned out, the president's sleep problem was related to his having been physically abused by his father. The present-day precipitant was that one of his closest advisers had commented to him that he was still compelled to fight his old ghosts by having people like him for his folksy manner. It is too bad that the producers of the show were not sufficiently informed about EMDR. Arkin's treating the president would have made great TV.)

As I have said, it is almost always necessary to continue processing the target memory or its associative links until the SUDS is 0 and the VOC is 7. My consultees and I have found that a client may wish to start on one target one week and then move to an unrelated target the next. Moving around too much opens up too many channels and leaves the door open for possible flooding. There must be a compelling reason to close down one target memory and switch to another one. The typical response I encounter from a client who wants to move on is, "It still bothers me, but I'm not feeling it now." This requires careful examination during Phase 8, because avoidance or fear of retraumatization may be present. The clinician may need to do some form of resourcing to help strengthen the client's coping abilities and reduce his or her fear of the memory, or possibly to unearth blocking beliefs that may have caused negative somatoform dissociation.

Another strategy is to have the client hold the original target memory in mind and do a very slow body scan. This helps ground the client in his or her body and reactivate state-dependent memories. The client can also do the body scan by holding the picture of the worst part of the memory in mind along with the negative cognition. These approaches usually stir something in the client, who may then elect to continue working on the target memory. If the client elects not to, then I do not press the issue.

10.11 The Three-Pronged Approach

Shapiro notes that the work is guided by the three-pronged EMDR protocol. She states, "While the standard EMDR procedure takes place during each reprocessing session, the standard three-pronged EMDR protocol guides the overall treatment of the client. ... Each reprocessing session must be directed at a particular target. The generic divisions of the targets are defined in the standard protocol as (1) the past experiences that have set the groundwork for the pathology, (2) the present situations or triggers that currently stimulate the disturbance, and (3) the templates necessary for appropriate future action. All of the specialized EMDR protocols (e.g., those regarding phobias or somatic disorders) are interfaced with this standard format" (2001, p. 76).

What remains implicit is that the therapeutic relationship plays a prominent relationship near the end of treatment as well. People want to get on with their lives.

They feel better by this point. So why do they need to continue at this point? Shapiro's reasons are sound; the future template gives more insurance that functional character trait change will remain. By rehearsing for future events and teaching new skills, the client is more likely to keep the gains he or she has made. By this time in treatment we have earned the respect and gratitude of our healing clients. If our client believes that he or she has done sufficient work, he or she will be ready to leave prematurely. Here the clinician needs to exert rational influence by reminding the client of the action plan that Kaslow (2002) speaks of, and the need to insure continued productive thinking that Bohart (2002) remarks on. Both stress the nature of a nonhierarchical structure, but one of co-participation. I am in agreement, but I will make one observation. The clinician, being the expert on treatment, raises his power (Gelso and Hayes, 1998) just a bit to remind the client of the reasoning to complete the future template. We, in private practice in the United States, need to be cognizant of our need to earn a living, and balance our needs against the need to do the full job. Dr. Shapiro used to tell a lovely story, at the end of Part 1 Training, of the young man who would one day be king. He traveled long and wide to find the wisest king of all. When he reached him and asked for his wisdom, the king gave him a test. He had to hold a bowl of water above his head for 24 hours; if he spilled one drop he would be instantly killed. However, if he succeeded, the king would give him wisdom. The young man carefully completed his task, and was given an immediate audience with the king. Hearing about the young man's success, the king gave him these words of wisdom. "Do you recall the care that you used to hold the bowl above your head?" asked the king. "Yes I do," answered the boy. "Just as you have used great care, being mindful of the water in the bowl, so am I mindful that each minute of the day I walk with God above my head. Make your decisions based upon that premise and you will govern wisely." May we all exert the necessary wisdom in a compassionate co-participatory manner as we head for the final leg of our journey.

10.11.1 The Case of Madeline – The Epilogue

A simple example would be the case of a client like Madeline, who came in with a driving phobia secondary to her accident. The first part of our work dealt with detraumatizing her from her near-death experience which led us back to old trauma. The second part dealt with identifying all current-day triggers (which included driving away from a stoplight when it turned green), and the future template involved imagining "running a movie" of herself driving, without negative arousal. If Madeline was still aroused during the future template, then she would open her eyes and process any disturbance. Then we would make a contract for her actually to drive, notice any disturbances, and journal them. These would be targeted in our next session. Fortunately, by the time we reached the future template, Madeline had no negative arousals and was successfully driving again.

However, when it came to her issues around feeling like running away from Richard because she could not tolerate her distress of experiencing one of his episodes, the wisdom of the three-pronged approach guided my treatment recommendations. Madeline would have been happy to end before the future template. It was our positive relationship, and a gentle reminder of the necessity to complete the work, that was the glue to help her stay in treatment until we were truly finished. The present-day referent was experiencing his distress; this led us to floatback to clusters of old traumas. After reprocessing those memories, we dealt with the present-day referent with good success. Now came installing the future template. We checked for any signs of distress while imagining her being with Richard during those challenging moments. She realized that she still had some anxiety, which led to her openness to completing the work. Richard's episodes were neurologically based, and though diminishing, would always be potentially "lurking" out there, like unexpected contact with her brother. We were able to desensitize her along with teaching and installing some mindfulness techniques and breathing exercises. This took one session. Finally, "we ran the movie" of her being with him during one of his spells. After successfully completing this part of treatment, I had Madeline keep a log of being with him during an episode. She reported that she experienced almost no distress, had compassion for him, and learned to take some proactive moves to help herself out when an episode occurred.

It is important for me to note two issues. The first is that Madeline believed herself to be finished before the future template was installed. While we could have congratulated ourselves on a job well done, we were not finished. Not completing the future template would have kept her at risk for future retraumatization. The second issue is the relative nature of living. I believe that it would have been foolish of me to expect an absolute resolution of any negative arousals during those episodes. There are real issues involved that may never completely resolve with Richard's condition (although, the neurological issues might. Even Richard's neurologist couldn't be certain). Imagine the love of your life having a condition that is permanent (Dana Reeves is one of my heroes). Can you imagine having no reactivity when a real life issue comes up? I can't. What I did with Madeline was to search out all possible experiential contributors, reprocess them, teach coping strategies, run the movie, and then have her experience, in vivo, one of these moments. After having been as thorough as possible, I had done my due diligence. Now we were done.

10.12 Terminating Therapy

Clients often are impatient to finish treatment. Many times they want to terminate before completing the protocol. I do my best to explain the necessity for comprehensive resolution by following this research-proven methodology. There are times when life interferes (other commitments, illness, or money issues). I try my best to illustrate problems that may come up as a result of premature termination, but people will be people. I have found peace in myself when I have done my best, and part of being in relationships is developing the ability to know when it is time to let go. I just make sure that the client knows that I do not consider the work to be completed, and that he or she is welcome back if the need arises.

Shapiro advises that we consider and relate to our clients three important issues: that the work may not be complete, that additional material may arise, and that the clients have the power to meet these challenges and to continue growing throughout their lives.

On the idea that the work may not be complete, Shapiro writes, "Do not assume that every possible unconscious dysfunction has been resolved within a given number of EMDR sessions" (2001, p. 217). She goes on to point out that there may be other dissociated memory networks that have not become activated during this treatment episode.

Shapiro also advises, "It is necessary to communicate to clients that other material may arise and that this is not evidence of failure on their part but, rather, a natural unfolding process" (2001, p. 218). She advises that clinicians teach our clients that now that they have become more functional, other memories may surface as a result. An example would be when a client comes to treatment with a work-related problem, such as not being able to stand up to his or her boss. History taking reveals physical abuse by the client's father. The client processes the old abuse and the present-day precipitants, and in learning more assertive ways of relating, he or she practices appropriately standing up to an irrational boss. The client may be quite on target with his or her assertions and may speak his or her mind. Often this scenario leads to a better working environment. But what happens if in asserting himself or herself appropriately, the client gets demoted or fired (because of the boss' old state-dependent memories). This may activate other maladaptive schemas and state-dependent memories for the client to work on. Relationally, it is important to work with the client on the pros and cons of any action to be taken, recognizing that life involves risk.

In my experience, it has happened that a client has reported an untoward event that led to an activation of my own state-dependent memories. There is no substitute for learning EMDR thoroughly. I can be as related as possible, but if I do not understand the method, and an untoward event occurs, there is much more chance that I will have a countertransference reaction. If I do know EMDR thoroughly, I may have such a reaction anyway, but at least I will be sure that I have practiced properly.

Shapiro also notes that "it is necessary to instill in clients a sense of self-empowerment and confidence in their ability to exercise post-therapy monitoring" (2001, p. 218). Life is what happens when we are busy making plans, or so they say. By urging clients to continue journaling, clinicians help them take action to mediate future situations. Not every life problem requires a new round of treatment. Shapiro has stated publicly that "our goal is to effect the most comprehensive change within the shortest period of time, without disturbing the stable parts of a person's life" (2004). The clinician's goal is to empower the client to take what he or she has learned in treatment, and, with the greatest amount of response flexibility available, to find novel solutions to new challenges.

Relational aspects are embedded in many of the practices of EMDR. My goal in communicating my vision of the relational imperative has been to elucidate these ideas and highlight the relational issues that are present in Shapiro's work but not explicitly expressed. My hope is that this book will help the mental health community to view EMDR through the relational and humanistic lens that I believe was intended for it. The standard methodology has many mechanistic parts, but the heart and soul of EMDR is to end the cycle of violence (Shapiro, personal communication, June 1, 1995). Clinicians all need to practice relationally to accomplish this goal.

I will leave you with the following story. I was given permission to publish it by its author, John Marquis, one of the original 36 trainees in Shapiro's first training in Sunnyvale, California. (John also obtained permission from the son of the woman whom the story is about.)

> In the first public EMD training in March 1990 in the United States, there were not yet rules against working with friends in practicum. I worked with a remarkable colleague named Helen Mehr, PhD. I share this because Helen told others about it when she was alive. Helen was a person who had a long history of remarkable work to promote peace and freedom as well as political and professional pioneering activities. In 1990 she devoted about half of her time to peace organizations and writing letters to the editors of newspapers. Although she had grown up in freedom in Canada, she had lost European relatives in the Holocaust. Anytime she was reminded of the Holocaust in any way, she pictured the emaciated bodies in the mass graves. She chose this as her target for EMD and

reported 10 SUDS, and a lump in her stomach. In those days we got a SUDS level after every set of eye movements. The anxiety numbers went down steadily to a 3, and then jumped back to a 7.

"It's the anger!"

"Okay, feel the anger," I said, raising my fingers.

"No! I don't want to lose the anger. That's what has motivated me all these years to fight for peace and justice."

I said, "Francine says that eye movements just get rid of the bad stuff."

"Okay," said Helen.

We continued processing. When we got to 1 SUDS, the grave was filled in, and with the next set, flowers grew on the grave. The anger was gone — and Helen went on fighting like a tiger for peace and justice, winning a special award from the American Psychological Association shortly before her death.

Appendix A
Trauma, PTSD, and Complex PTSD

Trauma can be described in many forms. Perhaps it would be useful to give the definition of post-traumatic stress disorder (PTSD). The Diagnostic and Statistical Manual of Mental Disorders IV-R defines PTSD as the result of having been exposed — either firsthand or as a witness — to an extreme situation or episode that is outside of the realm of normal, expectable daily experience. One example is a threat to oneself physically, emotionally, or sexually. Other circumstances could include witnessing events such as 9/11 or the death of a loved one, or being in a situation, such as a hurricane, where there was a perceived threat to one's wellbeing. Not everyone exposed to life-threatening situations develops full-blown PTSD or any symptoms of trauma. The meaning of the event, the amount of social support available, and a person's physiological hardiness can all mitigate against the development of symptoms.

PTSD is a formal diagnosis and includes symptoms of intrusive thoughts and recollections, avoidance behaviors, and states of hyperarousal that have been present for at least one month after the traumatic event. Examples of intrusive states are recurrent and distressing recollections of the traumatic event, nightmares about it, flashbacks, and a physical reactivity to events with similar components (sight, sound, or smells, for example). Avoidance behaviors include avoiding thinking about the incident, staying away from places and activities that remind one of it, psychological amnesia for part or all of the trauma, diminished participation in activities that usually are pleasurable, feelings of detachment, preventing oneself from feeling (sometimes going as far as feeling numb — called psychic numbing), and believing that as a result of the event or situation,

215

one will not have a full life. Symptoms of hyperarousal include difficulty falling or staying asleep; bursts of anger, agitation, or irritability; problems concentrating; hypervigilance (being constantly on guard when there is no objective reason for it); and an exaggerated startle response.

Traumatic stress is not limited to the symptoms described in the formal diagnosis of PTSD, however. People exposed to traumatic events may develop a condition called Acute Stress Disorder. The essential features of this disorder include anxiety and dissociation, and the symptoms usually resolve within 4 weeks' time. After those 4 weeks, the diagnosis may change to PTSD, or these symptoms may remain in a subacute phase where certain symptoms may be present from time to time but do not meet the criteria for a full-blown psychiatric syndrome. This subacute phase may contain elements of intrusive thoughts, avoidance, and hyperarousal, and it may last anywhere from a few days after the event to a lifetime.

Traumatic stress frequently results from extreme situations; however, other unpleasant events may be experienced in such a way that the brain is not able to process this information to an adaptive conclusion. The response to these unpleasant events may contain elements of intrusive states, avoidance, and hyperarousal. Present-day situations that seem innocuous to some or only mildly annoying to others can be very disconcerting to the person who has experienced a past unpleasant event of which this current stressor implicitly reminds him or her. The person's brain is not able to take in the sights, sounds, smells, and sensations of this event and naturally process them to an adaptive conclusion. The person reacts in a way that others may view as an overreaction. The next time you feel yourself ready to say that someone is overreacting, remind yourself that the person might simply be reacting with an intensity suggesting that other painful memories have become stimulated neurologically and activated physiologically. Depending on whether you are a friend or the treating clinician, a more appropriate response might be to say, "I'm sorry you feel so agitated" or "What old memories might be getting activated by this event?" This is a humanistic way of transmitting information to the person.

I am indebted to Shapiro (personal communication, Feb. 20, 1995) for redefining and broadening the concept of trauma to include any memory that the brain cannot process to an adaptive conclusion. The adaptive information processing model of EMDR states that the brain has the inherent ability to take in information and process it to a productive conclusion. When something prevents this, the information stays in the brain in state-dependent form. It is as if the brain videotapes these traumatic moments and stores them with the painful sensations attached. This causes the painful energy of the unpleasant event(s) to be experienced in the present. The information about the traumatic experience may not be in the conscious mind. It is often in a dissociated state.

When experiences occur in a person's life that he or she is able to process to adaptive completion, lessons are learned and stored away for further usage. Whatever is no longer needed is forgotten and released. The culmination of this neurological process is declarative memory. However, when a person encounters a situation — be it a personal betrayal, a natural disaster, or an act of terrorism — his or her coping processes diminish. When the pain cannot be contained or tolerated, dysfunctional thinking patterns ensue, and the person's ability to function in the world is hampered. If these thinking patterns are not caught immediately, the person may act in dysfunctional manners, such as overeating. Depending on how long a stressor lingers, the dysfunctional behavior may continue. If it does, it usually becomes conscious, since people around the person will likely comment on it.

The original reasons for the behavior are usually somewhat difficult to retrieve. The cognitive sciences have much to say in this realm. When adequate coping is not available, the person fights, flees, freezes, or faints. Though not exactly analogous, these responses equate to hyperarousal, avoidance, and dissociation. When memories of the traumatic event come to consciousness, the person feels the suffering acutely. When this happens, it can be said that a physiological reexperiencing is occurring, as described by van der Kolk (1994). Depending on many variables, the person's physiological arousal interacts with other parts of the brain and personality so that his or her coping abilities diminish, sometimes momentarily (we have all had the experience of being caught off guard), sometimes for longer and longer periods. If the stressors are continuous (e.g., living in a concentration camp or a home where a father molests his son), the person's whole coping style, lifestyle, and fixated characteristics prevail as an unmovable part of his or her personality. This is usually the case in what we call complex PTSD. These poor souls usually end up with Axis 2 diagnoses, e.g., borderline. This is also when pathological dissociation occurs. I have found it helpful to use the formulations of Nijenhuis et al. (2004) in their elegant explanation of the structural model of dissociation.

According to Herman, complex PTSD is the syndrome that results from prolonged and repeated trauma (1992). Another name for this is Disorders of Extreme Stress, Not Otherwise Specified (DESNOS). There are six deficit areas of DESNOS:

1. Dysregulation of affect and impulses
2. Disorders of attention and consciousness

3. Disorders of self-perception
4. Distorted interpersonal relations
5. Distortions of systems of meaning
6. Somatization of external stress manifesting in the body as disease or physical disorders

These deficit areas are not currently covered in the DSM IV-R. Herman, van der Kolk, and others have been lobbying for their inclusion. They have an excellent point. This condition is well known in the field of traumatology, yet its exclusion from the general nomenclature of mental heath presents many problems. Aside from perpetuating undue and incorrect diagnostic problems, this glaring omission means that DESNOS is not a reimbursable diagnosis in the ever-narrowing mentality of the world of managed care.

DESNOS also presents special relational problems in treatment. A client who is dysregulated and distorting cannot feel safe. Without safety, a prolonged period of stabilization is needed before doing any active trauma work. Prospective clients often tell clinicians that they want to start the active trauma work of EMDR as soon as possible, only to find on evaluation that they are not ready. Early in my EMDR career, I was not as conservative with this group of clients as I am now, and a few had their problems unnecessarily complicated by my desire to heal them quickly. In my opinion, the best EMDR strategy for stabilizing these clients is Resource Development and Installation (RDI).

For traumatized clients who are beginning treatment, Dr. Patti Levin's article on trauma would be a good reference article to give them. I want to thank Patti for giving permission to include it in this book.

Dr. Patti Levin[1]

After a trauma, people may go though a wide range of normal responses.

Such reactions may be experienced not only by people who experienced the trauma firsthand, but by those who have witnessed or heard about the trauma or been involved with those immediately affected. Many reactions can be triggered by persons, places, or things associated with the trauma. Some reactions may appear totally unrelated.

Here is a list of common physical and emotional reactions to trauma, as well as a list of helpful coping strategies. These are NORMAL reactions to ABNORMAL events.

Physical reactions

- Aches and pains like headaches, backaches, stomachaches
- Sudden sweating and/or heart palpitations (fluttering)
- Changes in sleep patterns, appetite, interest in sex
- Constipation or diarrhea

- Easily startled by noises or unexpected touch
- More susceptible to colds and illnesses
- Increased use of alcohol or drugs and/or overeating

Emotional reactions

- Shock and disbelief
- Fear and/or anxiety
- Grief, disorientation, denial
- Hyperalertness or hypervigilance
- Irritability, restlessness, outbursts of anger or rage
- Emotional swings — like crying and then laughing
- Worrying or ruminating — intrusive thoughts of the trauma
- Nightmares
- Flashbacks — feeling like the trauma is happening now
- Feelings of helplessness, panic, feeling out of control
- Increased need to control everyday experiences
- Minimizing the experience
- Attempts to avoid anything associated with trauma
- Tendency to isolate oneself
- Feelings of detachment
- Concern over burdening others with problems
- Emotional numbing or restricted range of feelings
- Difficulty trusting and/or feelings of betrayal
- Difficulty concentrating or remembering
- Feelings of self-blame and/or survivor guilt
- Shame
- Diminished interest in everyday activities or depression
- Unpleasant past memories resurfacing
- Loss of a sense of order or fairness in the world; expectation of doom and fear of the future

Helpful coping strategies

- Mobilize a support system — reach out and connect with others, especially those who may have shared the stressful event
- Talk about the traumatic experience
- Cry
- Hard exercises like jogging, aerobics, bicycling, walking
- Relaxation exercises like yoga, stretching, massage
- Humor
- Prayer and/or meditation
- Hot baths

- Music and art
- Maintain a balanced diet and sleep cycle as much as possible
- Avoid overusing stimulants like caffeine, sugar, or nicotine
- Commit to something personally meaningful and important every day
- Hug those you love
- Eat warm turkey, boiled onions, baked potatoes, cream-based soups — these are tryptophan activators, which help you feel tired but good (like after Thanksgiving dinner)
- Proactive responses toward personal and community safety — organize or do something socially active
- Write about your experience — in detail, just for yourself or to share with others

People are usually surprised that reactions to trauma can last longer than they expected. It may take weeks, months, and, in some cases, years to fully regain equilibrium. Many people will get through this period with the help and support of family and friends. But sometimes friends and family may push people to "get over it" before they're ready. Let them know that such responses are not helpful for you right now, though you appreciate that they are trying to help. Many people find that individual, group, or family counseling are helpful. Either way, the key word is CONNECTION — ask for help, support, understanding, and opportunities to talk.

The Chinese character for *crisis* is a combination of two words — danger and opportunity. Hardly anyone would choose to be traumatized as a vehicle for growth. Yet our experience shows that people are incredibly resilient, and the worst traumas and crises can become enabling, empowering transformations.

Appendix B
The EMDR International Association and the Definition of EMDR

The EMDR International Association (EMDRIA) is a membership organization of mental health professionals dedicated to the highest standards of excellence and integrity in EMDR. To that end, the association distributes brochures, publishes a quarterly newsletter, holds an annual conference, evaluates training programs, and maintains programs and listings of EMDRIA Certified Therapists and Approved Consultants, and Providers of Basic EMDR Training.

EMDRIA is the ongoing support system for EMDR-trained practitioners and provides the mechanism for the continued development of EMDR in a professional manner. Through EMDRIA, practitioners have access to the latest clinical information and research data on EMDR. EMDRIA, as well as the EMDR Institute, offers many excellent advanced training opportunities for EMDR clinicians to become more proficient in their skills.

EMDRIA
P.O. Box 141925
Austin, TX 78714-1925
Tel: (512) 451-5200
Fax: (512) 451-5256
Email: info@emdria.org
Website: www.emdria.org

The material in this appendix has been provided by the EMDRIA, which holds the copyright.

I. Purpose of Definition

The purpose of this definition is to serve as the foundation for the development and implementation of policies in all EMDRIA's programs in the service of its mission. This definition is intended to support consistency in EMDR training, standards, credentialing, continuing education, and clinical application while fostering the further evolution of EMDR through a judicious balance of innovation and research. This definition also provides a clear and common frame of reference for EMDR clinicians, consumers, researchers, the media, and the general public.

II. Foundational Sources and Principles for Evolution

Francine Shapiro, PhD, developed EMDR based on clinical observation, controlled research, feedback from clinicians whom she had trained, and previous scholarly and scientific studies of information processing. The original source of EMDR is derived from the work of Shapiro as it is described in her writings (Shapiro, 2001). Shapiro made clear that she is committed to the development of EMDR in a way that balances clinical observations and proposed innovations with independent empirical validation in well-designed and executed scientific studies. Previously held and newly proposed elements of EMDR procedure or theory that cannot be validated must give way to those that can.

III. Aim of EMDR

In the broadest sense, EMDR is intended to alleviate human suffering and assist individuals and human society to fulfill their potential for development while minimizing risks of harm in its application. For the client, the aim of EMDR treatment is to achieve the most profound and comprehensive treatment effects in the shortest period of time, while maintaining client stability within a balanced family and social system.

IV. Framework

EMDR is an approach to psychotherapy that is comprised of principles, procedures, and protocols. It is not a simple technique characterized primarily by the use of eye movements. EMDR is founded on the premise that each person has both an innate tendency to move toward health and wholeness, and the inner capacity to achieve it. EMDR is grounded in psychological science and is informed by both psychological theory and research on the brain.

EMDR integrates elements from both psychological theories (e.g., affect, attachment, behavior, bioinformational processing, cognitive, humanistic, family systems, psychodynamic, and somatic) and psycho-therapies (e.g., body-based, cognitive–behavioral, interpersonal, person-centered, and psychodynamic) into a standardized set of procedures and clinical protocols. Research on how the brain processes information and generates consciousness also informs the evolution of EMDR theory and procedure.

V. Hypotheses of the EMDR Model

The Adaptive Information Processing model is the theoretical foundation of the EMDR approach. It is based on the following hypotheses:

1. Within each person is a physiological information processing system through which new experiences and information are normally processed to an adaptive state.

2. Information is stored in memory networks that contain related thoughts, images, emotions, and sensations.

3. Memory networks are organized around the earliest related event.

4. Traumatic experiences and persistent unmet interpersonal needs during crucial periods in development can produce blockages in the capacity of the adaptive information processing system to resolve distressing or traumatic events.

5. When information stored in memory networks related to a distressing or traumatic experience is not fully processed, it gives rise to dysfunctional reactions.

6. The result of adaptive processing is learning, relief of emotional distress, and the availability of adaptive responses and understanding.

7. Information processing is facilitated by specific types of bilateral sensory stimulation. Based on observational and experimental data, Shapiro has referred to this stimulation as bilateral stimulation (1995) and dual attention stimulation (2001).

8. Alternating, left–right, bilateral eye movements, tones, and kinesthetic stimulation, when combined with the other specific procedural steps used in EMDR, enhance information processing.

9. Specific, focused strategies for sufficiently stimulating access to dysfunctionally stored information (and in some cases, adaptive information) generally need to be combined with bilateral stimulation in order to produce adaptive information processing.

10. EMDR procedures foster a state of balanced or dual attention between internally accessed information and external bilateral stimulation. In this state the client experiences simultaneously the distressing memory and the present context.

11. The combination of EMDR procedures and bilateral stimulation results in decreasing the vividness of disturbing memory images and related affect, facilitating access to more adaptive information and forging new associations within and between memory networks.

VI. Method

EMDR uses specific psychotherapeutic procedures to 1) access existing information, 2) introduce new information, 3) facilitate information processing, and 4) inhibit accessing of information (Lipke, 1999). Unique to EMDR are both the specific procedural steps used to access and process information, and the ways in which sensory stimulation is incorporated into well-defined treatment procedures and protocols, which are intended to create states of balanced or dual attention to facilitate information processing.

EMDR is used within an eight-phase approach to trauma treatment (Shapiro, 1995, 2001) in order to insure sufficient client stabilization and reevaluation before, during and after the processing of distressing and traumatic memories and associated stimuli. In Phases 3 – 6, standardized steps must be followed to achieve fidelity to the method. In the other 4 phases there is more than one way to achieve the objectives of each phase. However, as it is a process, not a technique, it unfolds according to the needs and resources of the individual client in the context of the therapeutic relationship. Therefore, different elements may be emphasized or utilized differently depending on the unique needs of the particular client.

To achieve comprehensive treatment effects, a three-pronged basic treatment protocol is used to first address past events. After adaptive resolution of past events, current stimuli still capable of evoking distress are processed. Finally, future situations are processed to prepare for possible or likely circumstances.

VII. Fidelity in Application Through Training and Observation

It is central to EMDR that positive results from its application derive from the interaction between clinician, method, and client. Therefore, graduate education in a mental health field (e.g., clinical psychology, psychiatry, social work, counseling, or marriage and family therapy) leading to eligibility for licensure, certification, or registration, along with supervised training, are considered essential to achieve optimal results. Meta-analytic research (Maxfield & Hyer, 2002) indicates that degree of fidelity to the published EMDR procedures is highly correlated with the outcome of EMDR procedures. Evidence of fidelity in procedure and appropriateness of protocol is considered central to both research and clinical application of EMDR.

Appendix C
Myths and Realities About EMDR

Myth #1: EMDR is all about the eye movements.
Reality #1: EMDR is an eight-phase, multimodal approach to the alleviation of traumatic stress, one phase of which uses bilateral stimulation, which may be eye movements, audio tones, or tapping.

Many new forms of psychotherapy have been developed as a result of academic findings based on research and scholarly applications of existing forms of treatment, but EMDR came into being as a result of a chance happening. In 1987, Francine Shapiro, then a doctoral student in clinical psychology, was taking a walk and thinking about something distressing. Her eyes spontaneously started to move rapidly, in a manner similar to that of REM sleep. Then she noticed she was no longer disturbed by her distressing thoughts. She experimented on herself and repeated the results.

Then she did the same with her colleagues and friends, using her fingers to lead them in back-and-forth eye movements. She replicated her results with many of them, but some got stuck in their disturbing thoughts. So she experimented with changing the variables: the speed of her fingers, different parts of the disturbing experiences, ways of opening and closing the eye movement sessions. As she continued to collect information on how initial subjects fared, she realized that she was discovering something that might be of use in anxiety reduction. Since this was her area of focus, and her primary orientation was behavioral, she named her procedure Eye Movement Desensitization (EMD).

It was because of this chance discovery and Shapiro's initial emphasis on eye movements, which had never been used in psychotherapy before for the alleviation of anxiety, that EMD became tagged with the myth that it was only about the eye movements. What was not highlighted sufficiently were the comprehensive strategies Shapiro developed, including history taking, affect tolerance, isolating the components of a target memory, and so on. Shapiro began to teach others her method and analyze the results that were reported. EMD came of age when she recognized that when used properly, it brought about both behavioral desensitization and cognitive restructuring. A paradigm shift occurred, and EMD became Eye Movement Desensitization and Reprocessing. EMDR was no longer seen as a simple desensitization technique. A new way of thinking, along with peace of mind, became the optimal outcome.

Myth #2: It's a three-session miracle cure.
Reality #2: It takes as long as it takes.

Shapiro has always stressed the importance of taking a comprehensive history and developing a treatment plan. These tasks alone take a minimum of two to three sessions, in my experience. Perhaps in certain cases of simple PTSD, a single traumatic memory can be detraumatized in three sessions. It is true that in 1995, a study by Wilson, Becker, and Tinker demonstrated that three sessions of EMDR were statistically effective in subjects with PTSD. In the discussion section of their paper these authors state,

> The present results suggest that EMDR was effective in decreasing symptoms and anxiety associated with traumatic memory and increasing positive cognition. EMDR effectiveness was demonstrated on different outcome measures after three ninety-minute treatment sessions, with effects being maintained at 90 days after treatment (1995, p. 235).

These results were presented in the prestigious peer-reviewed *Journal of Consulting and Clinical Psychology*. The authors also did a 15-month follow-up study and found that the treatment results held (1997).

Myth #3: EMDR is a cult.
Reality #3: Neither the EMDR Institute, founded by Shapiro, nor the EMDR International Association (EMDRIA), a nonprofit membership organization not affiliated with the Institute, requires indoctrination and obedience of its members.

It always makes me laugh when I hear this myth. As an EMDR facilitator blessed with a deep and commanding voice, it falls to me to get everyone back into the EMDR Institute trainings after breaks. It's like herding cats. EMDR clinicians are very independent human beings. The idea that

Shapiro requires cult-like devotion is also a myth. Many of us have taken her on, challenging her ideas and methods. Some clinicians have developed variations, such as Maureen Kitchur's developmental strategic model for EMDR. Some have filled in missing pieces, such as Leeds and Korn (who developed RDI). This book represents the first book-length examination of how the therapeutic relationship plays a vital and unexplored role in EMDR methodology.

Myth #4: It's a pyramid money-making scheme.
Reality #4: EMDRIA sets training and certification standards. Those who have met the qualifications may be designated as Approved Consultants, Approved Trainers, or Specialty Presenters.

Show me a type of therapy where senior members do not tutor those with less experience. I have run a no-fee study group once a month for the past 4 years in the hope of encouraging EMDR clinicians to continue their education. Enough said.

Myth #5: Part 1 and Part 2 (which used to be called Level 1 and Level 2) of the EMDR Institute training are all one needs to become proficient at EMDR.
Reality #5: Additional training and consultation are necessary to become proficient in the practice of EMDR.

When trainees complete Part 2, they receive a "Certificate of Completion for the Two-Part EMDR Basic Training." Nowhere on this certificate does it indicate that the trainee did anything but show up. Currently, to become certified in EMDR, 20 hr of consultation by an approved EMDR consultant, 10 of which must be individual consultation, must be completed. For information on advanced training and consultation opportunities, see www.EMDR.com and www.EMDRIA.org or contact the EMDR Institute at (831) 761-1040 or EMDRIA at (512) 451-5200.

Myth #6: EMDR is a panacea; it can be used for just about any troubling condition.
Reality #6: EMDR can be applied to a human being's experience-based problems in living that have caused psychopathology.

There is a wide range of applicability in EMDR, and it can be used with many populations. However, it cannot cure cancer or schizophrenia. The proper application can help people release the traumatic effects associated with the experiential contributors of problems that hold them back from having a more robust life. See Appendix D: EMDR Clinical Applications For Diverse Clinical Populations.

These may include such problems as PTSD, but EMDR can also be applied to other conditions that may not meet this diagnosis. Examples include times when problems in living exacerbate already difficult problems. Other applications have been developed to *assist* various populations that may have difficulties that cannot be completely healed, such as obsessive-compulsive disorder. Properly applied, EMDR can help the client with OCD, for example, deal with the problems that the disorder has created for him or her.

Mark Grant (Grant, 1999) has developed protocols for dealing with the psychological aspects of pain. Sandra Foster, Jennifer Lendl, and David Grand use applications of EMDR for performers and athletes whose abilities are inhibited by negative self-limiting beliefs that cause them to underachieve in their respective fields. Marsha Whisman has developed protocols to deal with anxiety problems, panic disorder, and OCD, and Silke Vogelman-Sine, Larry F. Sine, Nancy Smyth, and A. J. Popky have developed protocols to deal with chemically dependent populations. Roger Solomon has developed protocols to deal with grief. Ricky Greenwald, Joan Lovett, Frankie Klaff, Bob Tinker, and others have developed and documented useful ways of using EMDR with children who have a variety of problems. All have made major contributions, but when it comes to children, they are our future. Each of these fine child clinicians has made sterling contributions. Joan Lovett, MD, a behavioral pediatrician, was one of the pioneers who developed adaptations of EMDR for use with children. In her book *Small Wonders: Healing Childhood Trauma with EMDR,* she describes her methods for integrating EMDR with play therapy and storytelling. Frankie Klaff ("mother" of integrating family systems theory and EMDR with children) has stated, "When you work with children and adolescents, if you don't have the relationship, you don't have the child" (personal communication, April 9, 2005). Tinker and Wilson, in their book *Through the Eyes of a Child* (1999), write about the importance of the relationship when dealing with attachment-disordered children.

> Myth #7: EMDR can be used on traumatized clients no matter what their level of functioning is.
> Reality #7: EMDR is the term for the entire methodology. Many misuse the term to refer to only the trauma-releasing phases of EMDR. Trauma release *cannot* be done on a client without careful consideration of his or her level of functioning and stability.

To attempt to detraumatize an unstable person is, at a minimum, unwise. Activating the information-processing system in unstable clients can destabilize them further. Having them focus on their trauma intensifies the felt stress of the event, and without the necessary containment skills, they can be catapulted into more pain and acting out.

> Myth #8: EMDR is just about dialoging with bilateral stimulation
> Reality #8: EMDR is a multiphasic, multimodal treatment approach. All eight phases are vital.

History taking, evaluating, and preparing the client are necessary in every case. After these steps are completed, using the procedural steps outline correctly with bilateral stimulation may be all that is needed to alleviate the client's traumatic stress. During bilateral stimulation, unless the client loops or blocks, Shapiro advises the clinician to stay out of the way because EMDR works by empowering the client's brain to do the healing; active intervention strategies are used only when information processing is blocked. There are some mental health clinicians who just dialogue with the client while doing continuous bilateral stimulation. I hope I have been clear enough that this is not EMDR.

> Myth #9: EMDR takes away necessary motivations and actions that the traumatic situation taught the person to use.
> Reality #9: EMDR releases the pain of old trauma, but it does not take away any important learning. Nor does it diminish motivation to accomplish one's goals, be they artistic creation or social justice.

This is a common fear among actors who use the technique of transfer of emotion, in which they create an emotion for a particular scene based on their past emotional experiences. It has also been a fear among certain activists who are concerned that by losing their anger, they will lose their motivation. For them, I refer them to the last case vignette in the book, at the end of Chapter 10: the story of Dr. Helen Mehr.

Appendix D[1]
EMDR Clinical Applications
for Diverse Clinical Populations

EMDR is conceptualized as a treatment for the experiential contributors of disorders and health. Expanding the standard protocols (Shapiro, 1995, 2001), additional applications have been developed in direct clinical practice by experts and consultants in a variety of specialty areas. As with all treatments for most of these disorders, little controlled research has been conducted, a state of affairs evident in an evaluation report by a task force set in motion by the Clinical Division of the American Psychological Association (Chambless, Baker, Baucom, Beutler, Calhoun, Crits-Christoph, et al., 1998). It revealed that only about a dozen complaints, such as specific phobias and headaches, had empirically well-supported treatments. Adding to this is the circumstance that many of the treatments listed as empirically validated had not been evaluated for the degree to which they provided substantial long-term clinical effects. For the latest listing see: http://therapyadvisor.com.

While EMDR protocols for PTSD have been widely investigated by controlled research, it is hoped that the additional applications will be thoroughly investigated. Suggested parameters have been thoroughly delineated (Shapiro, 2001, 2002). To aid researchers in identifying protocols available for study, and to assist clinicians in obtaining supervision for proposed applications, published materials and conference presentations are listed below. Many presentations have been taped and are available from the conference coordinators. Presenters may also be accessed directly through the EMDR International Association: http://www.emdria.org.

Positive therapeutic results with EMDR have been reported with a wide range of populations. As previously noted, however, most of the clinical disorders listed have no empirically validated treatments, and widespread investigation with controlled research is needed in all orientations (see Chambless et al., 1998). EMDR clinical applications are based upon the adaptive information processing model (see Shapiro, 2001, 2002) which posits that the reprocessing of experiential contributors can have a positive effect in the treatment of a variety of disorders. To date, while numerous controlled studies have supported EMDR's effectiveness in the treatment of PTSD, other clinical applications are based on clinical observations and are in need of further investigation.

Since the initial efficacy study (Shapiro, 1989a), positive therapeutic results with EMDR have been reported with a wide range of populations, including the following:

1. Combat veterans from Desert Storm, the Vietnam War, the Korean War, and World War II who were formerly treatment resistant and who no longer experience flashbacks, nightmares, and other PTSD sequelae (Blore, 1997a; Carlson, Chemtob, Rusnak, & Hedlund, 1996; Carlson, Chemtob, Rusnak, Hedlund, & Muraoka, 1998; Daniels, Lipke, Richardson, & Silver, 1992; Lipke, 2000; Lipke & Botkin, 1992; Silver & Rogers, 2001; Thomas & Gafner, 1993; White, 1998; Young, 1995).

2. Persons with phobias and panic disorder who revealed a rapid reduction of fear and symptomatology (De Jongh & ten Broeke, 1998; De Jongh, ten Broeke, & Renssen, 1999; De Jongh, van den Oord, & ten Broeke, 2002; Doctor, 1994; Feske & Goldstein, 1997; Goldstein, 1992; Goldstein & Feske, 1994; Kleinknecht, 1993; Nadler, 1996; O'Brien, 1993; Protinsky, Sparks, & Flemke, 2001a). Some controlled studies of spider phobics have revealed comparatively little benefit from EMDR, (e.g., Muris & Merckelbach, 1997; Muris, Merkelbach, Holdrinet, & Sijsenaar, 1998; Muris, Merckelbach, van Haaften, & Nayer, 1997), but evaluations have been confounded by lack of fidelity to the published protocols (see De Jongh et al., 1999; Shapiro, 1999; and Appendix D). One evaluation of panic disorder with agoraphobia (Goldstein, de Beurs, Chambless, & Wilson, 2000) also reported limited results (for comprehensive discussion per Shapiro, 2001, 2002; see also Appendix D).

3. Crime victims, police officers, and field workers who are no longer disturbed by the aftereffects of violent assaults and/or the stressful nature of their work (Baker & McBride, 1991; Dyregrov, 1993;

Jensma, 1999; Kitchiner & Aylard, 2002; Kleinknecht & Morgan, 1992; McNally & Solomon, 1999; Page & Crino, 1993; Shapiro & Solomon, 1995; Solomon, 1995, 1998; Solomon, & Dyregrov, 2000; Wilson, Becker, Tinker, & Logan, 2001).

4. People relieved of excessive grief due to the loss of a loved one or to line-of-duty deaths, such as engineers no longer devastated with guilt because their train unavoidably killed pedestrians (Lazrove et al., 1998; Puk, 1991a; Shapiro & Solomon, 1995; Solomon, 1994, 1995, 1998; Solomon & Kaufman, 2002).

5. Children and adolescents healed of the symptoms caused by trauma (Chemtob, Nakashima, Hamada, & Carlson, 2002; Cocco & Sharpe, 1993; Datta & Wallace, 1994, 1996; Fernandez, Gallinari, & Lorenzetti, 2004; Greenwald, 1994, 1998, 1999, 2000, 2002; Jaberghaderi, Greenwald, Rubin, Dolatabadim, & Zand, in press; Johnson, 1998; Korkmazler-Oral & Pamuk, 2002; Lovett, 1999; Pellicer, 1993; Puffer, Greenwald, & Elrod, 1998; Russell & O'Connor, 2002; Scheck, Schaeffer, & Gillette, 1998; Shapiro, 1991; Soberman, Greenwald, & Rule, 2002; Stewart & Bramson, 2000; Taylor, 2002; Tinker & Wilson, 1999).

6. Sexual assault victims who are now able to lead normal lives and have intimate relationships (Edmond, Rubin, & Wambach, 1999; Hyer, 1995; Parnell, 1994, 1999; Puk, 1991a; Rothbaum, 1997; Scheck, Schaeffer, & Gillette, 1998; Shapiro, 1989b, 1991, 1994; Wolpe & Abrams, 1991).

7. Victims of natural and manmade disasters able to resume normal lives (Chemtob et al., 2002; Fernandez et al., 2004; Grainger, Levin, Allen-Byrd, Doctor, & Lee, 1997; Jarero, Artigas, Mauer, Lopez Cano, & Alcala, 1999; Knipe, Hartung, Konuk, Colleli, Keller, & Rogers, 2003; Shusta-Hochberg, 2003).

8. Accident, surgery, and burn victims who were once emotionally or physically debilitated and who are now able to resume productive lives (Blore, 1997b; Hassard, 1993; McCann, 1992; Puk, 1992; Solomon & Kaufman, 1994).

9. Victims of marital and sexual dysfunction who are now able to maintain healthy relationships (Keenan & Farrell, 2000; Kaslow, Nurse, & Thompson, 2002; Levin, 1993; Protinsky, Sparks, & Flemke, 2001b; Snyder, 1996; Wernik, 1993).

10. Clients at all stages of chemical dependency, and pathological gamblers, who now show stable recovery and a decreased tendency to relapse (Henry, 1996; Shapiro & Forrest, 1997; Shapiro, Vogelmann-Sine, & Sine, 1994; Vogelmann-Sine, Sine, Smyth, & Popky, 1998).

11. People with dissociative disorders who progress at a rate more rapid than that achieved by traditional treatment (Fine, 1994; Fine & Berkowitz, 2001; Lazrove, 1994; Lazrove & Fine 1996; Marquis & Puk, 1994; Paulsen, 1995; Rouanzoin, 1994; Twombly, 2000; Young, 1994).

12. People engaged in business, performing arts, and sport who have benefited from EMDR as a tool to help enhance performance (Crabbe, 1996; Foster & Lendl, 1995, 1996; Graham, 2004).

13. People with somatic problems/somatoform disorders, including chronic pain, who have attained a rapid relief of suffering (Brown, McGoldrick, & Buchanan, 1997; Dziegielewski & Wolfe, 2000; Grant, 1999; Grant & Threlfo, 2002; Gupta & Gupta, 2002; Ray & Zbik, 2001; Wilson et al., 2000).

14. Clients with a wide variety of PTSD and other diagnoses who experience substantial benefit from EMDR (Allen & Lewis, 1996; Brown, McGoldrick, & Buchanan, 1997; Cohn, 1993; Fensterheim, 1996; Forbes, Creamer, & Rycroft, 1994; Gelinas, 2003; Ironson, et al., 2002; Korn & Leeds, 2002; Lee et al., 2002; Manfield, 1998; Manfield & Shapiro, 2003; Madrid, Skolek, Shapiro, in press; Marcus, Marquis, & Saki, 1997; Marquis, 1991; McCullough, 2002; Parnell, 1996, 1997; Pollock, 2000; Power et al., 2002; Protinsky, Sparks, & Flemke, 2001a; Puk, 1991b; Renfrey & Spates, 1994; Ricci, in press; Rittenhouse, 2000; Shapiro & Forrest, 1997; Spates & Burnette, 1995; Spector & Huthwaite, 1993; Sprang, 2001; Vaughan et al., 1994; Vaughan, Wiese, Gold, & Tarrier, 1994; Wilson, Becker, & Tinker, 1995, 1997; Wolpe & Abrams, 1991; Zabukovec, Lazrove, & Shapiro, 2000).

Appendix E
Confusion Regarding Research on EMDR

There have been charges that EMDR is pseudoscience. In their 2002 paper in the *Journal of Clinical Psychology,* "A Critical Evaluation of Current Views Regarding Eye Movement Desensitization and Reprocessing (EMDR): Clarifying Points of Confusion," Perkins and Rouanzoin confront the misperceptions and misinterpretations of problems that researchers have published, such as the claim by Rosen et al. that EMDR is nothing more than a simple exposure therapy (1998a, 1998b). They also cite other authors, such as MacCulloch and Feldman (1996), who give reasons for the uniqueness of EMDR, dealing with the rapid dearousal reflex.

In traditional exposure therapy, the client is exposed to prolonged uninterrupted negative stimuli. EMDR uses short bursts of exposure to traumatic events with free association. Then the client's experience is covaried with attention to present-day experience. This is part of the dual-attention stimulation that Shapiro writes about, where the client is stimulated into state-dependent memory, bilateral stimulation is applied briefly, and then the client reports whether changes have occurred on visual, auditory, or sensory motor channels. Following this reporting, the client is reexposed to negative stimulation briefly again, and then again brought back to current-day experience to report what changes have occurred in his or her information processing. This process is specifically distinct from exposure therapy.

Other problems researchers have reported regarding EMDR's supposed ineffectiveness result from methodological and fidelity issues in their outcome studies. Maxfield and Hyer found that the results obtained in treatment outcome studies are intrinsically related to the methods employed to evaluate outcomes. Research design, type of measures, sample selection and size, treatment delivery, and assessment may all influence treatment outcomes (2002). They cite the Gold Standard Scale developed by Foa and Meadows (1997). Elements of this scale include

1. Clearly defined target symptoms

2. Reliable and valid measures with good psychometric properties

3. Use of blind evaluators

4. Assessor training with demonstrated interrater reliability

5. Manualized replicable specific treatment programs to ensure consistent and replicable treatment delivery

6. Unbiased assignment treatment

7. Treatment adherence, evaluated by treatment fidelity ratings

Maxfield and Hyer added three additional gold standards, including: no concurrent treatment, multimodal assessment, and adequate course of treatment (2002). For example, if an insufficient course of treatment were given to a specific population of traumatized individuals, (for example, combat veterans) where only one traumatic experience was treated, one could not expect that EMDR would be found effective in alleviating the symptoms of PTSD. This was the case in Jenson's 1994 study. When Jenson is compared to studies such as Carlson et al.'s 1998 study, it is clear that multiply traumatized veterans required longer and more comprehensive treatment of all traumatic experiences during their Vietnam tours of duty. This was one of the landmark studies that convinced the Department of Defense to include EMDR in its list of acceptable treatments for veterans.

Some critics say that EMDR provides nothing more than a placebo effect. McNally (1999) and Lohr, Lilienfeld, Tolin, and Herbert (1999) have expressed this view. Perkins and Rouanzoin (2002) confront this challenge by citing a study by Van Etten and Taylor, in which they concluded "from their meta-analysis that the effect sizes of EMDR tended to be larger than those of controlled conditions such as pill placebo and supportive psychotherapy, indicating that placebo is not a plausible interpretation of achieved results" (1998). Van Etten and Taylor go on to state that the treatment effects of EMDR are much larger and longer lasting than the treatment effects of behavior therapy, and that empirical evidence does not support the placebo hypothesis (p. 79).

Appendix F
Trauma Case Conceptualization Questionnaire

Mark Dworkin, CSW, LCSW
251 Mercury Street, East Meadow, NY 11554
(516) 731-7611
mdworkin@optonline.net

Purpose: To develop an initial understanding of whom the client is; what he or she is struggling with, and how his or her struggles initially affect the clinician.

Instructions: When filling out this form please keep notes on any reactions you may have to your client's presentation of his or her problems.

Age _____ Gender _____ Ethnicity_____ Marital status_____
Highest level of education _____
Occupation _____
Religious affiliation _____
Spiritual path _____
Cultural identification _____
Current family system (including marital status) and social support system_____
_____
_____

Medical conditions (list)_____
_____

_____

Medications_____

_____

_____

Substance abuse or compulsive/obsessive life patterns _____

_____

_____

_____

DES score_____
Genetic predispositions _____

1. Presenting problem(s) (include duration and length of problem; why treatment now?)

_____

_____

_____

Time in treatment _____

Most disturbing picture? _____

_____

_____

Core negative beliefs spoken spontaneously? _____

_____

_____

_____

Somatosensory experience of the trauma? (also note the lack of feelings or sensations associated) _____

_____

_____

_____

2. What strategies has the client used to deal with this current problem? What has worked? _____

_____

_____

_____

_____

_____

What strategies have not worked, and why? _____

_____

_____

_____

_____

_____

_____

3. What old painful memories (feeder memories), *especially of the original cause of the problem, if remembered,* does this presenting problem stir up in the client? (List all relevant ones. Also list other traumas client has suffered.) If none, can the client simply not recall or make connections to old traumas of the same type? Or is this truly a single-incident trauma?

a) _____

_____

_____

b) _____

_____

_____

c) _____

_____

_____

d) _____

_____

_____

e) _____

_____

_____

f) _____

_____

_____

g) _____
   _____
   _____
   _____

h) _____
   _____
   _____
   _____

4. What are the core negative beliefs this clients holds, and how does the client apply them to each of the traumatic memories?_____
   _____
   _____
   _____
   _____
   _____

5. What resources (including ego strengths, coping skills, self-capacities) did the client use to attempt to deal with these old memories?
   _____
   _____
   _____
   _____

6. What psychoform and somatoform types of dissociative symptoms does client present with? For example:

        positive psychoform — flashbacks
        negative psychoform — psychogenic amnesia
        positive somatoform — any physical pain that has been ruled out
            by a physician as having a physical cause
        negative somatoform — psychic numbing

   _____
   _____
   _____
   _____
   _____

7. Clinician's assessment of client's ability to tolerate intense abreactive experience
      Adequate ____
      Inadequate ____
      Rationale_____

      _____
      _____
      _____

8. Clinician's assessment of client's body awareness
      Adequate ____
      Inadequate ____
      Rationale _____

      _____
      _____
      _____

9. List general resources, including ego strengths, coping skills, self-capacities_____

      _____
      _____
      _____

10. Past treatment episodes and the diagnoses _____

      _____
      _____
      _____
      _____

11. Past responses to treatment, both positive and negative _____

      _____
      _____
      _____
      _____

12. Past responses to previous clinicians and reasons why _____

      _____
      _____
      _____
      _____

How does the client appear to initially relate to you? _____

_____
_____

_____

_____

What old memories, negative cognitions, and feeling states does the client induce IN YOU? _____

_____

_____

_____

_____

13. Significant symptoms and defenses of client (also note how you are affected by these symptoms and defenses) _____

_____

_____

_____

_____

14. What is the desired outcome of treatment? _____

_____

_____

_____

15. What are the desired positive cognitions at the start of treatment, and what are the client's current VOC ratings? _____

_____

_____

_____

_____

16. Are there any current constraints to beginning active trauma work (e.g., never start active trauma work with a tax accountant on April 1st)? _____

_____

_____

_____

_____

_____

17. Trauma case conceptualization summary (including possible transferential and countertransferential reactions) _____

_____

_____

_____

_____

Appendix G
Clinician Self-Awareness Questionnaire

This is Version 6 of the questionnaire.

Purpose: To assist in raising awareness of what old state-dependent memories may become activated in you, to assess what may be coming from you and what may be coming from the client, and to develop EMDR relational strategies. Sometimes problems occur in Phase 1 when the client shares information that evokes negative arousal, in Phase 2 when the client has trouble understanding the elements of preparation or wants to start processing trauma prematurely, or in Phase 3 when there is a problem structuring the assessment piece. Sometimes client information may not evoke negative arousal until Phase 4 when the client is actively processing. Often, clinicians' triggers are from old memories. These memories may be explicit or implicit (somatosensory). Noticing these moments in yourself may aid you in continuing productive processing.

Instructions: Whenever an EMDR treatment session becomes *problematic,* consider this self-administered instrument when reflecting on this session.

How many times have you seen this client? _____

Gender M___ F___ Marital status M   D   S   W

Children? Y__ N__ Gender and ages _____

Occupation (of client)_____

Religious/spiritual affiliation_____

1. Is this the first time you have felt state-dependent memories activated by this client? Y__ N__

2. If No, is this the same issue that has activated you previously with this client? Y___ N___

3. Do you get activated by the same issue with other clients? Y___ N___

4. Have you ever been traumatized? Y___ N___

5. Do you believe that you are struggling with compassion fatigue, vicarious traumatization, or secondary traumatic stress? Y___ N___

6. Describe the presenting problem (or present-day referents):

_____

_____

_____

_____

_____

_____

_____

7. What old trauma(s) are related to Question 6?

_____

_____

_____

_____

_____

_____

8. Describe what state-dependent memories of yours become activated NOW. How are you triggered?

_____

_____

_____

_____

_____

9. Why do you believe that your state-dependent memories are being activated NOW?

_____

_____

_____

_____

_____

_____

10. Describe this client's presentation style (avoidant, aggressive, straight-forward, shameful, guilt ridden, etc.):

_____

_____

_____

_____

_____

_____

11. What activates your state-dependent memories about the client's presentation style?

_____

_____

_____

_____

_____

_____

12. When you think of the problem you are experiencing with this client, what picture comes to your mind NOW?

_____

_____

_____

_____

_____

13. When you see this picture in your mind, what negative cognition do you get about yourself NOW?

_____

_____

_____

_____

14. When you link the picture with the negative cognition, what unpleasant sensations do you experience right NOW? Where in your body do you experience these sensations?

_____

_____
_____
_____
_____

15. Does your client notice your getting activated? Y__ N__. If yes, how does the client respond?

    Ignores it____
    Gets anxious_____
    Gets annoyed_____
    Attacks_____
    Feels guilt_____
    Feels shame_____
    Is curious_____
    Is suspicious_____

16. What does your client do with his or her reactions to your reactions? (To answer this, reconstruct a piece of process that became problematic between the two of you).

_____
_____
_____
_____
_____
_____
_____
_____
_____
_____
_____

17. After examining this piece of process, how would you NOW reconceptualize this treatment problem interpersonally?

_____
_____
_____
_____
_____
_____
_____
_____
_____
_____

_____

_____

18. What relational strategy(s) can you develop NOW to overcome this problem?

_____

_____

_____

_____

_____

_____

_____

PRACTICUM

(When this questionnaire is part of a workshop or study group, you may have the option of processing this issue to possible closure, including debriefing. Consider using Browning and Zangwill's floatback technique when stuck in the present without old memories available.)

Present-day referent (in the treatment moment):

_____

_____

_____

_____

_____

Old memory:

_____

_____

_____

_____

Picture:

_____

_____

_____

Negative cognition:

_____

_____

_____

Positive cognition:

_____

_____

_____

VOC ___

SUDS ___

Emotion:

_____

Body:

_____

Based on your experiential work, how do you NOW reconceptualize this problem relationally?

_____
_____
_____
_____
_____
_____
_____
_____
_____

What relational strategy might you consider NOW to help work this problem out?

_____
_____
_____
_____
_____
_____
_____
_____

Appendix H
International Treatment Guidelines and EMDR Research

I. International Treatment Guidelines

- American Psychiatric Association. (2004). *Practice guideline for the treatment of patients with acute stress disorder and posttraumatic stress disorder.* Arlington, VA: American Psychiatric Association.

  EMDR is given the same status as cognitive–behavioral therapy (CBT) as an effective treatment for ameliorating symptoms of both acute and chronic PTSD.

- Bleich, A., Kotler, M., Kutz, I., & Shalev, A. (2002). *Guidelines for the assessment and professional intervention with terror victims in the hospital and in the community.* Jerusalem: National Council for Mental Health.

  EMDR is one of only three methods recommended for treatment of terror victims.

- Chambless, D. L., et al. (1998). Update of empirically validated therapies, II. *The Clinical Psychologist, 51,* 3–16.

  According to a task force of the Clinical Division of the American Psychological Association, the only methods empirically supported for the treatment of any posttraumatic stress disorder population were EMDR, exposure therapy, and stress inoculation therapy.

- Clinical Resource Efficiency Support Team of the Northern Ireland Department of Health, Social Services, and Public Safety. (2003).

The management of post traumatic stress disorder in adults. Belfast: Ireland: Author.

Of all the psychotherapies, EMDR and CBT were stated to be the treatments of choice.

- Department of Veterans Affairs and Department of Defense. (2004). *VA/DoD clinical practice guideline for the management of post-traumatic stress.* Washington, DC: Author.

  EMDR was one of four therapies recommended and given the highest level of evidence. Available online at http://www.oqp.med.va.gov/cpg/PTSD/PTSD_cpg/frameset.htm.

- Quality Institute Heath Care CBO/Trimbos Institute. (2003). Dutch National Steering Committee Guidelines Mental Health Care: Multi-disciplinary Guideline Anxiety Disorders. Utrecht, Netherlands: Author.

  EMDR and CBT are both treatments of choice for PTSD.

- Foa, E. B., Keane, T. M., & Friedman, M. J. (2000). *Effective treatments for PTSD: Practice guidelines of the International Society for Traumatic Stress Studies.* New York: Guilford Press.

  These guidelines list EMDR as an efficacious treatment for PTSD.

- French National Institute of Health and Medical Research. (2004). *Psychotherapy: An evaluation of three approaches.* Paris: Author.

  Of the different psychotherapies, EMDR and CBT were stated to be the treatments of choice for trauma victims.

- Sjöblom, P. O., Andréewitch, S., Bejerot, S., Mörtberg, E., Brinck, U., Ruck, C., et al. (2003). *Regional treatment recommendation for anxiety disorders.* Stockholm: Medical Program Committee/Stockholm City Council.

  Of all psychotherapies, CBT and EMDR are recommended as treatments of choice for PTSD.

- Personal Improvement Computer Systems. (2004). *Therapy advisor.*

  An NIMH-sponsored Web site, available online at http://www.therapyadvisor.com, listing empirically supported methods for a variety of disorders. EMDR is one of three treatments listed for PTSD.

United Kingdom Department of Health. (2001). *Treatment choice in psychological therapies and counselling evidence based clinical practice guideline.* London: Author.

Best evidence of efficacy was reported for EMDR, exposure, and stress inoculation.

II. Meta-analyses

- Davidson, P. R., & Parker, K. C. H. (2001). Eye movement desensitization and reprocessing (EMDR): A meta-analysis. *Journal of Consulting and Clinical Psychology, 69,* 305–316.

  EMDR is equivalent to exposure and other cognitive behavioral treatments. It should be noted that exposure therapy uses 1 to 2 hr of daily homework and EMDR uses none.

- Maxfield, L., & Hyer, L. A. (2002). The relationship between efficacy and methodology in studies investigating EMDR treatment of PTSD. *Journal of Clinical Psychology, 58,* 23–41.

  A comprehensive meta-analysis reported the more rigorous the study, the larger the effect.

- Van Etten, M., & Taylor, S. (1998). Comparative efficacy of treatments for post-traumatic stress disorder: A meta-analysis. *Clinical Psychology and Psychotherapy, 5,* 126–144.

  This meta-analysis determined that EMDR and behavior therapy were superior to psychopharmaceuticals. EMDR was more efficient than behavior therapy, with results obtained in one-third the time.

III. Randomized Clinical Trials

- Carlson, J., Chemtob, C. M., Rusnak, K., Hedlund, N. L, & Muraoka, M. Y. (1998). Eye movement desensitization and reprocessing (EMDR): Treatment for combat-related post-traumatic stress disorder. *Journal of Traumatic Stress, 11,* 3–24.

  Twelve sessions of EMDR eliminated posttraumatic stress disorder in 77% of the multiply traumatized combat veterans studied. Effects were maintained at follow-up. This is the only randomized study to provide a full course of treatment with combat veterans. Other studies (e.g., Pitman et al./Macklin et al.) evaluated treatment of only one or two memories, which, according to the International Society for Traumatic Stress Studies practice guidelines, is inappropriate for multiple-trauma survivors. The VA/DoD practice guideline also indicates that these studies (often with only two sessions) offered insufficient treatment doses for veterans.

- Chemtob, C. M., Nakashima, J., & Carlson, J. G. (2002). Brief treatment for elementary school children with disaster-related PTSD: A field study. *Journal of Clinical Psychology, 58*, 99–112.

  EMDR was found to be an effective treatment for children with disaster-related PTSD who had not responded to another intervention. This is the first controlled study for disaster-related PTSD and the first controlled study examining the treatment of children with PTSD.

- Edmond, T., Rubin, A., & Wambach, K. (1999). The effectiveness of EMDR with adult female survivors of childhood sexual abuse. *Social Work Research, 23*, 103–116.

  EMDR treatment resulted in lower scores (fewer clinical symptoms) on all four of the outcome measures at the 3-month follow-up, compared to those in the routine treatment condition.

- Edmond, T., & Rubin, A. (2004). Eighteen month follow-up study of the effectiveness of EMDR with adult female survivors of childhood sexual abuse. *Journal of Child Sexual Abuse, 13 (1)*, pp. 69–86.

  This article reports on the 18-month follow-up from the 1991 study. The EMDR group improved on all standardized measures.

- Edmond, T., Sloan, L., & McCarty, D. (2004). Sexual abuse survivors' perceptions of the effectiveness of EMDR and eclectic therapy: A mixed-methods study. *Research on Social Work Practice, 14*, 259–272.

  Combination of qualitative and quantitative analyses of treatment outcomes with important implications for future rigorous research. Survivors' narratives indicate that EMDR produces greater trauma resolution, while within eclectic therapy, survivors more highly value their relationship with their therapist, through whom they learn effective coping strategies.

- Ironson, G. I., Freund, B., Strauss, J. L., & Williams, J. (2002). Comparison of two treatments for traumatic stress: A community-based study of EMDR and prolonged exposure. *Journal of Clinical Psychology, 58*, 113–128.

  Both EMDR and prolonged exposure produced a significant reduction in PTSD and depression symptoms. Study found that 70% of EMDR participants achieved a good outcome in three active treatment sessions, compared to 29% of persons in the prolonged exposure condition. EMDR also had fewer dropouts.

- Jaberghaderi, N., Greenwald, R., Rubin, A., Dolatabadim S., & Zand, S. O. (2004). A comparison of CBT and EMDR for sexually abused Iranian girls. *Clinical Psychology and Psychotherapy,* II(5), pp. 358–386.

Both EMDR and CBT produced significant reduction in PTSD and behavior problems. EMDR was significantly more efficient, using approximately half the number of sessions to achieve results.

• Lee, C., Gavriel, H., Drummond, P., Richards, J., & Greenwald, R. (2002). Treatment of post-traumatic stress disorder: A comparison of stress inoculation training with prolonged exposure and eye movement desensitization and reprocessing. *Journal of Clinical Psychology, 58,* 1071–1089.

Both EMDR and stress inoculation therapy plus prolonged exposure (SITPE) produced significant improvement, with EMDR achieving greater improvement on PTSD intrusive symptoms. Participants in the EMDR condition showed greater gains at 3-month follow-up. EMDR required 3 hr of homework compared to 28 hr for SITPE.

• Marcus, S., Marquis, P., & Sakai, C. (1997). Controlled study of treatment of PTSD using EMDR in an HMO setting. *Psychotherapy, 34,* 307–315.

Funded by Kaiser Permanente. Results show that 100% of single-trauma and 80% of multiple-trauma survivors were no longer diagnosed with posttraumatic stress disorder after six 50-min sessions.

• Marcus, S., Marquis, P., & Sakai, C. (2004). Three- and Six-month follow-up of EMDR treatment of PTSD in an HMO setting. *International Journal of Stress Management, 11,* 195–208.

Funded by Kaiser Permanente, this follow-up evaluation indicates that a relatively small number of EMDR sessions result in substantial benefits that are maintained over time.

• Power, K. G., McGoldrick, T., Brown, K., et al. (2002). A controlled comparison of eye movement desensitization and reprocessing versus exposure plus cognitive restructuring, versus waiting list in the treatment of post-traumatic stress disorder. *Journal of Clinical Psychology and Psychotherapy, 9,* 299–318.

Both EMDR and exposure therapy plus cognitive restructuring (with daily homework) produced significant improvement. EMDR was more beneficial for depression and required fewer treatment sessions.

• Rothbaum, B. (1997). A controlled study of eye movement desensitization and reprocessing in the treatment of post-traumatic stress disordered sexual assault victims. *Bulletin of the Menninger Clinic,* *61,* 317–334.

Three 90-min sessions of EMDR eliminated posttraumatic stress disorder in 90% of rape victims.

• Scheck, M., Schaeffer, J. A., & Gillette, C. (1998). Brief psychological intervention with traumatized young women: The efficacy of eye movement desensitization and reprocessing. *Journal of Traumatic Stress, 11,* 25–44.

Two sessions of EMDR reduced psychological distress scores in traumatized young women and brought scores within one standard deviation of the norm.

• Shapiro, F. (1989). Efficacy of the eye movement desensitization procedure in the treatment of traumatic memories. *Journal of Traumatic Stress Studies, 2,* 199–223.

This seminal study appeared the same year as the first controlled studies of CBT treatments. Three-month follow-up indicated substantial effects on distress and behavioral reports. Marred by lack of standardized measures and the originator's serving as sole therapist.

• Soberman, G. B., Greenwald, R., & Rule, D. L. (2002). A controlled study of eye movement desensitization and reprocessing (EMDR) for boys with conduct problems. *Journal of Aggression, Maltreatment, and Trauma, 6,* 217–236.

The addition of three sessions of EMDR resulted in large and significant reductions of memory-related distress and problem behaviors by 2-month follow-up.

• Taylor, S., et al. (2003). Comparative efficacy, speed, and adverse effects of three PTSD treatments: Exposure therapy, EMDR, and relaxation training. *Journal of Consulting and Clinical Psychology, 71,* 330–338.

The only randomized study to show exposure statistically superior to EMDR on two subscales (out of 10). This study used therapist assisted *in vivo* exposure, where the therapist takes the person to previously avoided areas, in addition to imaginal exposure and 1 hr of daily homework (@ 50 hr). The EMDR group used only standard sessions and no homework.

• Vaughan, K., Armstrong, M. F., Gold, R., O'Connor, N., Jenneke, W., & Tarrier, N. (1994). A trial of eye movement desensitization compared to image habituation training and applied muscle relaxation in post-traumatic stress disorder. *Journal of Behavior Therapy & Experimental Psychiatry, 25,* 283–291.

All treatments led to significant decreases in PTSD symptoms for subjects in the treatment groups as compared to those on a waiting list, with a greater reduction in the EMDR group, particularly with respect to intrusive symptoms. In the 2 to 3 weeks of the study, 40 to 60 additional minutes of daily homework were part of the treatment in the other two conditions.

- Wilson, S., Becker, L. A., & Tinker, R. H. (1995). Eye movement desensitization and reprocessing (EMDR): Treatment for psychologically traumatized individuals. *Journal of Consulting and Clinical Psychology, 63,* 928–937.

  Three sessions of EMDR produced clinically significant change in traumatized civilians on multiple measures.

- Wilson, S., Becker, L. A., & Tinker, R. H. (1997). Fifteen-month follow-up of eye movement desensitization and reprocessing (EMDR) treatment of post-traumatic stress disorder and psychological trauma. *Journal of Consulting and Clinical Psychology, 65,* 1047–1056.

  Follow-up at 15 months showed maintenance of positive treatment effects with 84% remission of PTSD diagnosis.

IV. Non Randomized Studies

- Devilly, G. J., & Spence, S. H. (1999). The relative efficacy and treatment distress of EMDR and a cognitive behavioral trauma treatment protocol in the amelioration of post-traumatic stress disorder. *Journal of Anxiety Disorders, 13,* 131–157.

  The only EMDR research study that found CBT superior to EMDR. The study is marred by poor treatment delivery and higher expectations in the CBT condition. Treatment was delivered in both conditions by the developer of the CBT protocol.

- Fernandez, I., Gallinari, E., & Lorenzetti, A. (2004). A school-based EMDR intervention for children who witnessed the Pirelli building airplane crash in Milan, Italy. *Journal of Brief Therapy, 2,* 129–136.

  A group intervention of EMDR was provided to 236 schoolchildren exhibiting PTSD symptoms 30 d post-incident. At 4-month follow-up, teachers reported that all but two children evinced a return to normal functioning after treatment.

- Grainger, R. D., Levin, C., Allen-Byrd, L., Doctor, R. M., & Lee, H. (1997). An empirical evaluation of eye movement desensitization and reprocessing (EMDR) with survivors of a natural catastrophe. *Journal of Traumatic Stress, 10,* 665–671.

  A study of Hurricane Andrew survivors found significant differences on the Impact of Event Scale and subjective distress in a comparison of EMDR and nontreatment condition.

- Puffer, M., Greenwald, R., & Elrod, D. (1997). A single session EMDR study with 20 traumatized children and adolescents. *Traumatology, 3*(2), Article 6.

  In this delayed treatment comparison, over half of the participants moved from clinical to normal levels on the Impact of Events Scale, and all but three showed at least partial symptom relief on several measures at 1 – 3 months following a single EMDR session.

- Silver, S. M., Brooks, A., & Obenchain, J. (1995). Eye movement desensitization and reprocessing treatment of Vietnam war veterans with PTSD: Comparative effects with biofeedback and relaxation training. *Journal of Traumatic Stress, 8,* 337–342.

  One of only two EMDR research studies that evaluated a clinically relevant course of EMDR treatment with combat veterans (e.g., more than one or two memories; see Carlson, Chemtob, Rusnak, Hedlund, & Muraoka, 1998, above). The analysis of an inpatient veterans' PTSD program ($N = 100$) found EMDR to be vastly superior to biofeedback and relaxation training on seven of eight measures.

- Silver, S. M., Rogers, S., Knipe, J., & Colelli, G. (in press). EMDR therapy following the 9/11 terrorist attacks: A community-based intervention project in New York City. *International Journal of Stress Management, 12*(1), p. 29–42.

  Clients made highly significant positive gains on a range of outcome variables, including validated psychometrics and self-report scales. Analyses of the data indicate that EMDR is a useful treatment intervention both in the immediate aftermath of disaster and later.

- Solomon, R. M., & Kaufman, T. E. (2002). A peer support workshop for the treatment of traumatic stress of railroad personnel: Contributions of eye movement desensitization and reprocessing (EMDR). *Journal of Brief Therapy, 2,* 27–33.

  Sixty railroad employees who had experienced fatal grade crossing accidents were evaluated for workshop outcomes and for the additive effects of EMDR treatment. Although the workshop was successful, in this setting, the addition of a short session of EMDR (5 – 40 min) led to significantly lower (subclinical) scores, which further decreased at follow-up.

- Sprang, G. (2001). The use of eye movement desensitization and reprocessing (EMDR) in the treatment of traumatic stress and complicated mourning: Psychological and behavioral outcomes. *Research on Social Work Practice, 11,* 300–320.

  In a multisite study, EMDR significantly reduced symptoms more often than the CBT treatment on behavioral measures and on four of five psychosocial measures. EMDR was more efficient, inducing change at an earlier stage and requiring fewer sessions.

V. Information Processing, Procedures, and Mechanism of Action

EMDR contains many procedures and elements that contribute to treatment effects. While the methodology used in EMDR has been extensively validated (see above), questions still remain regarding mechanism of action. An information-processing model (Shapiro, 2001, 2002a) is used to explain EMDR's clinical effects and to guide clinical practice. This model is not linked to any specific neurobiological mechanism since the field of neurobiology is as yet unable to determine the neurobiological concomitants of any form of psychotherapy (nor of many medications). However, since EMDR achieves clinical effects without the need for homework or the prolonged focus used in exposure therapies, attention has been paid to the possible neurobiological processes that might be evoked. Although the eye movements (and other dual-attention stimulation) comprise only one procedural element, this element has come under the greatest scrutiny. Controlled studies evaluating the mechanism of action of the eye movement component follow this section.

- MacCulloch, M. J., & Feldman, P. (1996). Eye movement desensitization treatment utilizes the positive visceral element of the investigatory reflex to inhibit the memories of post-traumatic stress disorder: A theoretical analysis. *British Journal of Psychiatry, 169,* 571–579.

  One of a variety of articles positing an orienting response as a contributing element (see Shapiro, 2001, for a comprehensive examination of theories and suggested research parameters). This theory has received controlled research support (see Barrowcliff, Gray, Freeman, & MacCulloch, 2004; Barrowcliff, Gray, MacCulloch, Freeman, & MacCulloch, 2003).

- Perkins, B. R., & Rouanzoin, C. C. (2002). A critical evaluation of current views regarding eye movement desensitization and reprocessing (EMDR): Clarifying points of confusion. *Journal of Clinical Psychology, 58,* 77–97.

  Reviews common errors and misperceptions of the procedures, research, and theory.

- Ray, A. L., & Zbik, A. (2001). Cognitive behavioral therapies and beyond. In C. D. Tollison, J. R. Satterhwaite, & J. W. Tollison (Eds.), *Practical pain management* (3rd ed.; pp. 189–208). Philadelphia: Lippincott.

  Note that the application of EMDR guided by its information-processing model appears to afford benefits to chronic pain patients not found in other treatments.

- Stickgold, R. (2002). EMDR: A putative neurobiological mechanism of action. *Journal of Clinical Psychology, 58,* 61–75.

  Comprehensive explanation of the potential links to the processes that occur in REM sleep. Controlled studies have evaluated these theories (see Christman, Garvey, Propper, & Phaneuf, 2003; Kuiken, Bears, Miall, & Smith, 2001–2002).

- Rogers, S., & Silver, S. M. (2002). Is EMDR an exposure therapy? A review of trauma protocols. *Journal of Clinical Psychology, 58,* 43–59.

  Theoretical, clinical, and procedural differences referencing 2 decades of CBT and EMDR research.

- Shapiro, F. (2001). Eye movement desensitization and reprocessing: Basic principles, protocols and procedures (2nd ed.). New York: Guilford Press.

  EMDR is an eight-phase psychotherapy with standardized procedures and protocols that are all believed to contribute to therapeutic effect. This text provides description and clinical transcripts.

- Shapiro, F. (Ed.). (2002). *EMDR as an integrative psychotherapy approach: Experts of diverse orientations explore the paradigm prism.* Washington, DC: American Psychological Association Books.

  EMDR is an integrative approach distinct from other forms of psychotherapy. Experts of the major psychotherapy orientations identify and highlight various procedural elements.

VI. Randomized Studies of Hypotheses Regarding Eye Movements

A number of international practice guideline committees have reported that the clinical component analyses reviewed by Davidson and Parker (2001) are not well designed (International Society for Traumatic Stress Studies/ISTSS; DoD/DVA). Davidson and Parker note that there is a trend toward significance for eye movements when the studies conducted with clinical populations are examined separately. Unfortunately, even these studies are flawed. As noted in the ISTSS guidelines (Chemtob et al., 2000), since these clinical populations received insufficient treatment doses to obtain substantial main effects, the studies are inappropriate for component analyses. However, as noted in the DoD/DVA guidelines, the eye movements used in EMDR have been separately evaluated by numerous memory researchers. These studies have found a direct effect on emotional arousal, imagery vividness, attentional flexibility, and memory association.

- Andrade, J., Kavanagh, D., & Baddeley, A. (1997). Eye-movements and visual imagery: A working memory approach to the treatment of post-traumatic stress disorder. *British Journal of Clinical Psychology, 36*, 209–223.

  Tested the working memory theory. Eye movements were superior to control conditions in reducing image vividness and emotionality.

- Barrowcliff, A. L., Gray, N. S., Freeman, T. C. A., & MacCulloch, M. J. (2004). Eye-movements reduce the vividness, emotional valence and electrodermal arousal associated with negative autobiographical memories. *Journal of Forensic Psychiatry and Psychology, 15*, 325–345.

  Tested the reassurance reflex model. Eye movements were superior to control conditions in reducing image vividness and emotionality.

- Barrowcliff, A. L., Gray, N. S., MacCulloch, S., Freeman, T. C. A., & MacCulloch, M. J. (2003). Horizontal rhythmical eye-movements consistently diminish the arousal provoked by auditory stimuli. *British Journal of Clinical Psychology, 42*, 289–302.

  Tested the reassurance reflex model. Eye movements were superior to control conditions in reducing arousal provoked by auditory stimuli.

- Christman, S. D., Garvey, K. J., Propper, R. E., & Phaneuf, K. A. (2003). Bilateral eye movements enhance the retrieval of episodic memories. *Neuropsychology, 17*, 221–229.

Tested cortical activation theories. Results provide indirect support for the orienting response/REM theories suggested by Stickgold (2002). Saccadic eye movements, but not tracking eye movements were superior to control conditions in episodic retrieval.

- Kavanagh, D. J., Freese, S., Andrade, J., & May, J. (2001). Effects of visuospatial tasks on desensitization to emotive memories. *British Journal of Clinical Psychology, 40,* 267–280.

  Tested the working memory theory. Eye movements were superior to control conditions in reducing within-session image vividness and emotionality. There was no difference at 1 week post.

- Kuiken, D., Bears, M., Miall, D., & Smith, L. (2001–2002). Eye movement desensitization reprocessing facilitates attentional orienting. *Imagination, Cognition and Personality, 21*(1), 3–20.

  Tested the orienting response theory related to REM-type mechanisms. Indicated that the eye movement condition was correlated with increased attentional flexibility. Eye movements were superior to control conditions.

- Sharpley, C. F., Montgomery, I. M., & Scalzo, L. A. (1996). Comparative efficacy of EMDR and alternative procedures in reducing the vividness of mental images. *Scandinavian Journal of Behaviour Therapy, 25,* 37–42.

  Results suggest support for the working memory theory. Eye movements were superior to control conditions in reducing image vividness.

- Van den Hout, M., Muris, P., Salemink, E., & Kindt, M. (2001). Autobiographical memories become less vivid and emotional after eye movements. *British Journal of Clinical Psychology, 40,* 121–130.

  Tested their theory that eye movements change the somatic perceptions accompanying retrieval, leading to decreased affect, and therefore decreasing vividness. Eye movements were superior to control conditions in reducing image vividness. Unlike control conditions, eye movements also decreased emotionality.

VII. Additional Neurobiological Evaluations

- Lamprecht, F., Kohnke, C., Lempa, W., Sack, M., Matzke, M., & Munte, T. (2004). Event-related potentials and EMDR treatment of post-traumatic stress disorder. *Neuroscience Research, 49,* 267–272.

- Lansing, K., Amen, D. G., Hanks, C., & Rudy, L. (in press). High resolution brain SPECT imaging and EMDR in police officers with PTSD. *Journal of Neuropsychiatry and Clinical Neurosciences.*
- Levin, P., Lazrove, S., & van der Kolk, B. A. (1999). What psychological testing and neuroimaging tell us about the treatment of posttraumatic stress disorder (PTSD) by eye movement desensitization and reprocessing (EMDR). *Journal of Anxiety Disorders, 13,* 159–172.
- van der Kolk, B., Burbridge, J., & Suzuki, J. (1997). The psychobiology of traumatic memory: Clinical implications of neuroimaging studies. *Annals of the New York Academy of Sciences, 821,* 99–113.

Appendix I
EMDR Clinician Resources:
The Humanitarian Assistance Program[1]

I. Purpose

"Our goal is to break the cycle of suffering that ruins lives and devastates families."

EMDR–Humanitarian Assistance Programs (HAP), a 501(c)(3) non-profit organization, can be described as the mental health equivalent of Doctors Without Borders: a global network of clinicians who travel anywhere there is a need to stop suffering and prevent the aftereffects of trauma and violence.

Our primary focus is on training local therapists within crisis or under-served communities to treat trauma with EMDR (Eye Movement Desensitization and Reprocessing), a therapeutic approach that has been proven effective for posttraumatic stress disorder in numerous controlled studies.

The HAP model emphasizes training and empowering local clinicians to continue the healing process.

EMDR becomes a powerful weapon for battling the aftereffects of trauma, whether from natural or manmade disaster. We also help local therapists and organizations set up infrastructures to support ongoing direct service to their communities. In this way, the healing power of EMDR is increased exponentially, continuing long after HAP clinicians leave an area.

Our Disaster Mental Health Recovery Network coordinates clinicians to treat victims and emergency service workers after crises such as the Oklahoma City bombing and the 9/11 terrorist attacks.

Other HAP projects have included work in the Balkans; Bangladesh; Columbine, Colorado; Central and South America; Milan, Italy; Dunblane, Scotland; Northern Ireland; Bombay; San Francisco; and Turkey, as well as for Palestinians and Israelis.

II. Donate to EMDR Humanitarian Assistance Programs

EMDR HAP depends on the financial support of donors, as well as the voluntary services of skilled EMDR educators, to bring its programs to traumatized communities and their caregivers across the United States and around the world. Donors receive the periodic HAP newsletter describing the projects their donations have funded.

You can help in this work with a tax-deductible financial contribution in any amount.

By mail, send your check in U.S. dollars payable to EMDR HAP to:

EMDR HAP
P.O. Box 6505
Hamden, CT 06517

By credit card, charged to VISA, Master Card, American Express, or Discover in U.S. dollars:

- **Online:** Go to our *secure site* and complete and submit the donation form provided.
- **By fax:** Print out the fax/mail donation form, provide all requested information including your signature, and fax to **(203) 288-4060**.

III. Frequent Flyer Miles

One of our greatest operating costs is the airfare to bring HAP volunteers to the sites of our projects. We are seeking recognition by major airline frequent flyer programs as one of "their" charities, so that miles in any amount can be donated to a fund for HAP's benefit. Until we get that status, we are able to benefit from donated miles only if an individual uses his or her miles to buy us a specific ticket. This is a cumbersome process, but still worthwhile for HAP.

If you would like to help in this way, you can register with us and pledge us your miles, adding to your pledge from time to time until you have enough for a ticket, domestic or international. (All miles must be in the program of a specific airline or its partner airlines to qualify for a ticket from any of the partner airlines.) We will then contact you and ask you to purchase a specific ticket for a current HAP project volunteer with those pledged miles. We have been informed that the IRS does not consider gifts of frequent flyer miles to have a cash value for purposes of tax deduction. But we assure you that such gifts have a great cash value for HAP.

EMDR HAP
P.O. Box 6505
Hamden, CT 06517
or fax to (203) 288-4060

IV. EMDR International Association (EMDRIA)

The EMDR International Association is a professional organization of EMDR-trained therapists and researchers devoted to promoting the highest possible standard of excellence and integrity in EMDR practice, research, and education for the public good.

EMDRIA further develops the existing body of empirical knowledge, theory, and clinical application of EMDR procedures and keeps its membership informed of changes. It is also involved in developing ethical standards for practice and training; creating clinical support materials; and educating other professional organizations and the general public about the benefits of EMDR.

For more information about EMDRIA, contact the association at P.O. Box 141925, Austin TX 78714-1925, Phone: (512) 451-5200, email info@emdria.org, or visit their Web site at http://www.emdria.org.

V. The EMDR Europe Association

The EMDR Europe Association is the governing body for all the national European EMDR Associations, including Israel. It performs a similar function to EMDRIA as the overseeing professional organization of European EMDR-trained therapists and researchers. It is also devoted to promoting the highest possible standard of excellence and integrity in EMDR practice, research, and education. Further details can be found via their website http:// www.emdr-europe.org or email: info@emdr-europe.org.

VI. EMDR Association of Canada

EMDRAC (the Eye Movement Desensitization and Reprocessing Association of Canada) is dedicated to establishing, maintaining, and promoting the highest standards of excellence and integrity in Eye Movement Desensitization and Reprocessing practice, research, and education. Further information can be found on their website at www.emdrac.ca.

Glossary

Adaptive resolution — A state that occurs as a result of complete information processing; learning takes place, and information is stored with appropriate affect and is available to guide future action (Shapiro & Maxfield, 2002).

Appraisal — The brain's assignment of meaning to a new stimulus, achieved by evaluating incoming data (by consulting the mental models that the brain has created based on past experiences) and determining whether that stimulus is good, bad, or neutral. Both internal and external factors play a role in this decision, as well as information about the social context (Siegel, 1999).

Arousal — Based on the appraisal (good, bad, or neutral) it has made, the brain directs the flow of energy through the system to prepare the rest of the brain and the body for action. The essential message of this arousal function is "Act!" This is internal emotional arousal, as opposed to external physiological arousal from a stimulant such as caffeine or exercise. Emotional forms of arousal result from the brain's having assigned an evaluated subjective meaning — positive or negative — to the stimulus. If the client appraises the clinician as genuinely interested, positive arousal occurs, and the client begins his or her narrative, such as "I've been thinking about what we've been working on, and I remembered that it was my older brother, not my father, who bullied me the most" (Siegel, 1999).

Attunement — This occurs when one person nonverbally perceives and feels another's experience. Similar to empathy, attunement creates an attachment bond. When something interferes with attunement, the clinician and client slip into what is called misattunement or malattunement (Siegel, 1999).

Compartmentalization — This occurs when a clinician has had a countertransferential reaction and mentally steps aside, without interrupting the client's trauma processing, in order to use his or her own resourcing strategies to return to a state of centeredness. If the countertransference has actually stopped processing, this self-resourcing technique is not appropriate; a relational interweave should be used instead.

Contingent communication — This is the attuned connection between two individuals' mental states, whereby the state of one affects the state of the other, and vice versa (Siegel, 1999).

Coregulation — The back-and-forth process where each person allows the other to influence his or her state (Siegel, 1999).

Countertransference — The activation of old mental models and states of mind from the clinician's relationships with important figures in the past, stimulated — intentionally or not — by the client.

Desensitization — The elimination or reduction of anxiety elicited by specific environment or internal stimuli (Shapiro & Maxfield, 2002).

Dysfunctionally stored information — A situation that occurs as a result of incomplete processing; information is stored in a memory network with a highly negative emotional charge and isolated from more adaptive information (Shapiro & Maxfield, 2002).

Emotional memory — A person's mood at the time of a past event.

Empathic resonance — See *Resonance.*

Explicit memory — Semantic and autobiographical memory; one's sense of oneself at a past time in one's life. Also called declarative memory, explicit memory is devoid of state-dependent traumatic memories.

Feeder memories — Old state-dependent memories, thematically related to a similar problem if not to the presenting problem.

Hyperarousal — A state of mind in which too much negative stimulation floods the client, either for the moment or chronically, as in the case of clients with poor attachment patterns.

Hypoarousal — A state of mind that appears to be in a shut-down mode; the client is usually blocked from knowledge of his or her body's reactions in life.

Implicit memory — Memories that include body or somatic memory, perceptual memory, emotional memory, and behavioral memory. Implicit memory is devoid of a sense of oneself or a sense of time. Also called nondeclarative memory. Parts of state-dependent memories may be dissociated into this memory system and stored in a dysfunctional way (Siegel, 1999).

Information processing — The process by which new perceptual information is sorted, connected with associated memory networks, encoded, and stored in memory (Shapiro & Maxfield, 2002).

Information processing system — A physiological-based system that is geared to process information to a state of adaptive resolution (Shapiro & Maxfield, 2002).

Intersubjective — Two people having mutually reciprocal influence on each other. Another way to express this is: the continuous feedback loops between clinician and client based upon each one's old mental models from relationships with important figures in their pasts. The interface of reciprocally interacting worlds of experience.

Memory — Broadly defined, memory is the way past events affect a person's future function.

Memory networks — Neurobiological associations of related memories, thoughts, images, emotions, and sensations (Shapiro & Maxfield, 2002).

Mental model — The generalizations made by the brain from past experiences. Mental models are consulted when the brain appraises a new stimulus. Mental models are basic components of implicit memory. They help the mind to seek out familiar objects or experiences and "know" what to expect from the environment (Siegel, 1999).

Mental state resonance — See *Resonance.*

Nonlinearity — The characteristic of a system when small changes in the components of the system lead to huge and unpredictable changes in its behavior. This unpredictability is due in part to the fact that the response is predicated on the content of the given system and in part to the fact that the system will have random activations that may or may not be reinforced by its environment.

Perceptual memory — A recollection of what things looked, sounded, smelled, and tasted like, and what they felt like to the touch.

Presentation style — The manner in which the client shows himself or herself to the world; it can also be a way a client describes or avoids describing trauma.

Reciprocal mutual influence — The ways in which client and clinician influence each other explicitly and implicitly.

Relational strategy — Any intervention that correctly identifies a breach in contingent communication between client and clinician and restores it, usually through recreating an atmosphere of safety and then targeting transferential material.

Relational interweave — A type of relational strategy where the clinician notices that misattunement has interfered with processing, takes rational responsibility for the moment (without necessarily sharing the content), and restarts the client's productive processing safely.

Reprocessing — The process of forging new associative links between dysfunctionally stored information and adaptive information, resulting in complete information processing and adaptive resolution (Shapiro & Maxfield, 2002).

Response flexibility — The ability to respond to new situations in appropriate ways, unhampered by the triggers or aftereffects of old trauma.

Resonance — A very deep form of attunement; a sensory motor state of vibratory identification. Mental state resonance is the sensitivity to signals and attunement between client and clinician involving the intermittent alignment of states of mind. As two individual states are brought into alignment, a form of what we call mental state resonance can occur in which each person's mental state both influences, and is influenced by, that of the other. Productive processing usually occurs in this state.

Somatic memory — Recollection of what the body felt like at the time of a past event.

Stabilization — A state of equilibrium maintained by the client prior to reprocessing of distressing events; includes safety, affect regulation, and impulse control (Shapiro & Maxfield, 2002).

State-dependent memory — A traumatic memory that is held dysfunctionally and developmentally frozen in time because the brain is unable to process it naturally into long-term storage. When any stimuli, external or internal, activate the neural network holding a state-dependent memory, a state of mind is activated in which these signals or information are released. This may cause changes in emotion, thought, and behavior. This kind of state of mind is usually not influenced sufficiently by more adaptive states of mind. This, in turn, causes consternation in the person because he or she knows that what he or she is experiencing is irrational yet feels powerless to change this state.

State of mind — refers to the cluster of brain activity (and mental modules) at a given moment in time. This "moment" can be brief or extended, and states of mind can have various degrees of sharpness or blurriness to their boundaries across time. The repeated activation of states of mind as time goes by – over weeks, months, and years – into a specialized, goal-directed set of cohesive functional units is what we are going to call a "specialized self" or "self state" (Siegel 1999).

Transference — The activation of old mental models and states of mind from the client's relationships with important figures in the past.

Working memory — The chalkboard of the mind, which allows an individual to reflect upon things perceived in the present and recalled from the past.

References

Allen, J. G., & Lewis, L. (1996). A conceptual framework for treating traumatic memories and its application to EMDR. *Bulletin of the Menninger Clinic, 60 (2)*, 238–263.

Baker, N., & McBride, B. (1991, August). *Clinical applications of EMDR in a law enforcement environment: Observations of the psychological service unit of the L.A. county sheriff's department.* Paper presented at the Police Psychology (Division 18, Police & Public Safety Sub-section) Mini-Convention at the American Psychological Association annual convention, San Francisco, CA.

Barlow, D., & Craske, M. (1989). *Mastery of your anxiety and panic.* New York: Graywind.

Beck, A. T. & Emery, G. (1985). *Anxiety Disorders and Phobias: A Cognitive Perspective.* New York: Basic Books.

Bergman, U. (2000). EMDR and ego state therapy: Treating the spectrum of personality disorders. EMDRIA annual conference.

Beutler, L., & Harwood, T. (2002). What is and can be attributed to the therapeutic relationship. *J. Contemporary Psychotherapy, 32*(1), 25–33.

Blore, D. C. (1997a). Reflections on "a day when the whole world seemed to be darkened." *Changes: An International Journal of Psychology and Psychiatry, 15*, 89–95.

Blore, D. C. (1997b). Use of EMDR to treat morbid jealousy: A case study. *British Journal of Nursing, 6*, 984–988.

Bohart, A. (2002). How does the relationship facilitate productive client thinking? *J. Contemporary Psychotherapy, 32*(1), 62–69.

Brown, K. W., McGoldrick, T., & Buchanan, R. (1997). Body dysmorphic disorder: Seven cases treated with eye movement desensitization and reprocessing. *Behavioural & Cognitive Psychotherapy, 25*, 203–207.

Browning, C. J. (1999, September). Floatback and float-forward: Techniques for linking past, present, and future. *EMDRIA Newsletter,* 12.

Carlson, J. G., Chemtob, C. M., Rusnak, K., & Hedlund, N. L. (1996). Eye movement desensitization and reprocessing treatment for combat PTSD. *Psychotherapy, 33*, 104–113.

Carlson, J. G., Chemtob, C. M., Rusnak, K., Hedlund, N. L., & Muraoka, M. Y. (1998). Eye movement desensitization and reprocessing for combat-related posttraumatic stress disorder. *J. Traumatic Stress, 11*, 3–24.

Chambless, D. L., Baker, M. J., Baucom, D. H., Beutier, L. E., Calhoun, K. S., Crits-Christoph, P., et al. (1998). Update on empirically validated therapies. *Clinical Psychologist, 51*, 3–16.

Chemtob, C. M., Nakashima, J., & Carlson, J. G. (2002). Brief treatment for elementary school children with disaster-related PTSD: A field study. *J. Clinical Psychol., 58*, 99–112.

Cocco, N., & Sharpe, L. (1993). An auditory variant of eye movement desensitization in a case of childhood post-traumatic stress disorder. *Journal of Behavior Therapy and Experimental Psychiatry, 24*, 373–377.

275

Cohn, L. (1993). Art psychotherapy and the new eye treatment desensitization and reprocessing (EMD/R) method, an integrated approach. In E. Dishup (Ed.), *California Art Therapy Trends* (pp. 275–290). Chicago, IL: Magnolia Street Publisher.

Crabbe, B. (1996, November). Can eye-movement therapy improve your riding? *Dressage Today,* 28–33.

Daniels, N., Lipke, H., Richardson, R., & Silver, S. (1992, October). *Vietnam veterans' treatment programs using eye movement desensitization and reprocessing.* Symposium presented at the International Society for Traumatic Stress Studies annual convention, Los Angeles, CA.

Datta, P. C., & Wallace, J. (1994, May). *Treatment of sexual traumas of sex offenders using eye movement desensitization and reprocessing.* Paper presented at the 11th Annual Symposium in Forensic Psychology, San Francisco.

Datta, P. C., & Wallace, J. (1996, November). *Enhancement of victim empathy along with reduction of anxiety and increase of positive cognition of sex offenders after treatment with EMDR.* Paper presented at the EMDR Special Interest Group at the Annual Convention of the Association for the Advancement of Behavior Therapy, New York.

Davidson, P. R., & Parker, K. C. H. (2001). Eye movement desensitization and reprocessing (EMDR): A meta-analysis. *J. Consulting Clinical Psychol., 69,* 305–316.

De Jongh, A., & Ten Broeke, E. (1998). Treatment of choking phobia by targeting traumatic memories with EMDR: A case study. *Clinical Psychology & Psychotherapy, 5,* 264–269.

De Jongh, A., Ten Broeke, E., and Renssen, M. R. (1999). Treatment of specific phobias with eye movement desensitization and reprocessing (EMDR): Protocol, empirical status, and conceptual issues. *Journal of Anxiety Disorders, 13,* 69–85.

De Jongh, A., van den Oord, H. J. M., & Ten Broeke, E. (2002). Efficacy of eye movement desensitization and reprocessing (EMDR) in the treatment of specific phobias: Four single-case studies on dental phobia. *Journal of Clinical Psychology, 58,* 1489–1503.

Devilly, G. J., & Spence, S. H. (1999). The relative efficacy and treatment distress of EMDR and a cognitive-behavioral trauma treatment protocol in the amelioration of posttraumatic stress disorder. *J. Anxiety Disorders, 13,* 131–157.

Devilly, G. J., Spence, S. H., & Rapee, R. M. (1998). Statistical and reliable change with eye movement desensitization and processing: treating a trauma within a veteran population. *Behav. Ther., 29,* 435–455.

Doctor, R. (1994, March). *Eye movement desensitization and reprocessing: A clinical and research examination with anxiety disorders.* Paper presented at the 14th annual meeting of the Anxiety Disorders Association of America, Santa Monica, CA.

Dworkin, M. (2003). Integrative approaches to EMDR: Empathy, the intersubjective, and the cognitive interweave. *J. Psychotherapy Integration, 13*(2), 171–187.

Dyregrov, A. (1993). EMDR-nymetode for tramebehandling. *Tidsskrift for Norsk Psykologforening, 30,* 975–981.

Dziegielewski, S., & Wolfe, P. (2000). Eye movement desensitization and reprocessing (EMDR) as a time-limited treatment intervention for body image disturbance and self-esteem: A single subject case study design. *Journal of Psychotherapy in Independent Practice, 1,* 1–16.

Edmond, T., Rubin, A., & Wambach, K. (1999). The effectiveness of EMDR with adult female survivors of childhood sexual abuse. *Soc. Work Res., 23,* 103–116.

Egendorf, A. (1986). *Healing from the war: Trauma and Transformation after Vietnam.* Boston: Shambhala.

Fensterheim, H. (1996). Eye movement desensitization and reprocessing with complex personality pathology: An integrative therapy. *Journal of Psychotherapy Integration, 6,* 27–38.

Fernandez, I., Gallinari, E., & Lorenzetti, A. (2004). A school-based EMDR intervention for children who witnessed the Pirelli Building airplane crash in Milan, Italy. *Journal of Brief Therapy, 2,* 129–136.

Feske, U., & Goldstein, A. (1997). Eye movement desensitization and reprocessing treatment for panic disorder: A controlled outcome and partial dismantling study. *Journal of Consulting and Clinical Psychology, 36,* 1026–1035.

Figley, C. R. (Ed.). (1995). *Compassion fatigue: Coping with secondary traumatic stress disorder in those who treat the traumatized.* London: Brunner-Routledge.

Figley, C. R. (Ed.). (2002). *Treating compassion fatigue.* Hove, England: Brunner-Routledge.

Fine, C. G. (1994, June). *Eye movement desensitization and reprocessing (EMDR) for dissociative disorders.* Presentation at the Eastern Regional Conference on Abuse and Multiple Personality. Alexandria, VA.

Fine, C., & Berkowitz, A. (2001). The wreathing protocol: The imbrication of hypnosis and EMDR in the treatment of dissociative identity disorder and other dissociative responses. *American Journal of Clinical Hypnosis, 43,* 275–290.

Foa, E. B., Keane, T., & Friedman, M. J. (Eds.). (2000). *ISTSS guidelines for PTSD.* New York: Guilford Press.

Foa, E. B., & Meadows, E. A. (1997). Psychological treatments for posttraumatic stress disorder: A critical review. *Annu. Rev. Psychol., 48,* 449–480.

Forbes, D., Creamer, M., & Rycroft, P. (1994). Eye movement desensitization and reprocessing in posttraumatic stress disorder: A pilot study using assessment measures. *Journal of Behavior Therapy and Experimental Psychiatry, 25,* 113–120.

Forgash, C. (2003). Improving Survivors Health with Integrated EMDR and Ego State Treatment. EMDRIA annual conference. EMDRIA annual conference.

Foster, S., & Lendl, J. (1995). Eye movement desensitization and reprocessing: Initial applications for enhancing performance in athletes. *Journal of Applied Sport Psychology, 7 (Supplement),* 63.

Foster, S., & Lendl, J. (1996). Eye movement desensitization and reprocessing: Four case studies of a new tool for executive coaching and restoring employee performance after setbacks. *Consulting Psychology Journal, 48,* 155–161.

Gelinas, D. J. (2003). Integrating EMDR into phase-oriented treatment for trauma. *Journal of Trauma and Dissociation, 4,* 91–135.

Gelso, C. (2002, Spring). Real relationship: The "something more" of psychotherapy. *J. Contemporary Psychotherapy, 32*(1), 35–40.

Gelso, C., & Hayes, J. (1998). *The psychotherapy relationship.* New York: Wiley.

Gendlin, E. (1981). *Focusing.* New York: Bantam Books.

Gendlin, E. (1996). *Focusing oriented psychotherapy.* New York: Guilford Press.

Gilson, G., & Kaplan, S. (2000). *The therapeutic interweave in EMDR.* Self-published.

Goldstein, A. (1992, August). *Treatment of panic and agoraphobia with EMDR: Preliminary data of the Agoraphobia and Anxiety Treatment Center, Temple University.* Paper presented at the Fourth World Congress on Behavior Therapy, Queensland, Australia.

Goldstein, A. J., de Beurs, E., Chambless, D. L., & Wilson, K. A. (2000). EMDR for panic disorder with agoraphobia: Comparison with waiting-list and credible attention-placebo control condition. *Journal of Consulting and Clinical Psychology, 68,* 947–956.

Goldstein, A., & Feske, U. (1994). Eye movement desensitization and reprocessing for panic disorder: A case series. *Journal of Anxiety Disorders, 8,* 351–362.

Graham, L. (2004). Traumatic swimming events reprocessed with EMDR. www.Thesportjournal.org, 7, (1)1–5.

Grainger, R. D., Levin, C., Allen-Byrd, L., Doctor, R. M., & Lee, H. (1997). An empirical evaluation of eye movement desensitization and reprocessing (EMDR) with survivors of a natural disaster. *Journal of Traumatic Stress, 10,* 665–671.

Grand, D. (1999). Defining and redefining EMDR. New York: Self-published.

Grand, D. (2001). *Emotional healing at warp speed.* New York: Harmony Books.

Grant, M. (1999). *Pain control with EMDR.* New Hope, PA: EMDR Humanitarian Assistance Program.

Grant, M., & Threlfo, C. (2002). EMDR in the treatment of chronic pain. *Journal of Clinical Psychology, 58,* 1505–1520.

Greenwald, R. (1994). Applying eye movement desensitization and reprocessing to the treatment of traumatized children: Five case studies. *Anxiety Disorders Practice Journal, 1,* 83–97.

Greenwald, R. (1998). Eye movement desensitization and reprocessing (EMDR): New hope for children suffering from trauma and loss. *Clinical Child Psychology and Psychiatry, 3,* 279–287.

Greenwald, R. (1999). *Eye movement desensitization and reprocessing (EMDR) in child and adolescent psychotherapy.* New Jersey: Jason Aronson Press.

Greenwald, R. (2000). A trauma-focused individual therapy approach for adolescents with conduct disorder. *International Journal of Offender Therapy and Comparative Criminology, 44,* 146–163.

Greenwald, R. (2001). *Eye movement desensitization and reprocessing: In child and adolescent psychotherapy.* Lanham, MD: Rowman & Littlefield.

Greenwald, R. (2002). Motivation-adaptive skills-trauma resolution (MASTR) therapy for adolescents with conduct problems: An open trial. *Journal of Aggression, Maltreatment, and Trauma, 6,* 237–261.

Greenwald, R. (2005a). *Child trauma handbook: A guide for helping trauma exposed children and adolescents.* New York: Haworth Press.

Greenwald, R. (2005b). *The peanut butter and jelly problem: In search of a better EMDR training model.* Submitted for publication.

Gupta, M., & Gupta, A. (2002). Use of eye movement desensitization and reprocessing (EMDR) in the treatment of dermatologic disorders. *Journal of Cutaneous Medicine and Surgery, 6,* 415–421.

Hassard, A. (1993). Eye movement desensitization of body image. *Behavioural Psychotherapy, 21,* 157–160.

Hayes, J. (2004). The inner world of the psychotherapist: A program of research on countertransference. *Psychotherapy Res., 14*(1), 21–36.

Hendricks, G., & Hendricks, K. (1993). *At the speed of life: A new approach to change in body-centered therapy.* New York: Bantam.

Henry, S. L. (1996). Pathological gambling: Etiological considerations and treatment efficacy of eye movement desensitization/reprocessing. *Journal of Gambling Studies, 12,* 395–405.

Herman, J. (1992, 1997). *Trauma and recovery.* New York: Basic Books.

Hyer, L. (1995). Use of EMDR in a "dementing" PTSD survivor. *Clinical Gerontologist, 16,* 70–73.

Ironson, G. I., Freund, B., Strauss, J. L., & Williams, J. (2002). Comparison of two treatments for traumatic stress: A community-based study of EMDR and prolonged exposure. *J. Clinical Psychol., 58,* 113–128.

Jaberghaderi, N., Greenwald, R., Rubin, A., Dolatabadim S., & Zand, S. O. (in press). A comparison of CBT and EMDR for sexually abused Iranian girls. *Clinical Psychol. Psychotherapy, II(5),* 358–368.

Jarero, I., Artigas, L., Mauer, M., Lopez Cano, T., & Alcala, N. (1999, November). *Children's post traumatic stress after natural disasters: Integrative treatment protocols.* Poster presented at the annual meeting of the International Society for Traumatic Stress Studies, Miami, FL.

Jeger, P., Hansjorg, Z., and Klaus, G., (2003). Increase in coherence in action control as a feature of successful psychotherapies: A sequential analytical examination of the therapist-patient interaction. *Psychotherapy Research, 13*(4), 415–428.

Jensma, J. (1999). Critical incident intervention with missionaries: A comprehensive approach. *Journal of Psychology & Theology, 27,* 130–138.

Jenson, J. A. (1994). An investigation of eye movement desensitization and processing (EMD/R) as a treatment for posttraumatic stress disorder (PTSD) symptoms of Vietnam combat veterans. *Behav. Ther., 23,* 311–32.

Johnson, K. (1998). *Trauma in the Lives of Children.* Alemeda, CA: Hunter House.

Kaslow, F. W. (2002, Spring). Shifting from treatment plans to action plans: Solidifying the therapeutic alliance. *J. Contemporary Psychotherapy, 32*(1), 83–92.

Kaslow, F. W., Nurse, A. R., & Thompson, P. (2002). EMDR in conjunction with family systems therapy. In F. Shapiro (Ed.), *EMDR as an integrative psychotherapy approach: Experts of diverse orientations explore the paradigm prism* (pp. 289–318). Washington, DC: American Psychological Association.

Keenan, P., & Farrell, D. (2000). Treating morbid jealousy with eye movement desensitization and reprocessing utilizing cognitive inter-weave: A case report. *Counselling Psychology Quarterly, 13,* 175–189.

Kernberg, O. (1985). *Borderline conditions and pathological narcissism.* New York: Jason Aronson.

Kitchiner, N., & Aylard, P. (2002). Psychological treatment of post-traumatic stress disorder: A single case study of a UK police office. *Mental Health Practice, 5,* 34–38.

Kleinknecht, R. A. (1993). Rapid treatment of blood and injection phobias with eye movement desensitization. *Journal of Behavior Therapy and Experimental Psychiatry, 24,* 211–217.

Kleinknecht, R. A., & Morgan, M.P. (1992). Treatment of post-traumatic stress disorder with eye movement desensitization and reprocessing. *Journal of Behavior Therapy and Experimental Psychiatry, 23,* 43–50.

Knipe, J., Hartung, J., Konuk, E., Colleli, G., Keller, M., & Rogers, S. (2003, September). *EMDR Humanitarian Assistance Programs: Outcome research, models of training, and service delivery in New York, Latin America, Turkey, and Indonesia.* Symposium presented at the annual meeting of the EMDR International Association, Denver, CO.

Korkmazler-Oral, U., & Pamuk, S. (2002). Group EMDR with child survivors of the earthquake in Turkey. *Association for Child Psychiatry and Psychology, Occasional Paper No. 19*, 47–50.

Korn, D. L., & Leeds, A. M. (2002). Preliminary evidence of efficacy for EMDR resource development and installation in the stabilization phase of treatment of complex posttraumatic stress disorder. *J. Clinical Psychol., 58*(12), 1465–1487.

Korner, A., Drapeau, M. Perry, J. C., Kurth, R., Pokorney, D., and Geyer, M. (2004). Self assessment of interpersonal schemas using the relationship patterns questionnaire: A quantitative approach. *Psychotherapy Research, 14*(4), 435–452.

Lansing, K., Amen, D. G., Hanks, C. & Rudy, L. (in press). High resolution brain SPECT imaging and EMDR in police officers with PTSD. *J. Neuropsychiatry Clinical Neurosciences.*

Lazrove, S. (1994, November). *Integration of fragmented dissociated traumatic memories using EMDR.* Paper presented at the 10th annual meeting of the International Society for Traumatic Stress Studies, Chicago, IL.

Lazrove, S., & Fine, C.G. (1996). The use of EMDR in patients with dissociative identity disorder. *Dissociation, 9*, 289–299.

Lazrove, S., Triffleman, E., Kite, L., McGlasshan, T., & Rounsaville, B. (1998). An open trial of EMDR as treatment for chronic PTSD. *American Journal of Orthopsychiatry, 69*, 601–608.

LeDoux, J. (1996). *The Emotional Brain: The mysterious underpinnings of emotional life.* New York: Simon & Schuster.

Lee, C., Gavriel, H., Drummond, P., Richards, J., & Greenwald, R. (2002). Treatment of post-traumatic stress disorder: A comparison of stress inoculation training with prolonged exposure and eye movement desensitization and reprocessing. *J. Clinical Psychol., 58*, 1071–1089.

Lendl, J., & Foster, S. (2003). EMDR performance enhancement for the workplace: A practioner's manual. Self-published. Write Sandra Foster, PhD, Corso Belvedue, 243, I-28823, Shiff, Italy.

Levin, C. (July/Aug. 1993). The enigma of EMDR. *Family Therapy Networker*, 75–83.

Levin, P., Lazrove, S., & van der Kolk, B. (1999). What psychological testing and neuroimaging tell us about the treatment of posttraumatic stress disorder by eye movement desensitization and reprocessing. *J. Anxiety Disorders, 13*(1–2), 159–172.

Levinson, E. (2000). *Interpersonal psychoanalysis monograph of the William Alanson White Institute.* New York.

Linehan, M. M. (1993). *Cognitive behavioral treatment of borderline personality disorder.* New York: Guilford Press.

Lipke, H., & Botkin, A. (1992). Brief case studies of eye movement desensitization and reprocessing with chronic post-traumatic stress disorder. *Psychotherapy, 29*, 591–595.

Lipke, H. (1999). *EMDR and psychotherapy integration: Theoretical and clinical suggestions with focus on traumatic stress.* Boca Raton, FL: CRC Press.

Lipke, H. (2000). *EMDR and psychotherapy integration.* Boca Raton: CRC Press.

Lohr, J. M., Lilienfeld, S. O., Tolin, D. F., & Herbert, J. D. (1999). Eye movement desensitization and reprocessing: An analysis of specific versus nonspecific treatment factors. *J. Anxiety Disorders, 13*, 185–207.

Lohr, M., Tolin, D., & Kleinknecht, R. (1996). An intensive investigation of eye movement desensitization and processing of claustrophobia. *J. Anxiety Disorders, 10*, 141–151.

Lovett, J. (1999). *Small wonders: Healing childhood trauma with EMDR.* New York: Free Press.

MacCulloch, M. J., & Feldman, P. (1996). Eye movement desensitization treatment utilizes the positive visceral element of the investigatory reflex to inhibit the memories of post-traumatic stress disorder: A theoretical analysis. *Br. J. Psychiatry, 169*, 571–579.

Madrid, A., Skolek, S., & Shapiro, F. (in press). Repairing failures in bonding through EMDR. Clinical Case Studies.

Manfield, P. (1998). *Extending EMDR.* New York: Norton.

Manfield, P., & Shapiro, F. (2003). The application of EMDR to the treatment of personality disorders. In J. F. Magnavita (Ed.), *Handbook of Personality: Theory and Practice.* New York: Wiley.

Marcus, S., Marquis, P., & Sakai, C. (1996). Controlled study of treatment of PTSD using EMDR in an HMO setting. *Psychotherapy, 34*, 307–315.

Marquis, J. N. (1991). A report on seventy-eight cases treated by eye movement desensitization. *Journal of Behavior Therapy and Experimental Psychiatry, 22*, 187–192.

Marquis, J. N., and Puk, G. (1994, November). *Dissociative identity disorder: A common sense and cognitive-behavioral view.* Paper presented at the annual meeting of the Association for Advancement of Behavior Therapy, San Diego, CA.

Maxfield, L., & Hyer, L. (2002). The relationship between efficacy and methodology in studies investigating EMDR treatment of PTSD. *J. Clinical Psychol., 58(1)*, 23–41.

McCann, D.L. (1992). Post-traumatic stress disorder due to devastating burns overcome by a single session of eye movement desensitization. *Journal of Behavior Therapy and Experimental Psychiatry, 23*, 319–323.

McCullough, L. (2002). Exploring change mechanisms in EMDR applied to "small t trauma" in short term dynamic psychotherapy: Research questions and speculations. *Journal of Clinical Psychology, 58*, 1465–1487.

McNally, R. J. (1999). Research on eye movement desensitization and reprocessing (EMDR) as a treatment for PTSD. *PTSD Res. Q., 10(1)*, 1–7.

McNally, V.J., & Solomon, R.M. (1999). The FBI's critical incident stress management program. *FBI Law Enforcement Bulletin, February*, 20–26.

Merleau-Ponty, M. (1968). *The visible and the invisible.* Evanston, IL: Northwestern University Press.

Muris, P., & Merckelbach, H. (1997). Treating spider phobics with eye movement desensitazation and reprocessing: A controlled study. *Behavioral and Cognitive Psychotherapy, 25*, 39–50.

Muris, P., Merkelbach, H., Holdrinet, I., & Sijenaar, M. (1998). Treating phobic children: Effects of EMDR versus exposure. *Journal of Consulting and Clinical Psychology, 66*, 193–198.

Muris, P., Merckelbach, H., van Haaften, H., & Nayer, B. (1997). Eye movement desensitization and reprocessing versus exposure in vivo. *British Journal of Psychiatry 171*, 82–86.

Nadler, W. (1996). EMDR: Rapid treatment of panic disorder. *International Journal of Psychiatry, 2*, 1–8.

Najavits, L., Griffen, G., Luborsky, L., Frank, A., Liese, B., Thompson, H., et al., (1995). Therapists' emotional reactions to substance abusers: A new questionnaire and initial findings. *Psychotherapy: Theory Research and Practice. 32*, 669–677.

Najavits, L. (1997). Psychotherapists' Implicit Theories of Therapy. *Journal of Psychotherapy Integration, 7*, 1–16.

Najavits, L., Crits-Christoph, P., and Dieberger, A. (2000). Clinicians' impact on the quality of substance abuse disordered treatment. *Substance Use and Misuse, 35(12–14)*, 2161–2190.

Nijenhuis, E. R. S., van der Hart, O., & Steele, K. (2002). The emerging psychobiology of trauma related dissociation and dissociative disorders. In H. D'Haenen, J. A. Den Boer, & P. Willner (Eds.), *Biological psychiatry* (pp. 1079–1098). London: Wiley.

Nijenhuis, E. R. S., Van der Hart, O., & Steele, K. (2004a). Strukturelle dissoziation der persönlichkeitsstruktur: Traumatischer ursprung, phobische residuen [Structural dissociation of the personality: Traumatic origins and phobic residues]. In L. Redemann, A. Hoffmann, & U. Gast (Eds.), *Psychotherapie der dissoziativen Störungen [Psychotherapy of dissociative disorders]* (pp. 47–69). Stuttgart: Thieme.

Nijenhuis, E. R. S., Van der Hart, O., & Steele, K. (2004b). Trauma-related structural dissociation of the personality. Retrieved Jan. 1, 2005, from http://www.trauma-pages.com/nijenhuis-2004.htm.

O'Brien, E. (Nov./Dec. 1993). Pushing the panic button. *Family Therapy Networker*, 75–83.

Page, A. C., & Crino, R. D. (1993). Eye-movement desensitization: A simple treatment for post-traumatic stress disorder? *Australian and New Zealand Journal of Psychiatry, 27*, 288–293.

Parnell, L. (1994, August). *Treatment of sexual abuse survivors with EMDR: Two case reports.* Paper presented at the 102nd annual meeting of the American Psychological Association, Los Angeles, CA.

Parnell, L. (1996). Eye movement desensitization and reprocessing (EMDR) and spiritual unfolding. *The Journal of Transpersonal Psychology, 28*, 129–153.

Parnell, L. (1997). *Transforming Trauma: EMDR.* New York: Norton.

Parnell, L. (1999). *EMDR in the treatment of adults abused as children.* New York: Norton.

Paulsen, S. (1995). Eye movement desensitization and reprocessing: Its use in the dissociative disorders. *Dissociation, 8*, 32–44.

Paulsen, S. (2003) EMDR and Ego State Therapy: Energizing Disowned Aspects of the self with dissociative table technique interwoven with EMDR.

Pearlman, L. A., & Saakvitne, K. W. (1995). *Trauma and the therapist.* New York: Norton.

Pellicer, X. (1993). Eye movement desensitization treatment of a child's nightmares: A case report. *Journal of Behavior Therapy and Experimental Psychiatry, 24,* 73–75.

Perkins, B. R., & Rouanzoin, C. C. (2002). A critical evaluation of current views regarding eye movement desensitization and reprocessing (EMDR): Clarifying points of confusion. *J. Clinical Psychol., 58*(1), 77–98.

Perls, F., Hefferline, R., & Goodman, P. (1951). *Gestalt therapy.* New York: Julian Press.

Perry, B. (1999). Memories of states. In J. Goodwin & R. Attias (Eds.), *Splintered reflections: Images of the body in trauma* (pp. 9–38). New York: Basic Books.

Pollock, P. (2000). Eye movement desensitization and reprocessing (EMDR) for post-traumatic stress disorder (PTSD) following homicide. *Journal of Forensic Psychiatry, 11,* 176–184.

Popky, J. A. (2002). De tur: A new way to address addictions and dysfunctional behaviors. EMDRIA annual conference.

Power, K. G., McGoldrick, T., Brown, K., et al. (2002). A controlled comparison of eye movement desensitization and reprocessing versus exposure plus cognitive restructuring, versus waiting list in the treatment of post-traumatic stress disorder. *J. Clinical Psychol. Psychotherapy, 9,* 299–318.

Protinsky, H., Sparks, J., & Flemke, K. (2001a). Eye movement desensitization and reprocessing: Innovative clincal applications. *Journal of Contemporary Psychotherapy, 31,* 125–135.

Protinsky, H., Sparks, J., & Flemke, K. (2001b). Using eye movement desensitization and reprocessing to enhance treatment of couples. *Journal of Marital & Family Therapy, 27,* 157–164.

Puffer, M. K., Greenwald, R., & Elrod, D. E. (1998). A single session EMDR study with twenty traumatized children and adolescents. *Traumatology, 3 (2).*

Puk, G. (1991a). Treating traumatic memories: A case report on the eye movement desensitization procedure. *Journal of Behavior Therapy and Experimental Psychiatry, 22,* 149–151.

Puk, G. (1991b, November). *Eye movement desensitization and reprocessing: Treatment of a more complex case, borderline personality disorder.* Paper presented at the annual meeting of the Association for Advancement of Behavior Therapy, New York, NY.

Puk, G. (1992, May). *The use of eye movement desensitization and reprocessing in motor vehicle accident trauma.* Paper presented at the eighth annual meeting of the American College of Forensic Psychology, San Francisco, CA.

Ray, A. L., & Zbik, A. (2001). Cognitive behavioral therapies and beyond. In C. D. Tollison, J. R. Satterhwaite, & J. W. Tollison (Eds.), *Practical Pain Management* (3rd ed.; pp. 189–208). Philadelphia: Lippincott.

Remen, R. N. (1996). *Kitchen table wisdom: Stories that heal.* New York: Riverhead.

Renfrey, G., & Spates, C. R. (1994). Eye movement desensitization and reprocessing: A partial dismantling procedure. *Journal of Behavior Therapy and Experimental Psychiatry, 25,* 231–239.

Ricci, R. (in press). Trauma resolution using eye movement desensitization and reprocessing with an incestuous sex offender: An instrumental case study. Clinical Case Studies.

Rittenhouse, J. (2000). Using eye movement desensitization and reprocessing to treat complex PTSD in a biracial client. *Cultural Diversity & Ethnic Minority Psychology, 6,* 399–408.

Rogers, C. (1961). *On becoming a person.* Boston: Houghton Mifflin.

Rogers, C. (1980). *A way of being.* Boston: Houghton Mifflin.

Rosen, G., McNally, R., & Lilienfeld, S. (1999). Eye movement magic. *Skeptic, 7*(4), 66–69.

Rosen, G., McNally, R., Lohr, J. M., Devilly, G. J., Herbert, J. D., & Lilienfeld, S. O. (1998a). Four points to consider before you buy EMDR products: A reply to Shapiro et al. *Calif. Psychologist, 31,* 15.

Rosen, G., McNally, R., Lohr, J. M., Devilly, G. J., Herbert, J. D., & Lilienfeld, S. O. (1998b). A realistic appraisal of EMDR. *Calif. Psychologist, 31,* 25–27.

Rothbaum, B. (1997). A controlled study of eye movement desensitization and reprocessing in the treatment of post-traumatic stress disordered sexual assault victims. *Bull. Menninger Clinic, 61,* 317–334.

Rouanzoin, C. (1994, March). *EMDR: Dissociative disorders and MPD.* Paper presented at the 14th annual meeting of the Anxiety Disorders Association of America, Santa Monica, CA.

Russell, A., & O'Connor, M. (2002). Interventions for recovery: The use of EMDR with children in a community-based project. *Association for Child Psychiatry and Psychology, Occasional Paper No. 19*, 43–46.

Scheck, M., Schaeffer, J., & Gillette, C. (1998). Brief psychological intervention with traumatized young women: The efficacy of eye movement desensitization and reprocessing. *J. Traumatic Stress, 11*, 25–44.

Schore, A. N. (1994). *Affect Regulation and the Origin of the Self: The neurobiology of emotional development.* Mahwah: NJ: Lawrence Erlbaum Associates.

Schore, A. N. (2003a). *Affect Dysregulation and Disorders of the Self.* New York: Norton.

Schore, A. N. (2003b). *Affect Regulation and the Repair of the Self.* New York: Norton.

Shapiro, F. (1989a). Efficacy of the eye movement desensitization procedure in the treatment of traumatic memories. *J. Traumatic Stress, 2*, 199–223.

Shapiro, F. (1989b). Eye movement desensitization: A new treatment for PTSD. *J. Behav. Ther. Experimental Psychiatry, 20*, 211–217.

Shapiro, F. (1991). Eye movement desensitization and reprocessing procedure: From EMD to EMDR—a new treatment model for anxiety and related traumata. *Behav. Therapist, 14*, 133–135.

Shapiro, F. (1994). Eye movement desensitization and reprocessing: A new treatment for anxiety and related trauma. In Lee Hyer (Ed.), *Trauma Victim: Theoretical and Practical Suggestions* (pp. 501–521). Muncie, Indiana: Accelerated Development Publishers.

Shapiro, F. (1995). *Eye movement desensitization and reprocessing: Basic principles, protocols and procedures.* New York: Guilford Press.

Shapiro, F., & Solomon, R. (1995). Eye movement desensitization and reprocessing: Neurocognitive information processing. In G. Everley (Ed.), *Innovations in disaster and trauma psychology, Vol. 1* (pp. 216–237). Elliot City, MD: Chevron Publishing.

Shapiro, F. (1996). Eye movement desensitization and reprocessing (EMDR): Evaluation of controlled PTSD research. *J. Behav. Ther. Experimental Psychiatry, 27*, 209–218.

Shapiro, F., & Forrest, M. (1997). *EMDR the breakthrough therapy for overcoming anxiety, stress and trauma.* New York: Basic Books.

Shapiro, F. (1998). EMDR: Accelerated information processing and affect driven constructions. *Crisis Intervention, 4*, 145–157.

Shapiro, F. (1999). EMDR and the anxiety disorders: Clinical and research implications of an integrated psychotherapy treatment. *J. Anxiety Disorders, 13*, 35–67.

Shapiro, F. (2001). *Eye movement desensitization and reprocessing: Basic principles, protocols, and procedures.* New York: Guilford Press.

Shapiro, F., and Maxfield, L. (2002). EMDR: An information processing treatment for PTSD. In session: *Journal of Clinical Psychology.* Special issue: Treatment of PTSD, *58*, 933–946.

Shapiro, F. (2002a). *EMDR: Adaptive information processing.* xxxxxxxxxxxxxxx: xxx, 000–000.

Shapiro, F., & Forrest, M. S. (1997). *EMDR: the breakthrough therapy for overcoming anxiety, stress, and trauma.* New York: Basic Books.

Shapiro, F., Vogelmann-Sine, S., & Sine, L. (1994). Eye movement desensitization and reprocessing: Treating trauma and substance abuse. *Journal of Psychoactive Drugs, 26*, 379–391.

Shapiro, F., & Maxfield, L. (2002a) Eye movement desensitization and reprocessing. *Encyclopedia of a Psychotherapy (1)*, 777–785.

Shapiro, F. (2002b). *EMDR as an integrative psychotherapy approach: Experts of diverse orientations explore the paradigm prism.* Washington, DC: American Psychological Association Press.

Shapiro, F., Eye Movement Desensitization and Reprocessing, Part 1 Training Manual, EMDR Institute, Inc., P. O. Box 750, Watsonville, CA.

Shaw, R. (2003). *The embodied psychotherapist.* Hove, England: Brunner-Routledge.

Shaw, R. (2004). The embodied psychotherapist: An exploration of the therapist's somatic phenomena within the therapeutic encounter. *Psychotherapy Res., 14*(3), 271–288.

Shusta-Hochberg, S. R. (2003). Impact of the World Trade Center disaster on a Manhattan psychotherapy practice. *Journal of Trauma Practice, 2*, 1–16.

Siegel, D. (1999). *The developing mind: Toward a neurobiology of interpersonal experience.* New York: Guilford Press.

Siegel, D., Plenery 2001 EMDRIA conference.

Silver, S., & Rogers, S. (2001). *Light in the heart of darkness: EMDR and the treatment of war and terrorism survivors.* New York: Norton.

Snyder, M. (1996). Intimate partners: A context for the intensification and healing of emotional pain. *Women and Therapy, 19*, 79–92.

Soberman, G. B., Greenwald, R., & Rule, D. L. (2002). A controlled study of eye movement desensitization and reprocessing (EMDR) for boys with conduct problems. *J. Aggression, Maltreatment, Trauma, 6*, 217–236.

Solomon, R. M. (1994, June). *Eye movement desensitization and reprocessing and treatment of grief.* Paper presented at 4th International Conference on Grief and Bereavement in Contemporary Society, Stockholm, Sweden.

Solomon, R.M. (1995, February). *Critical incident trauma: Lessons learned at Waco, Texas.* Paper presented at the Law Enforcement Psychology Conference, San Mateo, CA.

Solomon, R.M. & Shapiro, F. (1997). Eye movement desensitization and reprocessing: An effective therapeutic tool for trauma and grief. In C. Figley (ed.) *Death and Trauma.* New York, Brunner Mazel.

Solomon, R.M. (1998). Utilization of EMDR in crisis intervention. *Crisis Intervention, 4*, 239–246.

Solomon, R., & Dyregrov, A. (2000). Eye movement desensitization and reprocessing (EMDR): Rebuilding assumptive words. *Tidsskrift for Norsk Psykologforening, 37*, 1024–1030.

Solomon, R.M., & Kaufman, T. (1994, March). *Eye movement desensitization and reprocessing: An effective addition to critical incident treatment protocols.* Paper presented at the 14th annual meeting of the Anxiety Disorders Association of America, Santa Monica, CA.

Solomon, R. M. & Kaufman, T. E. (2002). A peer support workshop for the treatment of traumatic stress of railroad personnel: Contributions of eye movement desensitization and reprocessing (EMDR). *Journal of Brief Therapy, 2*, 27–33.

Spates, R. C., & Burnette, M. M. (1995). Eye movement desensitization and reprocessing: Three unusual cases. *Journal of Behavior Therapy and Experimental Psychiatry, 26*, 51–55.

Spector, J., & Huthwaite, M. (1993). Eye-movement desensitisation to overcome post-traumatic stress disorder. *British Journal of Psychiatry, 163*, 106–108.

Spierings, J. J. (1999). *Multi-culti EMDR.* Self-published. Write EMDR-HAP, 64 Hall st., P.O. Box 6506, Hammden, CT 06512.

Sprang, G. (2001). The use of eye movement desensitization and reprocessing (EMDR) in the treatment of traumatic stress and complicated mourning: Psychological and behavioral outcomes. *Research on Social Work Practice, 11*, 300–320.

Stewart, K., & Bramson, T. (2000). Incorporating EMDR in residential treatment. *Residential Treatment for Children & Youth, 17*, 83–90.

Stickgold, R. (2002). EMDR: A putative neurobiological mechanism of action. *J. Clinical Psychol., 58*(1), 61–75.

Stolorow, R. D., & Atwood, G. E. (1992). *Contexts of being.* Hillsdale, NJ: Analytic Press.

Stolorow, R. D., & Atwood, G. E. (1996). The intersubjective perspective. *Psychoanalytic Rev., 83*, 181–194.

Stolorow, R. D., & Atwood, G. E. (1997). Deconstructing the myth of the neutral analyst: An alternative from intersubjective systems theory. *Psychoanalytic Q., 66*, 431–449.

Stolorow, R., Atwood, G., and Brandchaft, B. (1994). The *Intersubjective Perspective.* Northvale, NJ: Jason Aronson, Inc.

Stolorow, R. D., Brandchaft, B., & Atwood, G. E. (2000). *Psychoanalytic treatment: An intersubjective approach.* Hillsdale, NJ: Analytic Press.

Stricker, G., & Gold, J. (1996). An assimilative model for psychodynamically oriented integrative psychotherapy. *Clinical Psychol.: Science Practice, 3*, 47–58.

Sullivan, H. S. (1953). *The interpersonal theory of psychiatry.* New York: Norton.

Taylor, R. (2002). Family unification with reactive attachment disorder: A brief treatment. *Contemporary Family Therapy: An International Journal, 24*, 475–481.

Taylor, S., et al. (2003). Comparative efficacy, speed, and adverse effects of three PTSD treatments: Exposure therapy, EMDR, and relaxation training. *J. Consulting Clinical Psychol., 71*, 330–338.

Thomas, R., & Gafner, G. (1993). PTSD in an elderly male: Treatment with eye movement desensitization and reprocessing (EMDR). *Clinical Gerontologist, 14*, 57–59.

Tinker, R., & Wilson, S. (1999). *Through the eyes of a child.* New York: Norton.

Twombly, J. (2000). Incorporating EMDR and EMDR adaptations into the treatment of clients with dissociative identity disorder. *Journal of Trauma and Dissociation, 1*, 61–81.

Van der Kolk, B. A. (1994). The body keeps the score: memory and the evolving psychobiology of post traumatic stress. *Harvard Rev. Psychiatry, 1*(5), 253–265.

Van der Kolk, B. A., McFarlane, A., & Weisaeth, L. (Eds.). (1996). *Traumatic stress.* New York: Guilford Press.

Van der Kolk, B. A., Pelcovitz, D., Roth, S., Mandel, F., McFarlane, A., & Herman, J. (1996). Dissociation, affect dysregulation and somatization: The complex nature of adaptation to trauma. *Am. J. Psychiatry, 153*(7), Festschrift Supplement, 83–93.

Van Etten, M. L., & Taylor, S. (1998). Comparative efficacy of treatments for PTSD: A metanalysis. *Clinical Psychol. Psychotherapy, 5,* 126–144.

Vaughan, K., Armstrong, M. F., Gold, R., O'Connor, N., Jenneke, W., & Tarrier, N. (1994). A trial of eye movement desensitization compared to image habituation training and applied muscle relaxation in post-traumatic stress disorder. *J. Behav. Ther. Experimental Psychiatry, 25,* 283–291.

Vaughan, K., Wiese, M., Gold, R., & Tarrier, N. (1994). Eye-movement desensitisation: Symptom change in post-traumatic stress disorder. *British Journal of Psychiatry, 164,* 533–541.

Vogelmann-Sinn, S., Sine, L. F., Smyth, N. J., & Popky, A. J. (1998). *EMDR chemical dependency treatment manual.* New Hope, PA: EMDR Humanitarian Assistance Programs.

Wachtel, P. L. (1977). *Psychoanalysis and behavior therapy: Toward an integration.* New York: Basic Books.

Watkins, J., & Watkins, H. (1997). *Ego states: Theory and therapy.* New York: Norton.

Watkins, J. G. (1971). The affect bridge: A hypnoanalytic technique. *Int. J. Clinical Experimental Hypnosis, 19,* 21–27.

Wernik, U. (1993). The role of the traumatic component in the etiology of sexual dysfunctions and its treatment with eye movement desensitization procedure. *Journal of Sex Education and Therapy, 19,* 212–222.

Whisman, M. (2001). Panic and phobias: Diagnosis, treatment and incorporation of EMDR with Ad de Jongh. EMDRIA annual conference.

White, G.D. (1998). Trauma treatment training for Bosnian and Croatian mental health workers. *American Journal of Orthopsychiatry, 63,* 58–62.

Wilson, D., Silver, S. M, Covi, W., & Foster, S. (1996). Eye movement desensitization and reprocessing: Effectiveness and autonomic correlates. *Behav. Ther. Experimental Psychiatry, 27,* 219–229.

Wilson, S. A., Becker, L. A., & Tinker, R. H. (1995). Eye movement desensitization and reprocessing (EMDR) treatment for psychologically traumatized individuals. *J. Consulting Clinical Psychol., 6*(3), 928–937.

Wilson, S. A., Becker, L. A., & Tinker, R. H. (1997). Fifteen-month follow-up of eye movement desensitization and reprocessing (EMDR) treatment for PTSD and psychological trauma. *J. Consulting Clinical Psychol., 5,* 1047–1056.

Wilson, S. A., Becker, L. A., Tinker, R. H., & Logan, C. R. (2001). Stress management with law enforcement personnel: A controlled outcome study of EMDR versus a traditional stress management program. *International Journal of Stress Management, 8,* 179–200.

Wilson, S. A., Tinker, R., Becker, L. A., Hofmann, A., & Cole, J. W. (2000, September). *EMDR treatment of phantom limb pain with brain imaging (MEG).* Paper presented at the annual meeting of the EMDR International Association, Toronto, Canada.

Wolpe, J. (1990). *The practice of behavior therapy* (4th ed.). New York: Pergamon Press.

Wolpe, J., & Abrams, J. (1991). Post-traumatic stress disorder overcome by eye movement desensitization: A case report. *Journal of Behavior Therapy and Experimental Psychiatry 22,* 39–43.

Young, J. E. (1990). *Cognitive therapy for personality disorders: A schema focused approach.* Sarasota, FL: Professional Resources Exchange.

Young, J. E., & Klosko, J. S. (1993). *Reinventing your life.* New York: Plume.

Young, J. E., Klosko, J. S., & Weishaar, M. E. (1993). *Schema therapy.* New York: Guilford Press.

Young, W. (1994). EMDR treatment of phobic symptoms in multiple personality. *Dissociation, 7,* 129–133.

Young, W. (1995). EMDR: Its use in resolving the trauma caused by the loss of a war buddy. *American Journal of Psychotherapy, 49,* 282–291.

Zabukovec, J., Lazrove, S., & Shapiro, F. (2000). Self-healing aspects of EMDR: The therapeutic change process and perspective of integrated psychotherapies. *Journal of Psychotherapy Integration, 10,* 189–206.

Notes

Chapter 2

1. Van der Kolk was once misquoted as saying that the relationship isn't that important in EMDR. This comment was made in relation to a training experience he took part in during a practicum at EMDR training. He corrected this impression in his 2004 plenary address at the EMDR International Association conference.

Chapter 10

1. You may remember that I postponed getting the positive cognition and VOC from Madeline in Phase 3 of one of the protocols because her verbal and analytic abilities completely deactivated her. However, I always include the positive cognition and VOC during Phase 5.

Appendix A

1. Copyright 1989 by Dr. Patti Levin.

Appendix D

1. Copyright by EMDR Institute, Inc.

Appendix I

1. Copyright 2002 EMDR Humanitarian Assistance Programs. All Rights Reserved.

Index

A

Abrams, J., 235, 236
Action control theory, 11
Action plan, defining, 11, 48, 205; *see also* Evaluation and preparation
Active coaching, 79–80, 116–118
Active therapeutic strategies
    case of Janice, 182–188
    case of Madeline, 177–180
    cognitive interweave, 36, 37, 109, 166–169
    dealing with transference/ countertransference binds, 182–188
    desensitization and, 115–116, 166
    empathic interweave, 188–189
    minimizing/repairing ruptures, 180–181
    need for intervention, 165–166
    processing transference directly, 181–182
    processing transference resistance, 176–177
    relational interweave, 18, 32, 39, 169–174
    vicarious traumatization of coutertransference, 174–176
Active trauma processing, *see* Desensitization (active trauma processing)
Active trauma work; *see also* Evaluation and preparation
assessment (trauma activation sequence)
    case of Ira, 97–99
    increasing trust, 102–103
    naming the related emotions, 100–101
    the negative cognition, 92–96
    overview of, 83–84
    the positive cognition and VOC, 96–99
    postponing the positive cognition, 99–100
    procedural steps outline, 85–86
    target selection, 86–90
    transference/countertransference views of, 143–147
    tuning in to body sensations, 101–102
    using dreams, 90–92
the body scan (intensive body awareness)
    case of Tricia, 198–200
    listening to the body, 197–198
    transference/countertransference views of, 151
desensitization (active trauma processing)
    active coaching, 116–118
    active therapeutic strategies, 115–116, 166
    case of Madeline, 107–111
    case of Stephanie, 119–124

clinician's self-knowledge,
113–115
completion process, 191–192
external constraints, 118
overview of, 105–106
transference/countertransference
views of, 147–150, 176
using a blocking belief, 108–111
using EMDR with couples,
111–112
using the stop signal/intermittent
debriefing, 113
working in a co-participatory
manner, 118–119
determining readiness for, 81
installation (linking the adaptive
perspective)
case of Madeline, 193–196
integration of positive self-
assessment, 192–193
proof of increased response
function, 196
transference/countertransference
views of, 150–151
orientation to, 69–71
Acute Stress Disorder, 216
Adaptive Information Processing model,
223–224; see also Information processing
system
Adaptive resolution, 217
Affect attunement exercise, 133–134
Affect bridge, 22, 87
Affect regulation, 52, 116
Affect tolerance, 33, 52, 71; see also Client
preparation (testing affect tolerance/
body awareness)
Alcala, N., 235
Alignment, defining, 16, 23
Allen, J. G., 236
Allen-Byrd, L., 235, 260
Alliance, see Therapeutic relationship, in
EMDR
Amen, D. G., 265
American Psychological Association
(APA), 233, 253
Analytic interpretation, 116
Andrade, J., 263, 264
Andréewitch, S., 254
Anticipatory anxiety, 134

Appraisal, defining, 14; see also
Neurobiology, of EMDR
Armstrong, M. F., 258
Arousal, defining, 15, 76, 217; see also
Neurobiology, of EMDR
Artigas, L., 11, 235
Assertiveness skills, 78
Assessment (trauma activation sequence);
see also Active trauma work
case of Ira, 97–99
increasing trust, 102–103
naming the related emotions, 100–101
the negative cognition, 92–96
overview of, 83–84
the positive cognition and VOC,
96–99
postponing the positive cognition,
99–100
procedural steps outline, 85–86
target selection, 86–90
transference/countertransference
views of, 143–147
tuning in to body sensations, 101–102
using dreams, 90–92
Assimilation, 167
Attachment disorders, 77
Attachment relationships, 49–50, 84
At the Speed of Life: A New Approach to
Change in Body-Centered Therapy
(Hendricks), 197
Attunement, defining, 15, 23; see also
Neurobiology, of EMDR
Atwood, G. E., 28, 37, 40, 126, 142, 153, 165
Audio scan, 202
Audio stimulation, 123
Avoidance, 113
Awareness technique, 76–77, 101–102
Aylard, P., 235

B

Baddeley, A., 263
Baker, M. J., 233
Baker, N., 234
Bandura, A., 79
Barlow, D., 76
Barrowcliff, A. L., 263
Baucom, D. H., 233
Bears, M., 264

Beck, A., 71

Becker, L. A., 37, 141, 154, 228, 235, 236, 259

Bejerot, S., 254

Bergmann, U., 25, 141

Berkowitz, A., 236

Beutler, L. E., 11, 233

Bilateral stimulation, aspects of, 67–69, 73, 97, 142, 223; *see also* Client preparation (testing affect tolerance/body awareness)

Bleich, A., 253

Blocked processing, 168, 171

Blocking beliefs, processing, 77, 108–111, 149–150

Blore, D. C., 234, 235

Body awareness, improving, 76–77

Body scan (intensive body awareness); *see also* Active trauma work
  case of Tricia, 198–200
  listening to the body, 197–198
  transference/countertransference
    views of, 151

Body sensations, awakening, 101–102

Bohart, A., 11, 12

Botkin, A., 234

Brain functions; *see also* Neurobiology, of EMDR
  definitions of, 14–15
  in therapy, 16–20, 217

Bramson, T., 235

Bridging positive cognition, 200

Brinck, U., 254

Brooks, A., 260

Browing, C., 22

Brown, K. W., 236, 257

Buchanan, R., 236

Burbridge, J., 265

Burnette, M. M., 236

C

Calhoun, K. S., 233

Carlson, J. G., 53, 234, 235, 238, 255, 256, 260

Certification, 221, 224–225, 229

Chambless, D. L., 233, 234, 253

Chemtob, C. M., 234, 235, 255, 256, 260, 263

Child Trauma Handbook: A Guide for Helping Trauma-Exposed Children and Adolescents (Greenwald), 156

Choice interweave, 167

Christman, S. D., 263

Client-centered clinicians, 8–9

Client history taking (trauma case conceptualization), 48–52, 134–140; *see also* Evaluation and preparation

Client preparation (testing affect tolerance/ body awareness); *see also* Evaluation and preparation
  bilateral stimulation, 67–69, 73, 97
  case of Sophie, 73–75
  completing the Safe Place exercise, 75
  creating a safe/control place, 71–73
  determining readiness for EMDR
    trauma processing, 81
  dual attention, 67, 73
  explaining state-dependent memory,
    66–67
  improving body awareness/reducing
    tension, 76–77
  orientation to active trauma work,
    69–71
  overview of, 65–66
  resourcing strategies, 77–81, 115, 207
  transference/countertransference
    views of, 140–143

Clinical trials (non randomized), 259–261

Clinical trials (randomized), 255–259

Clinician-client dyad, 19, 64

Clinician Self-Awareness Questionnaire, 175, 247

Clinician's self-knowledge, 113–115

Clinician's self-regulation skills, 159–163

Closure and reevaluation; *see also* Active trauma work
  closure (debriefing), 151, 152,
    200–202
  reevaluation (the forgotten phase),
    152, 202–205
  transference/countertransference
    views of, 151–152

Closure (debriefing), 151–152, 200–202

Coaches, inner, 79–80, 116–117; *see also* Active coaching

Cocco, N., 235

Cognitive-behavioral therapy, 1, 10

Cognitive interweave, 36, 37, 109, 166–169

Cognitive Therapy for Personality Disorders: A Schema Focused Approach (Young), 56

Cohn, L., 236
Collaborative alliance, 4, 47, 180–181
Colleli, G., 235, 260
Compartmentalization strategy, 161, 175
Compassion fatigue, 106, 119, 155, 156; see also Vicarious traumatization
Complete closure, 151; see also Closure and reevaluation
Complex PTSD, see Post-traumatic stress disorder (PTSD), aspects of
Congruence, 169
Connectionism, 93
Constraints, external, 118
Contexts of Being (Stolorow & Atwood), 153
Controlled breathing exercises, 71
Control place, see Safe Place exercise
Co-participatory roles, 84, 87, 105, 118–119
Coping strategies, 218–220
Co-regulation, defining, 16, 87; see also Neurobiology, of EMDR
Cornelius, D., 79, 116, 117, 162
Coughlin, E. P., 79, 116, 117, 162
Countertransference
    affect attunement exercise, 133–134
    clinician's self-regulation skills, 159–163
    clinician's use of self, 127
    definition of, 18, 125–127
    increasing trust and, 102
    intersubjective theory, 152–154
    relational interweave and, 182–188
    transference and, 134–152, 181–182
        phase 1: client history taking/treatment planning, 134–140
        phase 2: client preparation, 140–143
        phase 3: assessment, 143–147
        phase 4: desensitization, 147–150, 176
        phase 5: installation, 150–151
        phase 6: the body scan, 151
        phase 7: closure, 151–152
        phase 8: reevaluation, 152
    vicarious traumatization and, 154–159, 174–176
    working with transference and, 127–128
        case of Dan, 148–149
        case of George, 128–129
        case of Janice, 182–188

case of Laurie, 146–147
case of Michael, 129–133
case of Sally, 144–145
Couples, using EMDR with, 111–112
Crabbe, B., 236
Craske, M., 76
Creamer, M., 236
Crino, R. D., 235
Crisis, concept of, 220
Crits-Christoph, P., 233
Cross-cultural issues, in EMDR, 38–39

D

Daniels, N., 71, 234
Datta, P. C., 235
Davidson, P. R., 255, 263
De Beurs, E., 234
Debriefing, intermittent, 113, 115–116
Debriefing (closure), 151–152, 200–202; see also Closure and reevaluation
"Deconstructing the Myth of the Neutral Analyst: An Alternative From Intersubjective Systems Theory" (Stolorow & Atwood), 37
De Jongh, A., 234
Dependency attachment, insecure, 19
Dependency issues, 66
Desensitization (active trauma processing); see also Active trauma work
    active coaching, 116–118
    active therapeutic strategies, 115–116, 166
    case of Madeline, 107–111
    case of Stephanie, 119–124
    clinician's self-knowledge, 113–115
    completion process, 191–192
    external constraints, 118
    overview of, 105–106
    transference/countertransference views of, 147–150, 176
    using a blocking belief, 108–111
    using EMDR with couples, 111–112
    using the stop signal/intermittent debriefing, 113
    working in a co-participatory manner, 118–119
Desensitization of Triggers and Urge Reprocessing (DeTUR) protocol, 90, 208

DESNOS (Disorders of Extreme Stress, Not
Otherwise Specified), 29, 217–218
DeTUR (Desensitization of Triggers and
Urge Reprocessing) protocol, 90, 208
The Developing Mind (Siegel), 153
Devilly, G. J., 259
Diagnostic and Statistical Manual of
Mental Disorders IV-R (DSM IV-R),
215, 218
Dialectical Behavior Therapy (Lineham), 78
Disorders of Extreme Stress, Not
Otherwise Specified (DESNOS), 29,
217–218
Dissociation, pathological, 53, 95, 217
Dissociative Experience Scale (DES), 53, 95
Dissociative Identity Disorder, 53
Distress-management skills, 78
Doctor, R. M., 234, 235, 260
Dolatabadim, S., 235, 256
Dreams, using, 90–92
Drummond, P., 257
Dual attention, 67, 73, 223
Dworkin, M., 32, 239
Dyer, W., 80
Dyregrov, A., 234, 235
Dysfunctional stored memory, 37, 93, 217
Dziegielewski, S., 236

E

Edmond, T., 235, 256
Egendorf, A., 7, 48
Ego States: Theory and Therapy (Watkins), 22
Ego state work, 77
Elrod, D. E., 235, 260
The Embodied Psychotherapist (Shaw), 170
EMD (Eye Movement Desensitization),
227–228
"EMDR: Adaptive Information
Processing" (Shapiro), 28
EMDR and Psychology Integration (Lipke), 5
EMDR Association of Canada, 269
*EMDR Chemical Dependency Treatment
Manual*, 90, 208
EMDR Europe Association, 269
EMDR Humanitarian Assistance Program
(HAP), 267–268
EMDRIA (EMDR International
Association), 115, 221, 222, 229, 269

EMDR International Association
(EMDRIA), 115, 221, 222, 229, 269
EMDR methodology, *see* Eye Movement
Desensitization and Reprocessing
(EMDR)
Emotional reactions, 219
Emotional regulation skills, 78
Empathic attunement, 24–26, 38, 136, 165,
170
Empathic interweave, 188–189; *see also*
Active therapeutic strategies
Empathic-introspective inquiry, 28
Empathic reflection, 85
Empathic resonance, defining, 15–16
Empathy, subtleties of, 23–26
Enhancement, 72
Evaluation and preparation; *see also* Eye
Movement Desensitization and
Reprocessing (EMDR)
client history taking and treatment
planning (trauma case
conceptualization)
case of Madeline, 60–64
case of Walter, 54–58
conclusion, 64
developing atmosphere of trust,
47–48
seeking feeder memories, 58–60
taking client history, 48–52
thinking in EMDR terms, 52–54
transference/countertransference
views of, 134–140
Trauma Case Conceptualization
Questionnaire, 51, 60, 239
client preparation (testing affect
tolerance/body awareness)
bilateral stimulation, 67–69, 73, 97
case of Sophie, 73–75
completing the Safe Place exercise,
75
creating a safe/control place,
71–73
determining readiness for EMDR
trauma processing, 81
dual attention, 67, 73
explaining state-dependent
memory, 66–67
improving body awareness/
reducing tension, 76–77

orientation to active trauma work,
69–71
overview of, 65–66
resourcing strategies, 77–81, 115,
207
transference/countertransference
views of, 140–143
Evaluation anxieties, 71
Extending EMDR (Manfield), 127
External constraints, 118
Eye Movement Desensitization and
Reprocessing (EMDR); *see also* Active
trauma work; Closure and reevaluation;
Evaluation and preparation in daily
clinical practice
case of Dan, 148–149
case of George, 128–129
case of Ira, 97–99
case of Janice, 182–188
case of Kristin, 171–174
case of Laurie, 146–147
case of Madeline, 41–45, 60–64,
107–111, 177–180, 193–196,
210–211
case of Michael, 129–133
case of Richard, 111–112
case of Sally, 144–145
case of Sophie, 73–75
case of Stephanie, 119–124
case of Tricia, 198–200
case of Walter, 54–58
flexibility in methodology, 205–207
introduction, 27–28
overview of treatment, 28–32
relational aspects of EMDR
differences in, 36–38
the eight phases, 32–35, 224
potential barriers, 38–39
relational interweave, 39
staying in charge, 207–208
treatment stages, 40
for diverse clinical populations,
233–236
foundational sources/principles of, 222
international treatment guidelines,
253–255
myths and realities about, 227–231
neurobiology of
brain functions in therapy, 16–20

introduction, 13–16
subtext of EMDR session, 20–23
subtleties of empathy, 23–26
relational imperative in
early history trauma treatment, 6–9
introduction, 1–6
state-dependent memory, 6
the therapeutic relationship, 9–12
research on
confusion regarding, 237–238
evidence of fidelity, 224–225
hypotheses regarding eye
movement, 263–264
information-processing model,
261–262
meta-analyses, 255
neurobiological evaluations,
264–265
non randomized studies, 259–261
randomized clinical trials,
255–259
theoretical foundation for, 86, 222–224
three-pronged protocol, 209–210
Eye Movement Desensitization (EMD),
227–228
Eye scan, 202

F

Family members, using EMDR with,
111–112
Farrell, D., 235
Feedback, *see* Reevaluation (the forgotten
phase)
Feeder memories, 31, 58–60
Feldman, P., 237, 261
Fensterheim, H., 236
Fernandez, I., 39, 235, 259
Feske, U., 234
Figley, C. R., 106, 155, 156
Fine, C. G., 236
Flashbacks, 137
Flemke, K., 234, 235, 236
Floatback technique, 22, 87, 109, 163
Foa, E. B., 238, 254
Forbes, D., 236
Forrest, M., 235, 236
Fosha, D., 188
Foster, S., 79, 80, 230, 236

Free association, 59, 205
Freeman, T. C. A., 263
Freese, S., 264
Freud, S., 125
Freund, B., 256
Friedman, M. J., 254

G

Gafner, G., 234
Gallinari, E., 235, 259
Garvey, K. J., 263
Gavriel, H., 257
Gelinas, D. J., 236
Gelso, C., 4, 9, 10, 47, 126, 132, 175, 210
Gender issues, in EMDR treatment, 38
Gendlin, E., 85, 151
Genuineness, defining, 9
Gestalt Therapy (Perls), 101, 197
Gillette, C., 235, 258
Gilson, G., 168
Gold, R., 236, 258
Gold Standard Scale, 238
Goldstein, A., 234
Goodman, P., 101, 197
Graham, L., 236
Grainger, R. D., 235, 260
Grand, D., 141, 230
Grant, M., 230, 236
Gray, N. S., 263
Greenwald, R., 156, 230, 235, 256, 257, 258, 260
Gupta, A., 236
Gupta, M., 236

H

Hanks, C., 265
Hansjorg, Z., 11
HAP (EMDR Humanitarian Assistance Program), 267–268
Hartung, J., 235
Harwood, T., 11
Hassard, A., 235
Hayes, J., 4, 9, 10, 47, 125, 126, 132, 175, 210
Health issues, 135
Hedlund, N. L., 234, 255, 260
Hefferline, R., 101, 197

Heisenberg Uncertainty Principle, 3
Hendricks, G., 197
Hendricks, K., 197
Henry, S. L., 235
Herbert, J. D., 238
Herman, J., 25, 47, 217, 218
History taking, *see* Client history taking (trauma case conceptualization)
Holdrinet, I., 234
Hubbard, D. R., 197
Humor techniques, 156
Huthwaite, M., 236
Hyer, L., 140, 142, 202, 225, 235, 238, 255
Hyperarousal, 215, 216

I

Imaginary exposure, 84
Implicit memory, 53, 56
Incomplete closure, 151; *see also* Closure and reevaluation
Information processing system, 5–6, 36, 37, 223–224, 261–262
Inner coaches, 79–80, 116–117
The Inner World of the Psychotherapist (Hayes), 125
Insecure dependency attachment, 19
Insighted-oriented alliance, 47
Insomnia, 89
Installation (linking the adaptive perspective); *see also* Active trauma work
  case of Madeline, 193–196
  integration of positive self-assessment, 192–193
  proof of increased response function, 196
  transference/countertransference views of, 150–151
Integrative conceptualization, *see* Countertransference
Intermittent debriefing, 113, 115–116; *see also* Closure and reevaluation
International treatment guidelines, 253–255
Intersubjectivity theory, 40, 152–154
Intervention strategies, need for, 165–166; *see also* Active therapeutic strategies; Relational interweave
  "The Invisible Volcano: Overcoming Denial of Rage" (Snyder), 127

Ironson, G. L., 236, 256
Isolation of minds, concept of, 153

J

Jaberghaderi, N., 256
Jacobson, A., 76
Jarero, I., 235
Jeger, P., 11
Jenneke, W., 258
Jensma, J., 235
Jenson, J. A., 238
Johnson, K., 235
Journaling, 201, 213
Journal of Clinical Psychology, 237
Journal of Consulting and Clinical Psychology, 228

K

Kaplan, S., 168
Kaslow, F. W., 11, 54, 210, 235
Kaufman, T. E., 235, 260
Kavanagh, D., 263, 264
Keane, T. M., 254
Keenan, P., 235
Keller, M., 235
Kindt, M., 264
Kitchen Table Wisdom (Remen), 23
Kitchiner, N., 235
Kitchur, M., 229
Klaff, F., 230
Klaus, G., 11
Klein, M., 187
Kleinknecht, R. A., 234, 235
Knipe, J., 235, 260
Kohnke, C., 264
Konuk, E., 235
Korkmazler-Oral, U., 235
Korn, D., 77, 80, 81, 236
Kotler, M., 253
Kuiken, D., 264
Kutz, I., 253

L

Lamangne, J., 188
Lamprecht, F., 264
Language, in EMDR, 38
Lansing, K., 265
Lazrove, S., 235, 236, 265

LeDoux, J., 25
Lee, C., 236, 257
Lee, H., 235, 260
Leeds, A., 22, 77, 236
Lempa, W., 264
Lendl, J., 230, 236
Levin, C., 235, 260
Levin, P., 32, 218, 265
Lewis, L., 236
Lilienfeld, S. O., 238
Linehan, M. M., 56, 78
Lipke, H., 5, 234
Lived body paradigm, 192
Logan, C. R., 235
Lohr, J. M, 238
Lopez Cano, T., 235
Lorenzetti, A., 235, 259
Lovett, J., 230, 235

M

MacCulloch, M. J., 237, 261, 263
Madrid, A., 236
Maladaptive memory, 166
Malattunement, 15
Malevolent transformation, 158
    "The Management of Countertransference" (Gelso & Hayes), 132
Manfield, P., 127, 236
Marcus, S., 236, 257
Marquis, J. N., 236, 257
Mastery resources, 78
Matzke, M., 264
Mauer, M., 235
Maxfield, L., 140, 142, 202, 225, 238, 255, 271, 272, 273, 274
May, J., 264
McBride, B., 234
McCann, D. L., 235
McCarty, D., 256
McCullough, L., 236
McFarlane, A., 19
McGoldrick, T., 236, 257
McNally, R. J., 235, 238
Meadows, F. A., 238
Mehr, H., 231
Memory, 78, 87, 216
Memory networks, 36, 37, 93, 205, 223
Mental models, defining, 15

Mental state resonance, 15–16, 23, 95
Merckelbach, H., 234
Merleau-Ponty, M., 170
Meta-analytic research, 225, 255
Metaphorical interweave, 168
Miall, D., 264
Mindfulness meditation, 75, 76
Misattunement, 15, 18, 169
Mitchell, R., 39
Montgomery, I. M., 264
Morgan, M. P., 235
Mörtberg, E., 254
Munte, T., 264
Muraoka, M. Y., 234, 255, 260
Muris, P., 234, 264
Muscle relaxation exercise, 71, 76

N

Nadler, W., 234
Najavits, L., 11
Nakashima, J., 235, 256
Nayer, B., 234
Negative cognition, 92–96; see also Active
    trauma work
Negative transference, see Transference
Neurobiology, of EMDR
    brain functions in therapy, 16–20
    introduction, 13–16
    subtext of EMDR session, 20–23
    subtleties of empathy, 23–26
Nijenhuis, E. R. S., 53
Numbing, psychic, 76
Nurse, A. R., 235
Nurturing alliance, 4, 47

O

Obenchain, J., 260
O'Brien, E., 234
O'Connor, M., 235, 258
On Becoming a Person (Rogers), 23
One-person psychology, 3
Orienting reflex, defining, 14

P

Page, A. C., 235
Pamuk, S., 235
Panic disorders, 93
Parallel distributed processing, 93

Parasympathic dearousal, 68
Parker, K. C. H., 255, 263
Parnell, L., 235, 236
Pathological dissociation, 53, 95, 217
Paulsen, S., 236
Pearlman, L. A., 102, 106, 154, 156, 157,
    158, 174
Pellicer, X., 235
Perkins, B. R., 237, 238, 262
Perls, F., 101, 197
Perry, B., 50, 96
Personal histories, in the therapeutic
    process, 1
Personality, 217
Pet bereavement, 129
Phaneuf, K. A., 263
Physical reactions, 218–219
Pollock, P., 236
Popky, A. J., 90, 208, 230, 235
Positive cognition; see also Active trauma
    work
        postponement of, 99–100
        VOC and, 96–99
Post-therapy monitoring, 212–214
Post-traumatic stress disorder (PTSD),
    aspects of, 6, 7, 215–217
Power, K. G., 236, 257
Preparation, see Evaluation and
    preparation
Projective identification, 187
Propper, R. E., 263
Protinsky, H., 234, 235, 236
Psyche, 194
Psychic numbing, 76, 215
Psychoanalysis and Behavior Therapy:
    Toward an Integration (Wachtel), 171
Psychoanalytic interpretations, 36
Psychodynamic therapy, 36
Psychoform dissociative state, 53, 89, 137,
    138
Psychological trauma, see Trauma, aspects of
Psychotherapy, 8, 10, 47, 85, 174
PTSD (post-traumatic stress disorder),
    aspects of, 6, 7, 215–217
Puffer, M. K., 235, 260
Puk, G., 235, 236

Q

Quinn, G., 48

R

Ray, A. L., 236, 262
Realism, defining, 9
Rearousal, 204
Reciprocal mutual influence, 26
Reenactments, 156, 158
Reevaluation (the forgotten phase), 152,
    202–205; *see also* Closure and
    reevaluation
Reflective empathy, 36, 116
Relational emotions, naming, 100–101
Relational interweave; *see also* Active
    therapeutic strategies
    case of Janice, 182–188
    case of Kristin, 171–174
    dealing with transference/
        countertransference binds, 182–188
    definition of, 18, 32, 39, 169–171
    sequence of events in, 174
Relational issues, 125; *see also* Therapeutic
    relationship, in EMDR
Relational resources, 78
Remen, R. N., 23, 24
Renfrey, G., 236
Renssen, M. R., 234
Reprocessing, 11, 68, 196
Resonance, defining, 15–16
Resource development and installation
    (RDI), 22, 36, 77, 78, 218
Resourcing strategies, 77–81, 115, 207
Response flexibility, defining, 16
Responsibility interweave, 167
Ricci, R., 236
Richards, J., 257
Richardson, R., 234
Rittenhouse, J., 236
Rogers, C., 9, 23, 24, 26, 36, 158, 169
Rogers, S., 234, 235, 260, 262
Rosen, G., 237
Rothbaum, B., 235, 257
Rouanzoin, C., 236, 237, 238, 262
Rubin, A., 225, 235, 256
Ruck, C., 254
Rudy, L., 265
Rule, D. L., 235, 258
Ruptures, repairing alliance, 180–181
Rusnak, K., 234, 255, 260
Russell, A., 235
Rycroft, P., 236

S

Saakvitne, K. W., 102, 106, 154, 156, 157,
    158, 174
Sack, M., 264
Safe Place exercise
    aspects of, 71–73, 116
    case of Sophie, 73–75
    completing the, 75
Safety, establishing, 48
Safety interweave, 167
Sakai, C., 236, 257
Salemink, E., 264
Scalzo, L. A., 264
Schaeffer, J., 235, 258
Scheck, M., 235, 258
Scheiner, Z., 149
Schema-Focused Questionnaire, 56, 79, 94,
    205
Schemas, 56–57, 94–95
Schore, A. N., 13, 14, 23, 25, 49, 142
Self-beliefs, seeking, 58–60, 144; *see also*
    Active trauma work
Self-management techniques, 156
Self-regulation skills, for clinicians,
    159–163
Self-soothing techniques, 156
Sensory awareness, 147
Sensory cueing, 78
Sexual abuse, 115
Shalev, A., 253
Shapiro, F., 4, 5, 8, 28, 30, 37, 48, 49, 67, 68,
    77, 78, 83, 93, 96, 105, 106, 116, 142, 156,
    166, 167, 192, 197, 210, 212, 213, 216,
    222, 223, 224, 227, 228, 231, 233, 234,
    235, 236, 237, 258, 261, 262, 271, 272,
    273, 274
Sharpe, L., 235
Sharpley, C., 264
Shaw, R., 170, 192
Shusta-Hochberg, S. R., 235
Siegel, D., 13, 14, 15, 16, 17, 23, 28, 49, 50,
    93, 137, 142, 153, 155, 170, 271, 272,
    274
Sijsenaar, M., 234
Silver, S. M., 234, 260, 262
Sine, L. F., 230, 235
Sjöblom, P. O., 254
Skolek, S., 236
Sloan, L., 256

Small Wonders: Healing Childhood Trauma with EMDR (Lovett), 230
Smith, L., 264
Smyth, N. J., 208, 230, 235
Snyder, M., 235
Snyker, L., 127
Soberman, G. B., 235, 258
Solomon, R. M., 230, 235, 260
Somatoform dissociative state, 53, 76, 89, 101, 138
Sparks, J., 234, 235, 236
Spates, C. R., 236
Spector, J., 236
Spence, S. H., 259
Spierings, J., 39
Sprang, G., 236, 261
Stabilization, 29, 77, 113, 137, 218
State-dependent memory; *see also* Active trauma work
    explaining aspects of, 6, 19, 55, 58, 66–67
    relational interweave and, 170
State of mind, 15, 86, 137
State-specific excitatory form, 106
Steele, K., 53
Stewart, K., 235
Stickgold, R., 262, 264
Stimulation, *see* Bilateral stimulation, aspects of
Stolorow, R. D., 28, 37, 40, 126, 142, 153, 165
Stop signal, 113, 115–116
Strauss, J. L., 256
Stressors, 59, 217
Stress-reduction techniques, 76–77
Subjective Units of Disturbance (SUDS) scale, 20, 87, 97; *see also* Active trauma work
Sullivan, H. S., 158
Suzuki, J., 265
Symbolic resources, 78
Sympathetic arousal, 68
Sympathy, 24

T

Target memory, *see* Target selection, pitfalls/best practices of
Target selection, pitfalls/best practices of, 86–90; *see also* Active trauma work
Tarrier, N., 236, 258

Task-focused client, 12
Taylor, S., 235, 238, 255, 258
Ten Broeke, F., 234
Tension, reducing, 76–77
Terminating therapy, 212–214
The Therapeutic Interweave (Gilson & Kaplan), 168
Therapeutic relationship, in EMDR; *see also* specific topics
    definitions of, 9–12
    early history of trauma treatment, 6–9
    information processing psychology, 5–6
    introduction, 1–6
    minimizing/repairing ruptures, 180–181
    state-dependent memory, 6
    from working alliance to, 3–5, 47–48, 102–103, 165
TheraTapper, 143, 202
Thomas, R., 234
Thompson, P., 235
Threlfo, C., 236
Through the Eyes of a Child (Tinker & Wilson), 230
Tinker, R. H., 37, 141, 154, 228, 230, 235, 236, 259
Tolin, D. F., 238
Trait change, 37, 168
Transference; *see also* Countertransference
    countertransference and, 134–152
        phase 1: client history taking/ treatment planning, 134–140
        phase 2: client preparation, 140–143
        phase 3: assessment, 143–147
        phase 4: desensitization, 147–150, 176
        phase 5: installation, 150–151
        phase 6: the body scan, 151
        phase 7: closure, 151–152
        phase 8: reevaluation, 152
    defining countertransference and, 18, 125–127, 181–182
    processing resistance, 176–177
    relational interweave and, 182–188
    working with countertransference and, 127–128
        case of Dan, 148–149
        case of George, 128–129
        case of Janice, 182–188

case of Laurie, 146–147
case of Michael, 129–133
case of Sally, 144–145
Trauma, aspects of, 2, 47, 48, 72, 215–220
Trauma activation sequence, *see* Assessment (trauma activation sequence)
Trauma and Recovery (Herman), 25
Trauma and the Therapist: Countertransference and Vicarious Traumatization in Psychotherapy with Incest Survivors (Pearlman & Saakvitne), 102, 154
Trauma Case Conceptualization, *see* Client history taking (trauma case conceptualization)
Trauma Case Conceptualization Questionnaire, 51, 60, 239
Trauma processing, *see* Desensitization (active trauma processing)
Traumatic stress, 216
Traumatic Stress (Van der Kolk), 18
Trauma treatment, early history of, 6–9
Treating Compassion Fatigue (Figley), 156
Treatment (action) plans, 11, 48, 205; *see also* Evaluation and preparation
Treatment overview, *see* Eye Movement Desensitization and Reprocessing (EMDR)
Trust development, *see* Therapeutic relationship, in EMDR
Twombly, J., 236
Two-person psychology, 3, 152

U

Unconditional positive regard, 23

V

Validity of Cognition (VOC) scale, 53, 78, 85, 96, 97, 99, 100; *see also* Active trauma work
Van den Hout, M., 264
Van den Oord, H. J. M., 234

Van der Hart, O., 53
Van der Kolk, B. A., 18, 19, 25, 50, 197, 217, 218, 265
Van Etten, M. L., 238, 255
Van Haaften, H., 234
Vaughan, K., 236, 258
Verbal cueing, 78
Verbal intervention, 115, 116
Vicarious traumatization, 102, 106, 119, 154–159, 174–176
Vogelmann-Sine, S., 208, 230, 235

W

Wachtel, P. L., 126, 171, 175
Wallace, J., 235
Wambach, K., 235, 256
Watkins, H., 22, 87
Watkins, J., 22, 87
Watzlawitz, P., 79
Wave Work, 117
Weisaeth, L., 19
Wernik, U., 235
Whisman, M., 230
White, G. D., 234
Wiese, M., 236
Williams, J., 256
Wilson, S. A., 37, 141, 154, 228, 230, 234, 235, 236, 259
Wolfe, P., 236
Wolpe, J., 235, 236
Wolpert, B., 115
Working alliance, 3–5; *see also* Therapeutic relationship, in EMDR

Y

Young, J. E., 56, 79, 168, 205, 234, 236

Z

Zabukovec, J., 236
Zand, S. O., 235
Zangwill, W., 22
Zbik, A., 236, 262